W.O.W.
Guaranteed Income

**Learn How
Weekly Option Winners
Can Give You a
Safe Weekly Income
You Can Count On**

By Chuck Hughes

Information within this publication contains "forward looking statements" within the meaning of Section 27A of the Securities Act of 1933 and Section 21B of the Securities Exchange Act of 1934. Any statements that express or involve discussions with respect to predictions, goals, expectations, beliefs, plans, projections, objectives, assumptions or future events or performance are not statements of historical fact and may be "forward looking statements." Forward looking statements are based on expectations, estimates and projections at the time the statements are made that involve a number of risks and uncertainties which could cause actual results or events to differ materially from those presently anticipated. Investing involves the risk of loss as well as the possibility of profit. All investments involve risk, and all investment decisions of an individual remain the responsibility of that individual. Option and stock investing involves risk and is not suitable for all investors. Past performance does not guarantee future results. No statement in this book should be construed as a recommendation to buy or sell a security. The author and publisher of this book cannot guarantee that the strategies outlined in this book will be profitable and will not be held liable for any possible trading losses related to these strategies.

All information provided within this publication pertaining to investing, options, stocks and securities is educational information and not investment advice. Legacy Publishing advises all readers and subscribers to seek advice from a registered professional securities representative before deciding to invest in stocks and options featured within this publication. None of the material within this publication shall be construed as any kind of investment advice. Readers of this publication are cautioned not to place undue reliance on forward-looking statements, which are based on certain assumptions and expectations involving various risks and uncertainties that could cause results to differ materially from those set forth in the forward looking statements. Please be advised that nothing within this publication shall constitute a solicitation or an invitation to buy or sell any security mentioned herein. The author of this publication is neither a registered investment advisor nor affiliated with any broker or dealer.

Although every precaution has been taken in the preparation of this publication, the publisher and author assume no liability for errors and omissions. This publication is published without warranty of any kind, either expressed or implied. Furthermore, neither the author nor the publisher shall be liable for any damages, either directly or indirectly arising from the use or misuse of the book. Users of this publication agree to indemnify, release and hold harmless Legacy Publishing, its members, employees, agents, representatives, affiliates, subsidiaries, successors and assigns (collectively, "The Companies") from and against any and all claims, liabilities, losses, causes of actions, costs, lost profits, lost opportunities, indirect, special, incident, consequential, punitive, or any other damages whatsoever and expenses (including, without limitation, court costs and attorneys' fees) ("Losses") asserted against, resulting from, imposed upon or incurred by any of The Companies as a result of, or arising out of this agreement and/or your use of this publication. This publication is designed to provide accurate and authoritative information in regard to the subject matter covered. It is sold with the understanding that the author and publisher are not engaged in rendering legal, accounting, or other professional services. If legal advice or other expert assistance is required, the services of a competent professional person should be sought. Use of the material within this publication constitutes your acceptance of these terms.

HYPOTHETICAL PERFORMANCE RESULTS HAVE MANY INHERENT LIMITATIONS, SOME OF WHICH ARE DESCRIBED BELOW. NO REPRESENTATION IS BEING MADE THAT ANY ACCOUNT WILL OR IS LIKELY TO ACHIEVE PROFITS OR LOSSES SIMILAR TO THOSE SHOWN. IN FACT, THERE ARE FREQUENTLY SHARP DIFFERENCES BETWEEN HYPOTHETICAL PERFORMANCE RESULTS AND THE ACTUAL RESULTS SUBSEQUENTLY ACHIEVED BY ANY PARTICULAR TRADING PROGRAM.

ONE OF THE LIMITATIONS OF HYPOTHETICAL PERFORMANCE RESULTS IS THAT THEY ARE GENERALLY PREPARED WITH THE BENEFIT OF HINDSIGHT. IN ADDITION, HYPOTHETICAL TRADING DOES NOT INVOLVE FINANCIAL RISK, AND NO HYPOTHETICAL TRADING RECORD CAN COMPLETELY ACCOUNT FOR THE IMPACT OF FINANCIAL RISK IN ACTUAL TRADING. FOR EXAMPLE, THE ABILITY TO WITHSTAND LOSSES OR TO ADHERE TO A PARTICULAR TRADING PROGRAM IN SPITE OF TRADING LOSSES ARE MATERIAL POINTS WHICH CAN ALSO ADVERSELY AFFECT ACTUAL TRADING RESULTS. THERE ARE NUMEROUS OTHER FACTORS RELATED TO THE MARKETS IN GENERAL OR TO THE IMPLEMENTATION OF ANY SPECIFIC TRADING PROGRAM WHICH CANNOT BE FULLY ACCOUNTED FOR IN THE PREPARATION OF HYPOTHETICAL PERFORMANCE RESULTS AND ALL OF WHICH CAN ADVERSELY AFFECT ACTUAL TRADING RESULTS.

Table of Contents

Weekly Option Winners

WOW! I love the sound of this title! Everyone can use a little WOW in their world. Let me explain. In life, we are unable to remember entire days. We remember moments. Some of these moments we remember for a while and then they are filed away or placed in the recycle bin of our brains, while other moments are etched into our minds for life. These moments make up what are known as our memories.

Like most people I live for my WOW moments. They are 'feel good' moments that I can relive over and over again in my mind. I can still remember the first time I was ever up in a plane gazing down at the world stretched before me. I will never forget the cry of my first born child coming into the world. I will forever remember the first time I saw the Pacific Ocean breaking upon the rocky shores.

These are for me some of my WOW moments. I was amazed; I was in awe, I was hoping these experiences would never end. I look back at these moments today still with a sense of wonder and excitement! These moments make me feel good! They expand my world, make me believe in all good things and most importantly help me get through life's less than stellar moments.

Yes, life not only deals WOW experiences, but also has a way of dealing out the complete opposite, I like to call them the BOO experience. We all know them, we all have had them. We all have a strong distaste for them!

During the last five years, a lot of people can conjure up a lot of negative experiences. Jobs have been scarce, markets have crashed and investment and retirement plans have been slashed or destroyed. For a lot of investors, their negative experiences have far outweighed the WOW in their life. The negative experience is upsetting, demoralizing, and heart breaking. It leaves you feeling like the visiting team walking out on to the field at the Linc during a Philadelphia Eagles home game. You feel like you want to hop on the bus and go home. You feel uncomfortable and confused. The roar of the crowd is not for you.

Just as my other WOW experiences have changed my life forever, my new weekly option income plan has changed the way I will invest and make money for the rest of my life. This life altering experience is the ultimate investing game changer for me and my entire investing team!

It is the ultimate WOW experience of investing! By using the same option trading strategies I have used for the last 27 years to trade weekly options, I am able to realize profits others have only dreamed of attaining!

Over the past five years, we have experienced a global financial meltdown, severe recession and bear market, high unemployment, increased market volatility and an uncertain economy. This financial turmoil has made it very difficult for the average investor to realize a consistent return on investment.

Despite these difficult market conditions, my option strategies produced over $3.3 million in actual profits over the past five years. My brokerage account statements displayed throughout this manual show $3,308,137.76 in profits with an average return of 69.3%. The average number of days in a trade was 67 days resulting in an annualized return of 377.5%. There were 335 winning trades and 21 losing trades resulting in 94.1% accuracy.

Option Investing Produces $3.3 Million in Actual Profits

Total Profits	Average Return	Average Days in Trade	Annualized Return	Winning Trades	Losing Trades	Percent Wins
$3,308,137.76	69.3%	67	377.5%	335	21	94.1%

Trading these strategies with the weekly options has helped magnify my profits to the maximum degree! The results are impressive and they can be yours! Now we're talking! That is a WOW! It is something special, something unique, and something to be remembered! Bring on the bulls, bring on the bears. We are now fully prepared!

Let's take a look at what another WOW strategy is capable of doing! Over the past 5 years I collected $7,485,348.68 in gross cash income from selling option premium. Selling option premium is the ideal strategy for profiting in difficult market conditions. Weekly options take this strategy to a new level as you get 52 opportunities each year to sell option premium compared to 12 opportunities a year with monthly options.

Weekly options are the ideal investment for turning a small amount of money into a large amount of money. I would like to personally invite you on our journey of success investing in weekly options.

Wishing You the Best in Investing Success,

Chuck Hughes

Chuck Hughes

Chapter 1

Prime Trade Select

Prime Trade Select is my option selection program that I have been using successfully for more than 27 years to trade options. In this Chapter we will learn how to use *Prime Trade Select* to select weekly options with the best profit potential.

When *Prime Trade Select* is on a 'Buy' signal we want to initiate bullish weekly option trades that profit as the underlying stock moves up in price. There are three types of bullish trades that utilize weekly options:

1) Purchasing call options

2) Purchasing call option spreads

3) Covered calls

When *Prime Trade Select* is on a 'Sell' signal we want to initiate bearish weekly option strategies that profit as the underlying stock moves down in price. There are also three types of bearish trades that utilize weekly options:

1) Purchasing put options

2) Purchasing put option spreads

3) Covered calls on bearish ETFs

Note: If you are not familiar with option trading, Chapter 2 covers in detail the basics you need to know to trade weekly options.

Options are 'derivatives' that derive their value from the price movement of the underlying stock or ETF. If we can select stocks or ETFs that are moving up in price, we can harness the tremendous profit potential available from trading weekly call options. And if we can select stocks or ETFs that are moving down in price we can harness the tremendous profit potential available from trading weekly put options.

Let's now focus on the *Prime Trade Select* trade selection process to identify stocks that are moving up in price so we can initiate bullish weekly option positions and to identify stocks that are moving down in price so we can initiate bearish weekly option positions.

Road Map to Trading Success

"What goes up must come down spinning wheel got to go around."

- Blood, Sweat and Tears

What really makes stock prices go up or down? Is it really as simple as what goes up must come down and vice versa? How do I select stocks with the best profit potential? Stock prices are constantly fluctuating and many times there seems to be no 'rhyme or reason' to this constant price fluctuation. The air waves and the Internet are flooded with analysts and experts who try to predict the future price moves for stocks.

Often they have no real answers to our same questions and are just as baffled by why a stock is going up or going down. Where does that leave us? Let's face it; to the average investor the stock market can seem complicated and confusing.

Stocks can go up or down for no apparent reason. Apple reports great earnings but the stock plummets. The price of oil drops and the inflation report is tame but the major stock market indexes dive. Pfizer reports terrible earnings but the stock rallies. With the spinning wheel, going round and round, the ups and downs of the markets can leave anyone's head going round and round. When it comes right down to it, the reason **why** stock prices are going up or down seems to be anybody's guess. You might as well try to read tea leafs.

Highly paid analysts would have us believe that a company's earnings outlook drive stock prices. Yet how many times have you seen the stock of companies with good earnings plummet while those with terrible earnings soar? Just like bad things happen to good people, big stock declines can happen to good companies. It is a fact of life with no true explanation.

But none of that matters for one simple reason. At the end of the day, if there are more buy orders for a stock than sell orders then the price of the stock will go up. And if there are more sell orders for a stock than buy orders, then the price of the stock will go down. It's just that simple. Everything else is just noise. Everything else does not matter.

To make real money in the stock or option markets you don't need to know *why* a stock price rises or falls, you just need to know two things: when to buy and when to sell. If you can quantitatively measure the buying and selling pressure of a stock then you will know in advance whether the price of a stock is likely to go up or down. And you will then know if you should take a bullish or bearish option position.

In other words, if you get a reading on the buying pressure and selling pressure for a stock you can successfully assess whether a stock is likely to go up or go down in price. There are numerous ways to measure the buying and selling pressure of a stock. I want to teach you several methods. That way you can use all the methods or just work with the methods you are most comfortable. Remember comfort and ease are what we are aim for!

Successful option trading can be reduced to two simple rules:

1) Buy call options on a stock if the buying pressure exceeds the selling pressure

2) Buy put options on a stock if the selling pressure exceeds the buying pressure

The best way to measure buying and selling pressure is to track the daily price movement of a stock. If the daily price of a stock is increasing then the buying pressure is exceeding selling pressure and the stock is a 'buy'. If the daily price of a stock is decreasing then the selling pressure is exceeding buying pressure and the stock is on a 'sell' signal.

One of the most important rules I learned as a novice investor was that you want to purchase a stock or call option only if the buying pressure exceeds selling pressure as indicated by the price of the stock trending up.

Trying to profit by investing in a stock with a price that is trending down is very difficult as it requires that you correctly predict when the price of the stock will 'bottom out' and resume a price up trend so that your stock or call option purchase can be profitable.

Buying a stock because it is cheap and then trying to predict when a stock's price will bottom out can be nearly impossible to forecast correctly on a regular basis. This 'crystal ball' type of approach can leave the investor in a vulnerable position. A safer approach would be to wait until a stock's price is in an uptrend before investing.

A stock's price movement reflects all of the known information about a company so let the price movement of the stock tell you when you should buy and sell!

One of the most effective ways to measure buying and selling pressure is to look at the daily price movement of a stock. There are numerous methods for tracking the daily price movement. I want to teach you one of my favorite and most effective ways. It is using a price chart.

Price charts are a great way to get a visual look at the daily price changes and the price trend of a stock. It is the price trend that will determine if the stock is on a 'buy' or 'sell' signal and whether a bullish or bearish option trade should be taken.

For example, if the daily price trend of a stock is increasing then the buying pressure is exceeding selling pressure and a bullish option position should be initiated. If the daily price trend of a stock is decreasing then the selling pressure is exceeding buying pressure and a bearish option position should be initiated. Let's take a closer look at price charts and how this tool will lead us to the path of success.

Daily Price Trend of a Stock Is Increasing = Bullish Option Position

Daily Price Trend of a Stock Is Deceasing = Bearish Option Position

Using Price Charts

Price charts are a great tool that helps us determine a stock's price trend. The daily price chart below displays the daily price movement for Apple stock over the past month. The horizontal axis at the bottom of the chart references the time period of the chart which is one month in this example from March 8th through April 8th. The vertical axis on the right side of the chart represents the price of Apple stock and in this example ranges from 218 to 242.

The vertical bars display the daily price movement of the stock. Each vertical bar has a horizontal line which represents the stock's closing price for the day. On March 22nd the daily bar shows that Apple stock traded in a range from about 220 to 226 (circled). The closing price on March 22nd which is represented by the horizontal bar was about 225.

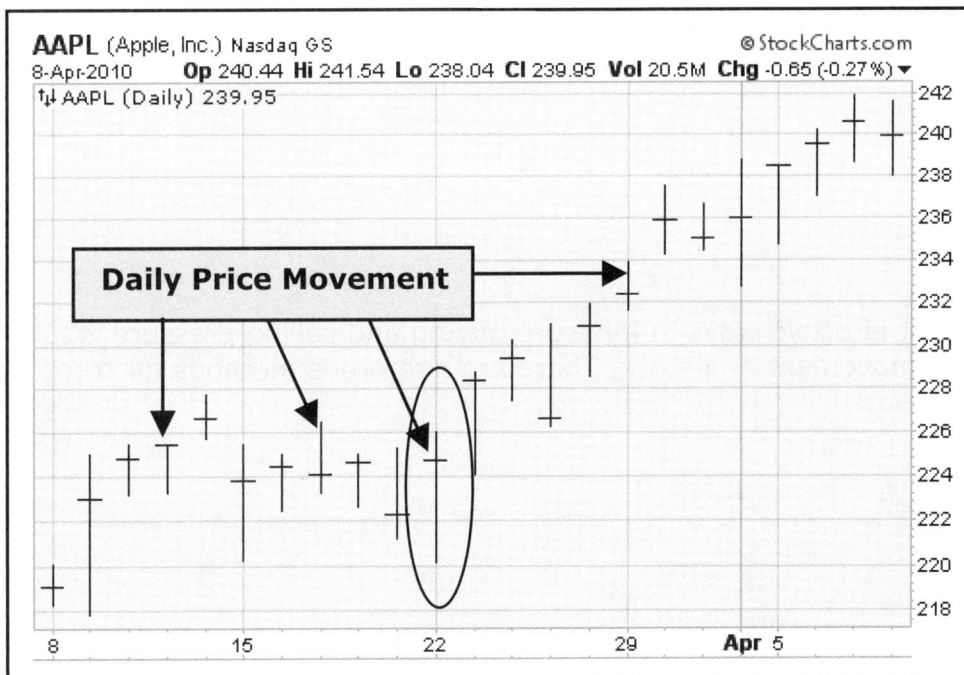

AAPL (Apple, Inc.) Nasdaq GS   ® StockCharts.com
8-Apr-2010   **Op** 240.44 **Hi** 241.54 **Lo** 238.04 **Cl** 239.95 **Vol** 20.5M **Chg** -0.65 (-0.27%) ▼
‡↓ AAPL (Daily) 239.95

Daily Price Movement

Determining the Price Trend

As noted previously we only want to buy a stock or call option if the buying pressure is exceeding the selling pressure as indicated by the price of the stock trending up. The best time to buy a stock is after the stock is already in a price up trend. We want to avoid stocks that are in a price down trend.

Daily price charts like the one just presented for Apple allow us to instantly see the price trend of a stock. I like to take this visual look at a stock's price movement one step further and actually measure the price movement. The easiest and simplest way to measure price movement is to use what are called 'moving average lines'.

Next, we are going to take a look at when to buy and when to sell. This concept always reminds me of an old Kenny Rogers song:

You got to know when to hold 'em, know when to fold 'em - Know when to walk away, know when to run.

Yes, with stocks you need to know when a stock is on a 'buy' signal or 'sell' signal. You are about to learn indicators that can quantitatively measure if a stock is moving up in price or moving down in price.

These indicators let us know in advance the most likely future price movement of a stock. We will then know if we want to establish bullish or bearish weekly option trades for a stock.

Determining the Most Likely Future Price Movement

Moving Average lines are a great trading tool that allows us to know in advance the most likely future price movement for a stock. I know the term Moving Average line may seem complicated but a Moving Average line is simply the average closing price of a stock over a specified time period. For example, the 50-Day Moving Average line represents the average closing price of a stock over the past 50 days.

Many times the real price trend of a stock can be obscured by the daily price fluctuations. The daily price chart below for Apple stock covers the 3 month period of November, December and January. As we learned in the previous price chart example for Apple, the vertical bars display the daily price movement of the stock.

This price chart shows a rally for Apple stock until mid-November and then a price decline into mid-December. This price decline is followed by another rally into the beginning of January followed by another price decline in January. Despite the daily price fluctuations the stock price was little changed over the 3 month period.

Three Month Price Action Shows No Clear Trend

11

Let's take another look at a price chart for Apple stock that covers a longer time period but includes the November, December and January period just mentioned. This price chart also includes the 100-Day Exponential Moving Average (EMA) line for Apple stock. I prefer to use Exponential Moving Averages over Simple Moving Averages as I have found Exponential Moving Averages to be more accurate in determining the price trend. Exponential Moving Averages give more weighting to recent price movements than Simple Moving Averages which give every day an equal weighting.

100-Day EMA Line is Sloping Up
Clearly Indicating a Price Up Trend

The 100-Day Exponential Moving Average (EMA) line is sloping up clearly indicating Apple stock is in a price up trend. Moving average lines give us an instant visual reference of the current price trend of a stock.

1) If the moving average line is sloping up, the stock is in a price up trend and buying pressure is exceeding selling pressure. Bullish option trades for the stock should be established.

2) If the moving average line is sloping down, the stock is in a price down trend and selling pressure is exceeding buying pressure. Bearish option trades for the stock should be established.

It is that simple! Moving averages tell us if a stock is on a 'buy' signal or 'sell' signal instead of trying to predict the future price movement of a stock. You can easily and quickly obtain moving average lines from numerous websites which will be covered shortly.

12

Buy and Sell Signals

One of the easiest ways to clarify whether a stock is a 'buy' or a 'sell' is to look at the shorter term 50-Day Exponential Moving Average (EMA) line in relation to the longer term 100-Day Exponential Moving Average (EMA) line.

If the shorter term 50-Day EMA line is **above** the longer term 100-Day EMA line it indicates the price momentum for the stock is to the upside which confirms the price up trend. We should initiate bullish option trades for the stock.

If the shorter term 50-Day EMA line is **below** the longer term 100-Day EMA line it indicates the price momentum for the stock is to the downside which confirms the price down trend. We should initiate bearish option trades for the stock.

50-Day EMA Line <u>Above</u> 100-Day EMA = Price Up Trend = Buy

50-Day EMA Line <u>Below</u> 100-Day EMA = Price Down Trend = Sell

---

Buying and Selling Pressure

When the shorter term 50-Day EMA line is **above** the longer term 100-Day EMA line it is an indication that the buying pressure for a stock is exceeding the selling pressure. And the most likely future price movement of the stock is up. The stock is on a 'buy' signal.

When the shorter term 50-Day EMA line is **below** the longer term 100-Day EMA line it is an indication that the selling pressure for a stock is exceeding the buying pressure. And the most likely future price movement of the stock is down. The stock is on a 'sell' signal .

50-Day EMA Line <u>Above</u> 100-Day EMA = Buying Pressure Exceeding Selling Pressure

50-Day EMA Line <u>Below</u> 100-Day EMA = Selling Pressure Exceeding Buying Pressure

---

'Buy' Signal Example

Let's look at an example of a 'buy' signal. The Apple stock daily price chart below displays the 50-Day EMA line and the 100-Day EMA line. The moving average lines indicate that Apple stock entered a price 'up' trend in April (circled) as the 50-Day EMA crossed above the 100-Day EMA line.

When the 50-Day EMA crossed above the 100-Day EMA it was a good indication that buying pressure was exceeding selling pressure and you want to take bullish option trades for Apple. As long as the 50-Day EMA line remains above the 100-Day EMA line Apple stock remains a 'buy' and bullish option trades should be maintained.

In this example the Apple 50-Day EMA line crossed above the 100-Day EMA line in April. I have been purchasing Apple stock and call options after the April buy signal as long as the 50-Day EMA line remains above the 100-Day EMA. Apple stock remains in a price 'up' trend as the 50-Day EMA line remains above the 100-Day EMA line indicating that buying pressure continues to exceed selling pressure. Monitoring the 50-Day and 100-Day EMA lines is an easy and effective way to determine the current price trend which tells us if we should be taking bullish or bearish option trades for Apple stock.

If the 50-Day EMA crosses *below* the 100-Day EMA it would indicate a reversal to a price 'down' trend as the selling pressure is now exceeding the buying pressure. You should take bearish option trades for the stock when this occurs. We will look at an example of a sell signal next.

50-Day EMA line Above 100-Day EMA line = Buy

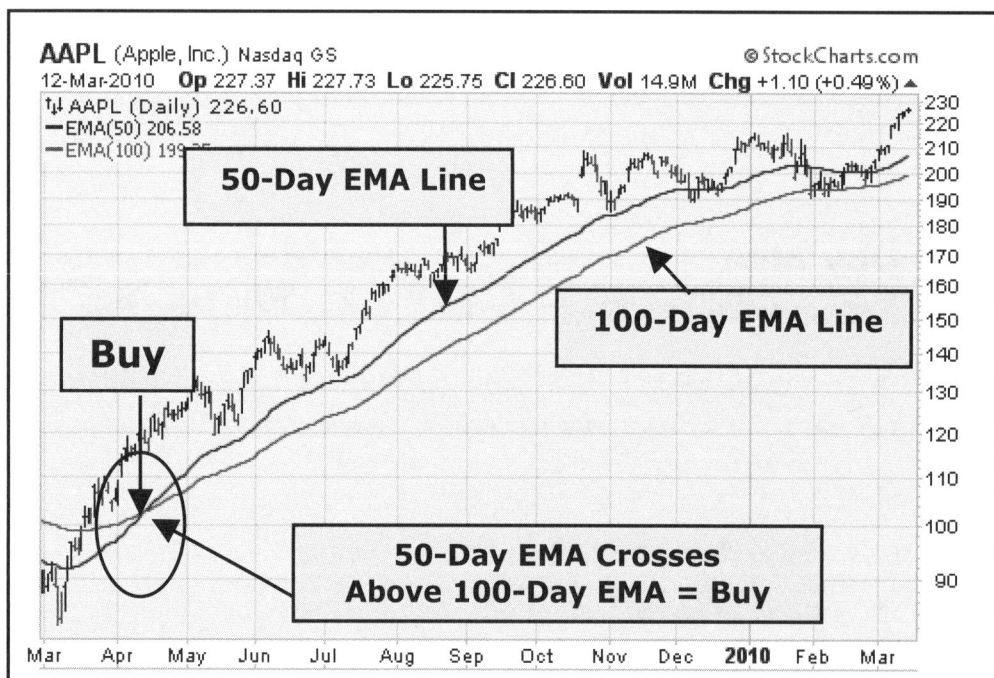

Sell Signal Example

Let's look at an example of a 'sell' signal. The daily price chart below shows the daily price movement and the 50-Day and 100-Day EMA lines for Merck stock. This chart reveals that in February the Merck 50-Day EMA line crossed below the 100-Day EMA line (circled) resulting in an *EMA System* 'sell' signal for Merck stock.

When the 50-Day EMA crossed below the 100-Day EMA it was a good indication that selling pressure was exceeding buying pressure and you want to establish bearish option positions for Merck stock. You want to hold on to the bearish option positions for Merck while the price trend is 'down' and at this point the length and severity of the price decline is still unknown.

As long as the 50-Day EMA line remains below the 100-Day EMA line Merck stock remains a 'sell'. Merck does not qualify as a buy until the 50-Day EMA line crosses above the 100-Day EMA line.

Monitoring the 50-Day and 100-Day EMA lines is an easy and effective way to determine the current price trend which tells us if we should be establishing bullish or bearish option positions for Merck stock.

50-Day EMA Below 100-Day EMA = Sell

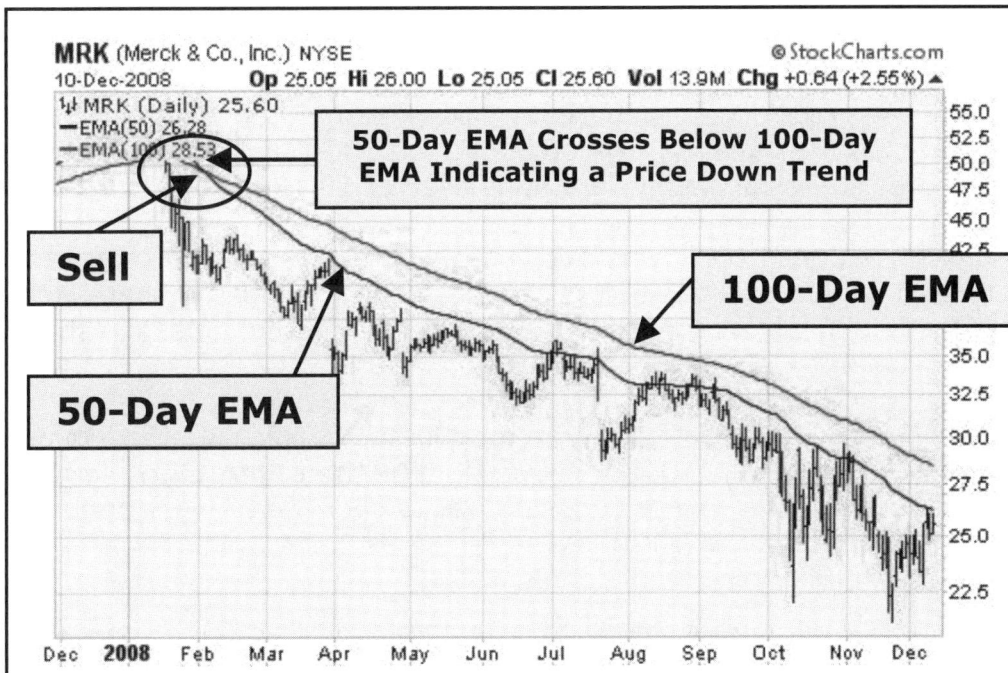

The 50/100-Day EMA trend following system is your road map to investing success. Trend following is a powerful, systematic approach that allows us to profit from the powerful profit opportunities available from trading weekly options.

Historical Results of *EMA System*

The 50/100-Day *EMA System* is a rule based system with clearly defined 'buy' and 'sell' rules. This enabled me to do historical testing with the help of the *Omega Research Trade Station* program using the 50/100-Day EMA Cross Over System just presented. Historical profit results are based on buying a stock when its 50-Day EMA line crosses above the 100-Day EMA and selling a stock when its 50-Day EMA line crosses below the 100-Day EMA. The profit/loss for each trade is calculated and a cumulative total is maintained for each testing period.

The *EMA System* is universal in nature and has been profitable for short term investing across a wide range of markets including: stocks, options, indexes, closed-end funds, zero coupon bonds, mutual funds, index funds and sector funds. The fact that the system is profitable in virtually every type of market confirms its credibility as a viable, robust approach to trading the financial markets.

Included on the following page are profit results for a well-diversified sampling of both growth and value stocks that represent a broad cross section of 26 different industry groups. This sampling includes small, mid and large cap stocks. Historical profit results were generated over a recent twenty four year period.

Profitable with Low Risk

Keep in mind that four bear markets occurred during this period. Results are based on trading one hundred shares of stock for each 'buy' signal and do not include commissions.

Let's review the tests conducted using the first stock tested Aetna Health Care (AET). The first time Aetna's 50-Day EMA crossed above the 100-Day EMA during the test period one hundred shares of Aetna were purchased at 10.18.

The profit/loss for each AET trade was calculated by the *Trade Station* software and the profits totaled $5,376 over the test period based on trading 100 shares for each buy signal. This $5,376 profit represents a 528% return on the initial investment of $1,018.

The software divides the total profits by the total losses to calculate the Reward to Risk Ratio. Aetna had a Reward to Risk Ratio of 3.9 as there were 3.9 dollars of profit for each 1 dollar of loss. There were 10 losing trades over the 24-year period and the average losing trade incurred a -$120 loss.

24-Years of Historical Results

Stock	Profit on 100 Shares	Profit Factor	Initial Cost 100 Shares	% Return on Initial Cost	Avg Loss
Aetna	$5,376	3.9	$1018	528%	-120
Adobe Systems	$5,679	4.4	$5	126200%	-173
Altria	$4,602	3.2	$220	2092%	-180
Analog Devices	$3,559	2.0	$92	3868%	-251
Applied Materials	$2,419	3.0	$3	96760%	-70
Auto Data Process	$2,878	3.5	$182	1581%	-98
Bunge	$3,282	100.0	$1,585	207%	0
Centex	$3,810	4.3	$216	1764%	-143
Cisco Systems	$5,474	10.1	$8	68425%	-100
Corning	$6,153	12.4	$178	3457%	-54
CVS Drug	$4,237	2.7	$505	839%	-250
Eaton Vance	$1,682	6.7	$10	16820%	-27
eBay	$2,453	3.7	$120	2044%	-156
EMC Corp	$7,257	80.0	$5	145140%	-18
Franklin Resources	$5,264	3.2	$5	112000%	-18
General Electric	$3,675	5.2	$130	2827%	-97
Golden West Fin'l	$3,700	4.4	$40	9250%	-78
Home Depot	$4,092	4.0	$4	102300%	-174
Illinois Tool Works	$5,924	4.8	$176	3366%	-225
Intel	$2,845	3.5	$39	7295%	-71
Johnson & Johnson	$4,877	4.5	$227	2148%	-181
KB Homes	$6,654	3.4	$840	792%	-202
Legg Mason	$4,212	7.1	$187	2252%	-78
Microsoft	$2,651	2.8	$10	26510%	-108
M&T Bank	$6,445	5.5	$37	17419%	-95
NVR Inc	$50,070	5.0	$1,080	4636%	-1050
PMC Sierra	$15,603	41.5	$225	6935%	-48
Procter & Gamble	$3,096	3.1	$223	1388%	-108
Sun Microsystems	$3,342	7.5	$25	13368%	-26
Texas Instruments	$4,227	3.7	$184	2297%	-111
Taro Pharma	$4,551	4.7	$87	5231%	-113
Unitedhealth	$7,627	9.5	$32	23834%	-91
Water Corp	$4,898	4.5	$375	1306%	-471
Yahoo!	$7,964	63.0	$132	6033%	-129
Totals / Averages	**$210,578**	**12.7**	**$8,204**	**2,567%**	**-150**

Average Yearly Return of 107%

The total initial investment required to buy 100 shares of each of the 34 stocks over the test period was $8,204. This $8,204 initial investment produced a total of $210,578 in profits over the test period which equates to a 2,567% return. The average yearly return was 107% which would enable us to double our initial investment every year on average. This average 107% annual return was achieved without the use of leverage or margin. Trading options instead of stock would have resulted in a much higher rate of return over the test period as options provide leverage.

The historical results demonstrate that the *EMA System* has the ability to produce handsome short term profits with very low risk. Of the trades that were losing trades, the average loss over the twenty four year period was $150 and when compared to the total profits of $210,578 demonstrates the ability of the system to keep losses to a minimum. The average Reward to Risk ratio was a very healthy 12.7 with over 12 dollars of profit for each 1 dollar of loss again demonstrating a very healthy risk-adjusted return.

The preceding investing results demonstrate the importance of 'investing with the trend' if you are a short term investor. The 50/100-Day *EMA System* allows us to know in advance the most likely future price movement of a stock and reduces the entry and exit timing risk associated with short term investing.

It is a versatile, effective method for profiting in any type of market and can quickly identify stocks on a 'buy' or 'sell' signal. This allows us to profit from trading weekly options by taking bullish option trades for a stock on a 50/100-Day *EMA System* 'buy' signal and taking bearish trades for a stock on a 50/100-Day *EMA System* 'sell' signal.

Equally important is the ability of the system to avoid large losses which can quickly ruin an investment plan. The system keeps losses to a minimum and almost always exits a trade before a big loss occurs. Following a discipline that keeps losses to a minimum is one of the most important characteristics of a successful short term investing program. Keep in mind that the worst bear market since 1932 occurred during this test period.

The 50-Day and 100 Day-EMA Lines Are
the 'Key' to Developing a Profitable Strategy

The stock market is in a constant state of flux. The constant up and down price movement of a stock makes it difficult at times to see the real price trend of a stock. That is why it is important for an investor to become comfortable with the 50/100-Day EMA lines.

The position of the 50-Day EMA in relation to the 100-Day EMA gives us a quick and accurate indication of a stock's current price trend. If the stock is in a price up trend bullish option trades should be initiated. And if the stock is in a price down trend bearish option trades should be initiated. In order to be a successful option investor we do not have to know what an analyst's rating is for a stock or the current earnings projection. All of that information is already reflected in a stock's price movement which can be quantitatively measured by the 50/100-Day EMA lines.

This simple but effective trend following system is mechanical in nature and instantly tells you if you should be taking a bullish or bearish option position. I prefer mechanical systems as they take the emotion out of trading. There is no judgment or interpretation involved. You don't have to rely on trying to predict future price movement.

Follow the Price Trend Instead of Trying to Predict It

"Prediction is very difficult, especially if it's about the future."
- Nils Bohr

The *50/100-Day EMA System* allows us to 'invest with the trend' instead of trying to predict the price direction of a stock. The historical studies presented demonstrate that price trends tend to continue in the same direction and can continue on longer than one may initially expect.

My investing experience confirms that the *50/100-Day EMA System* allows us to know in advance the most likely future price movement of a stock and whether we should be initiating bullish or bearish option trades.

Downloading On the 50/100-Day EMA Lines

The 50/100-Day EMA Lines can be easily downloaded from www.StockCharts.com. On the home page type in the stock symbol and click "Go". In this example I typed in the symbol for Apple stock AAPL.

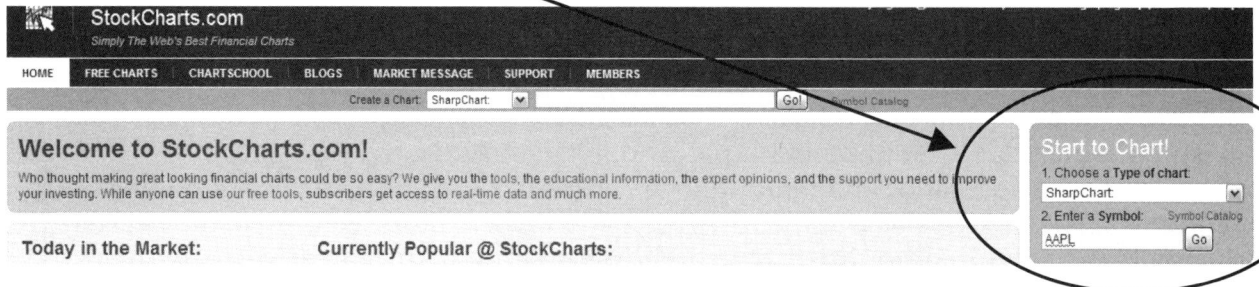

Once you click "Go" the default chart for Apple will appear. Below the default chart for Apple select "Daily" under Periods and "1 Year" under Range. Under Overlays select "Exp Mov. Avg" and Under Parameters select "50". Then select "Exp Mov. Avg" on the second row and Under Parameters select "100".

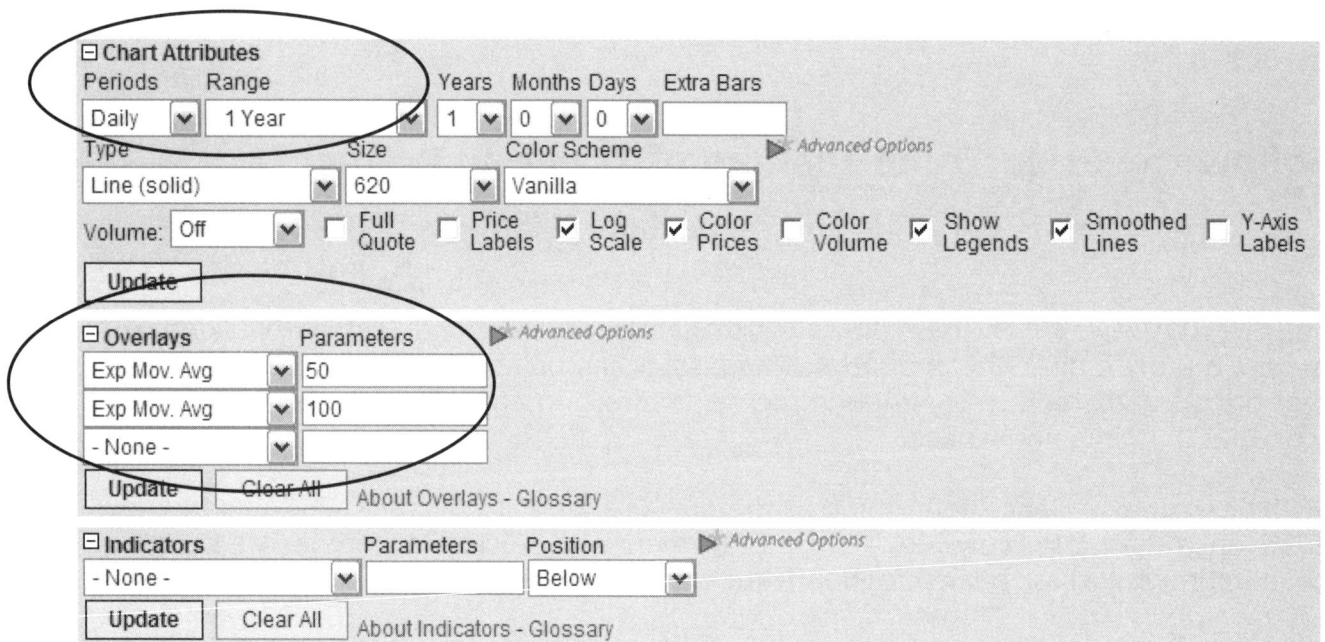

Click "Update" and the Apple price chart with the 50/100-Day EMA Lines will be displayed (see price chart on the following page).

Apple One Year Price Chart with 50/100-Day EMA Lines

AAPL (Apple, Inc.) Nasdaq GS   © StockCharts.com
15-Apr-2010   **Open** 245.78 **High** 249.03 **Low** 245.51 **Close** 248.92 **Volume** 13.4M **Chg** +3.23 (+1.31%) ▲
↑↓ AAPL (Daily) 248.92
— EMA(50) 224.19
— EMA(100) 212.38

Taking Short Positions

As we learned in the beginning of this Chapter we utilize three types of short trades when trading weekly options; purchasing put options, purchasing bearish put option spreads and covered calls using bearish ETFs.

These short positions profit as the underlying stock or ETF declines in price. I have learned through many years of experience that if you want to take a short position it is useful to check the long term trend of a stock or ETF. Short trades are more accurate when the long term price trend of a stock is down.

Trading with the long term trend helps prevent short trades from getting 'whipsawed' when counter-trend rallies occur. I have found that the 1-Month price of a stock in relation in relation to its 20-Month Exponential Moving Average (EMA) is an excellent way to identify the long term trend of a market.

If the 1-Month Price (shorter-term) is above the 20-Month Exponential Moving Average (EMA) (longer-term) a bullish long term trend is indicated.

And if the 1-Month Price is below the 20-Month EMA a bearish long term trend is indicated.

I refer to the 1-Month/20-Month EMA system as the *Major Trend System*.
This simple system has been very effective in correctly identifying major trends in global currency, fixed income, energy, commodity and equity markets.

Major Trend System 'Buy' Signal
- **1-Month Price is Above 20-Month EMA**

Major Trend System 'Sell' Signal
- **1-Month Price is Below 20-Month EMA**

Downloading the 1-Month/20-Month EMA Charts

The 1-Month Price and 20-Month EMA charts can be downloaded from www.stockcharts.com with the basic subscription. The steps involved in downloading the 1-Month Price and 20-Month EMA will be covered shortly.

For example, the price chart below displays the 1-Month/20-Month EMA price for the Emerging Markets ETF (EEM). The price chart shows that the major price trend for EEM was bullish from 2004 until June of 2008 when the 1-Month price was above the 20-Month EMA. During this bullish price trend, bullish EEM option positions should be established and short positions should be exited (chart courtesy of stockcharts.com).

In June of 2008 the 1-Month price crossed below the 20-Month EMA indicating a major price down trend and a Major Trend System 'Sell' signal. Bullish option positions should be closed out and bearish option positions should be initiated.

Emerging Markets 1-Month/20-Month EMA Price Chart

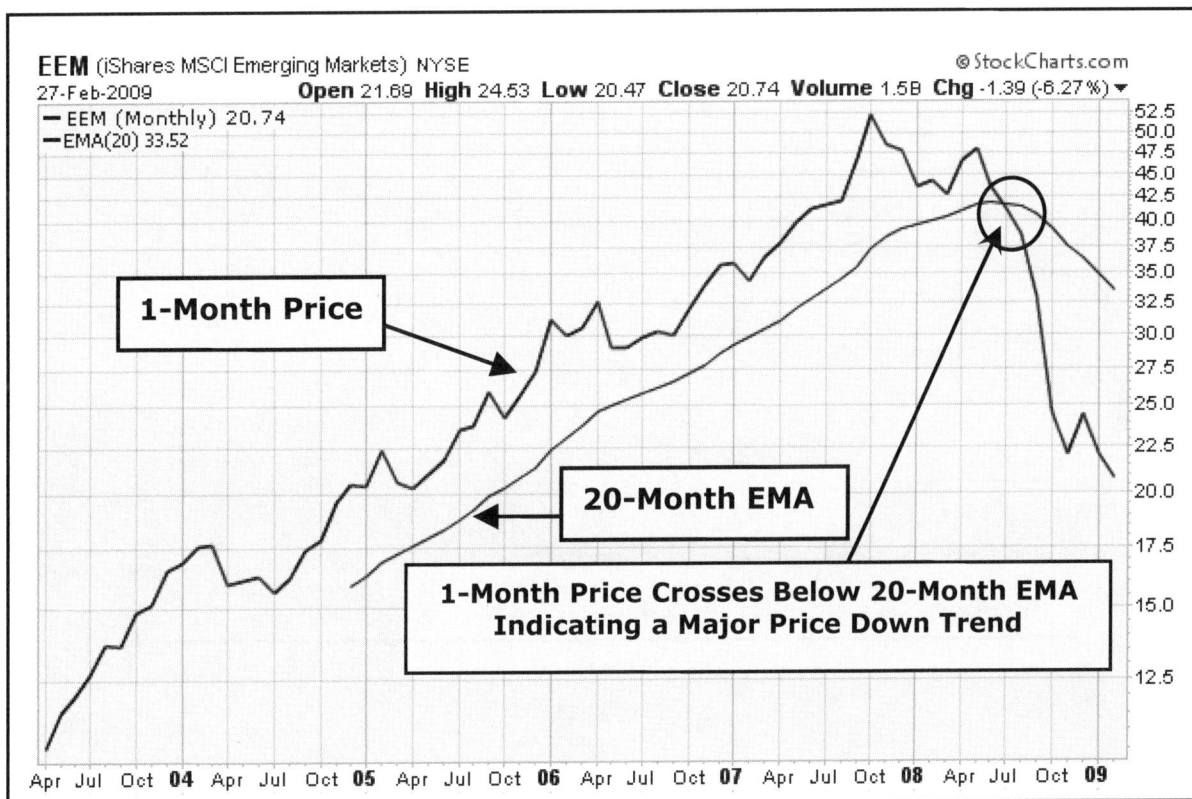

EEM (iShares MSCI Emerging Markets) NYSE   © StockCharts.com
27-Feb-2009   Open 21.69 High 24.53 Low 20.47 Close 20.74 Volume 1.5B Chg -1.39 (-6.27%) ▼
— EEM (Monthly) 20.74
—EMA(20) 33.52

1-Month Price

20-Month EMA

1-Month Price Crosses Below 20-Month EMA Indicating a Major Price Down Trend

Ten Year Price Chart

The chart below displays a longer term 1-Month/20-Month EMA price chart for the S&P 500 Index over a ten year period.

The price chart shows that the major price trend for the S&P 500 was bullish during the late 1990s, and then turned bearish in October 2000 when the 1-Month price crossed below the 20-Month EMA when bearish option positions should be taken.

In May of 2003 the major trend turned bullish when the 1-Month price crossed above the 20-Month EMA. Bullish S&P 500 Index option positions should be established and short positions should be exited (chart courtesy of stockcharts.com).

In December of 2007 the 1-Month price crossed below the 20-Month EMA indicating a major price down trend. Long option positions should be exited and short option positions should be initiated.

S&P 500 Index 1-Month/20-Month EMA Price Chart

24

S&P 500 Index Down 14% Over 10 Year Period

The S&P 500 Index incurred a 14% decline over the 10 year period just presented. Long term "buy and hold" investors would have incurred a 14% loss investing in the S&P 500 Index over this ten year period.

14% Loss versus 191% Return

The *Major Trend System* takes both long and short positions and over the same ten year period the system produced a 191% profit demonstrating the versatility of the system. Short positions profit as a stock or index declines in price.

The profit graph below displays the profit growth from trading the S&P 500 Index over the same ten year period using the *Major Trend System*. Over the ten year period, a $10,000 investment grew to $29,139 using the system resulting in a $19,139 profit and a 191% return.

Major Trend System Produces
191% Return Over 10 Year Period

Major Trend System
S&P 500 Index 10-Year Profit Results

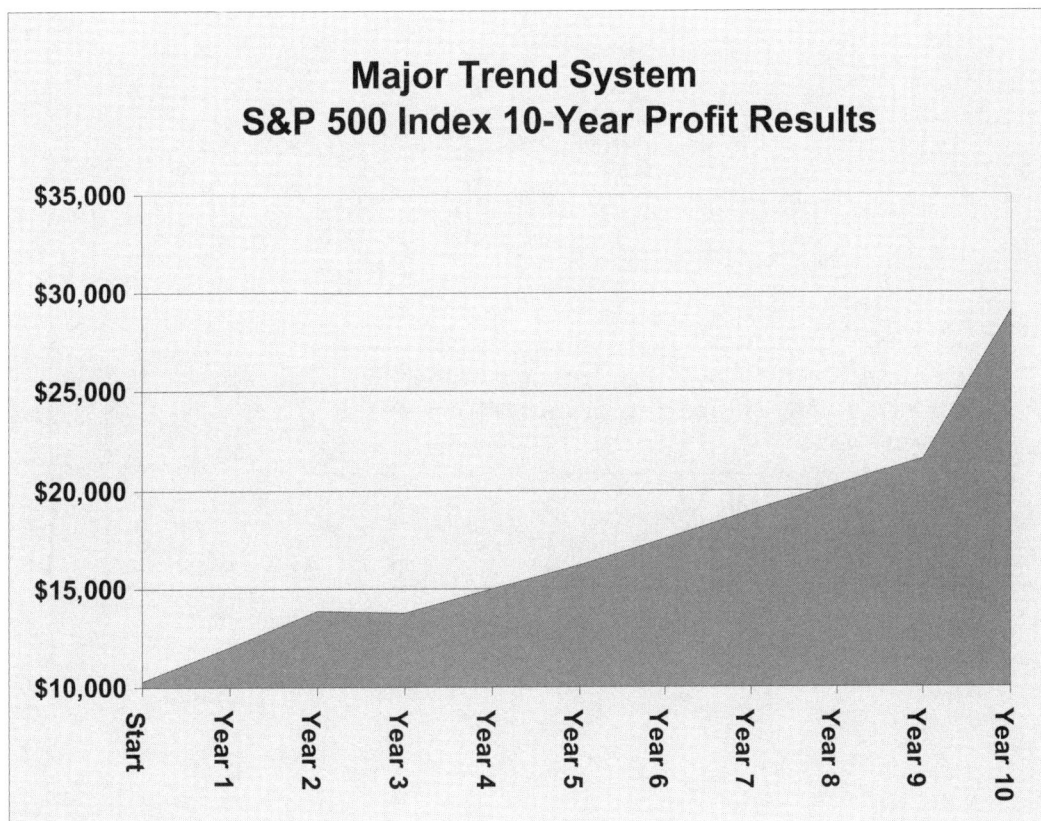

Using The Major Trend Indicator as a Filter

As mentioned earlier, I have found the 1-Month/20-Month EMA *Major Trend System* to be particularly useful when taking short option positions. The *Major Trend System* can be used as a filter by only taking short option positions when the *Major Trend System* is on a 'Sell' signal with the 1-Month Price below the 20-Month EMA.

The filter can improve the profit performance and reduce the risk of taking short positions using the shorter-term 50-Day/100-Day EMA System. The *Major Trend System* 'confirms' the trend indicated by the shorter-term 50-Day/100-Day EMA System.

The 50-Day/100-Day EMA System allows us to instantly see the 'Big Picture' when trading stocks and ETFs. The iShares Emerging Market Index ETF (EEM) daily price chart below shows the 50-Day EMA line crossing below the 100-Day EMA line in June indicating that this ETF is in a short-term price down trend (chart courtesy of Yahoo Finance).

iShares Emerging Market Index Daily Price Chart

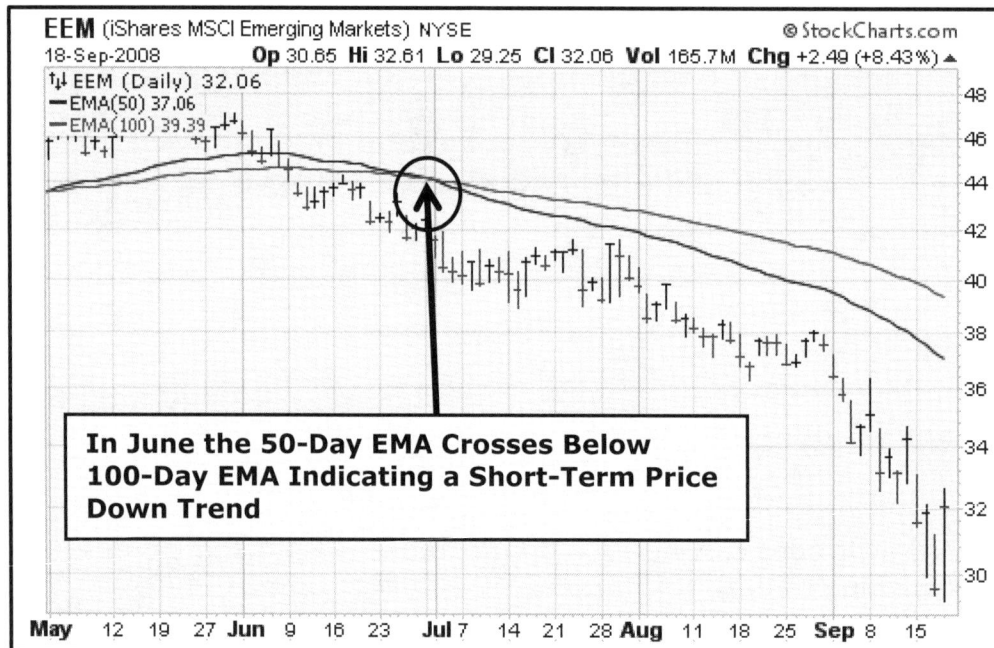

Trend Confirmation

The iShares Emerging Markets (EEM) monthly price chart below shows the 1-Month price crossing below the 20-Month EMA in June indicating a major price down trend.

The *Major Trend System* confirms the shorter term 50/100-Day EMA sell signal. Both the 50-Day/100-Day EMA and Major Trend systems turned bearish in June and short positions can be initiated (chart courtesy of stockcharts.com).

EEM (iShares MSCI Emerging Markets) NYSE © StockCharts.com
12-Sep-2008   Op 39.37 Hi 39.71 Lo 34.35 Cl 36.54 Vol 630.8M Chg -3.51 (-8.76%) ▼
— EEM (Monthly) 36.54
— EMA(20) 42.70

1-Month Price Crosses Below 20-Month EMA Confirming 50/100-Day EMA Shorter Term Sell Signal

Trend Confirmation Reduces Losses

The 1-Month/20-Month EMA filter only allows us to trade in the direction of the major trend. This helps prevent 'whipsaw' trades when counter-trend rallies occur. Preventing whipsaw trades can increase profits, reduce losses and increase the percentage of winning trades.

For example, the 1-Month/20-Month EMA price chart below for the Emerging Markets ETF (EEM) shows that the major price trend for EEM was bullish from 2004 until June of 2008. In June of 2008 the 1-Month price crossed below the 20-Month EMA indicating a major price down trend (chart courtesy of stockcharts.com).

During the 4 year period from 2004 until 2008 when EEM was in a major price up trend, the shorter-term 50-Day/100-Day EMA system issued three counter-trend 'sell' signals all of which turned out to be losing trades. Using the 1-Month/20-Month EMA as a filter for the 50-Day/100-Day EMA System would have avoided these three losing whipsaw trades.

50-Day/100-Day EMA System Issued 3 Counter-Trend 'Sell' Signals During Bullish 2004 - 2008 Period

The 1-Month/20-Month EMA price chart below for the S&P 500 Index is another example of how the system helps prevent whipsaw trades.

The 1-Month/20-Month EMA price chart below indicates the major price trend for S&P 500 Index was bullish from mid-2003 until December of 2007. In December of 2007 the 1-Month price crossed below the 20-Month EMA indicating a major price down trend.

During the 4½ year period the S&P 500 was in a major price up trend, the shorter-term 50-Day/100-Day EMA system issued five counter-trend "sell" signals all of which turned out to be losing trades. This is another example of how the 1-Month/20-Month EMA filter helps prevent whipsaw trades (chart courtesy of stockcharts.com).

50-Day/100-Day EMA System Issued 5 Counter-Trend 'Sell' Signals During Bullish 2003 - 2007 Period

Surviving the Financial Armageddon

By John Weston

There are times in your life that you will never forget. Dates that you know exactly where you were and what you were doing. In our family we have this thing about remembering where you were on significant events in history. My Grandfather would always say that he was out looking for his kids the day Pearl Harbor was attacked. My Dad was collecting glass bottles for money on the beach the day that the stock market crashed in 1929. My Mom was home watching TV the day President Kennedy was assassinated. I was at the office during the terrorist attack on September 11th. I remember sitting there watching the TV with utter disbelief and terror.

Unfortunately, I now have another unpleasant day to remember. I am thankful that no one has injured or killed. But the loss of people's dreams and financial security became palpable. That day would be September 15, 2008. This day will go down in history as the beginning of the worst financial crisis in the United States since the Great Depression. Due to the Lehman Brothers and Fannie Mae bankruptcy, the Merrill Lynch buyout and the AIG insurance company insolvency, today could be considered one of the worst global financial storms in history. Some call it a 'Financial Armageddon'. Over thirty trillion dollars of highly leveraged mortgage securities that went bad have caused a financial meltdown that has frozen global credit.

The day of September 15, 2008 started out no different than most. I was cruising into my desk that morning nursing my second cup of coffee, entertaining thoughts of when the market volatility is going to give us a decisive trend. Well, be careful what you wish for . . . the market was about to show us and the rest of the world a very decisive trend. The market began a precipitous sell off. Of course, Chuck Hughes was already on top of it . . . in the early AM hours he knew the Asian markets were selling off. He had a feeling already that things were going south and the ride was going to be a rough one.

Fortunately, Chuck's *Major Trend System* had already positioned us on the right side of the trend in the global currency, commodity and equity markets. In Chuck Hughes' August blog he recommended that readers take short positions in the global markets just as he had done over the summer. The *Major Trend System* issued 'go short' signals for most foreign currencies, commodities and equity markets in the June – July time frame.

By the end of the day the Dow Jones Industrial Average had lost over 500 points in ONE DAY! But Chuck's ETF option trading accounts **had a positive return for the day**. The copy of his brokerage account Profit/Loss Report that follows shows $14,987.22 in closed trade profits on September 15th and his open trades had a 14.5% return for the day. His other three global ETF trading accounts had similar returns.

Chuck Hughes locked in solid profits today and also created option spread trades that increase the profit potential of existing option trades and help preserve profits. Protecting profits is a very important requirement for profitable trading during volatile markets.

14.5% Return in One Day While Dow Dropped 504 Points

Account Reports: Profit/Loss Report 🖨 PRINT

Give your accountant a break. View profits/losses for all trades executed on one specific date or during a range of dates. Track by position, whether it's closed, or still opened. Download to a spreadsheet for easy manipulation, processing and tax reporting.

Trade date: « | 9/15/2008 | » | SELECT DATE

Trade date: « | | » | SELECT DATE

Symbol: Submit ▶ ☐ Show detailed unrealized positions

* To see all transactions within specified date range leave symbol blank

Click here to download data

Sept 15ᵗʰ Closed Trades

Realized P&L on Closed Positions

Symbol	Date Bought	Date Sold	Shares	Cost Basis	Sales Price	Gain-loss
+EWYMH	8/27/2008 3:35:11 PM	9/15/2008 10:52:32 AM	4	$6,302.00	$7,093.95	$791.95
+EWYMH	8/27/2008 3:35:11 PM	9/15/2008 10:52:41 AM	1	$1,575.50	$1,778.49	$202.99
+FLNOD	9/8/2008 2:57:00 PM	9/15/2008 10:51:53 AM	5	$10,727.50	$10,032.43	-$695.07
+FLNOD	9/11/2008 11:38:18 AM	9/15/2008 10:51:53 AM	5	$11,227.50	$10,032.43	-$1,195.07
+JIKOH	9/3/2008 3:27:07 PM	9/15/2008 10:34:02 AM	5	$9,827.50	$11,622.42	$1,794.92
+RSXWX	8/26/2008 3:51:00 PM	9/15/2008 9:58:34 AM	5	$6,527.50	$9,572.43	$3,044.93
EEV	8/26/2008 2:39:36 PM	9/15/2008 9:46:40 AM	100	$9,681.50	$11,910.13	$2,228.63
EEV	8/26/2008 2:39:36 PM	9/15/2008 9:46:40 AM	100	$9,701.50	$11,910.13	$2,208.63
EEV	8/26/2008 2:39:36 PM	9/15/2008 9:46:40 AM	100	$9,681.50	$11,920.13	$2,238.63
EFU	8/26/2008 2:32:13 PM	9/15/2008 9:44:26 AM	236	$25,458.42	$28,890.29	$3,431.87
EFU	8/26/2008 2:32:13 PM	9/15/2008 9:44:26 AM	64	$6,903.98	$7,838.80	$934.82

Total Realized Gain-Loss: $14,987.22

Open Trade Profit

Unrealized P&L on Open Positions

Symbol	Description	Position	Avg Price	Cost Basis	Market Value	Type	Unrealized Val.
+EEVLD	Proshares Tr Ultr Shrt Msci Dec 2008 120.00 Call	-3	-$19.9182	$5,975.45	-$10,080.00	Stock Option	-$4,104.55
+EWYMH	Ishares Inc Msci S Korea Jan 2009 60.00 Put	5	$17.5550	$8,777.50	$9,800.00	Stock Option	$1,022.50
+JIKOH	Claymore Exchange Traded Fd Tr Bny Bri&c Ptf Mar 2009 60.00 Put	5	$21.4550	$10,727.50	$12,650.00	Stock Option	$1,922.50
+RSXWX	Market Vectors Etf Tr Russia Etf Nov 2008 50.00 Put	5	$16.0550	$8,027.50	$11,500.00	Stock Option	$3,472.50
EEV	Proshares Tr Ultr Shrt Msci	300	$107.0817	$32,124.50	$42,240.00	Equities	$10,115.50
EFU	Proshares Tr Ultr Shrt Msci	300	$114.0817	$34,224.50	$40,059.00	Equities	$5,834.50

Total Unrealized Gain-Loss: $18,262.95

Steps for Downloading the 1-Month Price and 20-Month EMA

1) Log on to StockCharts.com
2) Type in the trading symbol under Symbol (in this example GLD for the Gold ETF)
3) Under Chart Attributes select 'Monthly' under Periods and select the desired
   Range (2 Years in this example)
4) Under Overlays select 'Exp Mov. Avg' and under Parameters select '20'
5) Click 'Update' to display chart (in this example the 2 year Gold ETF chart)

Note: The basic StockCharts.com subscription is required for this chart

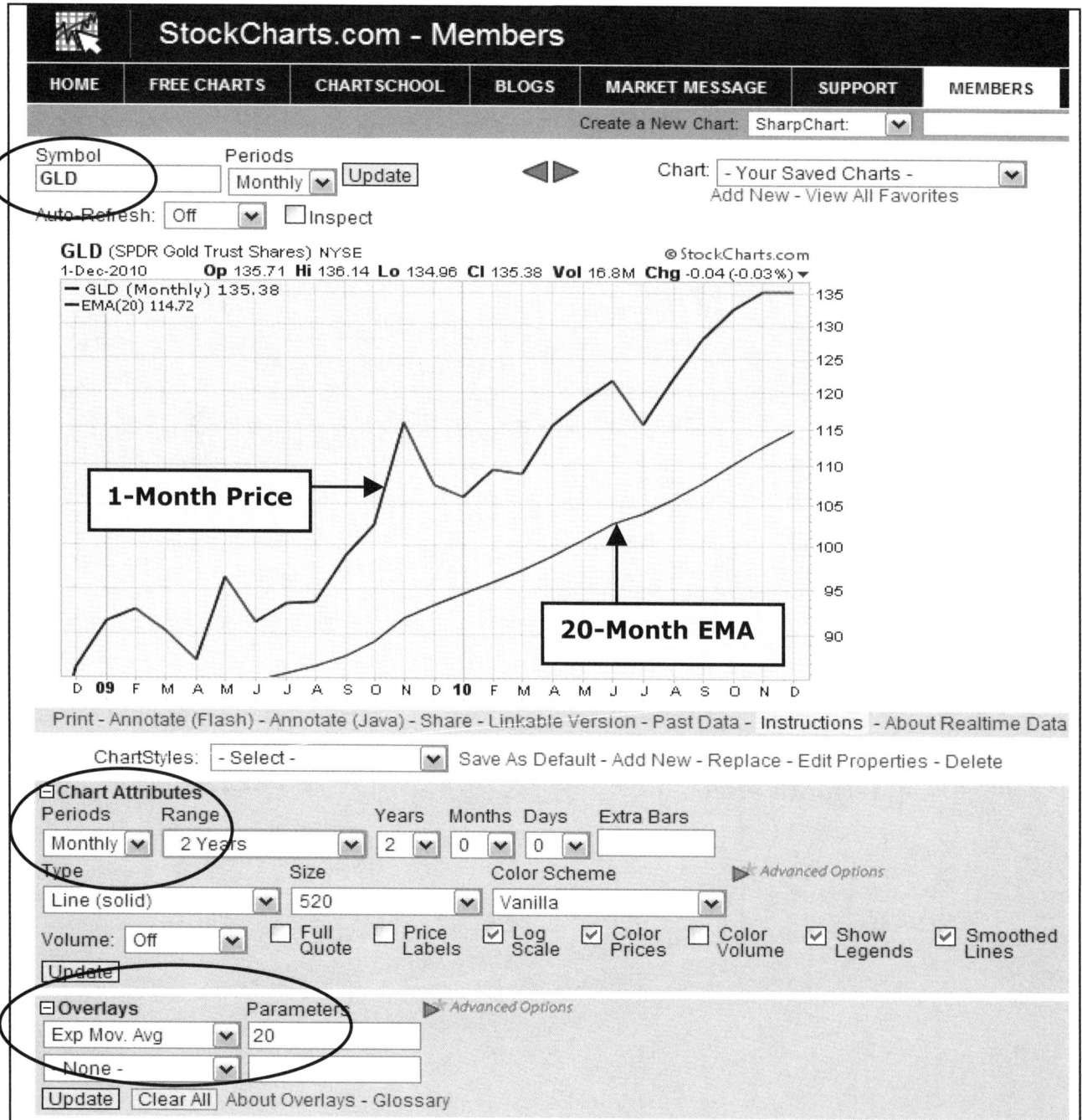

Major Trend System Trade Signal Examples

The monthly price graphs below show examples of Major Trend System 'Buy' and 'Sell' signals.

MON (Monsanto Co.) NYSE — @StockCharts.com
1-Dec-2008 **Open** 76.55 **High** 76.59 **Low** 70.57 **Close** 70.92 **Volume** 6.3M **Chg** -8.02 (-10.16%) ▼
— MON (Monthly) 70.92
— EMA(20) 90.81

Labels: 1-Month Price, 20-Month EMA, Buy, Sell

PBR (Petroleo Brasileiro (Petrobras)) NYSE — @StockCharts.com
1-Dec-2008 **Open** 18.58 **High** 18.68 **Low** 17.24 **Close** 17.35 **Volume** 23.0M **Chg** -2.97 (-14.61%) ▼
— PBR (Monthly) 17.35
— EMA(20) 39.04

Labels: 1-Month Price, 20-Month EMA, Buy, Sell

Major Trend System Historical Results

The *Major Trend* 1-Month/20-Month EMA system is a rule based system with clearly defined "buy" and "sell" rules which allow for historical profit testing.

Historical profit results are based on buying a market when the 1-Month price crosses above the 20-Month EMA and closing out long positions and going short a market when the 1-Month price crosses below the 20-Month EMA.

I conducted historical testing on a diversified portfolio of eight global markets including crude oil, the Euro currency, bonds and equities listed below:

Diversified Global Portfolio

Crude Oil		Euro Currency
MSCI Emerging Market Index		20-Year Treasury Bonds
iShares Latin America		MSCI Brazil
iShares Europe		S&P 500 Index

The historical profit results that follow were conducted over a 14 year period (or ETF inception). Results are based on an initial investment of $10,000 divided equally among the eight global markets and compounding the results thereafter and do not include commissions. The historical results do not reflect the use leverage or margin.

Major Trend System Global Portfolio Historical Results

Initial Investment	$10,000
Number Years	13.75
Profit	$111,031
Total Return	1,110%
Average Annual Return	80.7%
Percent Winning Trades	81.0%
Total Profits	$113,549
Total Losses	$2,518
Profit:Loss Ratio	45.1 to 1
Largest Losing Trade	-9.2%
Average Losing Trade	-3.2%

Major Trend System Global Portfolio Profit Results

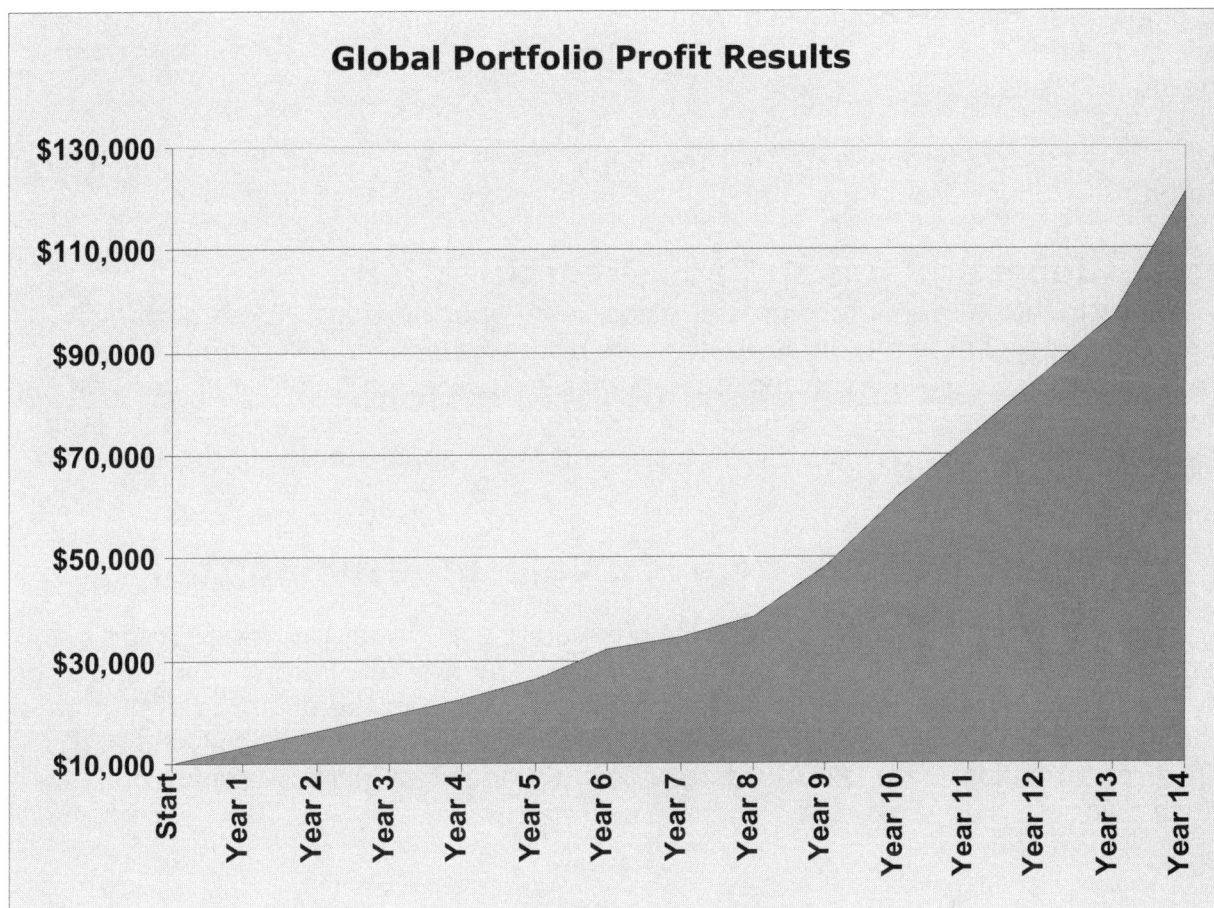

Global Portfolio Profit Results

Historical results reveal that the *Major Trend System* produced impressive profits with very low risk. A $10,000 investment grew to $121,031 and after deducting the initial $10,000 investment, the total profits were $111,031 (before commissions) which equates to a 1,110% return on the initial $10,000 investment.

Over the almost fourteen year test period this translates to an 80.7% average annual return. This is an excellent annual return for a system that does not use leverage or margin! Eighty-one percent of trades were profitable and all years were profitable.

$45 of Profit for Each 1 Dollar of Loss

The system produced $113,549 in total profits and only $2,518 in total losses. Dividing the total profits by the total losses results in a Profit to Loss Ratio of 45.1 to 1. This translates to more than 45 dollars of profit for each 1 dollar of loss.

A high Profit to Loss Ratio indicates that the *Major Trend System* keeps losses to a minimum by exiting losing trades before they develop into a large loss.

The *Major Trend System* normally exits a trade before a big loss occurs and provides you with the discipline necessary to become a successful trader. Keep in mind that two global bear markets occurred during this period including the worst bear market since 1932 during which the S&P 500 Index lost 50% of its value and the NASDAQ suffered a 76% loss.

These profit results demonstrate that the *Major Trend System* is a versatile, effective method for profiting from long or short trades in any type of market.

Broad Global and Asset Class Diversification

Most investment programs recommend diversifying your portfolio across different industry groups. One of the great advantages of the *Major Trend System* is that it allows you to also diversify your portfolio by asset class which further reduces risk and can result in higher returns. The ability of the *Major Trend System* to take both long and short trades also increases the diversity and profit opportunities of the system.

Major Trend System is a Valuable Trading Tool

Regardless of which indicator or methodology you use to trade, the *Major Trend System* can be a valuable trading tool for virtually any market. Before I take a long or short position I normally check to make sure I am trading in the direction of the major trend. Trading in the direction of the major trend provides a constant tailwind and helps prevent whipsaw trades. Avoiding whipsaw trades can increase profits and reduce risk.

GPS Major Trend System Individual Market Profit Results

The historical profit results that follow are based on an initial investment of $10,000 in a market and compounding the results thereafter and do not include commissions. The historical results do not reflect the use leverage or margin.

Emerging Market Index ETF Results

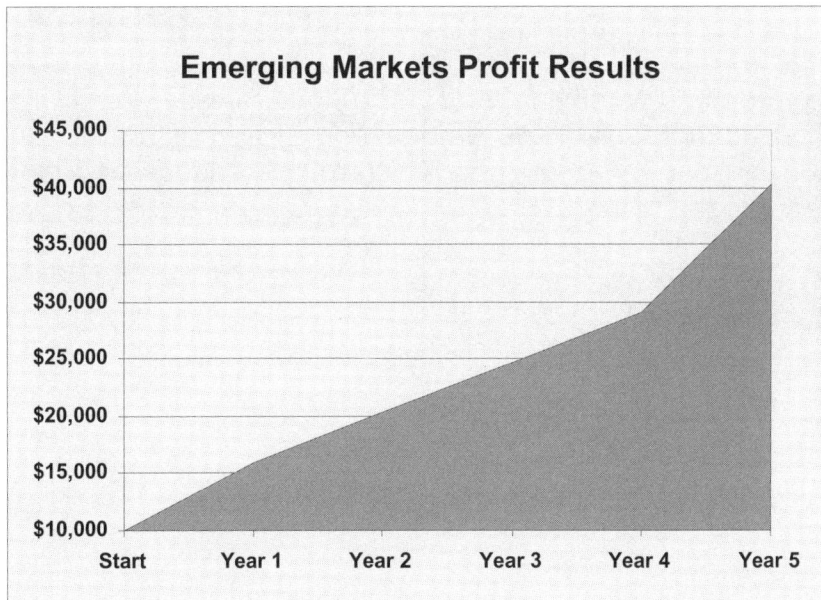

Emerging Markets Profit Results

Initial Investment	$10,000
Number Years	5
Profit	$30,334
Total Return	303%
Avg Annual Return	61%
% Winning Trades	100%
Profit:Loss Ratio	No Losses

S&P 500 Index ETF Profit Results

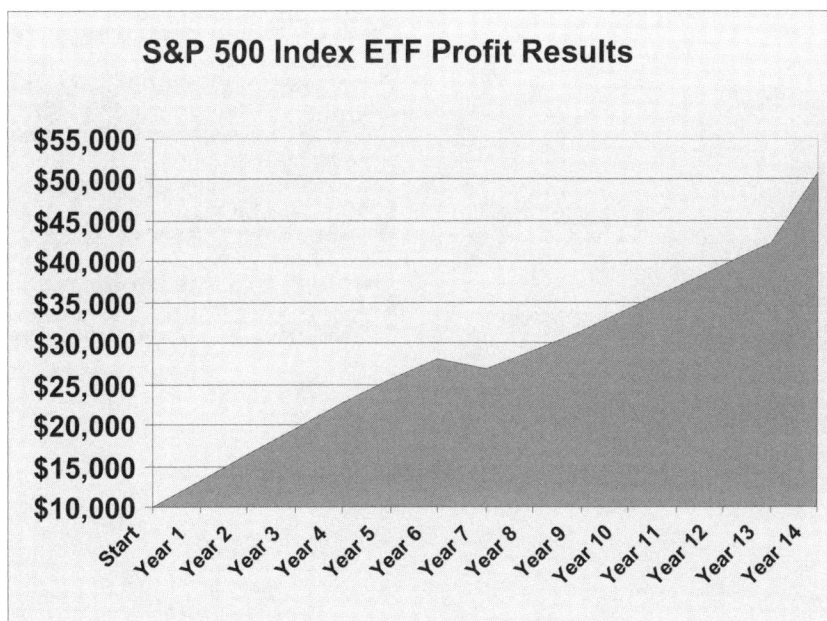

S&P 500 Index ETF Profit Results

Initial Investment	$10,000
Number Years	14
Profit	$40,847
Total Return	408%
Avg Annual Return	29%
% Winning Trades	67%
Profit:Loss Ratio	12 to 1

Euro Currency ETF Profit Results

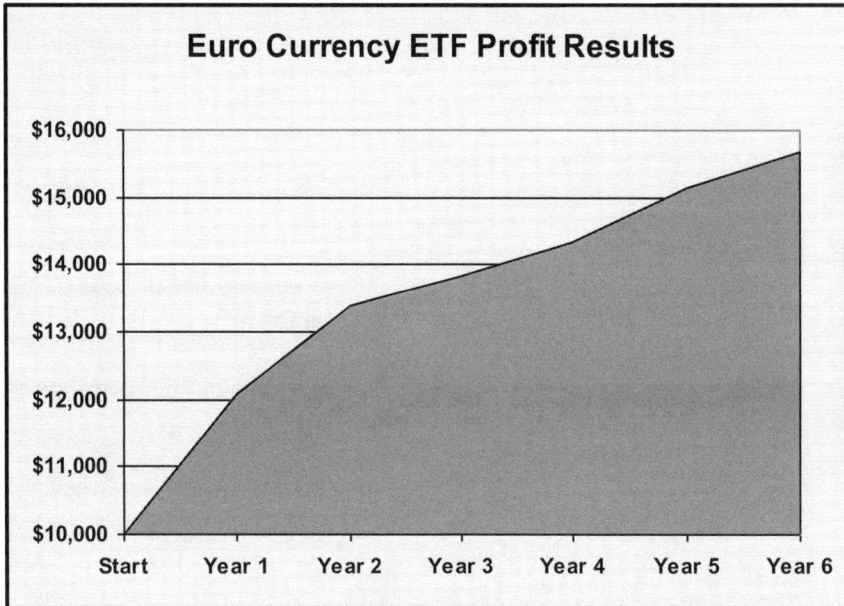

Euro Currency ETF Profit Results

Initial Investment	$10,000
Number Years	6
Profit	$5,823
Total Return	58%
Avg Annual Return	10%
% Winning Trades	67%
Profit:Loss Ratio	43 to 1

Brazil ETF Profit Results

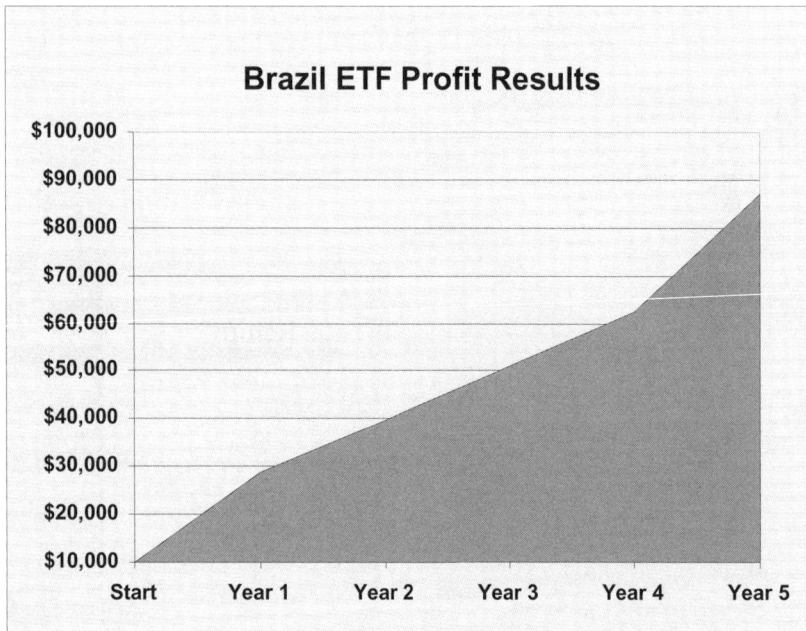

Brazil ETF Profit Results

Initial Investment	$10,000
Number Years	5
Profit	$77,035
Total Return	770%
Avg Annual Return	154%
% Winning Trades	100%
Profit:Loss Ratio	No Losses

Crude Oil Profit Results

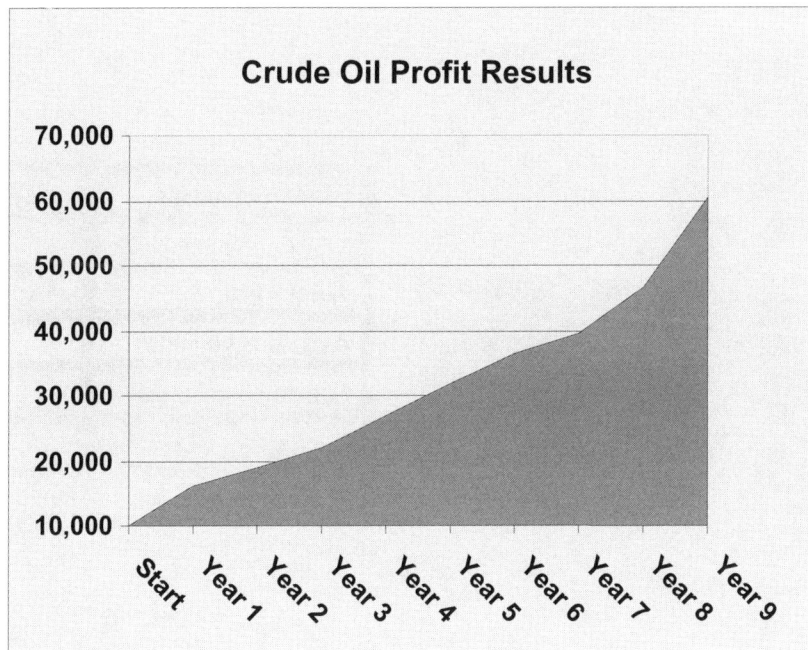

Crude Oil Profit Results

Initial Investment	$10,000
Number Years	9
Profit	$50,599
Total Return	506%
Avg Annual Return	56%
% Winning Trades	60%
Profit:Loss Ratio	19 to 1

Latin America ETF Profit Results

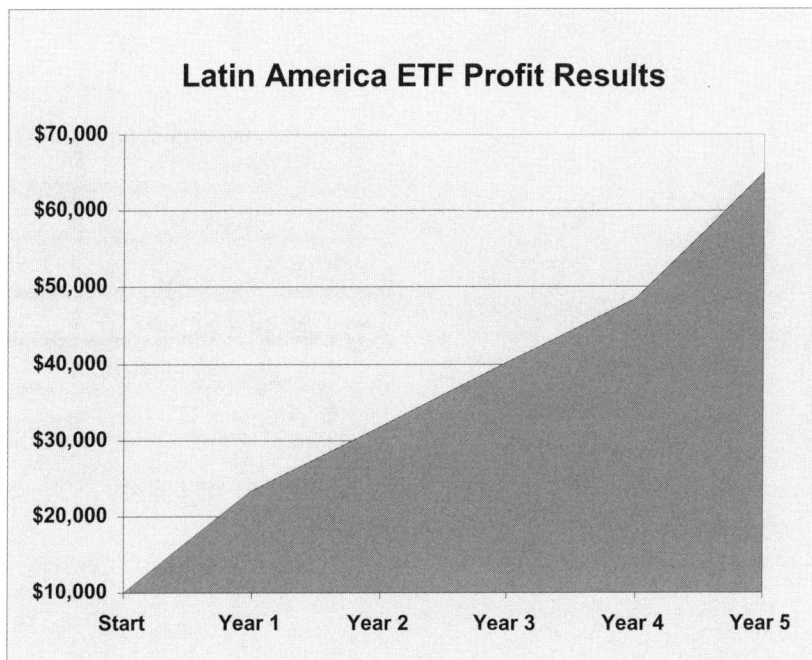

Latin America ETF Profit Results

Initial Investment	$10,000
Number Years	5
Profit	$55,106
Total Return	551%
Avg Annual Return	110%
% Winning Trades	100%
Profit:Loss Ratio	No Losses

Europe ETF Profit Results

Europe Index Profit Results

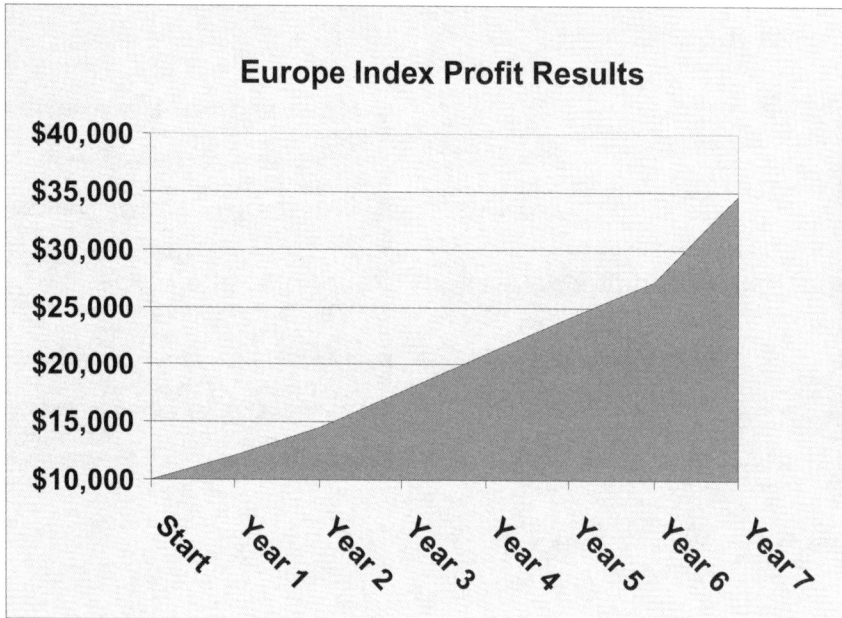

Initial Investment	$10,000
Number Years	7
Profit	$24,546
Total Return	245%
Avg Annual Return	35%
% Winning Trades	100%
Profit:Loss Ratio	No Losses

Treasury Bond ETF Profit Results

Treasury Bond ETF Profit Results

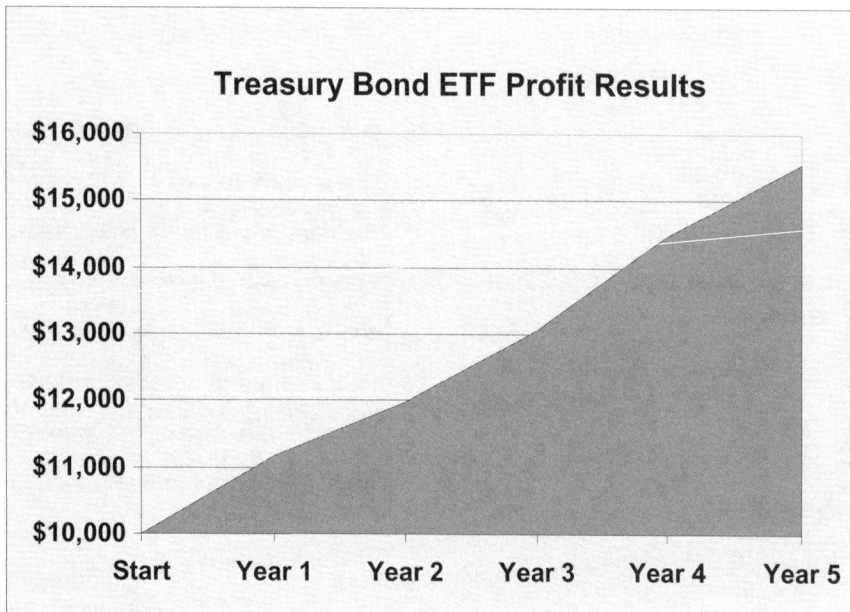

Initial Investment	$10,000
Number Years	5
Profit	$5,540
Total Return	55%
Avg Annual Return	11%
% Winning Trades	100%
Profit:Loss Ratio	No Losses

Finding the Best Profit Opportunities

On any given day there can be hundreds of stocks and ETFs on a 'buy' or 'sell' signal using the *50/100-Day EMA System*. The challenge lies in narrowing down the list of 'buys' to the stocks/ETFs with the best profit potential so that we may establish bullish weekly option trades. And narrowing down the list of 'sells' to the stocks/ETFs with the best profit potential so that we may establish bearish weekly option trades.

My *Prime Trade Select* process is a simple, systematic, three-step approach for finding stocks/ETFs with the best profit potential for both bullish and bearish weekly option trades. This systematic approach has produced consistent profits during all types of market conditions.

Prime Trade Select uses three steps to finding stocks with the best profit opportunities:

1) **Determine the price trend**

2) **Confirm the price trend**

3) **Select an entry point**

Let's review what we have learned thus far. We learned that the *50/100-Day EMA System* is a simple but effective way to measure the price trend of a stock. If the price trend is up and the stock/ETF is on a 'buy' signal we establish bullish weekly option positions. And if the stock/ETF is on a 'sell' signal we establish bearish weekly option positions. Before taking a bearish option position we want to make sure the stock/ETF is on a *Major Trend System* 'sell' signal which can help prevent unprofitable 'whipsaw' trades when a counter-trend rally occurs.

The second Step in the *Prime Trade Select* process is confirming the price trend. In my experience, one of the simplest but most effective methods for confirming the price trend is volume flow. Prices do not move without buyers and sellers.

Volume flow precedes price and is the key to measuring the validity and sustainability of a price trend.

My favorite volume indicator is the On Balance Volume line. On Balance Volume measures volume flow. When a stock closes up for the day, volume is added to the line and when a stock closes down volume is subtracted from the line. A cumulative total of the volume additions and subtractions form the On Balance Volume line.

On Balance Volume Indicator

- **When Close is Up Volume is Added**

- **When Close is Down Volume is Subtracted**

- **A Cumulative Total of Additions and Subtractions Form the OBV Line**

Let's now look at an example of how we use the On Balance Volume indicator to confirm the price trend. The price chart below displays the daily price movement for Riverbed stock. Below the price chart is an example of the On Balance Volume line for Riverbed stock.

The numerical value of the On Balance Volume line is not important. We simply want to see an up sloping line to confirm a price up trend.

We can see from chart below that the On Balance Volume line is sloping up. An up sloping line indicates that the volume is heavier on up days and buying pressure is exceeding selling pressure. Buying pressure must continue to exceed selling pressure in order to sustain a price up trend. So On Balance Volume is a simple indicator to use that confirms the price up trend and the sustainability of the price up trend.

Normally we only want to establish bullish weekly option positions on stocks/ETFs with an up sloping On Balance Volume line. Limiting bullish weekly option trades to stocks/ETFs with an up sloping On Balance Volume line helps us further narrow down our list of potential stocks/ETFs to trade.

Let's now look at an example of how we use the On Balance Volume indicator to confirm a price down trend. The price chart below displays the daily price movement for the Brazil ETF. Below the price chart is an example of the On Balance Volume line for the Brazil ETF. As previously mentioned, the numerical value of the On Balance Volume line is not important. We simply want to see a down sloping line to confirm a price down trend.

We can see from chart below that the On Balance Volume line is sloping down. A down sloping line indicates that the volume is heavier on down days and selling pressure is exceeding buying pressure. Selling pressure must continue to exceed buying pressure in order to sustain a price down trend. The On Balance Volume is confirming the price down trend and the sustainability of the price down trend.

Normally we only want to establish bearish weekly option positions on stocks/ETFs with a down sloping On Balance Volume line. Limiting bearish weekly option trades to stocks/ETFs with a down sloping On Balance Volume line helps us further narrow down our list of potential stocks/ETFs to trade.

Up Sloping On Balance Volume Line

- Volume is Heavier On Days Stock Closes Up

- Volume is Lighter On Days Stock Closes Down

- Buying Pressure is Exceeding Selling Pressure

- Helps Sustain Price Up Trend

Down Sloping On Balance Volume Line

- Volume is Heavier On Days Stock Closes Down

- Volume is Lighter On Days Stock Closes Up

- Selling Pressure is Exceeding Buying Pressure

- Helps Sustain Price Down Trend

**On Balance Volume Is a Useful
Tool to Confirm the Price Trend
For Virtually Any Market**

The price chart below displays the daily price movement for Home Depot stock. Below the price chart is the On Balance Volume line for Home Depot stock. We can see from chart that the On Balance Volume line is sloping up indicating volume is heavier on up days and buying pressure is exceeding selling pressure. The up sloping On Balance Volume line confirms the price up trend and the sustainability of the price up trend.

Confirmed Up Trend

- Stock price is trending up with 50-Day EMA line above 100-Day EMA line
- Volume is increasing on days a stock closes up
- Volume is decreasing on days a stock closes down

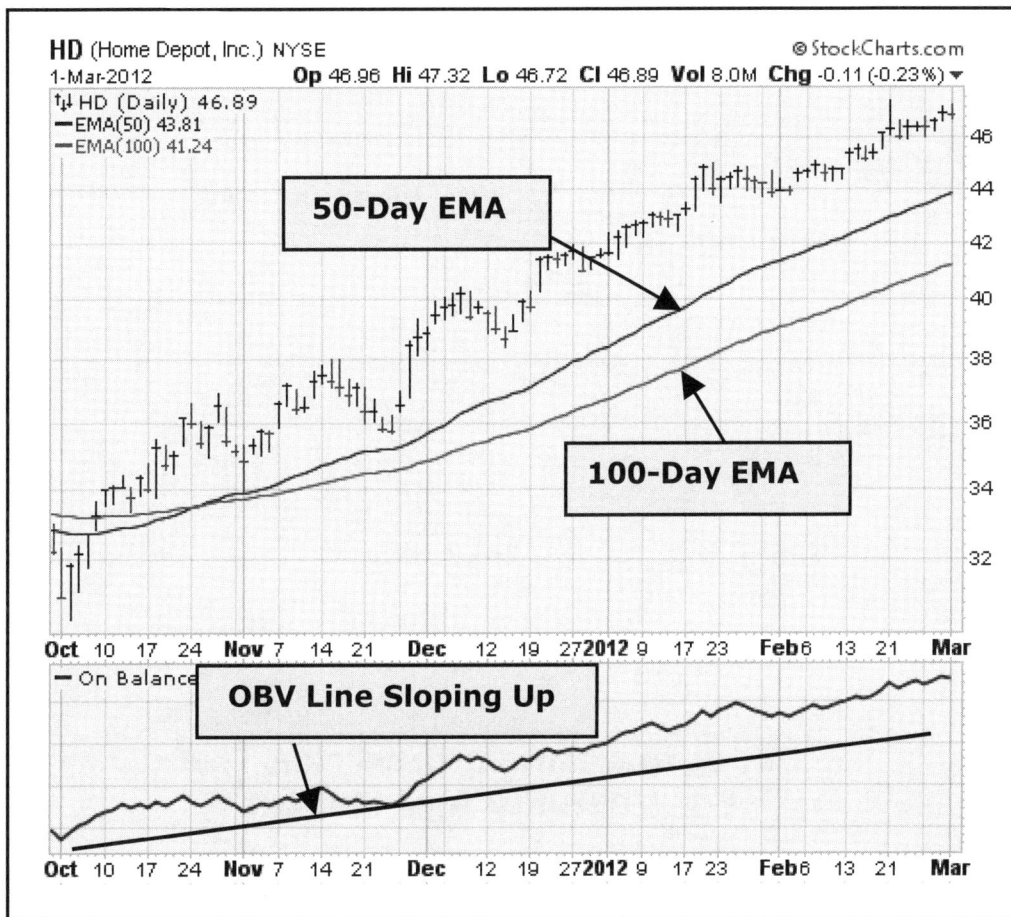

And the price chart below displays the daily price movement for the Brazil ETF. Below the price chart is the On Balance Volume line for the Brazil ETF. We can see from chart that the On Balance Volume line is sloping down indicating volume is heavier on down days and selling pressure is exceeding buying pressure. The down sloping On Balance Volume line confirms the price down trend and the sustainability of the price down trend.

Confirmed Down Trend

- Stock price is trending down with 50-Day EMA line below 100-Day EMA line
- Volume is increasing on days a stock closes down
- Volume is decreasing on days a stock closes up

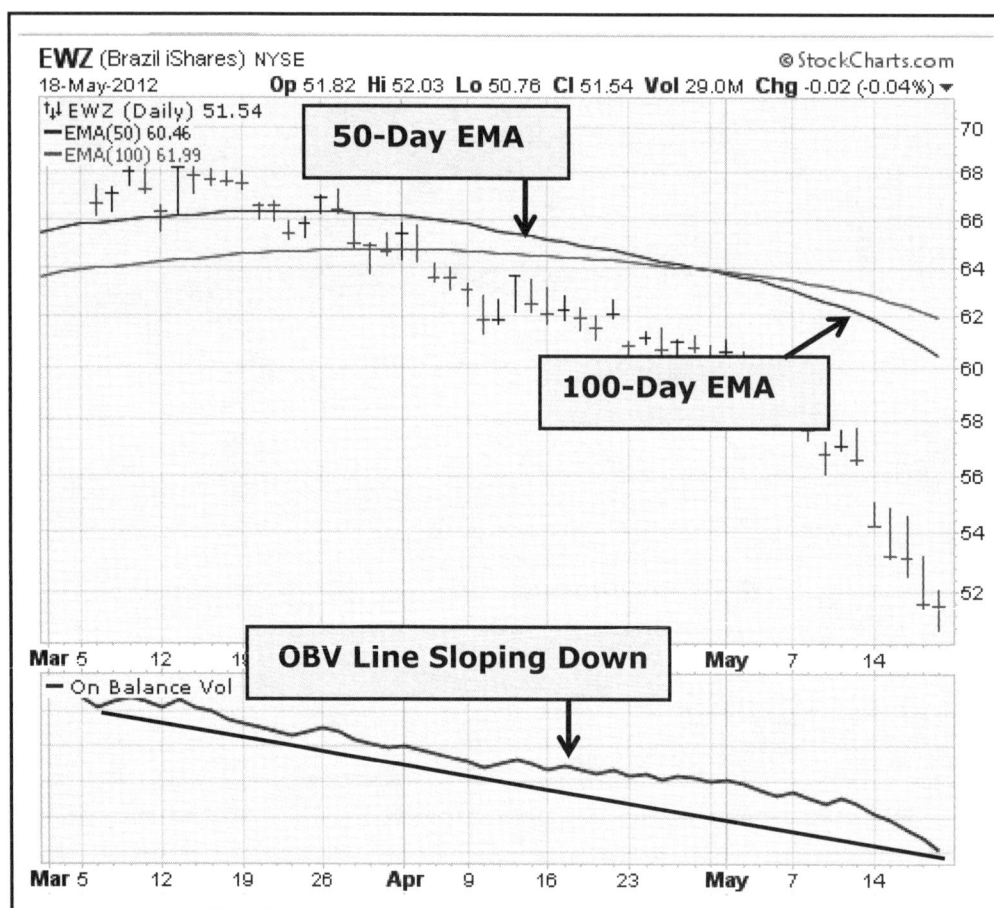

Downloading On Balance Volume

On Balance Volume can be easily downloaded from www.StockCharts.com. On the home page type in the stock symbol and click "Go". In this example I typed in the symbol for Apple stock AAPL.

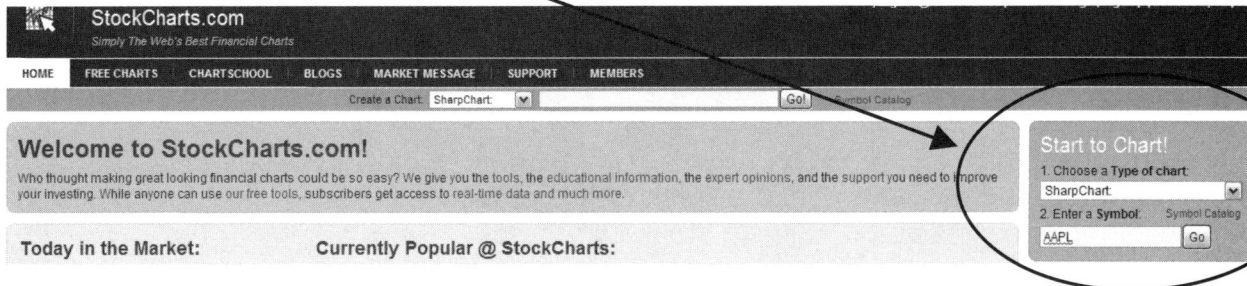

Once you click "Go" the default chart for Apple will appear. Below the default chart for Apple select "Daily" under Periods and "1 Year" under Range. Under Indicators select "On Balance Volume".

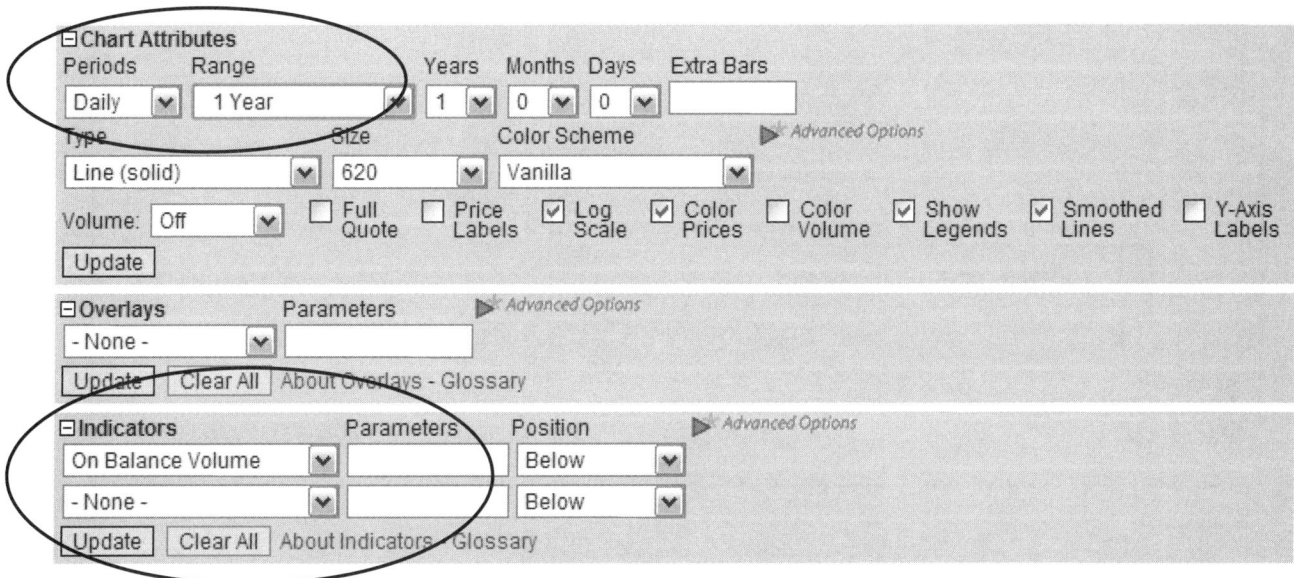

Click "Update" and the Apple price chart with the On Balance Line will be displayed (see price chart on the following page).

Apple One Year Price Chart with On Balance Volume Line Below

AAPL (Apple, Inc.) Nasdaq GS   © StockCharts.com
15-Apr-2010   **Open** 245.78 **High** 249.03 **Low** 245.51 **Close** 248.92 **Volume** 13.4M **Chg** +3.23 (+1.31%) ▲

— AAPL (Daily) 248.92

— On Balance Vol

On Balance Volume Line

New 52-Week High List

Another simple but effective method for confirming a price up trend is the new 52-Week high list. A stock is added to the new 52-Week high list when it trades at a higher price than its highest price over the past 52 weeks. For example, today Abbott Labs (circled below) traded at a high of 57.66 which is highest price the stock has traded over the past 52-Weeks. So Abbott Labs was added to today's new 52-Week high list.

The new 52-Week high list below lists the stocks that traded at a new 52-Week high price today. There is a new 52-Week High list published daily when the market is open for trading.

US Exchanges 52 Week Highs Thursday, Mar 8th, 2012   FlipCharts ☒

Stocks that have traded for a year that have matched or made a new 52-Week High during the current trading session.

Filter: US Exchanges ⌄   ⑦ HELP   **Main View** » Technical » Performance » Custom View

Sym	Name	Last	Change	Percent	High	Low	Volume	Time	Links
ABCB	Ameris Bancorp	11.65	-0.10	-0.85%	11.96	11.50	19,336	13:47	
ABCO	The Advisory Board	82.92	+0.92	+1.12%	82.99	82.01	46,468	13:52	
ABT	Abbott Laboratories	57.62	+1.36	+2.42%	57.66	56.90	6,720,538	13:54	
ABV	Companhia De Bebidas	40.59	+0.63	+1.58%	40.71	40.24	1,035,693	13:54	
ACAT	Arctic Cat Inc.	40.28	+1.25	+3.20%	40.48	39.26	291,507	13:53	
ACET	Aceto Corp.	8.75	+0.30	+3.55%	8.72	8.45	170,997	13:54	
ADS	Alliance Data System	122.77	+1.62	+1.34%	123.46	121.74	218,143	13:52	
AEO	American Eagle Outfi	15.74	+0.20	+1.29%	16.43	15.70	8,107,124	13:54	
AGEN	Agenus Inc.	4.10	-0.39	-8.69%	4.92	4.01	591,365	13:53	
AGN	Allergan	92.00	+1.36	+1.50%	92.45	90.99	1,535,740	13:54	
AIS	Antares Pharma	2.91	+0.16	+5.82%	2.97	2.81	1,546,090	13:53	
ALOG	Analogic Corp.	62.00	+2.57	+4.32%	62.17	59.63	101,952	13:53	
AMRB	American River Banks	7.15	+0.15	+2.14%	7.22	7.07	28,027	12:04	
AMTG	Apollo Residential	19.42	+0.13	+0.67%	19.52	19.12	375,895	13:53	
ARG	Airgas	82.73	+1.17	+1.43%	82.87	81.72	94,651	13:50	
ASRV	Ameriserv Financial	2.70	unch	unch	2.75	2.65	16,610	13:48	
ATHN	Athenahealth	74.17	+1.92	+2.66%	75.00	72.40	396,535	13:53	
AVD	American Vanguard	19.33	+0.66	+3.54%	19.39	18.79	170,259	13:53	
AZO	Autozone	384.80	+1.06	+0.28%	386.00	383.01	203,491	13:54	
BAP	Credicorp Ltd	127.53	+1.65	+1.31%	127.95	125.48	77,534	13:52	
BIG	Big Lots	44.88	-0.02	-0.04%	45.00	44.64	502,805	13:54	
BIP	Brookfield Infrastru	30.53	+0.35	+1.16%	30.60	30.32	130,327	13:52	
BUD	Anheuser-Busch Inbev	69.86	+2.99	+4.47%	69.93	68.58	1,164,405	13:54	
CALL	Vocaltec Communicati	22.64	-1.00	-4.23%	24.00	22.34	333,234	13:53	
CBB	Cincinnati Bell Inc	3.94	+0.01	+0.25%	3.98	3.81	984,457	13:54	
CBS	Cbs Corp.	30.19	+0.40	+1.34%	30.60	29.91	4,473,549	13:54	
CCI	Crown Castle Interna	53.87	+1.28	+2.43%	54.42	53.55	6,368,206	13:54	
CDI	Cdi Corp.	16.50	+0.23	+1.41%	16.61	16.30	24,339	13:51	
CERN	Cerner Corp.	76.22	+0.68	+0.90%	76.54	75.58	486,025	13:53	
CHD	Church & Dwight Comp	48.33	+0.55	+1.15%	48.50	47.98	442,288	13:53	
CHG	Ch Energy Group	66.94	-0.01	-0.01%	67.03	66.71	24,410	13:53	
CHKR	Chesapeake Granite	29.07	+0.41	+1.43%	29.25	28.68	220,433	13:53	

In my trading experience, I discovered that stocks that are making a new 52-Week high tend to continue their price up trend. A stock that makes a new 52-Week high 'confirms' the price up trend and allows you to further narrow down your buy list to stocks with the greatest profit potential.

Stocks that are included in the new 52-Week high list represent the very best profit opportunities available out of the universe of more than 6,000 common stocks currently trading.

Plain and simple . . . A stock does not make the new 52-Week high list unless it is in a very powerful price up trend.

Research tip: Even though trend confirmation is Step 2 in our *Prime Trade Select* process, downloading the new 52-Week high list is actually a good initial starting point for the 3 Step stock selection process. Most of the stocks on the new 52-Week high list are also in a price up trend with the 50 EMA line above the 100-Day EMA line.

The number of stocks on the new 52-Week high list will vary according to market conditions. I literally check the new 52-week high list almost every trading day. I normally will select one stock from an industry group and include 5 to 8 different industry groups in my bullish weekly option portfolio for diversification.

The price chart below shows the daily price action for Home Depot stock. We can see that HD stock has been making a series of new 52-Week highs each month. In this example, buying Home Depot stock or weekly call options when it was trading at a new high price has produced substantial profits.

New 52-Week Low List

When initiating bearish weekly option positions, we want to confirm the price down trend for a stock by checking the new 52-Week Low list. A stock is added to the new 52-Week low list when it trades at a lower price than its lowest price over the past 52 weeks. For example, today Alcoa (circled below) traded at a low of 8.29 which is lowest price the stock has traded over the past 52-Weeks. So Alcoa was added to today's new 52-Week low list.

The new 52-Week low list below lists the stocks that traded at a new 52-Week low price today. There is a new 52-Week Low list published daily when the market is open for trading.

US Exchanges 52 Week Lows — Friday, Jun 1st, 2012 — FlipCharts ☒

Stocks that have traded for a year that have matched or made a new 52-Week Low during the current trading session.

Filter: US Exchanges ⌄ ⓘ HELP   **Main View »** Technical » Performance » Custom View

Sym	Name	Last	Change	Percent	High	Low	Volume	Time	Links
AA	Alcoa Inc.	8.30	-0.25	-2.92%	8.48	8.29	24,656,500	06/01/12	
AAV	Advantage Oil & Gas	2.63	-0.14	-5.05%	2.73	2.57	282,400	06/01/12	
AB	Alliance Capital Man	12.43	-0.47	-3.64%	12.87	12.35	211,500	06/01/12	
ABB	Abb Ltd	15.63	-0.18	-1.14%	15.65	15.39	4,296,300	06/01/12	
ABFS	Arkansas Best Corp.	12.63	-0.02	-0.16%	12.84	12.30	314,600	06/01/12	
ACH	Aluminum Corporation	10.01	-0.65	-6.10%	10.17	10.00	290,300	06/01/12	
ACI	Arch Coal	6.23	-0.11	-1.74%	6.43	6.08	18,549,799	06/01/12	
ACM	Aecom Technology Cor	15.98	-0.31	-1.90%	16.15	15.78	1,038,100	06/01/12	
ADK	Adcare Health System	3.36	-0.04	-1.18%	3.39	3.29	17,500	06/01/12	
AIN	Albany International	17.93	-0.31	-1.70%	18.01	16.75	266,800	06/01/12	
AIR	Aar	11.56	-0.49	-4.07%	11.97	11.52	579,900	06/01/12	
AMBO	Ambow Education	4.10	-0.05	-1.20%	4.22	4.00	93,400	06/01/12	
ANF	Abercrombie & Fitch	32.14	-1.40	-4.17%	32.89	31.82	4,050,500	06/01/12	
ANR	Alpha Natural Resour	10.43	-0.05	-0.48%	10.75	9.91	13,726,699	06/01/12	
AP	Ampco-Pittsburgh Cor	15.55	+0.02	+0.13%	15.78	15.20	57,100	06/01/12	
APKT	Acme Packet	22.60	-0.28	-1.22%	22.74	21.80	1,800,400	06/01/12	
ARGN	Amerigon Incorporate	11.84	-0.14	-1.17%	11.95	11.41	623,000	06/01/12	
ARUN	Aruba Networks	12.93	-0.21	-1.60%	13.05	12.70	4,309,300	06/01/12	
ARX	Aeroflex Holding	6.10	-0.37	-5.72%	6.48	6.06	74,300	06/01/12	
ASTE	Astec Industries	26.96	-0.49	-1.79%	27.41	26.48	227,800	06/01/12	
ATI	Allegheny Technologi	30.33	-1.79	-5.57%	31.46	30.23	3,359,800	06/01/12	

Stocks that are making a new 52-Week low tend to continue their price down trend. A stock that makes a new 52-Week low 'confirms' the price down trend and allows you to further narrow down your list of stocks with the greatest profit potential for short positions. Similar to the new 52-Week High list, stocks that are included in the new 52-Week Low list represent the very best shorting opportunities available out of the universe of more than 6,000 common stocks currently trading.

A stock does not make the new 52-Week Low list unless it is in a very powerful price down trend. The number of stocks on the new 52-Week Low list will vary according to market conditions.

The price chart below shows the daily price action for Alcoa stock. We can see that Alcoa stock has been making a series of new 52-Week lows. In this example, buying Alcoa weekly put options when Alcoa was trading at a new low price has been very profitable.

Down Loading the New 52-Week High/Low List

The new 52-Week High/Low list can be easily downloaded from www.barchart.com

Step 1: Log on to www.barchart.com and click 'Stocks'

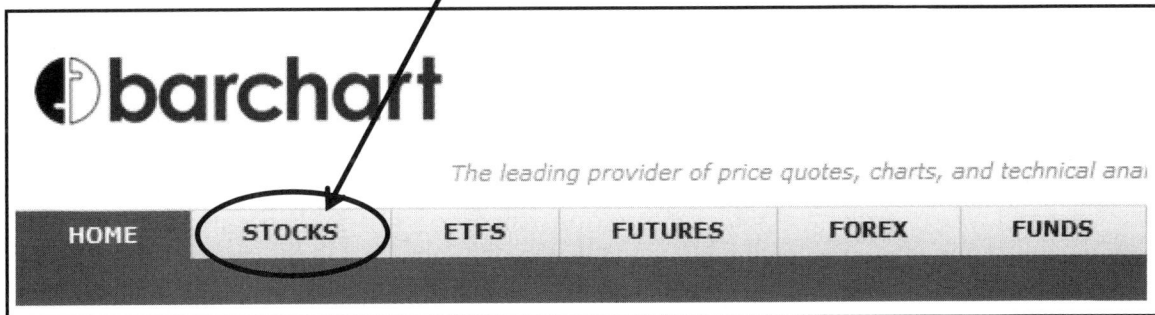

Step 2: Click '52 Week Highs' to display the current new 52-Week High List and click '52-Week Lows' to display the new 52-Week Low list

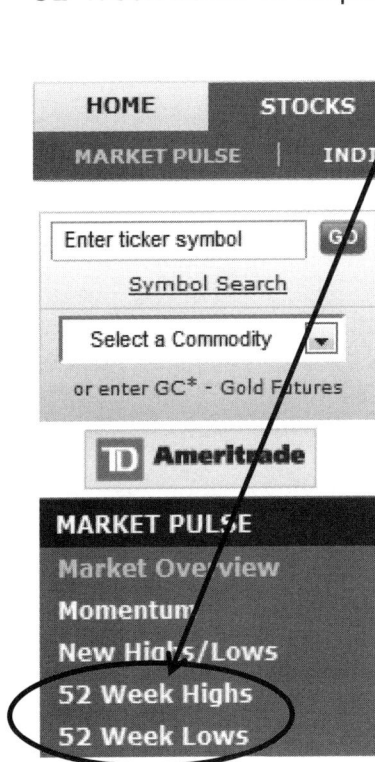

Industry Grouping

I check the new 52-Week High list almost every trading day. I discovered that when you check this list daily you start to notice stocks in certain industry groups that make new highs almost daily. These are the leading industry groups I like to focus on to narrow down my list to the stocks with the greatest profit potential for bullish weekly option positions.

Quantitative research suggests that approximately one half of a stock's price movement is due to the industry grouping of a stock. Focusing on the top performing industry groups provides a constant 'tail wind' (in pilot's terms) to your trading success. It allows you to not only narrow down your list of stocks on a 'buy' but also provides you stocks with the best profit potential. *Investors Business Daily* also provides industry rankings which help you focus on the top performing industry groups.

When initiating bearish weekly option positions, I like to focus on the weakest industry groups. This allows me to narrow down my list of stocks on a 'sell' signal and provides stocks with the best profit potential for bearish option positions.

We will next look at Step 3 of the *Prime Trade Select* process which is timing our entry point.

Timing is Everything

Step 3: Selecting an Entry Point

Now that we know how to determine a price trend and confirm the trend, the next step for the *Prime Trade Select* process is timing our entry point for entering bullish and bearish weekly option trades. We will look at selecting a buy point for bullish trades first.

One of the simplest but most effective entry timing indicators are the Keltner Channels which can quickly and easily be downloaded from investing websites such as www.StockCharts.com. Steps for down loading the Keltner Channels follow.

The Keltner Channels function as an overbought/oversold indicator that can help us select a buy point for stocks and weekly call options that are in a confirmed price up trend. Overbought is a term used to describe a stock that has been increasing in price over a period of weeks or months with very few price pullbacks. Oversold is a term used to describe a stock that has been decreasing in price over a period of weeks or months with very few prices increases.

Stocks in a price up trend do not advance in a straight line. There are always price corrections or retrenchments along the way. Like the tide there is an ebb and flow in the price movements in stocks. This is the natural order of the markets . . . stocks advance and then the price declines inevitably as profit taking occurs.

Stocks can remain in an overall price up trend as these price declines occur as long as the price decline is not severe enough to cause the 50-Day EMA line to cross below the 100-Day EMA line which signals a trend reversal from a price up trend to a price down trend. When this occurs a stock should be sold.

The Keltner Channels are a valuable timing tool as the channels can help us prevent buying stocks when they are in an overbought condition. When stocks become overbought they are vulnerable to profit taking and minor price declines within the context of remaining in a price up trend. The Keltner Channels can help us avoid buying stocks when they become overbought and instead buy stocks and call options when they become oversold.

When you avoid buying stocks that are overbought and instead buy stocks when they are oversold (but still in a price up trend) you greatly increase your odds of selecting a profitable trade.

Let's take a look at an example of the Keltner Channels and how they can help us select our entry point. The price chart below displays the daily price movement for Apple stock along with the three Keltner Channels. There is an upper channel, middle channel (which is the dotted line) and a lower channel.

When a stock trades near the upper channel it is an indication the stock is becoming overbought and will most likely encounter selling pressure and then trade back down towards the middle or lower channel.

When a stock trades near the lower channel it is an indication the stock is becoming oversold and will most likely encounter buying pressure and then trade back up towards the middle or upper channel.

If you are considering buying Apple stock or weekly call options, you don't want to buy if the stock is trading near the upper channel as there is a good chance the stock will encounter selling pressure near the upper channel and then decline in price.

It is better to wait until the stock trades near the middle or lower channel before buying. This results in a better entry as the stock most likely will trade back up towards the upper channel.

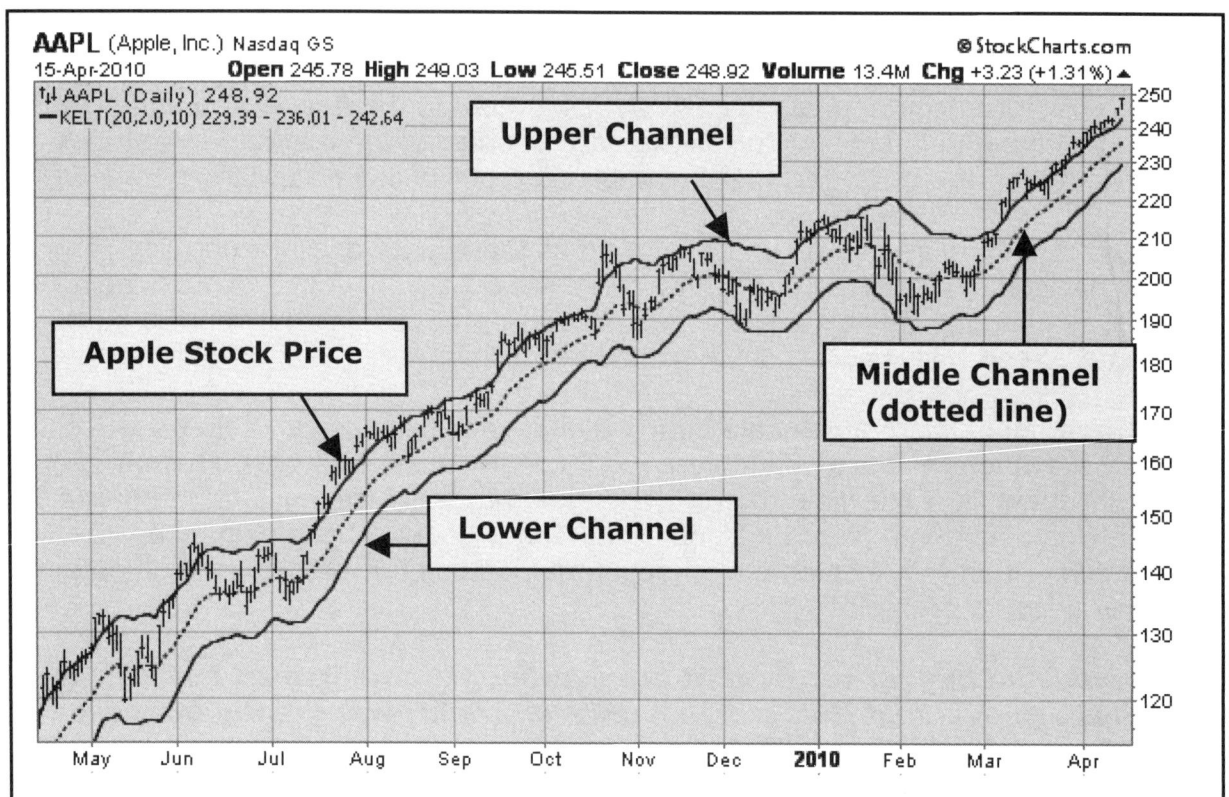

Circled below are examples of Apple stock trading above the upper channel. When a stock is trading above the upper channel it is better to wait for the stock to decline towards the middle or lower channel before buying.

When a stock is trading near the middle or lower channel there is a good probability that it will rally back towards the upper channel.

In each of these examples, after the stock traded above the upper channel it declined back towards the middle or lower channel within a week or two except for the example that occurred in mid-July. In this example the retracement took a little longer as the stock traded near the upper channel in mid-July and did not retrace back to the middle channel until mid-August. This happens occasionally in strong bull markets.

Currently Apple is trading above the upper channel and has stayed above the upper channel for several weeks not presenting any buying opportunities. In my experience this is very rare. Currently Apple stock would have to decline to about 236 before it touches the middle channel.

Don't Buy When a Stock Is Trading Near the Upper Channel

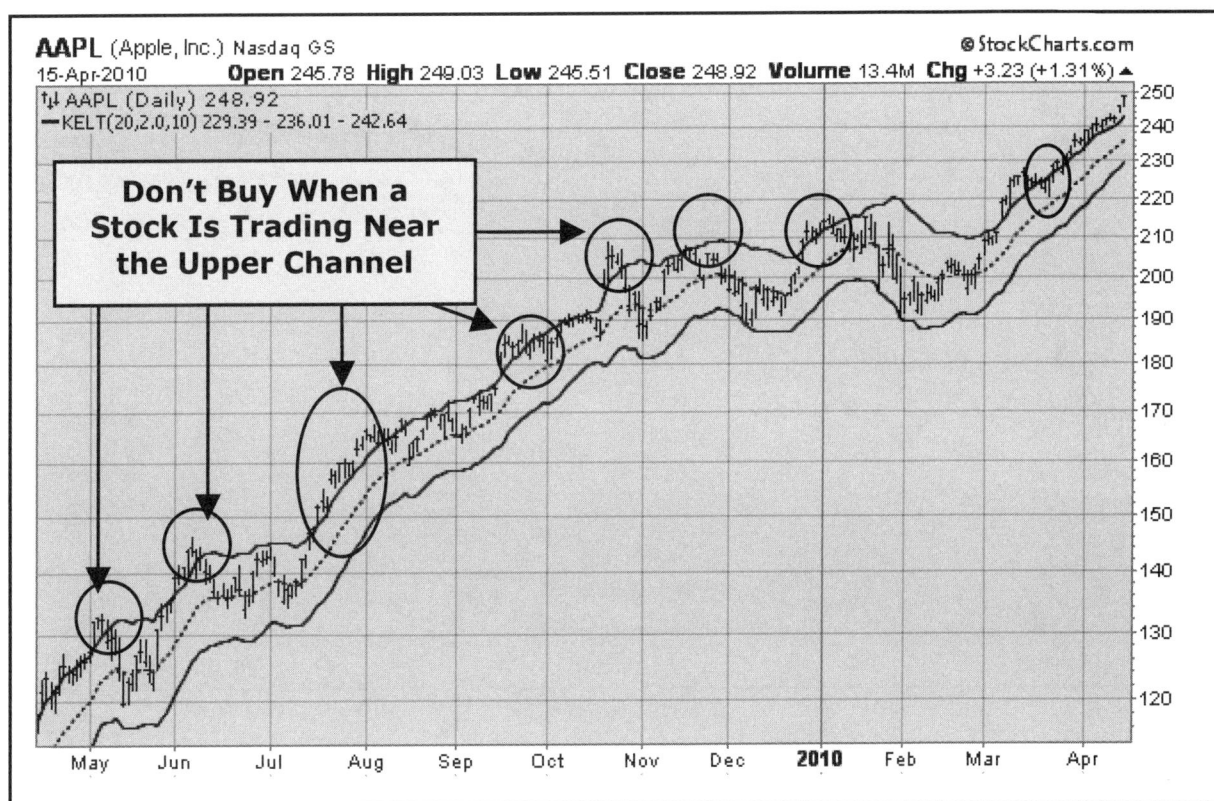

Identifying the Keltner Channel Price Levels

Whenever you download a Keltner Channel price chart, the price chart will list the price levels for the Lower, Middle and Upper Channel. Currently the Lower Channel price level is 229.39 (circled below). The Middle Channel price level is 236.01 and the Upper Channel price level is 242.64 (circled below).

Lower Channel Currently at 229.39 Price Level

Middle Channel Currently at 236.01 Price Level

Upper Channel Currently at 242.64 Price Level

If you are considering buying Apple stock or weekly call options, you would want to wait until the price of the stock declines to the middle or lower channel price level which is the 236.01 to 229.39 price level in this example.

Actual Trade Examples Using the Keltner Channels

My brokerage account trade confirmations below list purchases I made for Apple stock. The confirmations list the date of purchase and purchase price.

Transactions	Check Summary	Deposit Summary	Categories	Reports	
Date	Type	View	Description (show categories)		Amount ($)
11/04/09	Bought		400 of AAPL @ $193.38 (Order #1687)		-77,359.99
12/09/09	Bought		100 of AAPL @ $197.40 (Order #1801)		-19,747.99
02/16/10	Bought		400 of AAPL @ $203.40 (Order #1883)		-81,367.99
02/18/10	Bought		400 of AAPL @ $203.65 (Order #1889)		-81,467.99

I used the Keltner Channels to help select my purchase entry point. I bought Apple stock and call options when the stock was trading near the middle or lower channel which lowers my entry risk of buying stock when it is overbought and due for a price correction. These actual entry points are circled below.

You can see from the price chart that Apple stock did not decline in price much below my entry points. Using the Keltner Channels to help time my entry points reduced the risk of my stock purchase. With Apple stock trading near 249 I now have a substantial profit for my stock purchases.

I Bought AAPL Stock When It Was Trading Near the Middle or Lower Channel

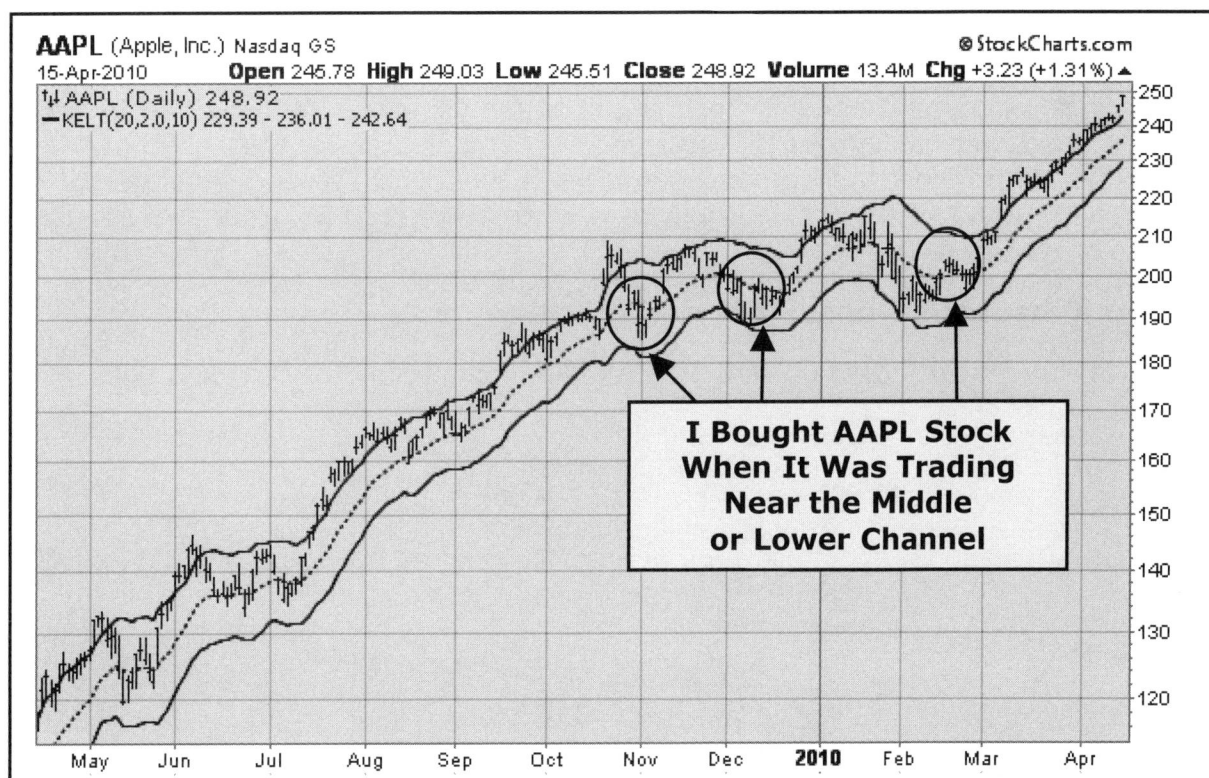

AAPL (Apple, Inc.) Nasdaq GS   © StockCharts.com
15-Apr-2010   **Open** 245.78 **High** 249.03 **Low** 245.51 **Close** 248.92 **Volume** 13.4M **Chg** +3.23 (+1.31%) ▲

AAPL (Daily) 248.92
KELT(20,2.0,10) 229.39 - 236.01 - 242.64

I Bought AAPL Stock When It Was Trading Near the Middle or Lower Channel

Timing Our Stock and Call Option Purchases

I have found the Keltner Channels to be a valuable timing tool that help me select a low risk entry point for my stock and call option purchases. Buying a stock when it is trading near the lower or middle channel can help prevent buying stocks when they are in an overbought condition and are vulnerable to price declines.

Buy Stocks When They Are Trading Near the Lower or Middle Channel

I like to buy a stock when the stock is trading near the middle or lower channel and is oversold. When a stock is oversold there is a good probability that it will rally back towards the upper channel providing us with a lower risk buy point.

I try to avoid buying a stock when it is trading near or above the upper channel and is overbought. When stocks become overbought they are vulnerable to profit taking and will most likely encounter selling pressure.

The Keltner Channels can help us avoid buying stocks and call options when they become overbought and instead buy stocks when they become oversold lowering the overall risk and increasing the profit potential of stock and option trading.

Let's review the three Step selection process so far for Apple stock. Apple stock is in a price up trend with its 50-Day EMA line above the 100-Day EMA line. The On Balance Volume line for Apple stock is sloping up indicating volume is heavier on up days and buying pressure is exceeding selling pressure. The up sloping On Balance Volume line confirms the price up trend and the sustainability of the price up trend. Apple stock is making a series of new 52-Week highs which also confirms the price up trend.

The last step is to purchase Apple stock or call option using the Keltner Channels to help identify a lower risk entry point. Currently the middle Keltner Channel is at the 236 price level and the lower Keltner Channel is at the 229.40 level. If Apple stock declines to the 236 to 229.40 level then we want to enter our buy order to purchase the stock or weekly call option.

Selection Process for Apple Stock or Call option

- Stock price is trending up with 50-Day EMA line above 100-Day EMA line

- On Balance Volume Line is sloping up

- Apple stock is making a series of new 52-Week highs

- Keltner Channels indicate a good buy point would be between 236 and 229.40

High Probability Buy Signals

The price chart below displays the Keltner Channels for Baidu stock. Occasionally the price of a stock will become very oversold even though the stock is on a 50/100-Day EMA 'buy' and will actually close below the lower Keltner Channel. Notice how the price of Baidu stock recently closed below the lower Keltner Channel (circled).

This oversold condition normally sets up a very powerful rally! If you purchase a stock or weekly call option when it closes below the lower Channel there is a high probability that your trade will be profitable. My brokerage confirmation below shows that I purchased 200 shares of Baidu at 98.17 when the stock closed below the lower Channel.

Bought 200 Shares BIDU @ 98.17

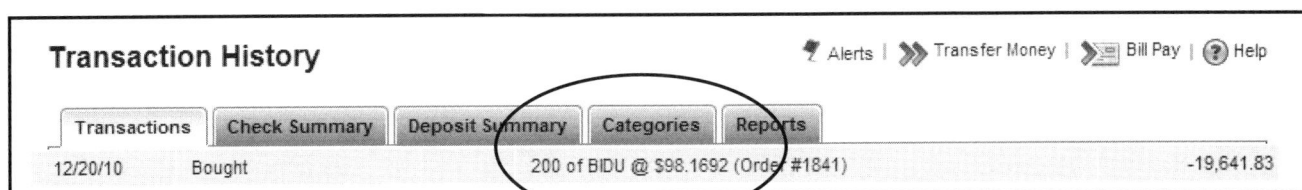

Transaction History   Alerts | Transfer Money | Bill Pay | Help

| Transactions | Check Summary | Deposit Summary | Categories | Reports |

| 12/20/10 | Bought | | 200 of BIDU @ $98.1692 (Order #1841) | | -19,641.83 |

Buying Baidu stock when it closed below the lower Keltner Channel has so far produced a 22% return. These high probability signals do not occur very often. I am always on the lookout for these type of high probability signals to make trade recommendations for my option advisory service.

The Keltner Channels are a very valuable timing tool that allows us to select lower risk entry points that have a high probability of being profitable. Some additional high probability trade examples follow.

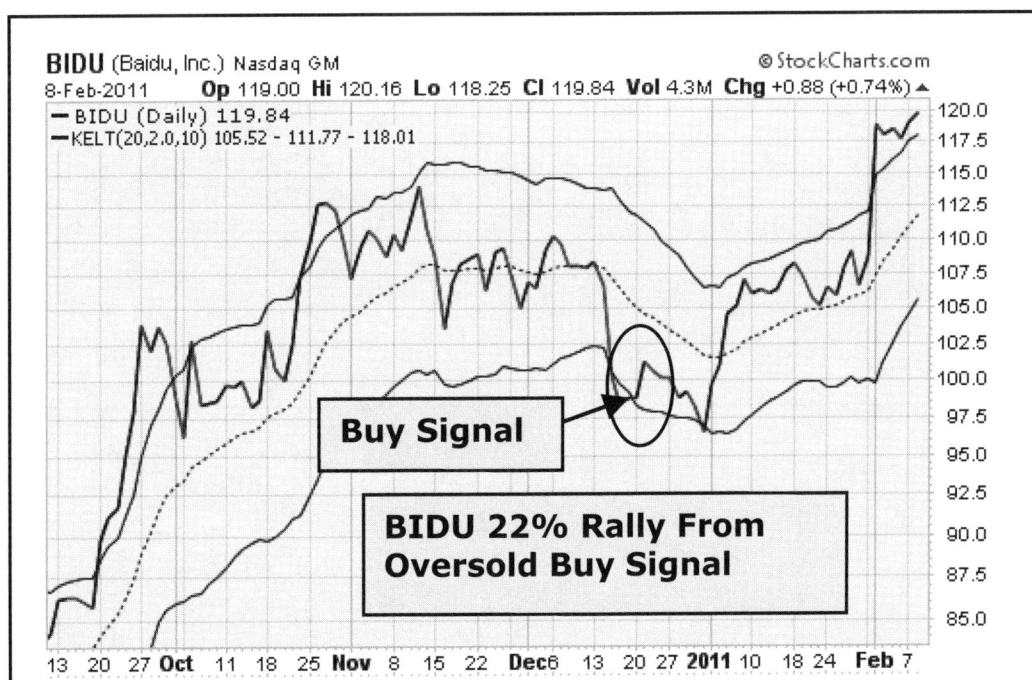

BIDU (Baidu, Inc.) Nasdaq GM
8-Feb-2011   Op 119.00 Hi 120.16 Lo 118.25 Cl 119.84 Vol 4.3M Chg +0.88 (+0.74%)
— BIDU (Daily) 119.84
— KELT(20,2.0,10) 105.52 - 111.77 - 118.01
© StockCharts.com

Buy Signal

BIDU 22% Rally From Oversold Buy Signal

High Probability Buy Signals

My brokerage confirmations that follow show that I have been buying stocks and ETFs on a 50/100-Day EMA System 'buy' after the stock or ETF closed below the lower Keltner Channel. Notice how these stocks and ETFs did not decline much after the high probability buy signal which created low risk entries. I also purchased call options on most of these stocks and ETFs.

Bought 100 Shares Nasdaq ETF @ 81.48
Bought 400 Shares Nasdaq ETF @ 81.89

High Probability Buy Signals

Bought 100 Shares AAPL @ 333.00
Bought 100 Shares AAPL @ 333.01

Date	Transaction	Action (Buy, Sell)	Symbol	Quantity	Price	Principal Amount
☐ 03/18/2011	06950341682	Bought	AAPL	100	333.00	33,300.00
☐ 03/18/2011	06950339263	Bought	AAPL	100	333.01	33,301.00

Bought 50 Shares AAPL @ 332.31
Bought 50 Shares AAPL @ 334.90

Transaction History

Alerts | Transfer Money | Bill Pay | Help

| Transactions | Check Summary | Deposit Summary | Categories | Reports |

| 03/18/11 | Bought | 50 of AAPL @ $332.31 (Order #2467) | -16,623.49 |
| 03/17/11 | Bought | 50 of AAPL @ $334.90 (Order #2094) | -16,752.99 |

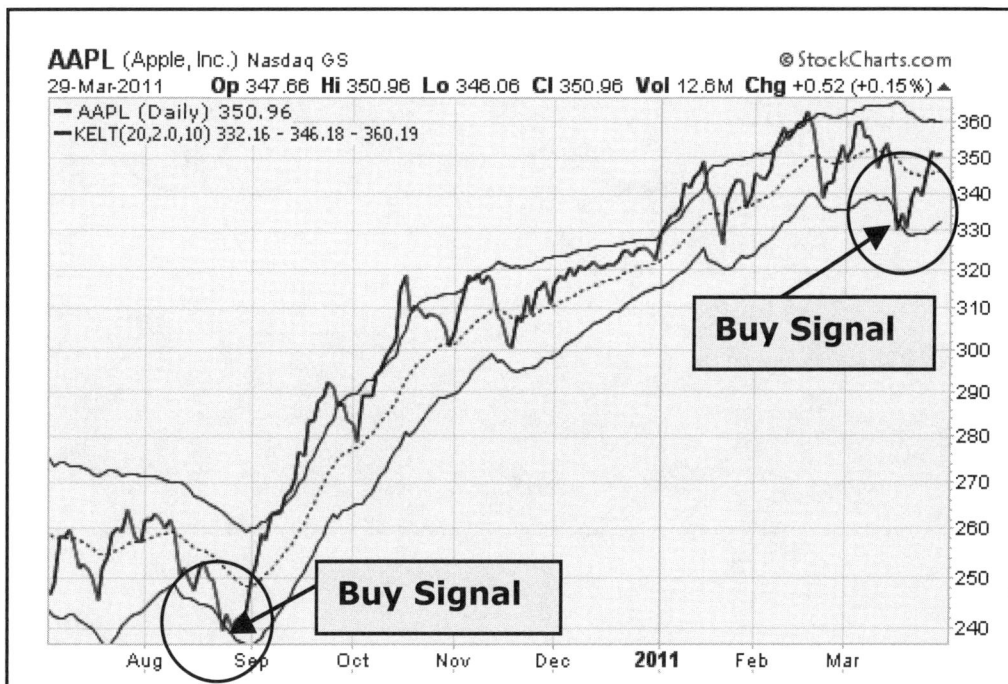

AAPL (Apple, Inc.) Nasdaq GS
29-Mar-2011 Op 347.66 Hi 350.96 Lo 346.06 Cl 350.96 Vol 12.6M Chg +0.52 (+0.15%) ▲
— AAPL (Daily) 350.96
— KELT(20,2.0,10) 332.16 - 346.18 - 360.19

Buy Signal

Buy Signal

High Probability Buy Signals

Bought 1,000 Shares S&P 500 ETF @ 49.04
Bought 400 Shares S&P 500 ETF @ 49.96
Bought 1,000 Shares S&P 500 ETF @ 49.96

Transaction History   Alerts | Transfer Money | Bill Pay | Help

Transactions	Check Summary	Deposit Summary	Categories	Reports

03/17/11	Bought	1,000 of SSO @ $49.04 (Order #2090)	-49,047.99
03/18/11	Bought	400 of SSO @ $49.96 (Order #2473)	-19,991.99
03/18/11	Bought	1,000 of SSO @ $49.96 (Order #2466)	-49,967.99

SSO (ProShares Ultra S&P 500 Fund) NYSE   © StockCharts.com
30-Mar-2011   Op 53.23 Hi 53.73 Lo 53.11 Cl 53.40 Vol 9.3M Chg +0.66 (+1.25%) ▲
— SSO (Daily) 53.40
—KELT(20,2.0,10) 49.17 - 51.73 - 54.29

Buy Signal

Oct   Nov   Dec   **2011**   Feb   Mar

High Probability Buy Signals

CVX (Chevron Corp.) NYSE — © StockCharts.com
8-Feb-2011 Op 97.87 Hi 97.99 Lo 97.11 Cl 97.74 Vol 5.7M Chg +0.08 (+0.08%) ▲
— CVX (Daily) 97.74
— KELT(20,2.0,10) 92.31 - 94.77 - 97.22

Chevron 45% Rally From Oversold Buy Signal

Buy Signal

NFLX (Netflix, Inc.) Nasdaq GS — © StockCharts.com
28-Jan-2011 Op 211.69 Hi 218.00 Lo 208.65 Cl 217.98 Vol 9.0M Chg +7.11 (+3.37%) ▲
— NFLX (Daily) 217.98
— KELT(20,2.0,10) 174.04 - 190.53 - 207.01

Netflix 102% Rally From Oversold Buy Signal

Buy Signal

High Probability Buy Signals

CAT (Caterpillar, Inc.) NYSE — © StockCharts.com
20-Dec-2010 Op 93.37 Hi 93.55 Lo 92.53 Cl 93.30 Vol 3.5M Chg +0.71 (+0.77%) ▲
— CAT (Daily) 93.30
— KELT(20,2.0,10) 85.98 - 89.20 - 92.42

Caterpillar 85% Rally

Buy Signal

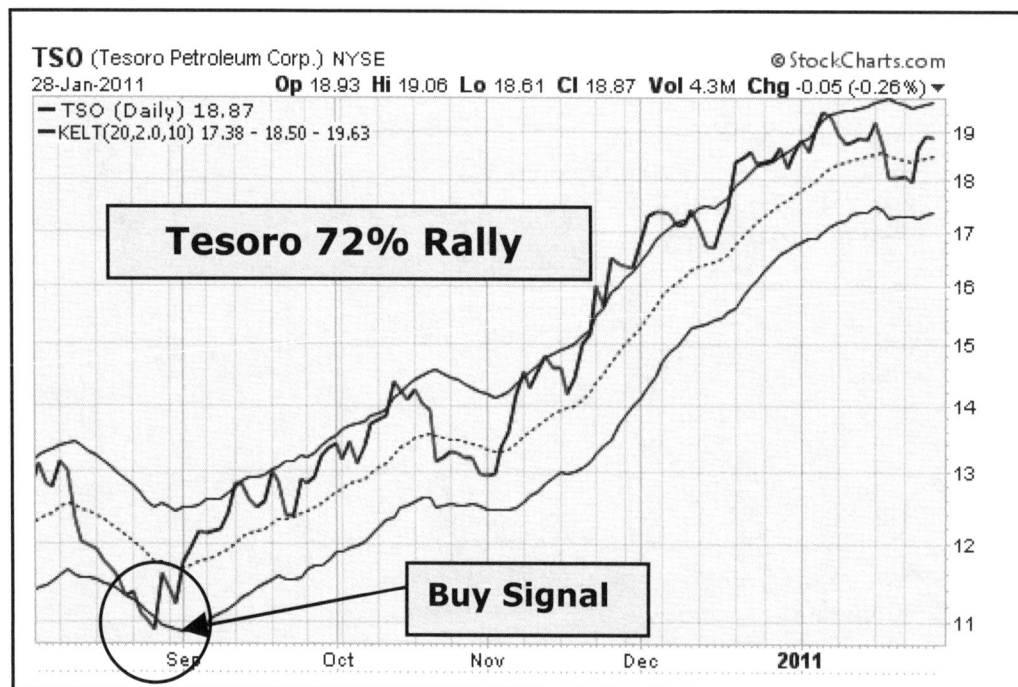

TSO (Tesoro Petroleum Corp.) NYSE — © StockCharts.com
28-Jan-2011 Op 18.93 Hi 19.06 Lo 18.61 Cl 18.87 Vol 4.3M Chg -0.05 (-0.26%) ▼
— TSO (Daily) 18.87
— KELT(20,2.0,10) 17.38 - 18.50 - 19.63

Tesoro 72% Rally

Buy Signal

Timing Bearish Entry Points

The Keltner Channels can also be used for timing bearish entry points. We want to establish bearish weekly option positions on stocks/ETFs that are in a confirmed price down trend but become temporarily over bought during counter-trend rallies.

The Keltner Channels indicate an overbought condition for a stock/ETF when the stock/ETF is trading near the mid to upper channel or above the upper channel.

Stocks in a price down trend do not decline in a straight line. There are always price rallies along the way. Stocks can remain in an overall price down trend as these price counter trend rallies occur as long as the price rally is not strong enough to cause the 50-Day EMA line to cross above the 100-Day EMA line which signals a trend reversal from a price down trend to a price up trend. When this occurs short positions should be closed out.

The Keltner Channels are a valuable timing tool as the channels can help us prevent establishing short weekly option positions when the underlying stock/ETF is in an oversold condition. When stocks become oversold they are vulnerable to counter trend rallies within the context of remaining in a price down trend. The Keltner Channels can help us avoid establishing short positions when the underlying stock/ETF becomes oversold and instead establish short option positions when the underlying stock/ETF becomes overbought.

When you avoid establishing short positions when the underlying stock/ETF is oversold and instead establish short positions when the underlying stock/ETF is overbought (but still in a price down trend) you greatly increase your odds of selecting a profitable short trade.

The price charts that follow are examples of stocks/ETFs that are in confirmed price down trend but became temporarily over bought when the stock/ETF price rallied back up to the middle or upper channel presenting numerous low risk entry points for establishing short option positions.

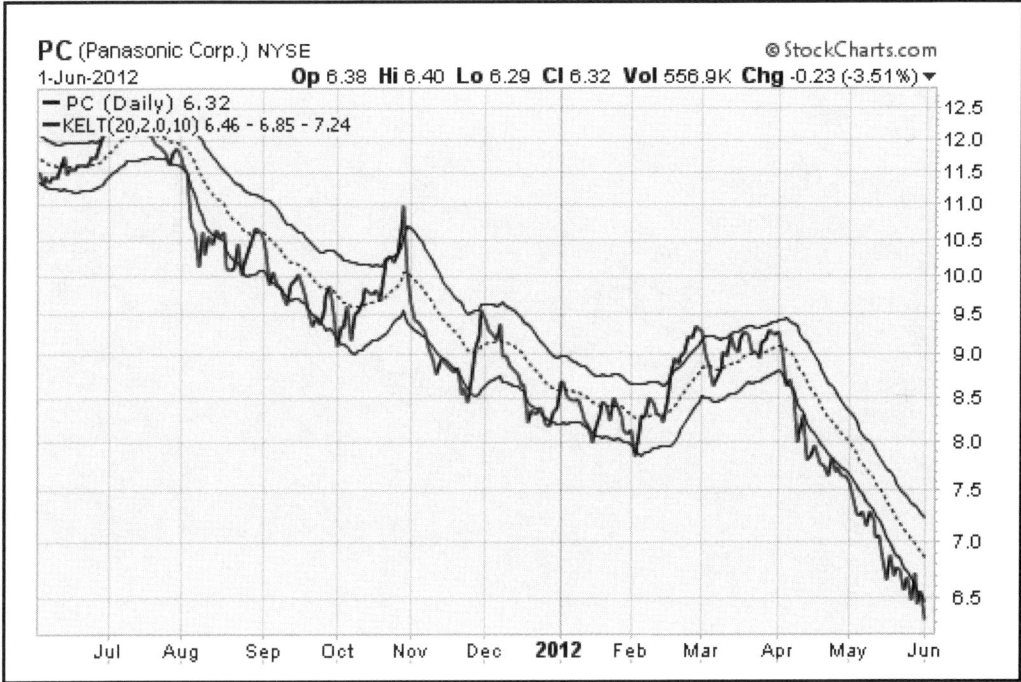

PC (Panasonic Corp.) NYSE
1-Jun-2012 Op 6.38 Hi 6.40 Lo 6.29 Cl 6.32 Vol 556.9K Chg -0.23 (-3.51%) ▼
— PC (Daily) 6.32
— KELT(20,2.0,10) 6.46 - 6.85 - 7.24
@ StockCharts.com

CEL (Cellcom Israel, Inc.) NYSE
1-Jun-2012 Op 7.06 Hi 7.10 Lo 6.97 Cl 6.97 Vol 388.3K Chg -0.27 (-3.73%) ▼
— CEL (Daily) 6.97
— KELT(20,2.0,10) 7.96 - 8.74 - 9.52
@ StockCharts.com

JRCC (James River Coal Company) Nasdaq GM   © StockCharts.com
1-Jun-2012 Open 2.38 High 2.49 Low 2.25 Close 2.42 Volume 1.7M Chg -0.09 (-3.59%) ▼
— JRCC (Daily) 2.42
— KELT(20,2.0,10) 2.74 - 3.37 - 4.00

CTRP (Ctrip.com Intl Ltd.) Nasdaq GS   © StockCharts.com
1-Jun-2012 Op 18.03 Hi 18.11 Lo 17.84 Cl 17.84 Vol 3.2M Chg -0.56 (-3.04%) ▼
— CTRP (Daily) 17.84
— KELT(20,2.0,10) 17.75 - 19.26 - 20.76

70

"I can see clearly now, the rain is gone,
I can see all obstacles in my way
Gone are the dark clouds that had me blind

It's gonna be a bright (bright), bright (bright)

Sun-Shiny day - "

Johnny Nash

Yes, the Keltner Channels clear the clouds of confusion and pave the way to clear decision making. Once you understand the channels of success it will become very clear when you should establish bullish and bearish option positions.

The Keltner Channels are a great tool that can help you establish low risk entry points for your option trades which in turn can increase the profit potential and accuracy of your option trades!

On the following page I will show you how to download the Keltner Channels and make them yours! For me, the Channels are the end all. There is no better guide to help me push away confusion and doubt. Securing a low risk entry point in trading is huge! This tool is invaluable! Learn it, embrace it, and use it!

In summary, I have experienced many years of success using the *Prime Trade Select* process to select option trades with the best profit potential. I hope you learn and embrace this valuable trading tool. In the next Chapter we will review option basics for those of you who are new to option trading.

Downloading the Keltner Channels

The Keltner Channels can be easily downloaded from www.StockCharts.com. On the home page type in the stock symbol and click "Go". In this example I typed in the symbol for Apple stock AAPL.

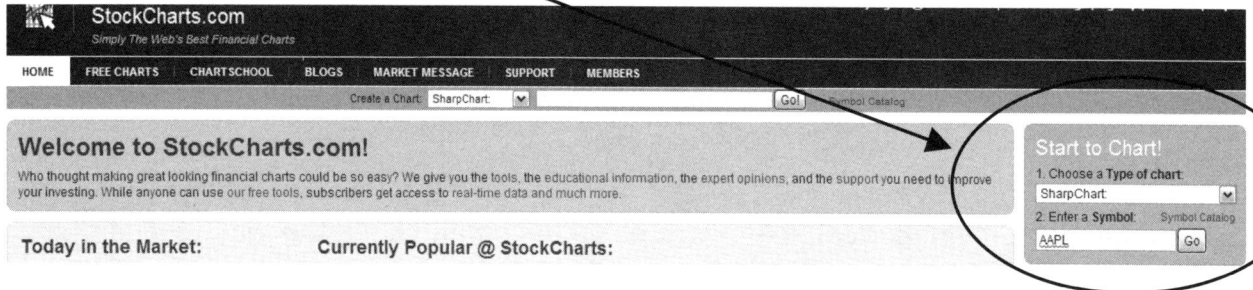

Once you click "Go" the default chart for Apple will appear. Below the default chart for Apple select "Daily" under Periods and "1 Year" under Range. Under Overlays select "Keltner Channels". The default Parameters are 20,2.0,10.

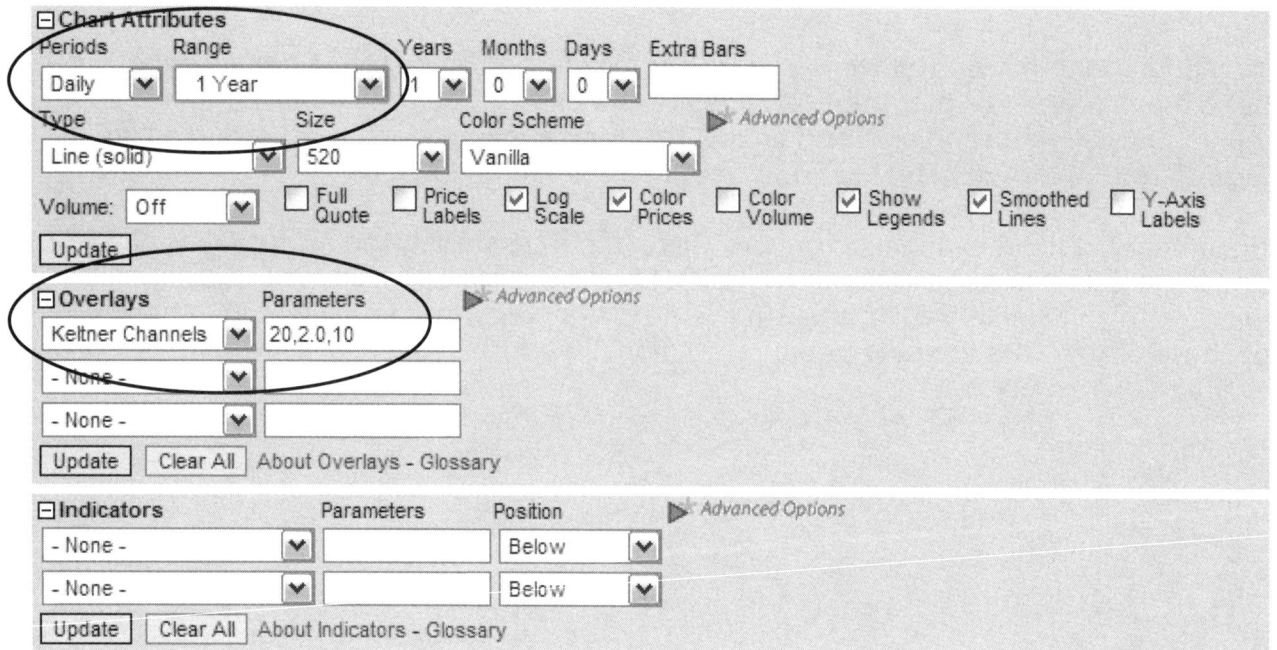

Click "Update" and the Apple price chart with the Keltner Channels will be displayed (see price chart on the following page).

Apple One Year Price Chart with Keltner Channels

AAPL (Apple, Inc.) Nasdaq GS
15-Apr-2010   Op 245.78 Hi 249.03 Lo 245.51 Cl 248.92 Vol 13.4M Chg +3.23 (+1.31%) ▲
— AAPL (Daily) 248.92
— KELT(20,2.0,10) 229.39 - 236.01 - 242.64
© StockCharts.com

Chapter 2

The Ins and Outs of Calls and Puts

The focus of this Chapter is to provide you with the practical knowledge you need to understand in order to trade weekly options. Learning the mechanics of option investing can be a bit overwhelming particularly if you have never invested in options before.

In Chapter 1 we learned about *Prime Trade Select*, a simple 3 Step trade selection process to identify options with the best profit potential for both bullish and bearish weekly option trades.

To be a successful options investor you don't need to know complicated mathematical formulas or Greek letters. You only need to know the basic mechanics of buying and selling options. In my 25 years of trading experience, option trading has been the most versatile and rewarding approach to profitable trading.

Option trading enables many different types of traders to achieve their specific investment goals. I have traded many types of option strategies with different investment goals. I favor the three limited risk option strategies listed below as I have had good success trading these strategies.

- Purchasing options to realize trading profits
- Trading option spreads that can profit during an up or down market
- Selling option premium to produce cash income

Successful Option Trading

The overall goal of my option investing is to achieve at least a 3 to 1 profit to loss ratio. To achieve this goal I must be ready to close out my losing trades before they develop into large losses and hold on to winning trades. I will normally sell an option before it incurs a 20 to 30% loss. Many option traders with good trading systems fail because they don't pay enough attention to risk. Maintaining a trading discipline that forces you to think in terms of reward versus risk can help you become a successful option trader.

If you are willing to risk 30% on an option trade, then you should be expecting a 90% profit on your winning trades in order to achieve a 3 to 1 profit to loss ratio. If you are willing to risk 50% on an option trade, then you should be expecting a 150% profit on your winning trades which is very difficult to achieve. I always think in terms of taking measured risks with every trade.

Also, if you have enough trading funds, don't risk more than 5 to 10% of your trading funds on any one trade. This helps prevent a large portfolio loss if one of your option trades experiences a big loss. This is especially important with options because they employ leverage.

Successful trade management can be summarized with three basics rules:

- Limit the size of your positions
- Close out your losing trades before they develop into large losses
- Don't limit your profits by selling winning trades with a small profit

There is no need to memorize all of the material presented in this Chapter. This Chapter can be used as a future reference when implementing a weekly option strategy.

Option Basics

Options are also known as derivatives because the option contract derives its price and value from the underlying asset on which it is based. The value of an option fluctuates as the price of the underlying asset rises or falls in price. Option values are also affected by other market conditions. These conditions could be a change in volatility due to sudden fluctuations of price in the underlying asset, interest rates, dividends or stock splits.

An option is the right, but not the obligation, to buy or sell a stock or index for a specified price on or before a specific date. A call option is the right to buy a stock/index, while a put option is the right to sell a stock/index. The investor who purchases an option, whether it is a put or call, is the option *"buyer"*. Conversely, the investor who sells the put or call "to open" is the option *"seller"* or *"writer"*.

Options are contracts in which the terms of the contract are standardized and give the buyer the right, but not the obligation, to buy or sell a particular stock/index at a fixed price (the strike price) for a specific period of time (until expiration). All option contracts traded on U.S. securities exchanges are issued, guaranteed and cleared by the Options Clearing Corporation (OCC). OCC is a registered clearing corporation with the SEC and has received 'AAA' credit rating from *Standard & Poor's Corporation*. The 'AAA' credit rating corresponds to OCC's ability to fulfill its obligations as counter-party for options trades.

The options markets provide a mechanism where many different types of investors can achieve their specific investment goals. An options investor may be looking for long term or short term profits, or they may be looking to hedge an existing stock or index position. Whatever your objectives may be, you need a thorough understanding of the markets you will be trading.

Options Share the Following General Characteristics:

- Options give you the right to buy or sell an underlying security or index

- If you buy an option, you are not obligated to buy the underlying security. You simply have the right to exercise the option

- If you sell an option, you are obligated to deliver the underlying security at the price at which the option was sold if the buyer exercises his/her right to take delivery

- Options are good for a specified period of time after which they expire and you lose the right to buy or sell the underlying security

- When options are purchased the buyer incurs a debit

- When options are sold the seller receives a credit

- Options are available in various strike prices representing the price of the underlying security

- The cost of an option is referred to as the option premium. The premium is comprised of time value and intrinsic value

- There are two kinds of options: calls and puts. Calls give you the right to buy the underlying security and puts give you the right to sell the underlying security

- Options (put or call) which have the same underlying security are called a class of options. For example, all the calls for General Electric constitute an option class.

- All options which are in one class and have the same strike price are called an option series. For example, all the General Electric options with a strike price of 25 constitute an option series.

- Most options are never exercised and are closed out before option expiration

Buying Options

Any investor can buy options if they have the required account established with their broker. Buying options limits the investor's risk to the amount of capital invested in the option purchase. Therefore the only requirement is that the investor has enough funds in their account to purchase the options. Since the purchase of an option contract results in a long position, a cash debit is subtracted from the buyer's account.

Selling Options

For every option buyer there is a seller or writer. If an option is exercised, the option writer is obligated by the option contract to deliver the specified number of shares of the underlying security at the specific strike price. Anyone can write options if they have the required account established with their broker.

Selling "naked" options can involve large capital loss risk and is not a suitable investment for all investors. Writing an option results in cash being credited to the seller's brokerage account. Since the writing of an option results in a short position, it requires that funds be held in margin to guarantee the writer's obligation. Margin requirements for writing naked options vary for different markets, and sometimes even for different stocks.

Underlying Security

The underlying security in options trading is defined as the financial instrument on which an option contract is based or derived. It is a stock or Exchange Traded Fund (ETF) that you have the right to purchase or sell. The symbol used for the underlying security in options trading is usually the symbol used by the exchange on which the underlying security is traded. For example, GE is used for General Electric and SPY is used for the S&P 500 Index ETF.

Strike Price

The strike price is the actual price at which the option holder may buy or sell the underlying security as defined in the option contract. For example, a GE Mar 09 20-Strike weekly call gives the buyer of the option the right to buy 100 shares of General Electric at $20 per share between now and the weekly option expiration on Friday March 9th.

Expiration Date

Weekly options start trading on Thursday and expire the following Friday and have a life of 6 trading day. The expiration date is the actual date that an option contract becomes void. Monthly options normally expire on the third Friday of each month. Be aware that in most cases, pending option contracts that are in-the-money at option expiration will be exercised automatically if the seller of that contract has not closed out (bought back) the short option prior to expiration or if the buyer of that contract has not closed out (sold) the long option prior to expiration.

Option Type

There are two types of options - call options and put options.

A call option *purchase* profits when the price of the underlying security moves higher.

A call option *short sale* profits when the price of the underlying security moves lower.

A put option *purchase* profits when the price of the underlying security moves lower.

A put option *short sale* profits when the price of the underlying security moves higher.

How to Read Option Symbols

An option symbol is comprised of several components that define the underlying stock or ETF and information about the specific option contract. A weekly option symbol consists of the stock or ETF trading symbol, year of expiration, month of expiration, expiration date, option type (call or put) and strike-price.

There are many financial websites available today that will give you option quotes. I like to use Yahoo Finance or the Chicago Board Options Exchange website at www.cboe.com to obtain option quotes.

The symbol for the General Electric Mar 09 19-Strike weekly call option is GE120309C00019000. Let's look at the components of this weekly option symbol.

GE, 12, 03, 09, C, 00019000

GE is the trading symbol for General Electric
12 is the expiration year 2012
03 is the expiration month of March
09 is the expiration date which is Friday March 9th in this example
C designates a call option (put options are designated with a "P")
00019000 designates a 19-Strike price

Stock Option Point Values

Normally, 1 stock option contract covers 100 hundred shares of the underlying stock. Therefore an option with a 3.5 point premium would cost $350 (100 shares x $3.5).

Exercise and Assignment

Exercise is the term used when the buyer of an option uses his/her right to purchase or sell the underlying security at the terms of the option contract. Assignment is the term used when the seller of an option is obligated to deliver the underlying security at the contract specification. When the option buyer exercises his/her option contract, the seller of that option contract receives a notice of assignment from their broker. The seller of the option contract must then deliver the underlying security at the specified price. Your broker handles the entire option exercise/assignment transaction, and the resulting cash profit/loss or stock position is transferred into or out of your account.

Section 1 Quiz

1. If you buy a Microsoft weekly call option you are obligated to buy Microsoft stock.
   A. True
   B. False

2. If you sell an option, you are obligated to deliver the underlying security at the strike price at which the option was sold if the buyer exercises his/her right to take delivery.
   A. True
   B. False

3. When options are sold the seller receives a cash credit.
   A. True
   B. False

4. Call options give you the right to sell the underlying security and put options give you the right to buy the underlying security.
   A. True
   B. False

5. Weekly options normally expire on Friday.
   A. True
   C. False

6. AAPL is the root symbol for Apple stock options. The symbol for the Apple May 04 2012 560-strike weekly put option is

   _____.
   A. AAPL120504C00560000
   B. AAPL130504P00560000
   C. AAPL120504P00560000
   D. AAPL120405P00560000

7. The IBM May 11 2012 100-strike weekly call option is quoted at 4.25. It would cost _____ to purchase one option contract at the current quote.
   A. $4.25
   B. $425
   C. $42.50
   D. $4,250

8. All listed stocks trade weekly options
   A. True
   B. False

9. Exercise is the term used when the buyer of an option uses his/her right to purchase or sell the underlying security at the terms of the option contract.
   A. True
   B. False

10. Most option contracts are never exercised.
    A. True
    B. False

11. Each stock option contract normally represents 100 shares of the underlying stock.
    A. True
    B. False

Section 1 Quiz Key

1. B, False
2. A, True
3. A, True
4. B, False
5. A, True
6. C, AAPL120504P00560000
7. B, $425
8. B, False
9. A, True
10. A, True
11. A, True

Option Characteristics

There are three major factors that determine the price of an option:

Strike Price in Relation to the Stock Price

The most important factor that determines the price of an option is the price of the underlying stock or ETF relative to the strike price. This determines whether an option is in-the-money or out-of-the-money and quantifies an option's intrinsic and time value. In-the-money options have more intrinsic value and are more expensive than out-of-the-money options. The deeper an option is in-the-money the more intrinsic value it will have and the more expensive it will be. In-the-money options are more expensive than at-the-money and out-of-the-money options.

Time Until Expiration

An option is considered a wasting asset, and as the option's expiration date gets closer, the value of the option decreases. The more time remaining until expiration, the more time value the option contract has. If the underlying security price falls far below or far above the strike price of the option, the underlying security becomes more dominant in determining the price of the option. On the day the option expires, the only value the option has is its intrinsic value, which is determined by the amount by which the option contract is in-the-money. If an option has no intrinsic value at expiration, it expires worthless.

The passage of time works against the options buyer, as the price of out-of-the-money options decreases at an accelerating rate as the expiration date approaches. This is called "time decay". The opposite is true for the option seller. The passage of time works for the option seller as time decay results in profits.

The longer an option has before expiration, the more expensive it will be. More time until expiration means more time value and a higher price.

Volatility

Volatility is the amount in annual percent terms that the underlying security has moved or is expected to move on an annual basis. This number can help predict short-term price ranges and also helps determine the relative value for an option price.

There are two types of volatility used in option analysis: The first is statistical volatility, which is volatility based on the historical price movement of the underlying security. This is sometimes referred to as historical volatility. This volatility number tells us what has happened in the past.

The second type of volatility is implied volatility, which is an implied value based on the current option prices for an underlying security. This kind of volatility can give insight into potential price movement.

When option prices rise because of increased trading volume or nervousness in the market this can signal a significant market event. When option prices rise, implied volatility rises as well. Therefore, implied volatility can be seen as a measurement of risk. Higher volatility means higher risk for the option seller and increased prices for option premiums.

The more volatile the stock, the more expensive the option will be. Because volatile stocks have larger price moves, there is a higher probability that an out-of-the-money option will become an in-the-money option with intrinsic value.

Option Pricing

Option premiums consist of intrinsic value and time value. At option expiration options lose all time value and consist of only intrinsic value. Intrinsic value is the difference between the option strike price and the current price of the underlying stock or ETF. The intrinsic value of a **call** option is calculated by subtracting the strike price of the option from the current stock price. For example, let's assume IBM stock is currently trading at 75.00 and the May 04 70-Strike weekly call option is priced at 7.00 points. The intrinsic value of this option would be 5.00 points.

Current Stock Price of 75.00 Minus Strike Price of 70.00 = 5.00 Intrinsic Value

The time value of an option is calculated by subtracting the intrinsic value from the total value of the option. In this example the 70-Strike option priced at 7.00 would have 2.00 points of time value.

Option Price of 7.00 Minus Intrinsic Value of 5.00 = Time Value of 2.00

In this example, if the IBM May 04 80-Strike call option is priced at 3.00 then this call option would have no intrinsic value and would only contain time value.

Current Stock Price of 75.00 Minus Strike Price of 80.00 = 0.00 Intrinsic Value

Option Price of 3.00 Minus Intrinsic Value of 0.00 = Time Value of 3.00

The intrinsic value of a **put** option is calculated by subtracting the current price of the stock from the strike price of the put. Let's assume again that IBM stock is trading at 75.00 and the IBM May 04 80-Strike weekly put option is priced at 8.00 points. The intrinsic value of this option would be 5.00 points and the time value would be 3.00 points.

Strike Price of 80.00 Minus Current Stock Price of 75.00 = 5.00 Intrinsic Value

Option Price of 8.00 Minus Intrinsic Value of 5.00 = Time Value of 3.00

In the above example, if the IBM May 04 70-Strike put option is priced at 2.00 then this put option would have no intrinsic value and would only contain time value.

Strike Price of 70.00 Minus Stock Price of 75.00 = 0.00 Intrinsic Value

Option Price of 2.00 Minus Intrinsic Value of 0.00 = Time Value of 2.00

When the price of a stock or ETF is below the strike price of a call option that option is said to be out-of-the-money. An option with a strike price that is closest to the price of the underlying security is at-the-money. A call option is in-the-money when the stock price is greater than the strike price. An in-the-money call option has intrinsic value equal to the amount the stock price exceeds the strike price.

A put option is just the opposite of a call option. A put option is out-of-the-money when the stock price is greater than the strike price. A put option is in-the-money when the stock is below the strike price. The intrinsic value of a put equals the amount by which the strike price exceeds the stock price. As with a call, a put will have value at expiration if the option is in-the-money. To clarify this concept, take a closer look at these terms:

	Call	**Put**
In the money	strike price<stock price	strike price>stock price
At the money	strike price=stock price	strike price=stock price
Out of the money	strike price>stock price	strike price<stock price

Time (or days remaining until expiration) and volatility are the main components of time value. Interest rates and stock dividends are smaller factors in the pricing of option premiums. The more time remaining until expiration, or the higher the stock volatility, the greater the risk to the option seller, and therefore the higher the option premium will be.

Dividends
Dividends reduce the value of call options and increase the value of put options. This is due to the fact that paying out a dividend normally reduces the stock price by the amount of the dividend. Dividends increase the attractiveness of holding stock compared to buying call options and holding cash. Conversely, short-sellers must pay out dividends so buying puts is more desirable than shorting stock.

Interest Rates
Rising interest rates increase the value of call premiums and decrease the value of put premiums. Higher rates increase the underlying security's forward price, which is the stock price plus the risk-free interest rate over the life of the option.

Advantages of Options Versus Stocks/Mutual Funds

When you purchase options you commit a limited amount of capital and thus have less total dollars at risk in the market compared to stocks and mutual funds. The surplus dollars can be placed in safe investments like a money market fund. Instead of buying stocks consider "leasing" them with options especially when your market expectations are likely to change more frequently with today's volatile markets. Set aside a small portion of your portfolio for weekly options to benefit from the frequent market swings that can create big profit opportunities for traders positioned to capitalize on market swings.

Options offer profit potential not only when the market rallies, but also when it declines. With stocks and most mutual funds you can only benefit from bullish markets. If you are bearish on the stock market cash is usually your only alternative. With options you can profit from both bullish and bearish markets.

A Lower Risk Alternative to "Going Short"

Put options are normally a better choice than selling short a stock or ETF. Option purchases normally do not require a margin account, whereas short selling a stock does require a margin account. In addition, a short stock position has virtually unlimited loss potential if a stock continues to rally in price. Conversely, the maximum loss for a put option purchase is limited to the purchase price of the option.

Options offer greater leverage than stocks or mutual funds. A 10% move in a stock can easily translate into a 100% move in the related option. Purchasing options offers profit leverage if you are correct in your market view but also offers limited risk if your market view is incorrect.

Options can allow for stock or mutual fund portfolios to be hedged without losing long-term capital gain status. This results in a more favorable tax treatment. This can improve the after-tax returns on stock holdings while allowing you to protect those stocks during market volatility.

Risk Management

The first step toward intelligent risk management is to trade weekly options only with that portion of your capital that can be comfortably devoted to speculation. This will permit you to trade rationally and to sleep soundly which is not possible if your 'Safe Money' is at risk. Never trade options with money needed to pay living expenses. Restrict your options trading to funds that can be lost without undue financial hardship.

Once you determine the amount of your available trading capital, allocate no more than 10% to any one trade. This should help mitigate losses when losing trades occur. This rule holds regardless of how successful you have been in the past and regardless of how attractive the next trade appears. There will always be losing trades. By compounding your capital after a few profitable trades, you are exposing yourself to potentially painful losses once that losing trade comes along.

Risk and Diversification

There are generally two types of portfolio risk: systematic and unsystematic.

Systematic Risk, also called non-diversifiable risk, is risk that cannot be eliminated. It arises from factors which cause the whole market to move up or down, and cannot be eliminated by diversification because it affects all securities. Examples of systematic risk are political or sociological changes that affect all securities. Some of the most common forms of systematic risk are changes in interest rates or inflation.

Unsystematic Risk, also called diversifiable risk can be reduced or eliminated by diversifying your portfolio. Unsystematic risk is risk that is unique to a certain industry, firm, or company. Examples of unsystematic risk include: a company's financial structure, weather and natural disasters, labor strife and a shortage of raw materials. Since unsystematic risk affects a single company or industry, it can be mitigated by investing in many companies across a broad range of industries.

Option positions should be diversified. A major advantage of option purchases is 'truncated risk', whereby your loss is limited to your initial investment yet your profit is virtually unlimited. Diversification will allow you to use truncated risk to its maximum advantage. While some of your positions will inevitably be unprofitable, each profitable trade can offset several unprofitable trades. Option positions should be established among many underlying stocks and indexes in unrelated industries. This gives you diversification, which can help mitigate sector weakness.

In order to trade options, your broker must first approve your account for option trading. There are various levels of option trading and each level has financial requirements that differ from broker to broker:

Level 1 Covered call writing
Level 2 Call and put purchases and covered put writing
Level 3 Spreads (requires margin)
Level 4 Uncovered call and put writing (requires margin)
Level 5 Index option writing (requires margin)

Be sure to ask your broker about their requirements for the level of options you plan to trade. Lastly, before you trade options, regulations require that you read *Characteristics and Risks of Standardized Options* prepared by the Options Clearing Corporation (OCC) and available from your broker.

Order Types

Listed below are definitions for a variety of popular orders that may be helpful.

• *Market Order*

A market order is simply an order without restrictions or limits that guarantees execution but not price. Because it lacks restrictions, it takes precedence over all other types of orders. A market order to buy is executed at the best offering price available, which is normally the "ask" price. A market order to sell is executed at the best bid price available which is normally the "bid" price.

• *Limit Order*

A limit order is an order in which an investor has placed a restriction or limit on the acceptable purchase or selling price. There are two types of limit orders: a buy limit order and sell limit order. A buy limit order sets the maximum amount an investor is willing to pay to purchase a security or option contract. A sell limit order sets the minimum price that an investor is willing to accept to sell their security or option contract.

• *Day Orders*

Day orders are only valid for one trading day. If you place the order during market hours, then it will expire at the end of the trading day if it is not executed. If you place a day order after the market close then it will be valid for the next trading day.

• *Good Until Canceled Orders (GTC)*

Normally each brokerage firm will establish time periods for which GTC orders are valid. Once a GTC order is placed, it will remain open until the option expires, the order itself expires, the order is filled, or the order is cancelled.

• *Stop Loss Orders*

A stop-loss order is normally used to protect a profit or prevent a further loss if you own a stock and the price of the stock starts to drop. Example: You purchase 100 shares of Microsoft stock at 25 and enter a GTC stop order to sell at 20. As long as Microsoft trades above 20 then the stop order will not be executed. If it trades at 20 or below, however, then the stop order automatically becomes a market order to sell 100 shares of Microsoft at the market. A stop order does not guarantee that you will be filled at the stop price. Using the above example, if Microsoft closes at 21 and opens the next trading day at 19 the stop order will be executed on the open at the best possible price but below the 20 stop-loss price.

Section 2 Quiz

1. Option premiums consist of intrinsic value and _____
   value.
   A. Dividend
   B. Payout
   C. Time
   D. Cash

2. Exxon stock is trading at 70. The Exxon May 11 65-strike
   weekly call option is priced at 8 points. The intrinsic value
   of this call option is ___ points.
   A. 8
   B. 3
   C. 65
   D. 5

3. The time value of the same Exxon 65-strike call option
   listed above is ___ points.
   A. 8
   B. 3
   C. 65
   D. 5

4. A call option is in-the-money when the strike price is
   _____ the current stock price.

   A. Less than
   B. Greater than
   C. Equal to

5. A put option is out-of-the-money when the strike price is
   _____ the current stock price.

   A. Less than
   B. Greater than
   C. Equal to

6. Time premium is normally the dollar amount the writer of
   an option is charging the buyer to assume the price
   movement risk of the option.
   A. True
   B. False

7. As an option's expiration date gets closer, the time value of an option increases.
   A. True
   B. False

8. On option expiration day, the only value an option has is its time value.
   A. True
   B. False

9. The most important factor that determines the price of an option is the price of the underlying security relative to the strike price of the option.
   A. True
   B. False

10. Higher volatility usually means higher risk for the option seller and increased prices for option premiums.
    A. True
    B. False

11. Dividends normally increase the value of call options and decrease the value of put options.
    A. True
    B. False

12. Rising interest rates normally decrease the value of call premiums and increase the value of put premiums.
    A. True
    B. False

13. Buying put options is normally a lower risk strategy than selling short stock.
    A. True
    B. False

14. Options offer greater leverage than buying stocks or mutual funds. A 10% move in a stock can translate into a 100% move in the related option.
    A. True
    B. False

15. One of the biggest differences between purchasing stock and purchasing weekly options is the fact that weekly options are time dependent.
    A. True
    B. False

16. Systematic risk normally can be eliminated with portfolio diversification.
    A. True
    B. False

17. A major advantage of option purchases is truncated risk, which limits your loss to your initial investment but allows for virtually unlimited profits.
    A. True
    B. False

18. Portfolio diversification will allow you to use truncated risk to its maximum advantage.
    A. True
    B. False

19. A market order is an order which an investor has placed a restriction or limit.
    A. True
    B. False

20. A limit order guarantees execution but not price.
    A. True
    B. False

21. A good until cancelled order remains in effect until the option expires, the order itself expires, the order is filled, or the order is cancelled.
    A. True
    B. False

22. A stop loss order guarantees that you will limit your loss to the stop loss price.
    A. True
    B. False

Section 2 Quiz Key

1. C, Time
2. D, 5
3. B, 3
4. A, Less than
5. A, Less than
6. A, True
7. B, False
8. B, False
9. A, True
10. A, True
11. B, False
12. B, False
13. A, True
14. A, True
15. A, True
16. B, False
17. A, True
18. A, True
19. B, False
20. B, False
21. A, True
22. B, False

Buying and Selling Calls and Puts

There are two ways to invest in options:

- **Buying options**
- **Selling short options**

Buying Options

The goal of buying an option is to 'Buy Low and Sell High'. Buying a call option is a bullish strategy as the value of a call option will increase as the price of the underlying stock increases. Conversely, if the price of the underlying stock decreases then the value of a call option also decreases. Buying calls is a strategy that can be used as an alternative to the outright purchase of the underlying security, giving the purchaser the added benefits of limited risk and increased leverage.

Buying a put option is a bearish strategy as the value of a put option will increase as the price of the underlying stock decreases. Conversely, if the price of the underlying stock increases then the value of a put option will decrease.

The risk for call or put option purchases is limited to the premium paid for the option. The profit potential is not limited.

The price you pay for an option is called the premium. When you buy an option, cash is deducted from your brokerage account to pay for the option premium. One option contract normally controls one hundred shares of the underlying stock. Purchasing an option with a 4.00 point premium would result in $400 being deducted from your brokerage account to pay for the premium (4.00 x 100 shares = $400). If you later sold this option for 6.00 points you would realize a $200 profit.

Buy at 4.00 and sell at 6.00 = 2.00 Profit

Conversely, if you later sell this option for 3.00 points you would realize a $100 loss.

Buy at 4.00 and sell at 3.00 = 1.00 Loss

Buyers of call options profit if the underlying stock increases in price

Buyers of put options profit if the underlying stock decreases in price

---

Selling Options

The goal of selling (to open) an option is to 'Sell High and Buy Low'. When you sell (to open) an option, cash is credited to your brokerage account. For example, if you sell an option for 6.00 points, $600 will be credited to your account ($6.00 x 100 shares = $600). This is just the opposite of purchasing an option. As noted previously, buying an option for 6.00 points would result in $600 being deducted from your account.

Selling (to open) a call option is a bearish strategy. An investor who sells a call option is also known as the 'writer'. Selling a call is also known as being 'short' a call. The value of a call option declines as the underlying stock decreases in price. Being 'short' a call option generates profits as the call option decreases in value.

If you sell (to open) a call option and the call option subsequently decreases in price then you can 'buy back' to close the short call at a lower price which will result in a profit for the call writer (Sell high and buy low). For example, if you sell (to open) a call option for 5.00 points and then later buy the call back to close for 3.00 points you would realize a 2.00 point profit.

Sell call at 5.00 and then buy back at 3.00 = 2.00 profit

This is a similar concept to 'shorting' a stock. If you short a stock that drops in price and then subsequently buy the stock back at a lower price to close you would realize a profit. For example, if you short IBM stock at 74.25 and subsequently buy the stock back to close at 70.00 you would realize a 4.25 point profit.

Short IBM at 74.25 and buy back at 70.00 = 4.25 profit

If you sell (to open) a call option for 5.00 points and then later buy the call back to close at a higher price let's say 7.00 points you would realize a 2.00 point loss.

Sell call at 5.00 and then buy back to close at 7.00 = 2.00 loss

Selling (to open) a put option is a bullish strategy. An investor who sells a put option is also known as the 'writer'. Selling a put is also known as being 'short' a put. The value of a put option declines as the underlying stock increases in price. If you sell (to open) a put option and the underlying stock subsequently increases in price then you can 'buy back' to close the short put at a lower price which will result in a profit for the put writer. For example, if you sell a put option for 5.00 points and then later buy the put back to close for 3.00 points you would realize a 2.00 point profit.

Sell put at 5.00 and then buy back to close at 3.00 = 2.00 profit.

If you sell (to open) a put option for 5.00 points and then later buy the put back to close at a higher price let's say 7.00 points you would realize a 2.00 point loss.

Sell put at 5.00 and then buy back to close at 7.00 = 2.00 loss

> **Selling a call option to open profits if the underlying stock decreases in price**
>
> **Selling a put option to open profits if the underlying stock increases in price**

Note: When you buy an option, you can sell the option any time prior to option expiration. When you sell to open an option you can buy to close the option any time prior to option expiration.

Let's review the types of option orders that you would give to your broker (or online) to make sure you understand this important concept.

Order		Result
Buy Call to Open		Establishes Long Call Position
Buy Put to Open		Establishes Long Put Position
Sell Call to Close		Closes Out Long Call Position
Sell Put to Close		Closes Out Long Put Position
Sell Call to Open		Establishes Short Call Position
Sell Put to Open		Establishes Short Put Position
Buy Call to Close		Closes Out Short Call Position
Buy Put to Close		Closes Out Short Put Position

Call Options versus Stock Ownership

It is important to understand the distinction between buying call options and owning stock. Unlike stocks, options have a limited life. If an investor purchases stock and the expected move does not occur with the stock he/she can continue to hold the stock indefinitely. This is not true with options as every option has an expiration date. At expiration a call option has only intrinsic value, which is the difference between its strike price and the current stock price. At expiration a call option is worthless if the stock closes at or below the strike price. Profiting from option purchases depends on your ability to predict both the direction and timing of a move in the price of the underlying stock.

Purchasing an in-the-money call has a higher probability of success than an out-of-the-money call, as there is a reduced requirement for the underlying stock to move in the right direction and a lower breakeven price. Sometimes new option traders will be tempted to buy weekly call options that are out-of-the-money because of the low cost. Everyone loves a bargain but these options are cheap for a reason: the option has little time left until expiration and the strike price and stock price are so far apart that it is highly unlikely that the option will be in the money before expiration day.

At-the-money and out-of-the-money calls have no intrinsic value; their entire price consists of time premium. At expiration, call buyers will lose their entire investment if the stock price is equal to or below the strike price.

If you choose to buy the cheapest options, you must be very precise in timing the move and calling the direction. You can also expect to have a higher percentage of losing trades when purchasing out-of-the money options.

In-the-Money Calls

Buying deep in-the-money call options offers a relatively conservative approach to options investing by giving an options trader more control over the time value and intrinsic value components of the option compared to at-the money and out-of-the-money options.

An important component of a deep in-the-money option is its substantial intrinsic value, which can comprise up to 90 to 95% or more of the total option premium. A major advantage of deep in-the-money options is the significantly lower level of time erosion of your option.

As options move deeper into the money, the amount by which an option's price will change for a one point move in the price of the underlying stock approaches 1.00 or 100% for a call option. This relationship between the price movement for an option compared to the price movement in the underlying security is referred to as an option's Delta. A deep in-the-money option behaves like the underlying stock by making a near point-for-point move with the price change in the underlying security. Therefore, these options are similar to owning the stock but with the advantages options provide:

- leverage resulting from a lower capital requirement

- limited risk

- higher percentage profit potential

Put Purchases

A put option purchase also known as being long a put is a bearish position. It gives the purchaser the right but not the obligation to sell the underlying security at a fixed price on or before the expiration. The risk for the purchaser is limited to the premium paid for the put option. The profit potential is not limited. The put purchase strategy benefits from a decrease in the price of the underlying security. Buying puts is a strategy that can be used as an alternative to short selling a stock, giving the purchaser the added benefits of limited risk and increased leverage.

Put Buying Advantages

• A put purchase is a limited risk alternative to shorting a stock which is a high-risk strategy

• Put purchases provide leverage without having to use margin

• Put purchases are limited risk but the profit potential is not limited

• Put purchasers do not have to pay dividends on the underlying stock, which is required of short sellers

Summary of Variables for Call and Put Purchases

Variable	Effect on a Call	Effect on a Put
Increase in Stock Price	Increases Call Value	Decreases Put Value
Decrease in Stock Price	Decreases Call Value	Increases Put Value
Higher Strike Price	Decreases Call Value	Increases Put Value
Lower Strike Price	Increases Call Value	Decreases Put Value
Longer Expiration	Increases Call Value	Increases Put Value
Shorter Expiration	Decreases Call Value	Decreases Put Value
Higher Interest Rate	Increases Call Value	Decreases Put Value
Lower Interest Rates	Decreases Call Value	Increases Put Value
Increased Dividends	Decreases Call Value	Increases Put Value
Decreased Dividends	Increases Call Value	Decreases Put Value
Increase in Volatility	Increases Call Value	Increases Put Value
Decrease in Volatility	Decreases Call Value	Decreases Put Value

Section 3 Quiz

1. Buying calls is a strategy that can be used as an alternative to the outright purchase of stock, giving the purchaser the added benefits of limited risk and increased leverage.
   A. True
   B. False

2. At expiration, call buyers will lose their entire investment if the underlying stock closes below the strike price of the call purchased.
   A. True
   B. False

3. The IBM 70-strike call option was purchased for 3 points. IBM stock would have to close at ___ at option expiration for this call purchase to breakeven.
   A. 67
   B. 70
   C. 73
   D. 76

4. In the above example if IBM stock closes at 80 at option expiration, a ___ point net profit (before commissions) would be realized on the call purchase.
   A. 7
   B. 3
   C. 10
   D. 8

5. Using the same IBM example, the maximum risk for purchasing the 70-strike call option for 3 points would be ___ points.
   A. 7
   B. 10
   C. 3
   D. 73

6. One advantage of purchasing deep in-the-money call options is the significantly lower level of time decay, as most of the option premium is composed of intrinsic value.
   A. True
   B. False

7. IBM stock is currently trading at 77. The IBM 55-
   strike in-the-money weekly call option is priced at 22.75
   points. This call option has ___ points of time value.
   A. 22
   B. .75
   C. 22.75
   D. 21.25

8. Purchasing an in-the-money call option has a lower
   probability of profit than an out-of-the-money call as there is
   an increased requirement for the underlying
   stock to move in the right direction.
   A. True
   B. False

9. As options move deeper in-the-money, the amount by which
   an option's price will change for a one point move in the price
   of the underlying stock approaches 1.00 or 100%. This is
   referred to as an option's Delta.
   A. True
   B. False

10. Buying put options is strategy that can be used as an
    alternative to short selling a stock, giving the buyer
    the added benefits of limited risk and increased leverage.
    A. True
    B. False

11. The Mastercard 120-strike weekly put option was purchased for 5
    points. Mastercard stock would have to close at ___ at
    option expiration for this put purchase to breakeven.
    A. 120
    B. 125
    C. 130
    D. 115

12. In the above example Mastercard stock closes at 130 at
    option expiration. This would result in a ____ point
    _____ for the put purchase.

    A. 10, profit
    B. 10, loss
    C. 5, profit
    D. 5, loss

Section 3 Quiz Key

1. A, True
2. A, True
3. C, 73
4. A, 7 (10 point value - 3 point cost = 7 point profit)
5. C, 3
6. A, True
7. B, .75
8. B, False
9. A, True
10. A, True
11. D, 115
12. D, 5, loss

Chapter 3

Starting on a Shoestring

In this Chapter we will explore the weekly option purchase strategy which allows investors to start with a small amount of money. We will learn how to trade a weekly option portfolio with just $270 and achieve average weekly returns as high as 83.6%.

I have been using *Prime Trade Select* for many years to select call and put options with the best profit potential. At the end of this Chapter my brokerage account Profit/Loss statements will show a total of $1,801,685.41 in real time profits over the past 5 years using *Prime Trade Select* for call and put option purchases. These option purchases had an average return of 85% and 91.2% winning trades.

Using *Prime Trade Select* to select weekly call and put option purchases can and will take you to places that no other investment opportunity will allow! With option investing a small investment can grow into a large fortune. It's pretty exciting stuff!

If you are not familiar with option investing then I recommend you read Chapter 2 *'The Ins and Outs of Calls and Puts'* before you go any further. Chapter 2 will teach you the basics of investing in weekly options. I know option investing may seem intimidating or complicated to some investors but I can tell you from experience that learning option investing is well worth the effort.

When I started investing in options 27 years ago I had a big mortgage payment and a young family. I started investing in options with only a $4,600 trading account as that is all I could scrape together at the time. But within the first two years I made $460,164 in profits which is more than I made at my airline job over the previous six years.

Knowing that I could support my family from my option trading business was very comforting and liberating for me as I finally achieved financial independence. I no longer depended on my job to support my family. At the end of this book I included copies of my 1985 and 1986 tax returns showing that $460,164 of profits during my first two years of option investing. I went on to make millions of dollars in profits investing in options using the option strategies you are about to learn.

Getting a high return with a small investment is the secret to becoming what I call a 'Shoestring Millionaire'. The key to achieving a high return is to use leverage. Stocks have historically provided an 11.6% average compounded rate of return over the long term.

While this rate of return far exceeds the historical returns for home prices and fixed income investments, it would take many years to turn a small investment into a large investment with an 11.6% annual return.

For example, it would take more than six years to double your investment with an 11.6% compounded rate of return.

Using Leverage

In my experience the best way to achieve a high rate of investment return is to invest in options. Options give you the 'leverage' you need to generate a high rate of return with a small investment which can enable us to become 'Shoestring Millionaires'.

In this Chapter we will explore purchasing call and put options which provide leverage that can enable you to realize a high rate of return over a short period of time. When you purchase a call or put option, the most you can lose is the cost of the option regardless of the price movement of the underlying stock. Even if the price of a stock drops to zero the most you can lose is the cost you paid for the option.

But because you can lose the funds you invest in options I recommend only investing that portion of your investing funds that you can afford to lose in options.

Purchasing options incurs limited risk as you can't lose more money than you invest. This is different from Forex trading or trading futures contracts which can result in losing more money than you invest. I have seen a lot of advertisements lately touting the '100 to 1' or even '200 to 1' leverage available from Forex trading. While this kind of leverage can produce high returns it can be dangerous to your financial health.

If you invest $10,000 in a '200 to 1' leveraged contract a 10% adverse move can wipe out your $10,000 investment and trigger a $190,000 margin call that will force you to pay the brokerage firm an additional $190,000 to meet the margin call.

Recently the Amaranth hedge fund 'blew up' as a result of margin calls the fund received on its energy futures contracts. These types of margin calls have occurred in the past and with the use of this type of leverage will probably occur again in the future. More often than not the use of this type of leverage eventually ends badly for investors.

**Options Can Provide a High Rate of Return
With a Small Investment Which Would
Allows Us to Become Shoestring Millionaires**

In Chapter 1 we learned the *Prime Trade Select* 3-Step process which identifies options with the greatest profit potential. *Prime Trade Select* identifies stocks and ETFs in a confirmed price up trend. If you can identify stocks/ETFs trending up in price, you can harness the tremendous profit opportunities available from purchasing call options.

Stocks that are in a confirmed price uptrend are excellent candidates for call option purchases as the value of a call option increases as the price of the underlying stock increases.

And stocks that are in a confirmed price down trend are excellent candidates for put option purchases as the value of a put option increases as the price of the underlying stock decreases.

Prime Trade Select lets us know in advance the most likely future price movement of a stock or ETF instead of trying to predict future price movement.

As noted previously, the greater return potential associated with options is due to the leverage that options provide. Let's take a look at some actual option examples so that you can understand the important concept of leverage and how leverage can provide a high rate of return.

The option quote table below contains actual call option prices (courtesy of Yahoo Finance) for Hewlett Packard (HPQ). Buying call options is a bullish strategy as the value of a call option will increase as the price of the underlying stock increases. Hewlett Packard stock is currently trading at 32.78. Let's focus on the March 35-Strike call option (circled).

Hewlett-Packard Co. (HPQ)   At 3:49PM ET: **32.78** ↓ 0.18 (0.55%)

CALL OPTIONS   **Expire at close Fri, Mar 17, 2006**

Strike	Symbol	Last	Chg	Bid	Ask	Open Int
25.00	HPQCE.X	7.90	0.00	7.60	7.80	303
27.50	HPQCY.X	5.40	↓1.00	5.10	5.30	479
30.00	HPQCF.X	2.80	↓0.15	2.65	2.75	4,797
32.50	HPQCZ.X	0.70	↓0.15	0.65	0.70	38,350
35.00	HPQCG.X	0.05	↓0.05	0.05	0.10	30,226

10% Stock Price Increase = 950% Option Return

Buying the 35-Strike call option gives us the right to buy 100 shares of HPQ at 35.00. If we were to purchase the 35-Strike call option we would expect to pay the 'ask' price of .10 cents or $10 per option (.10 x 100 shares = $10).

Let's assume HPQ stock increases 10% in price from the current price of 32.78 to 36.05. With a stock price of 36.05 the 35-Strike call option would be worth 1.05 points or $105 (stock price of 36.05 minus 35-Strike price = 1.05 option value). When you purchase options you can sell them any time prior to option expiration. So the option we purchased for .10 points could be sold for 1.05 points. Selling the 35-Strike call at 1.05 would produce a 950% return (1.05 sale price minus .10 cost = .95 profit divided by .10 cost = 950% return).

9.5 to 1 Leverage = Profit Opportunity

Options Are Highly Leveraged and Can Provide a High Rate of Return

---

Stock Investor
- **Buys HPQ Stock at 32.78**
- **Stock Increases 10% to 36.05**

Results:
- **Big Investment $3,278**
- **Small Profit 10%**

Option Investor
- **Buys 35-Strike Call Option for $10**
- **Stock Increases 10% to 36.05**
  Call Option is Worth $105 (Stock Price of 36.05 minus 35.0 Strike = 1.05 Option Value)

   $105 Option Value Minus $10 Cost = $95 Profit
   $95 Profit Divided by $10 Cost = 950% Return

Results:
- **Small Investment $10**
- **Big Profit 950%**

A 10% Price Increase in Stock = 950% Call Option Return
Which Allows Us to Achieve a High Rate of Return

102

The Power of Leverage

The table below compares the profit potential of purchasing Hewlett Packard stock at today's price of 32.78 versus the HPQ March 35-strike call option at .10 points. If HPQ stock increases to 38.00 stock investors realize a 15.9% return but option investors realize a 2,900% return. If HPQ stock increases to 40 stock investors realize a 22% return but option investors realize a 4,900% return.

"Progress always involves risks. You can't steal second base and keep your foot on first."

- Frederick B. Wilcox

15.9% Stock Return = 2,900% Option Return = 29 to 1 Leverage

22% Stock Return = 4,900% Option Return = 49 to 1 Leverage

Hewlett Packard Stock Price	35.00	36.00	37.00	38.00	39.00	40.00
Stock Profit	2.22	3.22	4.22	5.22	6.22	7.22
Stock % Return	6.8%	9.8%	12.9%	15.9%	19.0%	22.0%
Value of 35-Strike Call Option	0.00	1.00	2.00	3.00	4.00	5.00
Option Profit	0.00	0.90	1.90	2.90	3.90	4.90
Option % Return	0.00	900%	1900%	2900%	3900%	4900%

Option Profits Are Derived From Stock Price Movement

Options are 'derivatives' that derive their value from the price of the underlying stock. The intrinsic value of a call option will increase one point for each point its underlying stock increases above the strike price.

Intrinsic Value of Call Option Increases One Point for Each Point Its Stock Increases above the Strike Price

---

A lot has been published about option strategies that invest in options based on whether an option is undervalued or overvalued according to the Black-Scholes Pricing Model. These option strategies are very complex and require high-level mathematical calculations to compute an option's Alpha, Beta, Delta, Gamma, Theta etc.

I never understood the logic of investing in an option because it was slightly under valued at the time of purchase. Undervalued options can become more undervalued. **The price movement of the underlying stock determines an option's value and the resulting profit/loss.** When you purchase a call option your profits are determined by the price movement of the underlying stock.

Let's refer again to the example for the Hewlett Packard 35-Strike call purchased at .10 points so that you fully understand this important concept. The table below clearly demonstrates that the price of HPQ stock determines the profit/loss of the 35-Strike call option. If we can select a stock moving up in price, purchasing a call option on that stock can produce enormous profits due to the leverage options provide.

Option intrinsic value increases 'dollar for dollar' once the stock price moves above the strike price of the option purchased

HPQ Stock Price	35.00	36.00	37.00	38.00	39.00	40.00
Value of 35-Strike Call Option	0.00	1.00	2.00	3.00	4.00	5.00
Option Profit/Loss	0.00	0.90	1.90	2.90	3.90	4.90
Option % Return	0.00	900%	1,900%	2,900%	3,900%	4,900%

If we can select a stock moving up in price, purchasing a call option on that stock can produce enormous profits and will allow us to harness the leverage provided from option investing.

Compounding Your Returns

Purchasing call options can provide the leverage that allows you to achieve a high return with a small investment. The table below contains current actual call option prices for Merck (MRK). Merck stock is currently trading at 41.03. Let's focus on the MRK 40-Strike call option (circled below). Purchasing this option would cost 1.10 points or $110 (plus commission) at the current trading price.

MRK			**41.03 -0.06**	
Calls	Last Sale	Bid	Ask	Open Int
06 Sep 30.00 (MRK IF)	11.10	10.90	11.10	231
06 Sep 32.50 (MRK IZ)	8.60	8.40	8.60	150
06 Sep 35.00 (MRK IG)	6.10	5.90	6.10	263
06 Sep 37.50 (MRK IU)	3.60	3.40	3.60	474
06 Sep 40.00 (MRK IH)	1.10	1.00	1.10	2,744

An ordinary investor would:

- Buy Merck at 41.03
- Let's Assume Stock Increases 10% to 45.13

Net Result:

- Large Investment: $4,103
- Small Profit: 10%

A "Shoestring Millionaire" would:

- Buy MRK 40-Strike call at 1.10
- Let's Assume Stock Increases 10% to 45.13

Net Result:

- Small Investment: $110
- Large Profit: 366% *

* Stock price of 45.13 Minus 40-Strike Price = Option Value of 5.13
5.13 Option Value Minus 1.10 Cost = 4.03 Option Profit
4.03 Profit Divided by 1.10 Cost = 366% Option Return

Let's assume we purchase 10 of the Merck 40-Strike call options previously mentioned. Our total investment would be $1,100 plus commission (10 X $110 option price = $1,100). And let's again assume that the price of Merck stock increases 10% from 41.03 to 45.13. The value of the 40-Strike call option would be 5.13 (stock price of 45.13 minus strike price of 40 = 5.13 option value).

After subtracting the 1.10 cost of the option from the current 5.13 value results in a 4.03 profit or $403 per option. Our total profit for purchasing 10 options would be $4,030. When purchasing options our risk is limited to the purchase price of the option. In this example our total risk for purchasing ten options would be $1,100.

Big Gains Do Not Require Big Risks

In order for a stock investor to realize a $4,030 profit from a 10% move in Merck stock they would have to purchase 982 shares which would require a $40,291 investment. Which brings up the question . . . Would you rather risk $40,291 to make a $4,030 profit (buying stock) or risk $1,100 to make the same $4,030 profit (buying options)? Options trading allows you to make big gains that do not require big risks.

The Power of Compounding

Let's take this example one step further. Let's assume that you were able to make several of these trades consecutively. I know that losing trades are inevitable with any strategy and that every trade cannot be a big winner but for the sake of demonstration just bear with me for a moment. If you invested $1,100 and made a 366% return it would only take four such trades for your $1,100 investment to grow to $518,724 and after five trades your $1,100 investment grows to $2,417,253. Again, these results are strictly hypothetical but clearly demonstrate the power of compounding.

Trade Number	Starting Value	Percent Return	Profit	Ending Value
1	$1,100	366%	$4,026	$5,126
2	$5,126	366%	$18,761	$23,887
3	$23,887	366%	$87,427	$111,314
4	$111,314	366%	$407,410	$518,724
5	$518,724	366%	$1,898,530	$2,417,254
6	$2,417,254	366%	$8,847,149	$11,264,403
7	$11,264,403	366%	$41,227,716	$52,492,119

Options can provide spectacular returns without big risks . . . why doesn't everyone invest in them?

I think that in general options trading has been shrouded in mystery for the average investor. Most investors don't invest in options because they don't understand options. They have heard too many myths and misconceptions concerning options trading. When something is not understood, it is often feared. I believe this is the case with option trading.

The biggest misconception related to option trading is that it is 'too risky'. But that is simply not true. In the previous example for Merck options we learned that a stock investor has to risk $40,291 to receive the same profit potential as the options investor who only risks $1,100. Trading stocks can be more risky than trading options because more of your money is at risk. Option trading is also more versatile as you can profit in up or down markets.

Option Portfolio Snapshot

$254,006.83 Profit, Average Return 114.9%

My brokerage portfolio statement below contains examples of call options I purchased using *Prime Trade Select*. This portfolio has an open trade profit of $254,006.83 and an average return of 114% with no losing trades.

Apple Option	+ 70.2%	Cameron Option	+ 117.8%
Freeport Option	+ 116.2%	Fluor Corp Option	+ 146.7%
Google Option	+ 2.2%	Google Option	+ 120.0%
Celgene Option	+ 0.6%	Nat'l Oil Option	+ 84.2%
Apple Option	+ 182.5%	RIMM Option	+ 167.9%
Transocean Option	+ 49.5%		

Note: In this portfolio, I traded multiple option contracts. Trading one contract would require considerably less trading capital.

Portfolios

Alerts | Transfer Money | Bill Pay | Help

| Portfolios | Performance & Value | Positions | Gains & Losses | Risk Analyzer | Portfolio Analyzer | Income Estimator BETA |

Market Value: $477,662.79 ($254,006.83 / 114.95%)   DJIA 13,775.48 ▲ +103.56   Nasdaq 2,797.30 ▲ +46.44

REFRESH | STREAMING QUOTES | EXPORT TO EXCEL   Results per Page: 200

Symbol		Last Trade	Change $	Change %	Day's Gain	Qty	Price Paid	Total Gain $	Total Gain %	Market Val	Edit
AXVAU	Trade	74.50	2.50	3.47%	$560.00	2	$43.85	$6,172.52	70.24%	$14,960.00	Edit
CAMAM	Trade	39.30	0.00	0.00%	-$1,260.00	14	$18.06	$29,834.78	117.81%	$55,160.00	Edit
FCXAO	Trade	36.10	0.00	0.00%	$5,200.00	16	$19.38	$36,076.04	116.21%	$67,120.00	Edit
FLRAA	Trade	49.90	0.00	0.00%	-$1,080.00	12	$25.62	$45,169.04	146.70%	$75,960.00	Edit
GOOAF	Trade	62.70	-1.30	-2.03%	$480.00	2	$64.85	$292.52	2.25%	$13,280.00	Edit
GOPAY	Trade	132.50	1.50	1.15%	$760.00	2	$60.50	$14,542.52	120.01%	$26,660.00	Edit
LQHAK	Trade	12.10	1.11	10.10%	$400.00	4	$12.00	$29.01	0.60%	$4,840.00	Edit
NOVKJ	Trade	22.20	-1.40	-5.93%	-$4,560.00	24	$12.08	$24,499.04	84.42%	$53,520.00	Edit
QAAAD	Trade	66.57	1.76	2.72%	$2,124.00	12	$23.52	$51,613.04	182.57%	$79,884.00	Edit
RFYAN	Trade	49.15	-1.25	-2.48%	$720.00	12	$19.00	$38,359.04	167.94%	$61,200.00	Edit
RIGAR	Trade	28.20	0.00	0.00%	-$160.00	8	$18.69	$7,419.28	49.53%	$22,400.00	Edit
Cash					2,678.79					$2,678.79	
				Totals	$3,184.00		$220,977.17	$254,006.83	114.95%	$477,662.79	

LEGEND: ⊞ collapsed (click to expand)   ⊟ expanded (click to collapse)   Real-time quotes

Call Option Trade Examples

My brokerage confirmation below shows I purchased 15 Apple October 130-Strike call options symbol APVJF at 14.00 points. I used *Prime Trade Select* to select this option.

Apple was in a confirmed price up trend. The AAPL 50-Day EMA was above the 100-Day EMA. Apple was making a series of new 52-Week highs and the On Balance Volume line was sloping up confirming the price up trend.

USD - US DOLLAR

Trades

Trade Date	Settlement Date	Trade Time	Action	Quantity	Symbol	Price
08/31/2007	09/04/2007	3:36:37 pm	Buy to Open	15	÷APVJF	14.000000

AAPL (Apple, Inc.) Nasdaq GS — © StockCharts.com
2-Nov-2007 Op 189.21 Hi 189.44 Lo 183.49 Cl 187.87 Vol 35.8M Chg +0.43 (+0.23%) ▲
↑↓ AAPL (Daily) 187.87
—EMA(50) 161.55
—EMA(100) 146.25

50-Day EMA Above 100-Day EMA

On Balance Volume Line Sloping Up

108

In this trade example, my brokerage confirmation below shows I purchased 10 of the FCX Jun 65-Strike call options at 7.20 points using *Prime Trade Select* which was on a 'buy' signal.

FCX was in a confirmed price up trend with the 50-Day EMA was above the 100-Day EMA. FCX was making a series of new 52-Week highs and the On Balance Volume line was sloping up confirming the price up trend.

USD - US DOLLAR

Trades

Trade Date	Settlement Date	Trade Time	Action	Quantity	Symbol	Price
05/18/2007	05/21/2007	3:57:03 pm	Buy to Open	10	+FCXFM	7.200000

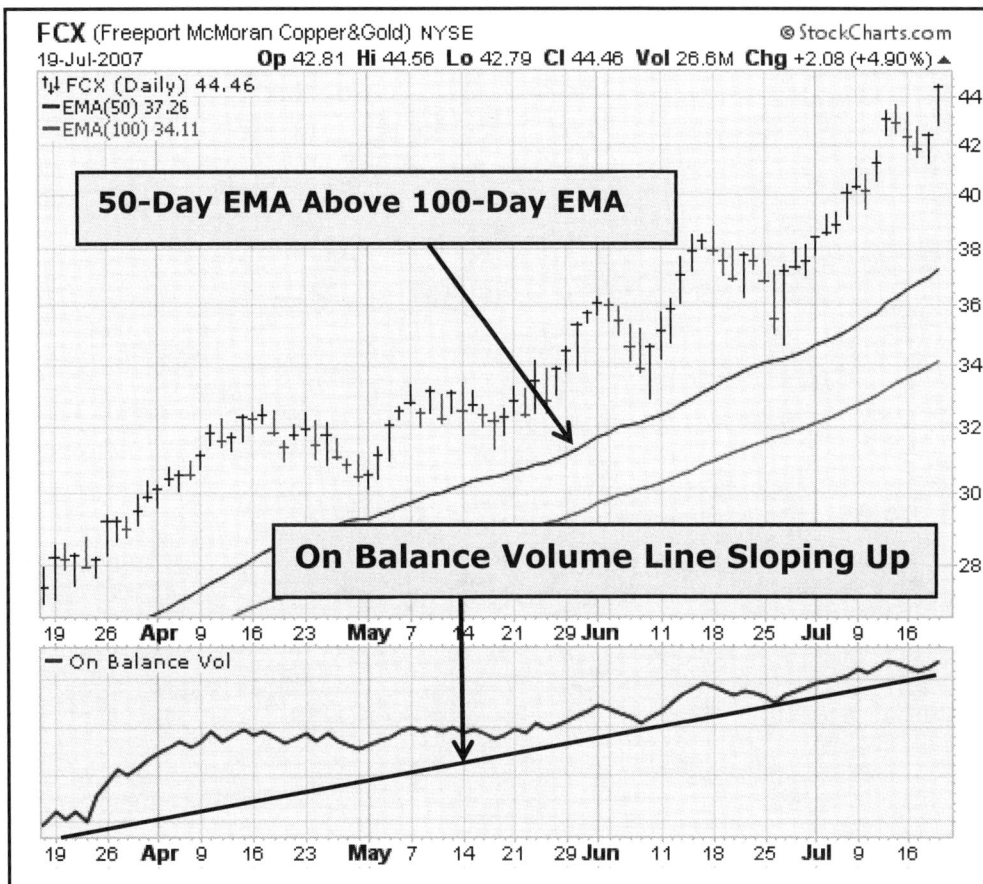

And in this trade example on April 23rd I purchased the Express Scripts Jun 80-Strike call option symbol XTQFP (ESRX subsequently had a stock split) at 10.18 using *Prime Trade Select* which was on a 'buy' signal.

Like Apple and FCX, Express Scripts was making a series of new 52-Week highs and the On Balance Volume line was sloping up confirming the price up trend.

USD - US DOLLAR

Trades

Trade Date	Settlement Date	Trade Time	Action	Quantity	Symbol	Price
04/23/2007	04/24/2007	3:57:55 pm	Buy to Open	10	+XTQFP	10.180000

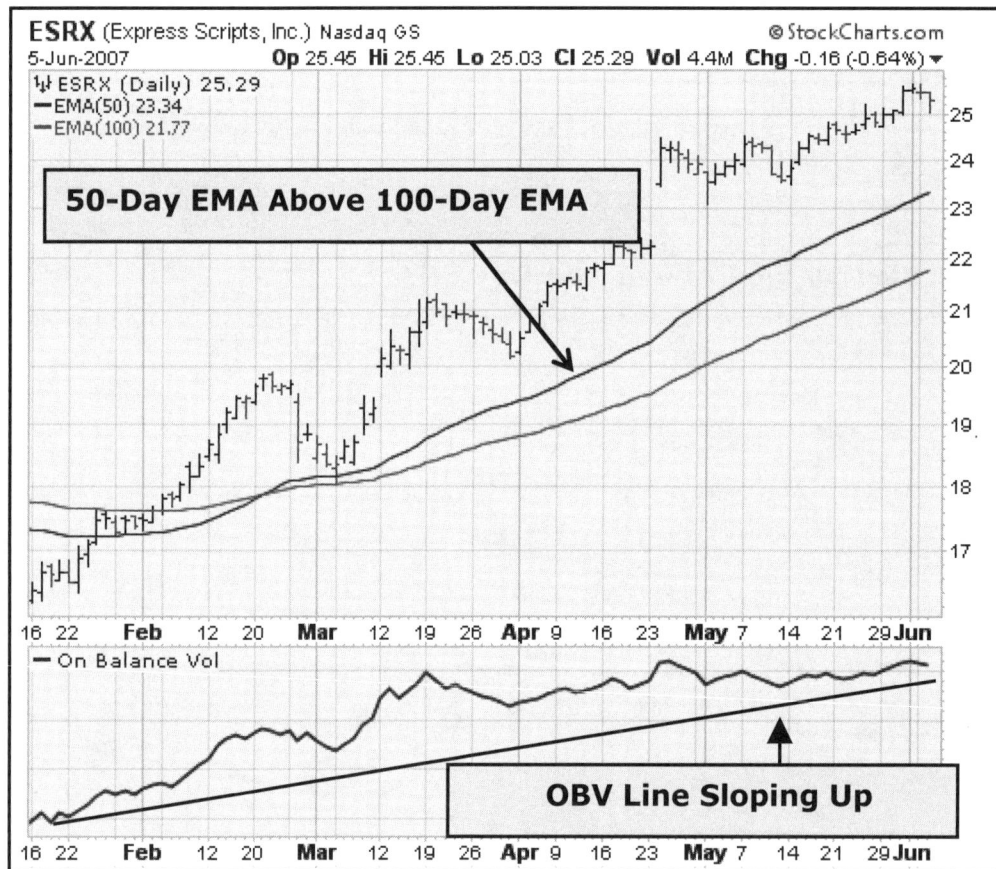

Let's take a look next at the details of the call option trade examples just presented so that you can understand the important concept of leverage and how leverage can provide a high rate of return.

Remember that even though these call option trades use leverage, they are all limited risk trades and you can't lose more than your initial investment regardless of adverse market moves.

My brokerage account Profit/Loss Report below shows that on October 5th I closed out the 15 Apple Oct 130-Strike call options at 30.30 points resulting in a $24,392.27 net profit after commissions and a 116% return for the option trade.

On August 31st when I purchased the AAPL options, Apple stock was trading at 139.20. When I sold the options on October 5th AAPL stock was trading at 158.40.

Purchasing Apple stock at 139.20 on August 31st and selling on October 5th at 158.40 would result in a 13.8% return. Over the same period of time my option trade produced a 116% return which is 8.4 times greater than the stock trade demonstrating the leverage available from trading options.

Option Return 8.4 Times Greater Than Stock Return

	Purchase Price	Sale Price	Point Profit	Percent Return
Stock	139.20	158.40	19.20	13.8%
Option	14.00	30.30	16.30	116.4%

13.8% Stock Return = 116% Option Return

Option Return 840% Greater Than Stock Return

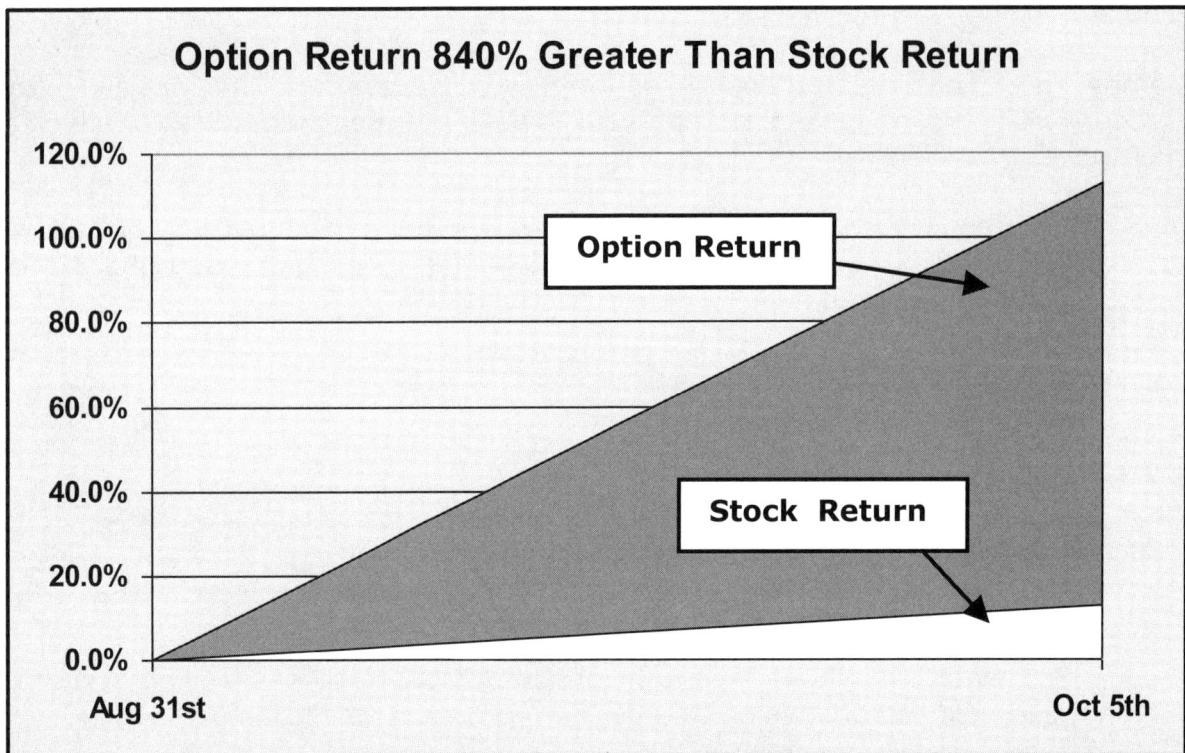

Aug 31st   Oct 5th

8.4 to 1 Leverage = Profit Opportunity

Options Are Highly Leveraged and Can Provide a High Rate of Return

Stock Investor
- Buys Apple Stock at 139.20
- Stock Increases 13.8% to 158.40

Results:
- Big Investment $13,920
- Small Profit 13.8%

Option Investor
- Buys 130-Strike Call Option for $1,400
- Stock Increases 13.8% to 158.40
- Call Option Increases in Value to 30.30

Results:
- Small Investment $1,400
- Big Profit 116% Which Allows a High Rate of Return

FCX and ESRX Trade Examples

My brokerage account confirmations below display the FCX and ESRX call option purchase examples previously presented. I purchased 10 of the FCX Jun 65-Strike call options symbol FCX at 7.20 points and 10 of the ESRX Jun 80-Strike call options symbol XTQFP at 10.18 points.

USD - US DOLLAR

Trades

Trade Date	Settlement Date	Trade Time	Action	Quantity	Symbol	Price
05/18/2007	05/21/2007	3:57:03 pm	Buy to Open	10	+FCXFM	7.200000

USD - US DOLLAR

Trades

Trade Date	Settlement Date	Trade Time	Action	Quantity	Symbol	Price
04/23/2007	04/24/2007	3:57:55 pm	Buy to Open	10	+XTQFP	10.180000

My brokerage account Profit/Loss Report below shows that I sold the FCXFM calls at 16.35 points and the XTQFP calls at 22.40 points. This resulted in a $9,099.72 profit and a 126% return for FCXFM and a $12,199.65 profit and a 119% return for XTQFP.

* To see all transactions within specified date range leave symbol blank						Guide to the Profit/Loss Report
Click here to download data						
Realized P&L on Closed Positions						
Symbol	Date Bought	Date Sold	Shares	Cost Basis	Sales Price	Gain-loss
+FCXFM	5/18/2007 3:57:03 PM	6/13/2007 12:25:45 PM	10	$7,225.00	$16,324.72	$9,099.72
+XTQFP	4/23/2007 3:57:55 PM	5/31/2007 1:41:25 PM	10	$10,205.00	$22,404.65	$12,199.65

Over the same time period purchasing FCX would have produced a 14.8% return compared to the 126% return for the option. The option purchase provided 8.5 to 1 leverage compared to the stock purchase.

FCX Option Return 8.5 Times Greater Than Stock Return

	Purchase Price	Sale Price	Point Profit	Percent Return
Stock	71.15	81.75	10.60	14.8%
Option	7.20	16.35	9.15	126%

And purchasing ESRX stock would have produced a 15.4% return over the same time period compared to the 119% return for the ESRX option. The option purchase provided 7.7 to 1 leverage compared to the stock purchase.

	Purchase Price	Sale Price	Point Profit	Percent Return
ESRX Option Return 7.7 Times Greater Than Stock Return				
Stock	88.30	101.90	13.60	15.4%
Option	10.18	22.40	12.22	119%

The Power of Leverage

On average these three option trade examples provided 8.2 times more profit compared to the purchase of their underlying stocks over the same time period. The 8.2 to 1 leverage provided by options can dramatically increase profit results.

Current Trade Results 198% Average Return

The snapshot of my brokerage account Profit/Loss Report below shows my current option purchase trades. I used *Prime Trade Select* to select these options. I currently have a profit of $22,491 on cost basis of $11,346 resulting in a 198% average return.

Trading	Markets	Account

ORDERS · POSITIONS · MESSAGES · SUMMARY · PERFORMANCE · HISTORY · BUY/SELL

Filter Off   + Select Columns ?

Position		QTY	Desc	Mark	Mark Chg	Market Value	Cost Basis	Cost Value	Open Mkt Gain
AAPL call	IN	+1	Jul12 3...	240.825	+10.525	24082....	54.90	5490.00	18592....
FAS call	!	+3	Apr12 1...	12.25	-1.20	3675.00	6.50	1950.00	1725.00
HD call	IN	+2	May12 ...	10.05	+0.00	2010.00	5.26	1052.00	958.00
HON call	IN	+2	Jun12 ...	10.85	-0.475	2170.00	8.51	1702.00	468.00
WFC call	IN	+2	Apr12 2...	9.50	+0.00	1900.00	5.76	1152.00	748.00
Portfolio Analysis							0.00		22491....

Trading ETF Options

In addition to stock options, I also like to trade options on ETFs which present some great profit opportunities. The four monthly price charts that follow show that these global markets were on a *Major Trend System* 'buy' signal from 2005 through mid-2008 with their 1-Month price above the 20-Month EMA. I used *Prime Trade Select* to select call options and call option spreads for these markets while they were on a buy signal. Option spreads will be covered in Chapter 6.

Global Energy

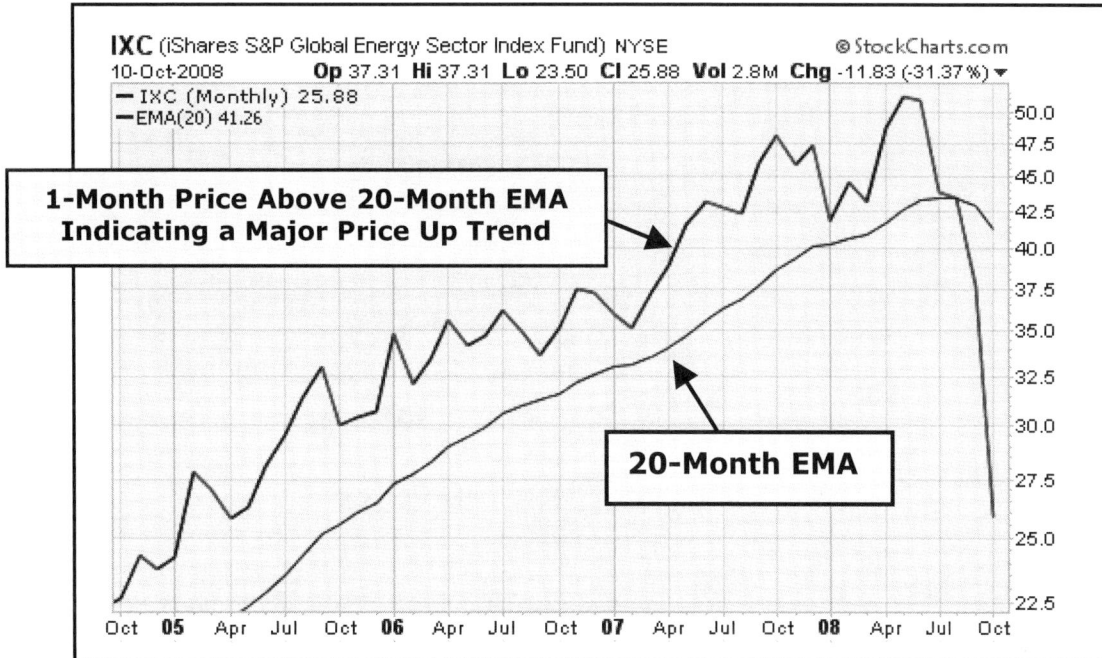

IXC (iShares S&P Global Energy Sector Index Fund) NYSE   © StockCharts.com
10-Oct-2008   Op 37.31 Hi 37.31 Lo 23.50 Cl 25.88 Vol 2.8M Chg -11.83 (-31.37%) ▼
— IXC (Monthly) 25.88
— EMA(20) 41.26

1-Month Price Above 20-Month EMA Indicating a Major Price Up Trend

20-Month EMA

Brazil Fund

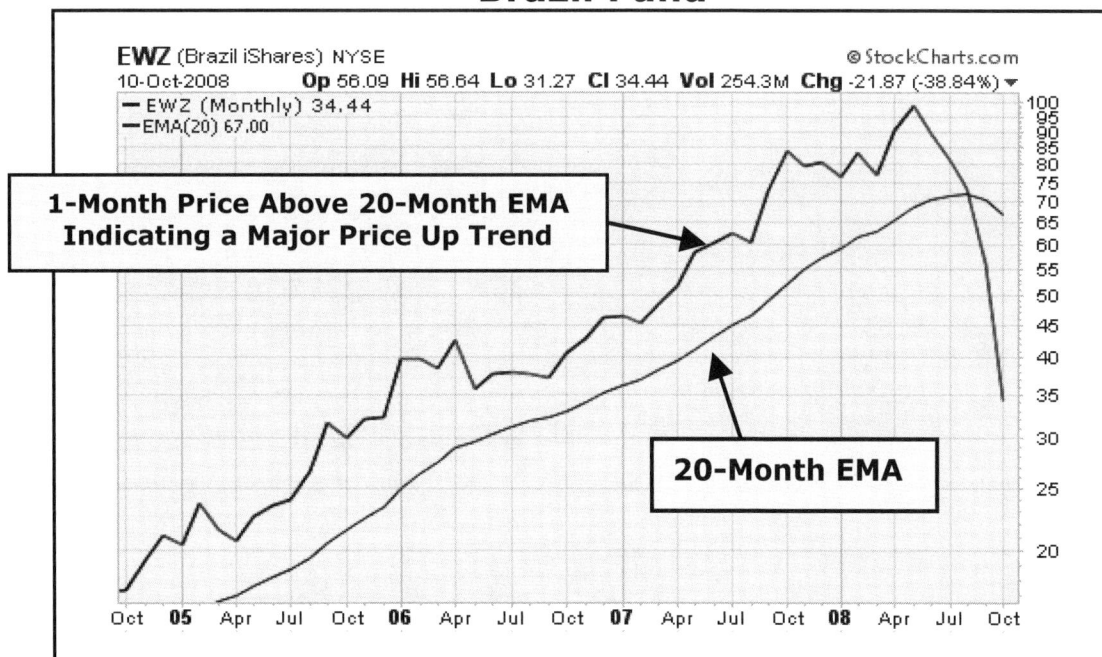

EWZ (Brazil iShares) NYSE   © StockCharts.com
10-Oct-2008   Op 56.09 Hi 56.64 Lo 31.27 Cl 34.44 Vol 254.3M Chg -21.87 (-38.84%) ▼
— EWZ (Monthly) 34.44
— EMA(20) 67.00

1-Month Price Above 20-Month EMA Indicating a Major Price Up Trend

20-Month EMA

Europe Australia & Far East Fund

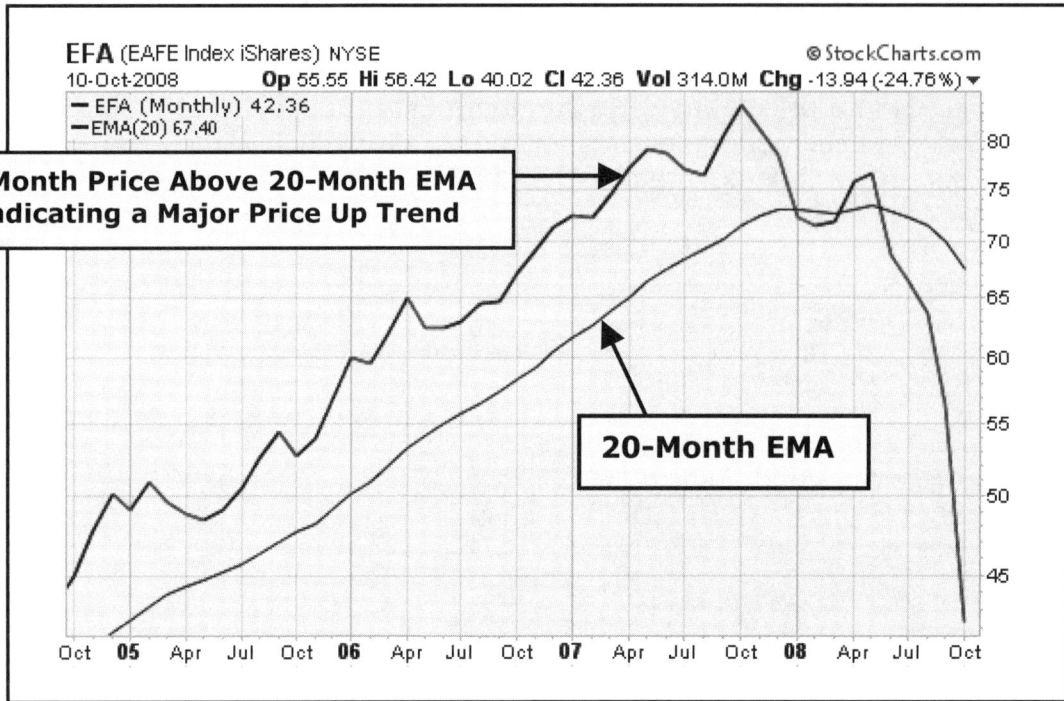

EFA (EAFE Index iShares) NYSE   © StockCharts.com
10-Oct-2008   Op 55.55 Hi 56.42 Lo 40.02 Cl 42.36 Vol 314.0M Chg -13.94 (-24.76%) ▼
— EFA (Monthly) 42.36
— EMA(20) 67.40

**1-Month Price Above 20-Month EMA
Indicating a Major Price Up Trend**

20-Month EMA

Oct **05** Apr Jul Oct **06** Apr Jul Oct **07** Apr Jul Oct **08** Apr Jul Oct

BLDRS Emerging Markets

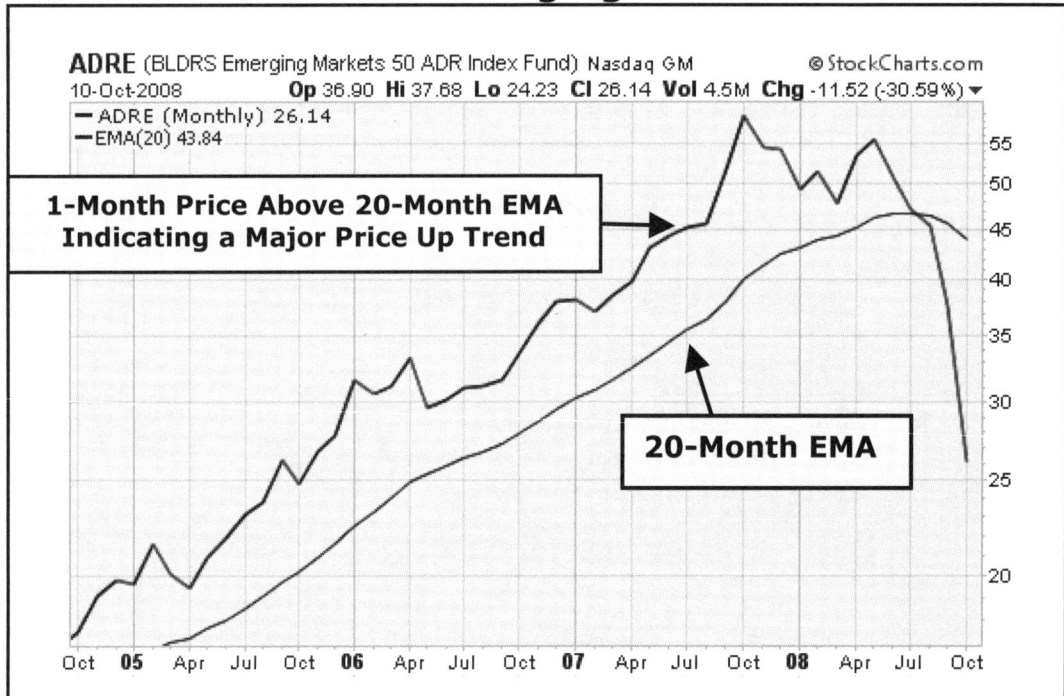

ADRE (BLDRS Emerging Markets 50 ADR Index Fund) Nasdaq GM   © StockCharts.com
10-Oct-2008   Op 36.90 Hi 37.68 Lo 24.23 Cl 26.14 Vol 4.5M Chg -11.52 (-30.59%) ▼
— ADRE (Monthly) 26.14
— EMA(20) 43.84

**1-Month Price Above 20-Month EMA
Indicating a Major Price Up Trend**

20-Month EMA

Oct **05** Apr Jul Oct **06** Apr Jul Oct **07** Apr Jul Oct **08** Apr Jul Oct

116

70% Average Return Over 7 Week Period

My brokerage account Profit/Loss Report below shows the purchase of call options and bullish option spreads on the four global markets just presented and other ETFs that were also on a *Prime Trade Select* 'buy' signal. The cost of the portfolio positions was $71,855.86 and the profit after commissions was $50,104 resulting in a 70% average return. The average holding period for these trades was seven weeks.

Note: In this portfolio, I traded 10 option contracts per trade. If you traded one contract per trade, this portfolio would only require $7,186 of trading capital and could be traded in a smaller account.

Account Reports: Profit/Loss Report   🖨 PRINT

Give your accountant a break. View profits/losses for all trades executed on one specific date or during a range of dates. Track by position, whether it's closed, or still opened. Download to a spreadsheet for easy manipulation, processing and tax reporting.

Trade date: « [   ] » SELECT DATE
Trade date: « [   ] » SELECT DATE
Symbol: [   ]   Submit ▶   ☐ **Show detailed unrealized positions**

To see all transactions within specified date range leave symbol blank Guide to the Profit/Loss Report

Unrealized P&L on Open Positions

Symbol	Description	Position	Avg Price	Cost Basis	Market Value	Type	Unrealized Val.
+BBHFP	Biotech Holdrs Tr Depostry Rcpts Jun 2007 180.00 Call	10	$11.1750	$11,175.00	$3,400.00	Stock Option	-$7,775.00
+BBHFR	Biotech Holdrs Tr Depostry Rcpts Jun 2007 190.00 Call	-10	-$3.8249	$3,824.94	-$100.00	Stock Option	$3,724.94
+EEMFE	Ishares Tr Msci Emerg Mkt Jun 2007 125.00 Call	-10	-$3.6649	$3,664.94	-$5,700.00	Stock Option	-$2,035.06
+EEMFT	Ishares Tr Msci Emerg Mkt Jun 2007 100.00 Call	10	$15.0050	$15,005.00	$29,200.00	Stock Option	$14,195.00
+EWZII	Ishares Inc Msci Brazil Sep 2007 45.00 Call	10	$8.2350	$8,235.00	$16,300.00	Stock Option	$8,065.00
+EWZIK	Ishares Inc Msci Brazil Sep 2007 55.00 Call	-10	-$4.9649	$4,964.92	-$7,800.00	Stock Option	-$2,835.08
+LXLAF	Ishares Tr Msci Eafe Idx Jan 2008 84.00 Call	-10	-$3.9649	$3,964.91	-$3,900.00	Stock Option	$64.91
+LXLAR	Ishares Tr Msci Eafe Idx Jan 2008 70.00 Call	10	$8.8850	$8,885.00	$14,100.00	Stock Option	$5,215.00
+OIHFJ	Oil Svc Holdrs Tr Depostry Rcpt Jun 2007 150.00 Call	10	$13.2650	$13,265.00	$24,200.00	Stock Option	$10,935.00
+OIHFK	Oil Svc Holdrs Tr Depostry Rcpt Jun 2007 155.00 Call	10	$14.2350	$14,235.00	$19,300.00	Stock Option	$5,065.00
+OIHFL	Oil Svc Holdrs Tr Depostry Rcpt Jun 2007 160.00 Call	-10	-$6.2949	$6,294.90	-$14,500.00	Stock Option	-$8,205.10
+OIHFM	Oil Svc Holdrs Tr Depostry Rcpt Jun 2007 165.00 Call	-10	-$10.1648	$10,164.82	-$9,800.00	Stock Option	$364.82
+QDFFH	Bldrs Index Fds Tr Emer Mk 50 Adr Jun 2007 34.00 Call	10	$5.2350	$5,235.00	$10,800.00	Stock Option	$5,565.00
+QDFFN	Bldrs Index Fds Tr Emer Mk 50 Adr Jun 2007 40.00 Call	-10	-$2.9649	$2,964.94	-$2,600.00	Stock Option	$364.94
+WFPAI	Select Sector Spdr Tr Sbi Materials Jan 2008 35.00 Call	10	$5.4350	$5,435.00	$7,100.00	Stock Option	$1,665.00
+WGTAI	Select Sector Spdr Tr Sbi Int-Utils Jan 2008 35.00 Call	10	$6.8350	$6,835.00	$6,800.00	Stock Option	-$35.00
+XBTGM	Select Sector Spdr Tr Sbi Int-Energy Jul 2007 65.00 Call	10	$4.5350	$4,535.00	$5,600.00	Stock Option	$1,065.00
+YECAC	Select Sector Spdr Tr Sbi Int-Energy Jan 2008 55.00 Call	10	$10.9350	$10,935.00	$16,500.00	Stock Option	$5,565.00
+YECAP	Select Sector Spdr Tr Sbi Int-Energy Jan 2008 68.00 Call	-10	-$5.9649	$5,964.90	-$6,700.00	Stock Option	-$735.10
+YOFAD	Ishares Tr Ftse Xnhua Idx Jan 2008 120.00 Call	-10	-$7.9649	$7,964.87	-$8,200.00	Stock Option	-$235.13
+YOFAW	Ishares Tr Ftse Xnhua Idx Jan 2008 90.00 Call	10	$17.4950	$17,495.00	$27,600.00	Stock Option	$10,105.00

Total Unrealized Gain-Loss: **$50,104.14**

Note: When most global markets reversed to a 'sell' signal in 2008 I took short option positions using *Prime Trade Select* as described in Chapter 1.

A 70% return over a 7 week period is a high rate of return which was possible due to the leverage that options provide. Let's take a look next at the details of some of the option trades above so that you can understand the important concept of leverage and how leverage can provide a high rate of return. Remember that even though these option trades use leverage, they are all limited risk trades and you can't lose more than your initial investment regardless of adverse market moves.

My brokerage account confirmation below shows that on December 12th I purchased 5 of the Emerging Market ETF June 100-Strike call options symbol EEMFT at 14.20 points (circled). The Emerging Market ETF was on a *Prime Trade Select* 'buy' signal.

USD - US DOLLAR

Trades

Trade Date	Settlement Date	Trade Time	Action	Quantity	Symbol	Price
12/12/2006	12/13/2006	11:13:26 am	Buy to Open	5	+YOFAW	16.200000
12/12/2006	12/13/2006	11:17:47 am	Buy to Open	5	+EWZFH	7.900000
12/12/2006	12/13/2006	11:18:47 am	Buy to Open	5	+EEMFT	14.200000

My brokerage account Profit/Loss Report below shows that on June 14th I sold the 5 EEMFT call options at 29.30 points resulting in a $7,514.77 net profit after commissions. This resulted in a 106% return for the option trade.

* To see all transactions within specified date range leave symbol blank   Guide to the Profit/Loss Report

Click here to download data

Realized P&L on Closed Positions

Symbol	Date Bought	Date Sold	Shares	Cost Basis	Sales Price	Gain-loss
+EEMFT	12/12/2006 11:18:47 AM	6/14/2007 11:49:01 AM	5	$7,127.50	$14,642.27	$7,514.77
+EEMFT	12/14/2006 3:28:40 PM	6/14/2007 11:49:01 AM	5	$7,877.50	$14,642.27	$6,764.77

On December 12th when I purchased the EEM options, the Emerging Markets ETF was trading at 111.30. On June 14th the ETF was trading at 129.20. Purchasing the Emerging Markets ETF at 111.30 on December 12th and selling on June 14th at 129.20 would result in a 16% return. Over the same period of time my option trade produced a 106% return which is 6.6 times greater than the ETF trade demonstrating the leverage available from trading options.

Option Return 6.6 Times Greater Than ETF Return

	Purchase Price	Sale Price	Point Profit	Percent Return
ETF	111.30	129.20	17.90	16.0%
Option	14.20	29.30	15.10	106.3%

16% ETF Return = 106% Option Return

Option Trade Provides 6.6 to 1 Leverage Compared to ETF

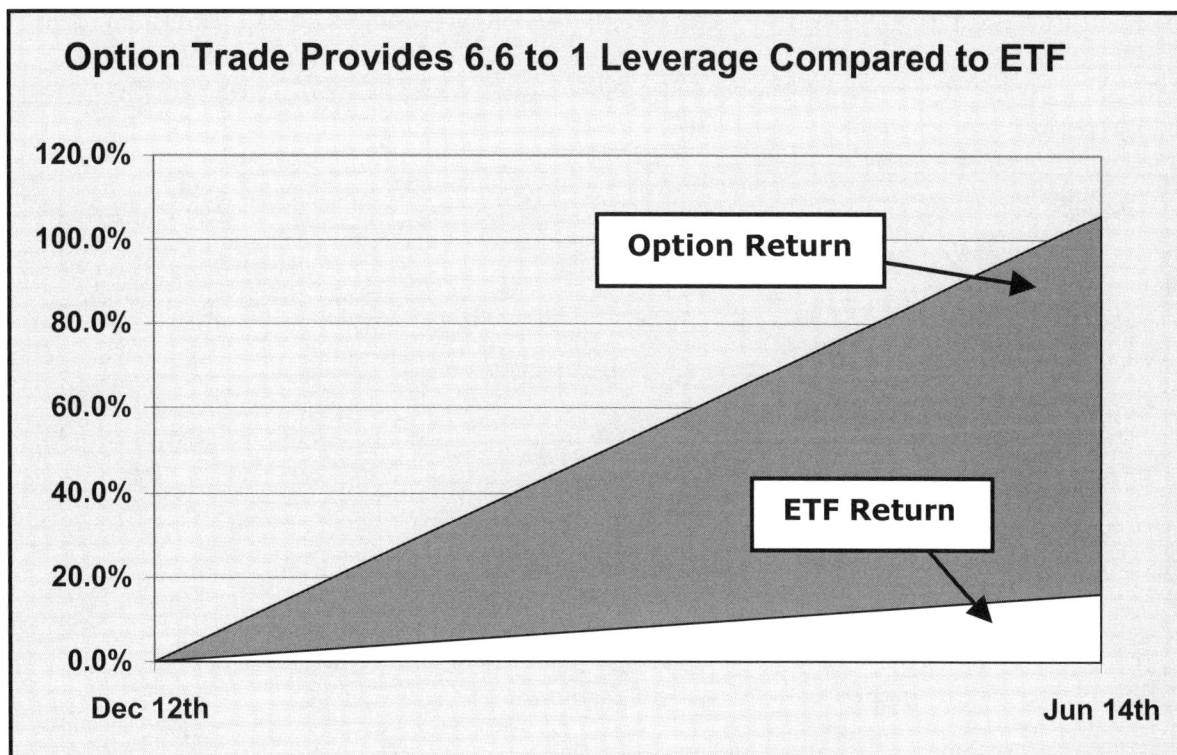

Option Return

ETF Return

Dec 12th — Jun 14th

(y-axis: 0.0%, 20.0%, 40.0%, 60.0%, 80.0%, 100.0%, 120.0%)

6 to 1 Leverage = Profit Opportunity

Options Are Highly Leveraged and Can Provide a High Rate of Return

ETF Investor
- Buys 100 Shares of Emerging Market ETF at 111.30
- ETF Increases 16% to 129.20

Results:
- Big Investment $11,130
- Modest Profit 16%

Option Investor
- Buys 100-Strike Call Option for $1,420
- ETF Increases 16% to 129.20
- Call Option Increases in Value to 29.30

Results:
- Small Investment $1,420
- Big Profit 106% Which Allows a High Rate of Return

Additional Trade Examples

My brokerage account confirmations below show additional examples of ETF option trades. I purchased 10 of the Brazil Index ETF 45-Strike call options symbol EWZII at 8.20 points and 10 of the Bldrs Emerging Mrkt ETF 34-Strike call options symbol QDFFH at 5.20 points. Both of these ETFs were on a *Prime Trade Select* confirmed price up trend.

USD - US DOLLAR

Trades

Trade Date	Settlement Date	Trade Time	Action	Quantity	Symbol	Price
04/04/2007	04/05/2007	11:21:24 am	Buy to Open	10	+EWZII	8.200000

USD - US DOLLAR

Trades

Trade Date	Settlement Date	Trade Time	Action	Quantity	Symbol	Price
01/17/2007	01/18/2007	9:42:56 am	Buy to Open	10	+IAHHH	6.500000
01/17/2007	01/18/2007	10:32:03 am	Buy to Open	10	+QDFFH	5.200000

My brokerage account Profit/Loss Report below shows that I sold the 10 EWZII calls at 14.90 points and the QDFFH calls at 10.6 points. This resulted in a $6,619.75 profit and an 82% return for EWZII and a $5,349.81 profit and a 104% return for QDFFH.

* To see all transactions within specified date range leave symbol blank   Guide to the Profit/Loss Report

Click here to download data

Realized P&L on Closed Positions

Symbol	Date Bought	Date Sold	Shares	Cost Basis	Sales Price	Gain-loss
+EWZII	4/4/2007 11:21:24 AM	6/11/2007 11:55:18 AM	10	$8,235.00	$14,854.75	$6,619.75
+QDFFH	1/17/2007 10:32:03 AM	6/13/2007 3:16:07 PM	10	$5,235.00	$10,584.81	$5,349.81

Over the same time period purchasing the Brazil Index ETF would have produced a 14% return compared to the 82% return for the option. The option purchase provided 5.9 to 1 leverage compared to the ETF purchase.

Brazil ETF Option Return 5.9 Times Greater Than ETF Return				
	Purchase Price	Sale Price	Point Profit	Percent Return
ETF	51.10	58.20	7.10	14%
Option	8.20	14.90	6.70	82%

And purchasing the Bldrs Emerging Mrkt ETF would have produced a 16.7% return over the same time period compared to the 103.8% return for the Bldrs Emerging Mrkt option. The option purchase provided 6.2 to 1 leverage compared to the ETF purchase.

Bldrs ETF Option Return 6.2 Times Greater Than ETF Return

	Purchase Price	Sale Price	Point Profit	Percent Return
ETF	38.20	44.60	6.40	16.7%
Option	5.20	10.60	5.40	103.8%

6.2 to 1 Leverage

On average these three ETF option trade examples provided 6.2 times more profit compared to the purchase of their underlying ETFs over the same time period. The 6.2 to 1 leverage provided by options can dramatically increase profit results.

Let's take a look at historical profit results for trading options instead of ETFs using the *Major Trend System*. Call options are purchased for *Major Trend System* 'buy' signals and put options are purchased for 'sell' signals. Let's assume in the historical testing that the option trades provided 6 to 1 leverage compared to ETF trades. Historical profit results are theoretical as options were not available for some ETFs at the beginning of the test period.

I conducted historical option testing on the same diversified portfolio of eight global markets that were used for historical ETF testing in Chapter 1. The eight global markets are listed below.

Diversified Global Portfolio

Crude Oil		Euro Currency
MSCI Emerging Market Index		20-Year Treasury Bonds
iShares Latin America		MSCI Brazil
iShares Europe		S&P 500 Index

The historical profit results that follow were conducted over a recent 14 year period (or ETF inception). Results are based on an initial investment of $4,600 divided equally among the eight global markets and compounding the results thereafter and do not include commissions. I chose the $4,600 initial investment because I started my options trading career in 1984 with a $4,600 trading account.

The *Major Trend System* option historical profit results for the diversified Global Portfolio of eight markets are displayed in the Profit Results Table and Profit Graph below.

Global Portfolio Option Historical Results

Initial Investment	$4,600
Number Years	13¾
Net Profit	$4,672,382
Total Return	101,573%
Average Annual Return	7,387%
Percent Winning Trades	81.0%
Total Profits	$4,892,509
Total Losses	$220,127
Profit:Loss Ratio	22.2 to 1

Global Portfolio Option Profit Results

$4,600 Grows to Over 4.6 Million Dollars!

Historical results reveal that the *Major Trend System* produced impressive profits trading ETF options with very low risk. A $4,600 investment grew to $4,676,982 over the 14 year test period. After deducting the initial $4,600 investment, the net profits were $4,672,382 (before commissions) which equates to a 101,573% return on the initial $4,600 investment. Over the almost fourteen year test period this translates to a 7,387% average annual return. This is an excellent annual return for a system with very low risk. All years were profitable.

$22 of Profit for Each 1 Dollar of Loss

The system produced $4,892,509 in total profits and $220,127 in total losses. Dividing the total profits by the total losses results in a Profit to Loss Ratio of 22.2 to 1 which translates to more than 22 dollars of profit for each 1 dollar of loss.

The Profit to Loss Ratio is a good measure of risk. A high Profit to Loss Ratio indicates that the *Major Trend System* keeps losses to a minimum by exiting losing trades before a big loss occurs. The *Major Trend System* normally exits a trade before a big loss occurs and provides you with the discipline necessary to become a successful options trader.

Keep in mind that two global bear markets occurred during this period including the worst bear market since 1932 during which the S&P 500 Index lost 50% of its value and the NASDAQ suffered a 76% loss. These profit results demonstrate that the *Major Trend System* is a versatile, effective method for trading options during any type of market condition.

Broad Global and Asset Class Diversification

Most trading programs recommend diversifying your option portfolio across different industry groups. One of the great advantages of the *Major Trend System* is that it allows you to also trade global markets with the best profit opportunities. The System also enables you to diversify your option portfolio by asset class which further reduces risk and can result in higher returns. The ability of the *Major Trend System* to take both bullish and bearish option trades also increases the diversity and profit opportunities of the system.

Major Trend System Individual Market Profit Results

The *Major Trend System* option historical profit results for individual markets are displayed in the Profit Results Equity Graphs and Profit Results Tables that follow.

Emerging Market Option Profit Results

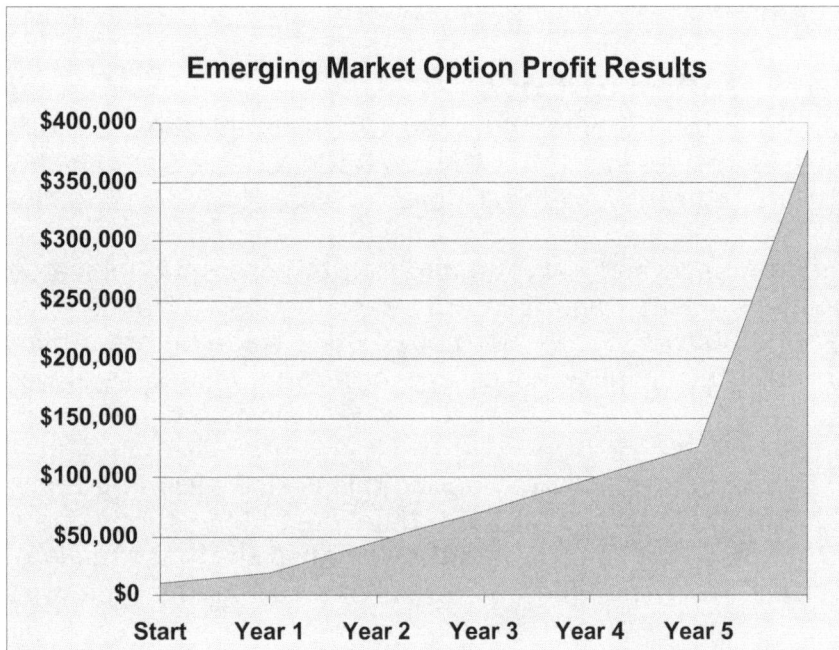

Emerging Market Option Profit Results

Initial Investment	$10,000
Number Years	5
Profit	$365,744
Total Return	3,657%
Avg Annual Return	731%
Profit:Loss Ratio	No Losses

Crude Oil Option Profit Results

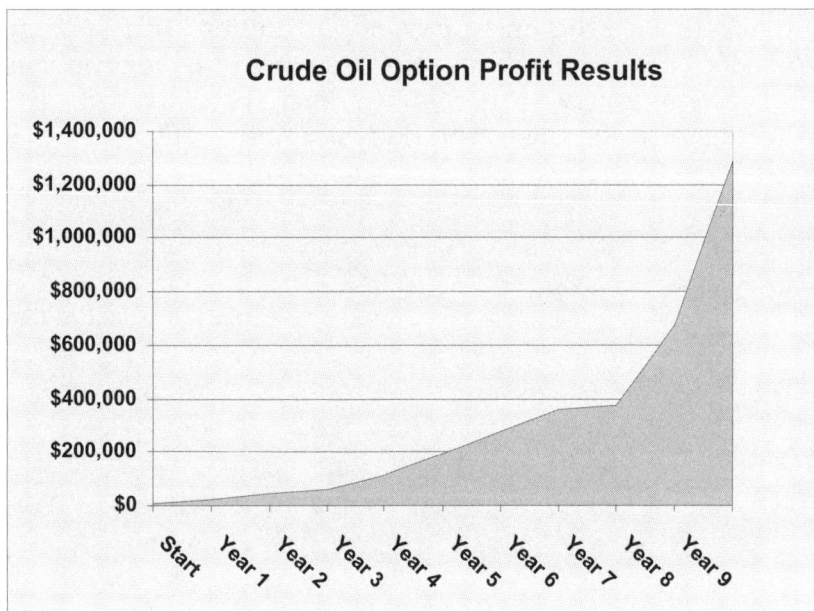

Crude Oil Option Profit Results

Initial Investment	$10,000
Number Years	9
Profit	$1,281,372
Total Return	12,813%
Avg Annual Return	1,423%
% Winning Trades	60%
Profit:Loss Ratio	10 to 1

Europe Index Option Profit Results

Europe Index Option Profit Results

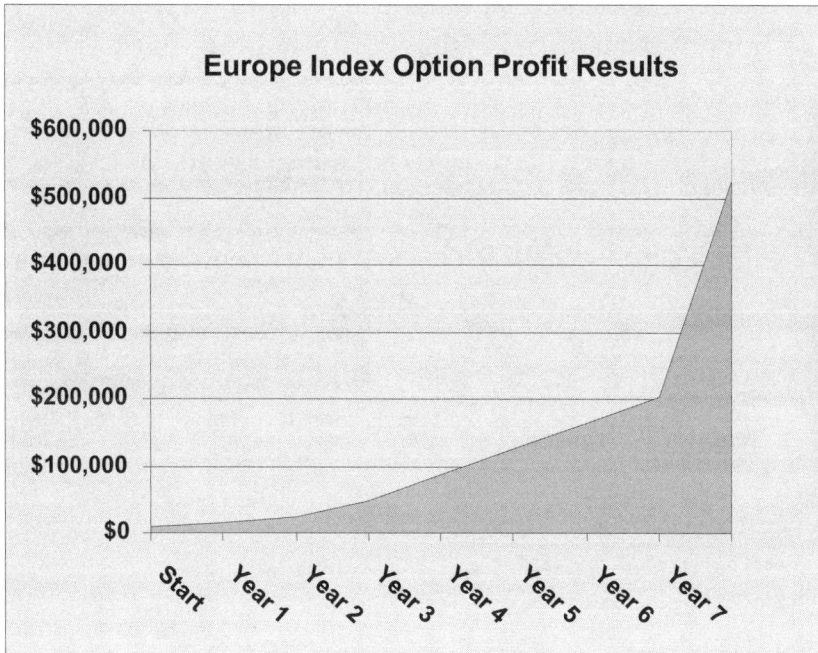

Initial Investment	$10,000
Number Years	7
Profit	$515,347
Total Return	5,153%
Avg Annual Return	736%
% Winning Trades	100%
Profit:Loss Ratio	No Losses

Treasury Bond Option Profit Results

Treasury Bond Option Profit Results

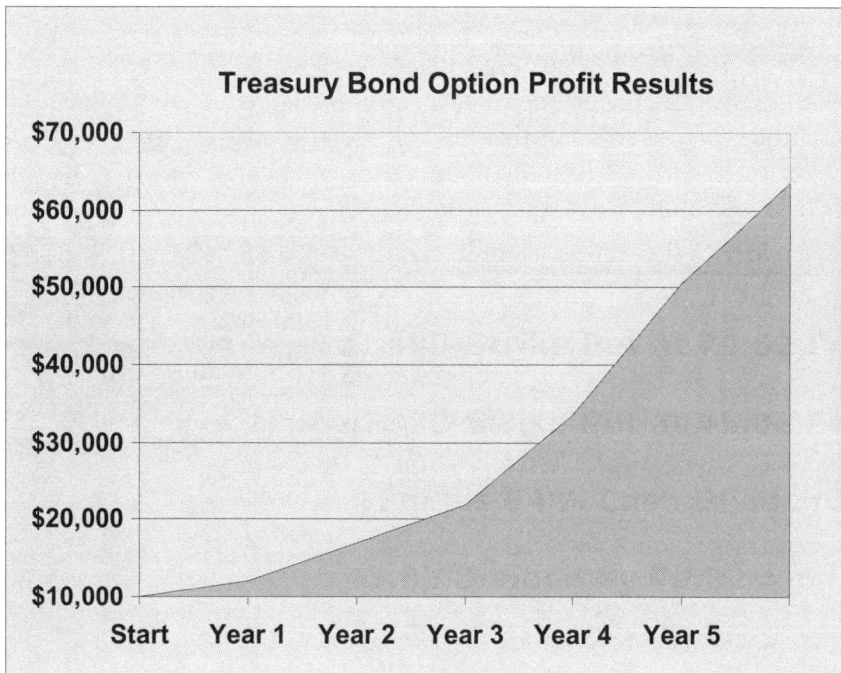

Initial Investment	$10,000
Number Years	5
Profit	$53,626
Total Return	536%
Avg Annual Return	107%
% Winning Trades	100%
Profit:Loss Ratio	No Losses

Brazil ETF Option Profit Results

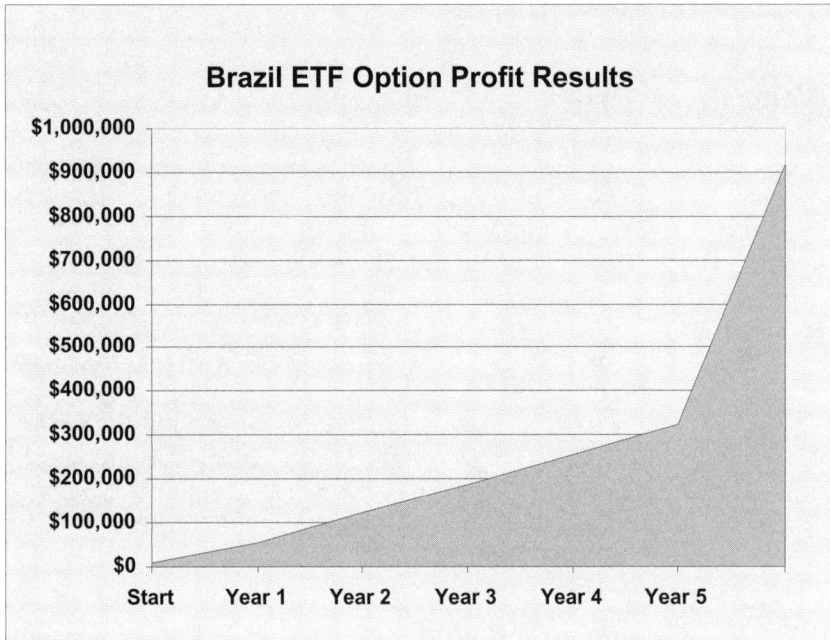

Initial Investment	$10,000
Number Years	5
Profit	$906,672
Total Return	9,066%
Avg Annual Return	1,813%
Profit:Loss Ratio	No Losses

S&P 500 Index Option Profit Results

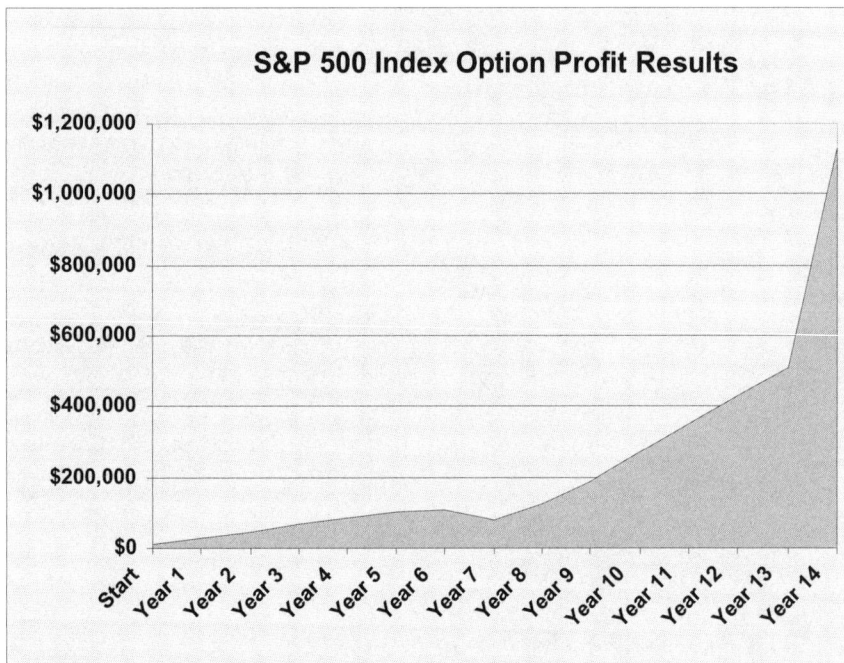

Initial Investment	$10,000
Number Years	14
Profit	$1,121,884
Total Return	11,218%
Avg Annual Return	801%
Profit:Loss Ratio	15 to 1

Euro Currency Option Profit Results

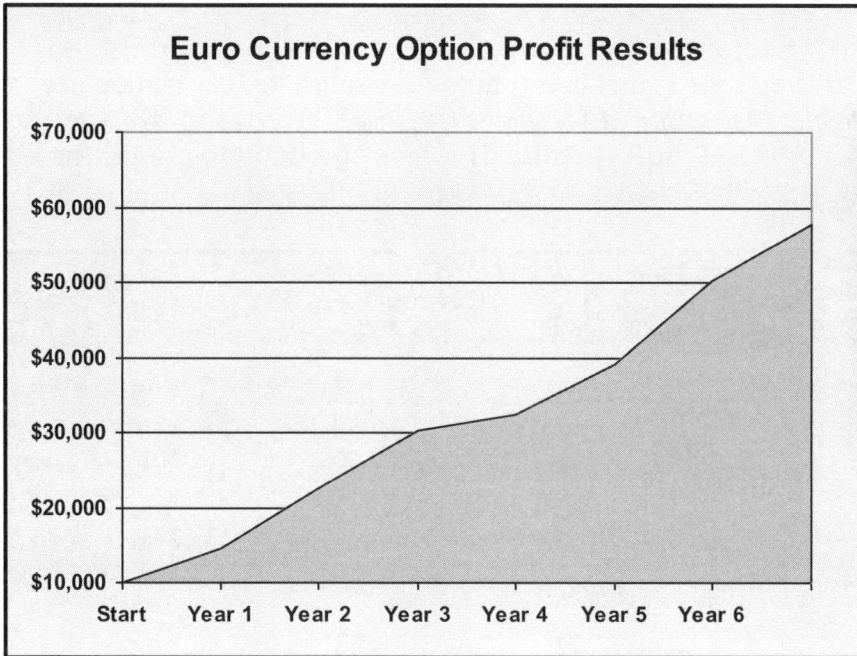

Euro Currency Option Profit Results

Initial Investment	$10,000
Number Years	6
Profit	$47,654
Total Return	476%
Avg Annual Return	79%
% Winning Trades	67%
Profit:Loss Ratio	25 to 1

Latin America ETF Option Profit Results

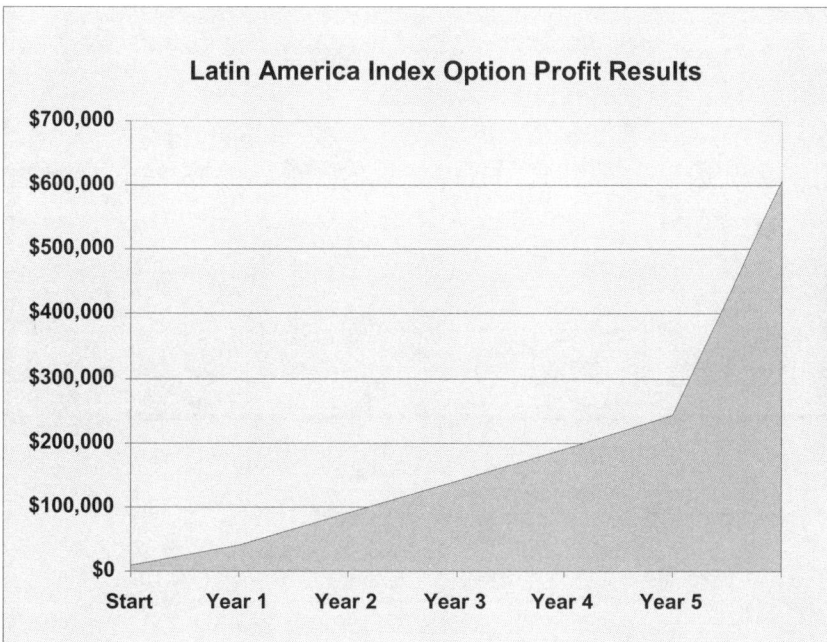

Latin America Index Option Profit Results

Initial Investment	$10,000
Number Years	5
Profit	$597,224
Total Return	5,972%
Avg Annual Return	1,194%
Profit:Loss Ratio	No Losses

Current Real Time Option Results
75.4% Average Return in Seven Weeks

My brokerage account Profit/Loss Report shows my current option portfolio with an average gain of 75.4 % for the option trades listed below. Five of the six trades are ETF option trades. I used *Prime Trade Select* to select these ETF trades in the energy, financial, small cap, NASDAQ and S&P 500 sectors. The average holding period for these trades is seven weeks.

Security	Open Date	Quantity	Open Unit Cost	Open Amount	Current Price	Current Value	Gain/Loss	Gain/Loss Percent
				$93.33		$93.33	$0.00	
				$93.33		$93.33	$0.00	
PCS CASH TR SER PRIME CASH		93.33	1	$93.33	1	$93.33	$0.00	
				$13759.40		$24212.00	$10452.60	75.97%
				$13759.40		$24212.00	$10452.60	75.97%
.CAT052111C80 CATERPILLAR INC CALL CAT 052111 80		2	11.772	$2354.40	26.15	$5230.00	$2875.60	122.14%
.DIG061811C43 PROSH ULTRA OIL&GAS ETF CALL DIG 061811 43		2	8.372	$1674.40	15.3	$3060.00	$1385.60	82.75%
.FAS041611C25 DRXN FIN BL 3X NEW ETF CALL FAS 041611 25		4	6.342	$2536.80	9.5	$3800.00	$1263.20	49.80%
.IWM031911C72 ISHRS RUSSELL 2000 ETF CALL IWM 031911 72		3	7.302	$2190.60	11.44	$3432.00	$1241.40	56.67%
.QLD041611C70 PROSH ULTRA QQQ ETF CALL QLD 041611 70		2	14.572	$2914.40	22.35	$4470.00	$1555.60	53.38%
.SSO031911C44 PROSH ULTRA S&P 500 ETF CALL SSO 031911 44		4	5.222	$2088.80	10.55	$4220.00	$2131.20	102.03%
				$13852.73		$24305.33	$10452.60	75.46%

Options Work Just as Well in a Down Market

Options work just as well in a down market. As noted in Chapter 1, I took short option positions in global markets in the summer of 2008 when *Prime Trade Select* reversed to a sell signal in most global markets allowing me to turn wealth destruction into wealth creation. The option quote table below contains actual put option prices (courtesy of Yahoo Finance) for Hewlett Packard (HPQ). Buying put options is a bearish strategy as the value of a put option increases as the price of the underlying stock decreases. Hewlett Packard stock is currently trading at 32.78. Let's assume that HPQ stock *declines* in price 10% from 32.78 to 29.50. Let's focus on the March 30-Strike put option (circled).

10% Stock Price Decrease = 900% Option Return

Buying the 30-Strike put option gives us the right to sell 100 shares of HPQ at 30.00. If we were to purchase the 30-Strike put option we would expect to pay the 'ask' price of .05 cents or $5 per option (.05 x 100 shares = $5). Let's assume HPQ stock decreases 10% in price from the current price of 32.78 to 29.50. With a stock price of 29.50 the 30-Strike put option would be worth .50 points or $50 (strike price of 30.00 minus 29.50 stock price = .50 option value). When you purchase options you can sell them any time prior to option expiration. So the option we purchased for .05 points could be sold for .50 points. Selling the 30-Strike put at .50 would produce a 900% return (.50 sale price minus .05 cost = .45 profit divided by .05 cost = 900% return).

Hewlett-Packard Co. (HPQ)   At 3:49PM ET: **32.78** ↓ 0.18 (0.55%)

PUT OPTIONS   **Expire at close Fri, Mar 17, 2006**

Strike	Symbol	Last	Chg	Bid	Ask	Open Int
27.50	HPQOY.X	0.05	0.00	N/A	0.05	13,200
30.00	HPQOF.X	0.05	0.00	N/A	0.05	21,661
32.50	HPQOZ.X	0.40	↓0.05	0.45	0.55	24,820
35.00	HPQOG.X	2.30	↑0.10	2.40	2.45	5,504
37.50	HPQOU.X	4.70	0.00	4.80	5.00	291

A 10% Increase in Stock Price = 950% Call Opt Return
A 10% Decline in Stock Price = 900% Put Option Return

Making Options the Most Profitable and Most Versatile Financial Investments Available Today

Trading Weekly Options

The preceding profit results and the $1,801,685.41 in real time option profits posted at the end of this Chapter demonstrate the ability of *Prime Trade Select* to successfully identify profitable option purchase opportunities.

Let's now take a look at using *Prime Trade Select* to select weekly option purchases. I have been trading weekly options since 2010 and have had great success using *Prime Trade Select* to trade weekly options. There are 52 opportunities per year to profit from weekly options compared to 12 opportunities per year for monthly options. Weekly options start trading on Thursday and expire the following Friday and have a life of 6 trading days.

Weekly Option Trade Examples

The daily price graph below shows Microsoft in a price up trend with the 50-Day EMA above the 100-Day EMA. The price up trend is confirmed with an up sloping On Balance Volume line and MSFT is making a series of new 52-Week highs.

Confirmed Price Up Trend for Microsoft:

- 50-Day EMA above 100-Day EMA = Buy
- MSFT making a series of new 52-Week highs
- On Balance Volume line is sloping up

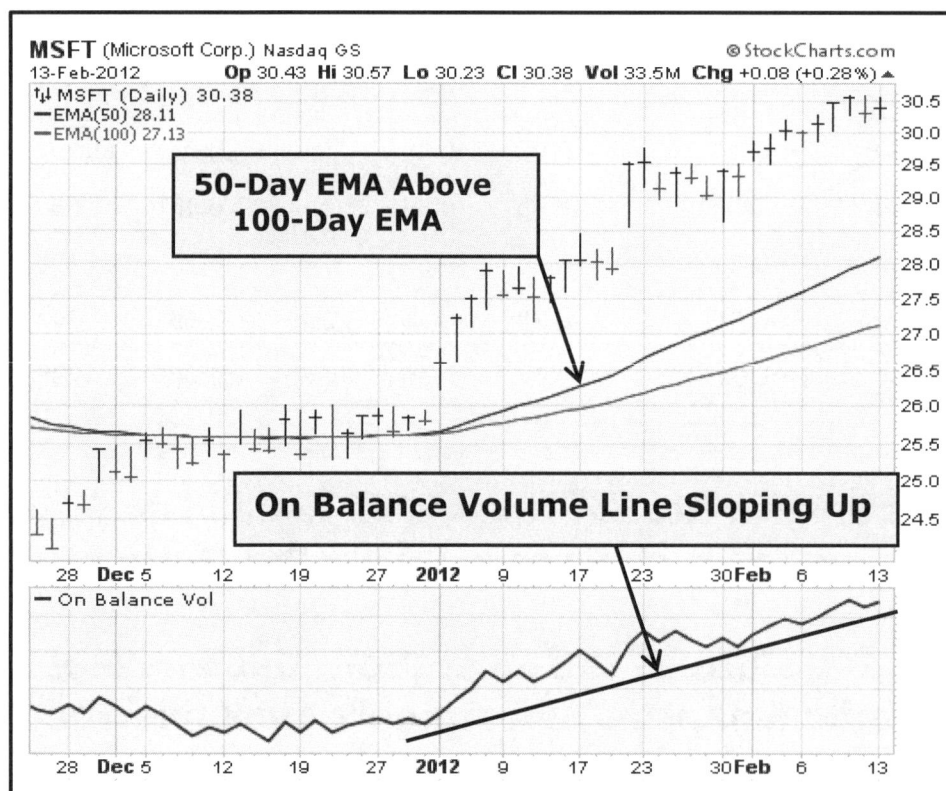

With Microsoft in a confirmed price up trend, I purchased weekly call options for Microsoft which profit when Microsoft stock moves up in price. My brokerage account Realized Gain/Loss Report below shows I purchased 5 of the MSFT Feb 18 30-Strike weekly calls at .52 points on February 14th and sold these calls four days later on February 17th at 1.18 points which resulted in a 126.6% return in four days.

Bought 5 MSFT Feb 18 30-Strike calls at .52 on Feb 14
Sold 5 calls at 1.18 on Feb 17 for 126.6% gain

Home	Accounts	Trade	Research & Ideas	Trading Tools	Planning & Retirement	Education	Client Services

Balances & Positions | Portfolio Planner | Gain/Loss | Watch Lists | History & Statements | Tax Center | Deposit/Withdraw | Online Cash Services

Sunday, March 11, 2012 02:30:29 PM EST   Export data | Printer-friendly page

Realized Gain/Loss ⚙ | Unrealized Gain/Loss ⚙ | Unsettled Closed Positions ⚙   Expand All   Edit your GainsKeeper cost basis

Security ▾	Trans type	Qty	Open date	Adj cost per share	Adj cost	Close date	Adj proceeds per share	Adj proceeds	Adj gain ($)	Adj gain (%)	Term
HD Feb 18 2012 46.0 Call	Sell to Close.FIFO	500	02/14/12	0.31	155.81	02/17/12	0.50	251.18	95.37	61.21	Short-term ▶
INTC Feb 18 2012 26.0 Call	Sell to Close.FIFO	500	02/14/12	0.62	310.81	02/17/12	1.46	731.17	420.36	135.25	Short-term ▶
MSFT Feb 18 2012 30.0 Call	Sell to Close.FIFO	500	02/14/12	0.52	260.81	02/17/12	1.18	591.17	330.36	126.67	Short-term ▶
WFC Feb 18 2012 30.0 Call	Sell to Close.FIFO	500	02/14/12	0.62	310.81	02/17/12	1.05	526.18	215.37	69.29	Short-term ▶
XLF Feb 18 2012 14.0 Call	Sell to Close.FIFO	500	02/14/12	0.62	310.81	02/17/12	0.75	376.18	65.37	21.03	Short-term ▶

Enter symbol   QUOTE ▾   Options: Enter underlying symbol and click Chain | Index: use "$" (e.g. $DJI)   CHAIN $? ☐ ☐

SnapTicket™   New cost-basis rules will change our tax reporting. | Symbol lookup | Quote disclaimer | Price Lock: On | Off   Streaming quotes: On | Off

Over the same four day period I owned the MSFT 30-Strike weekly call options, the price of Microsoft stock increased 3.2%. In this example the MSFT weekly option out performed Microsoft stock 39 to 1 (126.6%/3.2% = 39.5) demonstrating the tremendous leverage available with weekly options.

Option Trade Provided 39 to 1 Leverage

- MSFT Option Trade Produced 126.6% Return

- Over the Same 4-Day Time Period MSFT Stock Increased 3.2%

- Option Trade Provided 39 to 1 Leverage Compared to Stock Trade

Option Trade Provided 39 to 1 Leverage

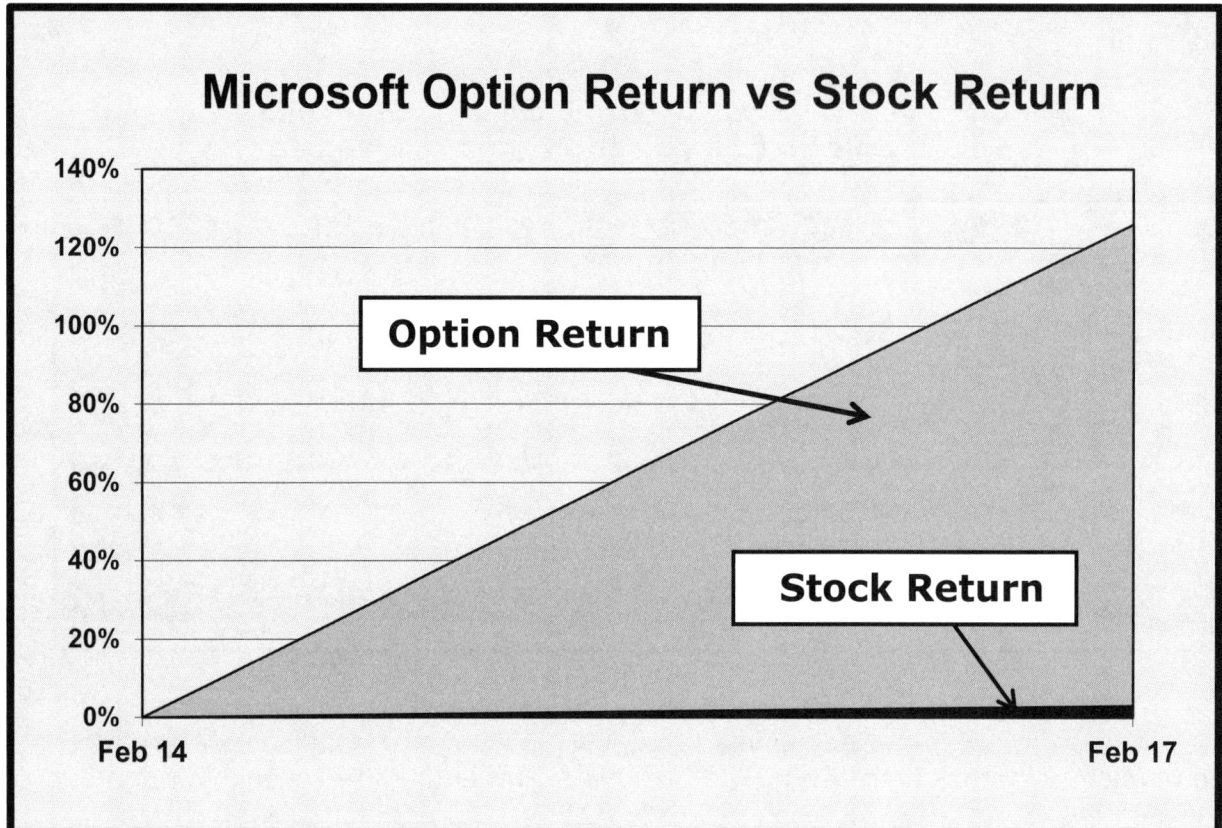

Microsoft Option Return vs Stock Return

Let's look at another example of a weekly option purchase trade. The daily price graph below shows Home Depot in a price up trend with the 50-Day EMA above the 100-Day EMA. The price up trend is confirmed with an up sloping On Balance Volume line and HD is making a series of new 52-Week highs.

Confirmed Price Up Trend for Home Depot:

- 50-Day EMA above 100-Day EMA = Buy

- HD making a series of new 52-Week highs

- On Balance Volume line is sloping up

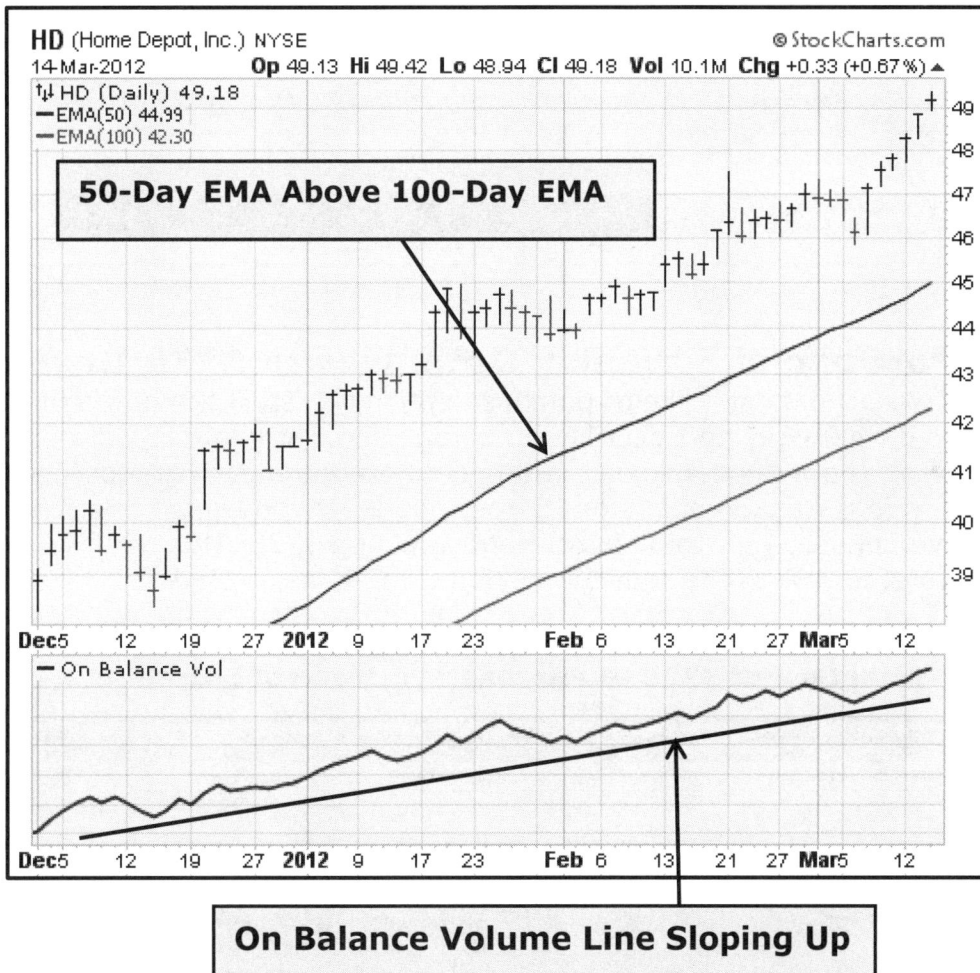

With Home Depot in a confirmed price up trend, I purchased weekly call options for Home Depot. My brokerage account Realized Gain/Loss Report below shows I purchased 5 of the HD Feb 18 46-Strike weekly calls at .31 points on February 14th and sold these calls four days later on February 17th at .50 points which resulted in a 61.2% return in four days.

Bought 5 HD Feb 18 46-Strike calls at .31 on Feb 14
Sold 5 calls at .50 on Feb 17 for 61.2% gain

Trade a Portfolio of 5 Weekly Options with $270 Investment

When I trade weekly options I like to purchase options on stocks in different industry groups to help diversify my portfolio. My brokerage account Realized Gain/Loss Report below shows I purchased options on stocks in 5 different industry groups. The average cost of these options was .54 points or $54 per option. If you traded one contract for each of the five options, your total investment would be $270. This portfolio had an average return of 82.7% over a four day period with no losing trades.

Average Weekly Return of 82.7%, Average Cost of $54 Per Option
Total Cost of $270 to Purchase Portfolio of 5 Options

And my brokerage account Realized Gain/Loss Report below shows another portfolio of weekly options I purchased recently in different industry groups.

The average cost of these options was .59 points or $59 per option. If you traded one contract for each of the four options your total investment would be $236. This week the Mar 02 weekly option portfolio had an average return of 83.6% over the one week period with no losing trades.

Average Weekly Return of 83.6%
Average Cost of $59 Per Option
Total Cost of $236 to Purchase Portfolio of 4 Options

Home	Accounts	Trade	Research & Ideas	Trading Tools	Planning & Retirement	Education	Client Services

Balances & Positions | Portfolio Planner | Gain/Loss | Watch Lists | History & Statements | Tax Center | Deposit/Withdraw | Online Cash Services

Tuesday, March 13, 2012 12:28:48 PM EST   Export data | Printer-friendly page

Realized Gain/Loss | Unrealized Gain/Loss | Unsettled Closed Positions   Expand All   Edit your GainsKeeper cost basis

Security	Trans type	Qty	Open date	Adj cost per share	Adj cost	Close date	Adj proceeds per share	Adj proceeds	Adj gain ($)	Adj gain (%)	Term
EEM Mar 02 2012 44.0 Call	Sell to Close.FIFO	500	02/24/12	0.54	270.81	03/02/12	0.61	306.18	35.37	13.06	Short-term
MSFT Mar 02 2012 31.0 Call	Sell to Close.FIFO	500	02/24/12	0.61	305.81	03/01/12	1.27	636.17	330.36	108.03	Short-term
WFC Mar 02 2012 30.0 Call	Sell to Close.FIFO	500	02/24/12	0.50	250.81	03/01/12	1.46	729.17	478.36	190.73	Short-term
XLF Mar 02 2012 14.0 Call	Sell to Close.FIFO	500	02/24/12	0.71	355.81	03/02/12	0.87	436.18	80.37	22.59	Short-term

Enter symbol   QUOTE ▼   Options: Enter underlying symbol and click Chain | Index: use "$" (e.g. $DJI)   CHAIN $?

SnapTicket™   New cost-basis rules will change our tax reporting. | Symbol lookup | Quote disclaimer | Price Lock On | Off   Streaming quotes: On | Off

Rolling Over Expiring Options with Spread Orders

When trading weekly options I like to use option spread orders to 'rollover' the expiring option into the new weekly option if the underlying stock/ETF is still on a *Prime Trade Select* 'buy' signal for call options or a 'sell' signal for put options.

Option spread orders help reduce commission costs and can help you to save on the 'bid/ask' spread costs associated with buying and selling options if you use a limit spread order that is mid-way between the bid/ask prices. I normally can get filled on spread orders at a limit price that is mid-way between the bid/ask prices. In this example the bid price for this spread was .90 and the ask price was .84. I was filled mid-way between the bid/ask price at .87. Because the closeout of the expiring options was a higher price than the purchase of the new options this was a credit spread order.

I used the option spread order below to close out the expiring MSFT Feb 24 30-Strike weekly call options into the new Mar 02 31-Strike weekly call options.

Sell to Close 5 MSFT Feb 24 30-Strike calls
Buy to Open 5 MSFT Mar 02 31-Strike calls

Options

| Single Order | Covered Call | **Rollout** | Straddle | Strangle |

⌐⌐ **Spread**   [?] Learn more about Vertical and Calendar Spreads

Vertical Call | Vertical Put | **Calendar Call** | Calendar Put

Underlying Symbol

msft   [View Calendar Call Spreads]   Symbol Lookup

MSFT MICROSOFT CORP COM
31.47 0.10 (0.32%) ⟳
Bid 31.46 Ask 31.47 Vol 25,999,639
Real Time Quote by NASDAQ @ 3:26:39 PM EST

Action   # of Contracts   Option Contract (Long)
Buy to Open ▼   5   MSFT Mar 02 2012 31.0 Call   Chain

MSFT **Mar 02 2012 31.0 Call**
Bid 0.59 Ask 0.61 ⟳
B/A Size 255X1279 Vol 2,209 Open Int 1121
Real Time Quote by OPRA @ 3:26:39 PM EST

Action   # of Contracts   Option Contract (Short)
Sell to Close ▼   5   MSFT Feb 24 2012 30.0 Call   Chain

MSFT **Feb 24 2012 30.0 Call**
Bid 1.45 Ask 1.49 ⟳
B/A Size 606X1007 Vol 17 Open Int 3262
Real Time Quote by OPRA @ 3:26:39 PM EST

Order Type [?]   **Premium**
Net credit ▼

MSFT **Calendar Call Spread** ⟳
Bid -0.90 Ask -0.84

Time-in-Force [?]
Day ▼

[Review order]

This option spread order was filled and I closed out the expiring Feb 24 options and bought the new Mar 02 options.

Rolling over expiring options can have several advantages. In this example, the profit on the closeout of the MSFT Feb 24 options exceeded the cost of the Mar 02 options thereby setting up a zero cost, no risk trade for the Mar 02 options.

When you rollover profitable trades, the profits can compound your returns and reduce risk. If you rollover your trades 52 times over the course of a year the profits can reduce your risk substantially or even eliminate your risk by reducing the cost basis to less than zero. The accumulated profits can compound your returns which in turn allows you to take additional trades and further compound your returns.

Rolling Over Options

- **Can reduce risk**

- **And allow you to compound returns**

Four Advantages of Options Investing

1. *Size Doesn't Matter*
Options can be traded in almost any size account. This allows traders with small trading accounts to take part in this opportunity. Options can be purchased for as little as a few hundred dollars and a diversified options portfolio can be established with just a few thousand dollars.

2. *Risk Is Limited*
Risk is limited to the purchase price of the call option regardless of how far the underlying stock may fall in price. With option purchases you are not required to add funds to your account with adverse market moves and there is no threat of margin calls.

3. *High Leverage*
Options provide substantially more leverage than stocks and mutual funds. A 10% price increase in a stock can easily produce a 50% return for the related call option.

4. *Profit Potential Is Not Limited*
Most importantly option profit potential is not limited. When you purchase a call option, the value of the option intrinsic value increases 'dollar for dollar' as the price of the underlying stock moves above the strike price of the call option purchased.

$1.8 Million in Real Time Profits Over the Past Five Years

Prime Trade Select has produced over $1.8 million in profits for the option purchase strategy over the past 5 years. My brokerage account Profit/Loss Reports that follow show $1,801,685.14 in profits and an average return of 85.0%. There were 178 profitable trades and 17 losing trades resulting in 91.2% accuracy. These results demonstrate the ability of *Prime Trade Select* to deliver substantial profits with high accuracy.

Option Strategy   **Profits $341,223.00**   **Average Return 86.6%**

Account Reports: Profit/Loss Report   PRINT

Give your accountant a break. View profits/losses for all trades executed on one specific date or during a range of dates. Track by position, whether it's closed, or still opened. Download to a spreadsheet for easy manipulation, processing and tax reporting.

Unrealized P&L on Open Positions

Symbol	Description	Position	Avg Price	Cost Basis	Market Value	Type	Unrealized Val.
+APVAJ	Apple Inc Jan 2008 150.00 Call	18	$20.0594	$36,107.00	$48,960.00	Stock Option	$12,853.00
+FCXAO	Freeport-Mcmoran Copper & Gold Jan 2008 75.00 Call	18	$21.8789	$39,382.00	$76,860.00	Stock Option	$37,478.00
+FLRKH	Fluor Corp New Nov 2007 140.00 Call	18	$15.6928	$28,247.00	$42,480.00	Stock Option	$14,233.00
+GOPKQ	Google Inc Cl A Nov 2007 570.00 Call	18	$37.3983	$67,317.00	$138,960.00	Stock Option	$71,643.00
+NOVKJ	National Oilwell Varco Inc Nov 2007 50.00 Call	18	$0.0000	$0.00	$50,940.00	Stock Option	$50,940.00
+RFYAN	Research In Motion Ltd Jan 2008 70.00 Call	18	$23.4178	$42,152.00	$80,730.00	Stock Option	$38,578.00
+RIGAR	Transocean Inc Ord Jan 2008 90.00 Call	18	$18.8233	$33,882.00	$48,960.00	Stock Option	$15,078.00

Total Unrealized Gain-Loss: $240,803.00

Account Reports: Profit/Loss Report   PRINT

Give your accountant a break. View profits/losses for all trades executed on one specific date or during a range of dates. Track by position, whether it's closed, or still opened. Download to a spreadsheet for easy manipulation, processing and tax reporting.

Unrealized P&L on Open Positions

Symbol	Description	Position	Avg Price	Cost Basis	Market Value	Type	Unrealized Val.
+APVKJ	Apple Inc Nov 2007 150.00 Call	20	$15.3450	$30,690.00	$44,100.00	Stock Option	$13,410.00
+FCXKO	Freeport-Mcmoran Copper & Gold Cl B Nov 2007 75.00 Call	20	$24.6700	$49,340.00	$75,800.00	Stock Option	$26,460.00
+FLRKH	Fluor Corp New Nov 2007 140.00 Call	20	$15.3250	$30,650.00	$37,400.00	Stock Option	$6,750.00
+NOVKT	National Oilwell Varco Inc Nov 2007 52.50 Call	20	$0.0000	$0.00	$46,800.00	Stock Option	$46,800.00
+RIGKR	Transocean Inc Ord Nov 2007 90.00 Call	20	$18.1000	$36,200.00	$43,200.00	Stock Option	$7,000.00

Total Unrealized Gain-Loss: $100,420.00

Option Strategy   Profits $154,821.03   Average Return 95.9%

Portfolios

Alerts | Transfer Money | Bill Pay | (?) Help

| Portfolios | Performance & Value | Positions | Gains & Losses | Risk Analyzer | Portfolio Analyzer | Income Estimator |

Market Value: $317,913.22 ($154,821.03 / 95.89%)   DJIA 13,779.14 ▲ +107.22 Nasdaq 2,799.37 ▲ +48.51

REFRESH | STREAMING QUOTES | EXPORT TO EXCEL®   Results per Page: 200

Symbol		Last Trade	Change $	Change %	Day's Gain	Qty	Price Paid	Total Gain $	Total Gain %	Market Val	Edit
AXVAU	Trade	74.50	2.50	3.47%	$560.00*	2	$44.50	$6,042.52*	67.76%*	$14,960.00*	Edit
CAMAM	Trade	39.30	0.00	0.00%	-$800.00*	8	$18.31	$16,757.78	114.14%	$31,440.00	Edit
FCXAO	Trade	36.10	0.00	0.00%	$2,925.00*	9	$20.60	$19,184.28*	103.30%*	$37,755.00*	Edit
FLRAA	Trade	49.90	0.00	0.00%	-$540.00*	6	$27.00	$21,751.53*	134.03%*	$37,980.00*	Edit
GOOAF	Trade	66.30	2.30	3.59%	$690.00	3	$64.27	$583.78	3.02%	$19,890.00	Edit
GOPAY	Trade	132.50	1.50	1.15%	$680.00*	2	$60.75	$14,412.52*	118.45%*	$26,580.00*	Edit
LQHAK	Trade	12.10	1.11	10.10%	$440.00*	4	$12.00	$69.01*	1.43%*	$4,880.00*	Edit
NOVKJ	Trade	22.20	-1.40	-5.93%	-$3,240.00*	18	$12.62	$17,579.28*	77.30%*	$40,320.00*	Edit
QAAAD	Trade	66.57	1.76	2.72%	$1,020.00*	6	$24.47	$25,191.53*	171.27%*	$39,900.00*	Edit
RFYAN	Trade	49.15	-1.25	-2.48%	$540.00*	9	$19.83	$28,019.28*	156.70%*	$45,900.00*	Edit
RIGAR	Trade	28.20	0.00	0.00%	-$240.00*	6	$19.05	$5,229.52*	45.67%*	$16,680.00*	Edit
Cash					1,628.22					$1,628.22	
				Totals	$2,035.00		$161,463.97	$154,821.03	95.89%	$317,913.22	

LEGEND: ⊞ collapsed (click to expand) ⊟ expanded (click to collapse)   Real-time quotes

Option Strategy   Profits $254,006.83   Average Return 114.9%

Portfolios

Alerts | Transfer Money | Bill Pay | Help

| Portfolios | Performance & Value | Positions | Gains & Losses | Risk Analyzer | Portfolio Analyzer | Income Estimator |

Market Value: $477,662.79 ($254,006.83 / 114.95%)   DJIA 13,775.48 ▲ +103.56   Nasdaq 2,797.30 ▲ +46.44

REFRESH | STREAMING QUOTES | EXPORT TO EXCEL   Results per Page: 200

Symbol		Last Trade	Change $	Change %	Day's Gain	Qty	Price Paid	Total Gain $	Total Gain %	Market Val	Edit
AXVAU	Trade	74.50	2.50	3.47%	$560.00*	2	$43.85	$6,172.52*	70.24%*	$14,960.00*	Edit
CAMAM	Trade	39.30	0.00	0.00%	-$1,260.00*	14	$18.06	$29,834.78*	117.81%*	$55,160.00*	Edit
FCXAO	Trade	36.10	0.00	0.00%	$5,200.00*	16	$19.38	$36,076.04*	116.21%*	$67,120.00*	Edit
FLRAA	Trade	49.90	0.00	0.00%	-$1,080.00*	12	$25.62	$45,169.04*	146.70%*	$75,960.00*	Edit
GOOAF	Trade	62.70	-1.30	-2.03%	$480.00*	2	$64.85	$292.52*	2.25%*	$13,280.00*	Edit
GOPAY	Trade	132.50	1.50	1.15%	$760.00*	2	$60.50	$14,542.52*	120.01%*	$26,660.00*	Edit
LQHAK	Trade	12.10	1.11	10.10%	$400.00*	4	$12.00	$29.01	0.60%	$4,840.00	Edit
NOVKJ	Trade	22.20	-1.40	-5.93%	-$4,560.00*	24	$12.08	$24,499.04*	84.42%*	$53,520.00*	Edit
QAAAD	Trade	66.57	1.76	2.72%	$2,124.00*	12	$23.52	$51,613.04	182.57%	$79,884.00	Edit
RFYAN	Trade	49.15	-1.25	-2.48%	$720.00*	12	$19.00	$38,359.04*	167.94%*	$61,200.00*	Edit
RIGAR	Trade	28.20	0.00	0.00%	-$160.00*	8	$18.69	$7,419.28*	49.53%*	$22,400.00*	Edit
Cash					2,678.79					$2,678.79	
				Totals	$3,184.00		$220,977.17	$254,006.83	114.95%	$477,662.79	

LEGEND: ⊞ collapsed (click to expand)   ⊟ expanded (click to collapse)   Real-time quotes

Option Strategy   Profits $81,942.94   Average Return 61.7%

E✱TRADE FINANCIAL

✱ Open An Account   ● Help Cente

Enter Symbol or Name [QUOTES] Enter Question or Keywords [SEARCH]

| Accounts | Trading & Portfolios | Quotes & Research | Mutual Funds, ETFs & Bonds | Advice & Retirement | Banking & Credit Cards |

Mortgages & Home Equity

| Trade Portfolios View Orders | Balances | Transaction History | IPO Center | Account Records | Active Trading | Global Trading |

Portfolios

⚡ Alerts | 》 Transfer Money | 》 Bill Pay | ● Help

| Portfolios | Performance & Value | Positions | Gains & Losses | Risk Analyzer | Portfolio Analyzer | Income Estimator |

Account/Watch List: 919 PSB   ⛁ Create / Edit List   View: Performance   Customize

Market Value: $216,344.91 ($81,942.94 / 61.69%)   DJIA 13,990.33 ▲ +72.11 Nasdaq 2,723.44 ▲ +23.95

[REFRESH ⟳] [STREAMING QUOTES] [EXPORT TO EXCEL ⬇]   Results per Page: 200

Symbol		Current Price	Change $	Change %	Day's Gain	Qty	Price Paid	Total Gain $	Total Gain %	Market Val	Edit
BGCHN	Trade	14.06	0.56	4.15%	$336.00	6	$11.00	$1,823.51	27.58%	$8,436.00	Edit
FCXHO	Trade	22.50	4.00	21.62%	$2,800.00	7	$11.00	$8,036.76	104.19%	$15,750.00	Edit
▣ FLRHT	Trade	21.80	2.02	10.21%	$1,414.00	7	$10.00	$8,246.76	117.59%	$15,260.00	Edit
GOPHV	Trade	42.00	0.90	2.19%	$270.00	3	$33.30	$2,599.76	26.00%	$12,600.00	Edit
IHHHJ	Trade	17.00	-1.40	-7.61%	-$280.00	2	$23.70	-$1,349.49	-28.41%	$3,400.00	Edit
IHHHK	Trade	13.80	-1.40	-9.21%	-$280.00	2	$19.20	-$1,089.49	-28.30%	$2,760.00	Edit
JECHJ	Trade	16.80	1.70	11.26%	$1,190.00	7	$9.00	$5,446.76	86.28%	$11,760.00	Edit
MALHJ	Trade	21.70	0.30	1.40%	$90.00	3	$17.40	$1,279.76	24.47%	$6,510.00	Edit
MALHK	Trade	18.30	0.10	0.55%	$40.00	4	$17.40	$349.01	5.01%	$7,320.00	Edit
MDRHN	Trade	23.65	0.00	0.00%	$0.00	6	$13.60	$6,017.51	73.63%	$14,190.00	Edit
NOVHS	Trade	22.50	2.00	9.76%	$1,400.00	7	$13.30	$6,426.76	68.93%	$15,750.00	Edit
PCPHB	Trade	17.70	0.00	0.00%	$0.00	6	$11.50	$3,707.51	53.63%	$10,620.00	Edit
PCUHQ	Trade	25.10	0.00	0.00%	$0.00	6	$10.00	$9,047.51	150.48%	$15,060.00	Edit
QAAHB	Trade	31.30	2.90	10.21%	$1,740.00	6	$14.20	$10,247.51	120.10%	$18,780.00	Edit
RFYHT	Trade	37.90	4.90	14.85%	$2,450.00	5	$22.10	$7,888.26	71.31%	$18,950.00	Edit
▣ RIGHR	Trade	19.70	2.00	11.30%	$1,200.00	6	$13.67	$3,599.52	43.79%	$11,820.00	Edit
UFBHS	Trade	25.00	0.00	0.00%	$0.00	5	$15.70	$4,638.26	59.00%	$12,500.00	Edit
▣ XTQHI	Trade	9.50	0.00	0.00%	$0.00	14	$5.90	$5,026.76	60.76%	$13,300.00	Edit
Cash						1,578.91				$1,578.91	
				Totals	$12,370.00		$132,823.06	$81,942.94	61.69%	$216,344.91	

141

Option Strategy   Profits $147,886.02   Average Return 81.7%

Account Reports: Profit/Loss Report   🖨 PRINT   Account: 033

Give your accountant a break. View profits/losses for all trades executed on one specific date or during a range of dates. Track by position, whether it's closed, or still opened. Download to a spreadsheet for easy manipulation, processing and tax reporting.

Trade date: « [   ] » [SELECT DATE]
Trade date: « [   ] » [SELECT DATE]
Symbol: [   ] [SUBMIT]   ☐ Show detailed unrealized positions

* To see all transactions within specified date range leave symbol blank   Guide to the Profit/Loss Report

Click here to download data

Realized P&L on Closed Positions

Symbol	Date Bought	Date Sold	Shares	Cost Basis	Sales Price	Gain-loss
+GOPHO	7/5/2007 3:53:51 PM	7/9/2007 9:30:25 AM	2	$9,914.50	$10,025.33	$110.83
+MROGY	6/18/2007 11:59:59 PM	7/12/2007 2:28:53 PM	10	$0.00	$5,775.39	$5,775.39
+MROGY	6/19/2007 11:59:59 PM	7/12/2007 2:28:55 PM	10	$0.00	$5,787.39	$5,787.39
+MROGZ	7/12/2007 2:26:53 PM	6/4/2007 11:36:43 AM	10	$1,568.50	$7,475.36	$5,906.86
+MROGZ	7/12/2007 2:26:53 PM	6/19/2007 11:59:59 PM	10	$1,568.50	$0.00	-$1,568.50
+UEXHH	7/5/2007 3:57:41 PM	7/9/2007 12:40:28 PM	10	$7,024.50	$7,475.36	$450.86

Total Realized Gain-Loss: $16,462.83

Unrealized P&L on Open Positions

Symbol	Description	Position	Avg Price	Cost Basis	Market Value	Type	Unrealized Val.
+APVHE	Apple Inc Aug 2007 125.00 Call	10	$11.7245	$11,724.50	$16,800.00	Stock Option	$5,075.50
+BGCHN	General Cable Corp Del New Aug 2007 70.00 Call	10	$11.0245	$11,024.50	$14,000.00	Stock Option	$2,975.50
+FCXGO	Freeport-Mcmoran Copper & Gold Jul 2007 75.00 Call	10	$8.4945	$8,494.50	$16,800.00	Stock Option	$8,305.50
+FLRHT	Fluor Corp New Aug 2007 100.00 Call	10	$10.0245	$10,024.50	$20,200.00	Stock Option	$10,175.50
+IHHHK	Intercontinentalexchange Inc Aug 2007 155.00 Call	7	$18.6296	$13,040.75	$12,600.00	Stock Option	-$440.75
+JECHJ	Jacobs Engr Group Inc Del Aug 2007 50.00 Call	10	$8.5245	$8,524.50	$15,600.00	Stock Option	$7,075.50
+MALGH	Mastercard Inc Cl A Jul 2007 140.00 Call	10	$12.9645	$12,964.50	$29,200.00	Stock Option	$16,235.50
+MDRHO	Mcdermott Intl Inc Aug 2007 75.00 Call	10	$9.0245	$9,024.50	$17,200.00	Stock Option	$8,175.50
+NOVGR	National Oilwell Varco Inc Jul 2007 90.00 Call	10	$12.3245	$12,324.50	$22,200.00	Stock Option	$9,875.50
+PCPHB	Precision Castparts Corp Aug 2007 110.00 Call	10	$10.0245	$10,024.50	$24,000.00	Stock Option	$13,975.50
+PCUHQ	Southern Copper Corp Aug 2007 85.00 Call	10	$10.0245	$10,024.50	$25,200.00	Stock Option	$15,175.50
+RFYHT	Research In Motion Ltd Aug 2007 200.00 Call	10	$22.1565	$22,156.50	$32,700.00	Stock Option	$10,543.50
+RIGGA	Transocean Inc Ord Jul 2007 105.00 Call	-10	-$2.4249	$2,424.94	-$1,850.00	Stock Option	$574.94
+RIGGS	Transocean Inc Ord Jul 2007 95.00 Call	10	$7.9750	$7,975.00	$10,800.00	Stock Option	$2,825.00
+UFBGS	Foster Wheeler Ltd Shs New Jul 2007 95.00 Call	10	$11.0245	$11,024.50	$22,400.00	Stock Option	$11,375.50
+XTQGW	Express Scripts Inc Jul 2007 47.50 Call	20	$0.0000	$0.00	$13,200.00	Stock Option	$13,200.00
+XTQGX	Express Scripts Inc Jul 2007 52.50 Call	-20	$0.0000	$0.00	-$3,700.00	Stock Option	$3,700.00

Total Unrealized Gain-Loss: $131,423.19

Option Strategy   Profits $155,361.56   Average Return 94.8%

E✱TRADE FINANCIAL®

* Open An Account   ● Help Cente

Enter Symbol or Name [QUOTES]   Enter Question or Keywords [SEARCH]

Accounts	Trading & Portfolios	Quotes & Research	Mutual Funds, ETFs & Bonds	Advice & Retirement	Banking & Credit Cards

Mortgages & Home Equity

Trade | Portfolios View Orders | Balances | Transaction History | IPO Center | Account Records | Active Trading | Global Trading

Portfolios

⚐ Alerts | ≫ Transfer Money | ≫ Bill Pay | ● Help

Portfolios	Performance & Value	Positions	Gains & Losses	Risk Analyzer	Portfolio Analyzer	Income Estimator

Account/Watch List: 597   ▩ Create / Edit List   View: Performance   ⚙ Customize

Market Value: $323,527.00   ($155,361.56 / 94.83%)   DJIA 13,986.26 ▲ +68.04 Nasdaq 2,723.49 ▲ +24 00

[REFRESH ⟳]   [▬▬▬▬▬▬]   [EXPORT TO EXCEL ⬇]   Results per Page: 200

Symbol		Current Price	Change $	Change %	Day's Gain	Qty	Price Paid	Total Gain $	Total Gain %	Market Val	Edit
BGCHL	Trade	22.30	0.00	0.00%	$0.00	9	$11.13	$10,027.27	99.85%	$20,070.00	Edit
FCXHM	Trade	31.00	3.99	14.77%	$2,394.00	6	$11.47	$11,699.52	169.55%	$18,600.00	Edit
FLRGS	Trade	26.00	2.01	8.38%	$1,005.00	5	$9.60	$8,188.26	170.17%	$13,000.00	Edit
FLRHT	Trade	21.80	2.02	10.21%	$808.00	4	$10.00	$4,709.01	117.40%	$8,720.00	Edit
GOPHV	Trade	42.00	0.90	2.19%	$360.00	4	$33.20	$3,509.01	26.40%	$16,800.00	Edit
IHHHJ	Trade	17.00	-1.40	-7.61%	-$560.00	4	$23.62	-$2,668.98	-28.19%	$6,800 00	Edit
IHHHK	Trade	13.80	-1.40	-9.21%	-$700.00	5	$20.10	-$3,161.74	-31.42%	$6,900.00	Edit
JECGJ	Trade	15.40	0.00	0.00%	$0.00	10	$0.00	$15,400.00	...	$15,400.00	Edit
JECHJ	Trade	18.80	1.70	11.26%	$340.00	2	$9.00	$1,550.51	85.69%	$3,360.00	Edit
MAGE	Trade	44.90	2.61	6.17%	$1,044.00	4	$16.00	$11,549.01	180.14%	$17,960.00	Edit
MDRHM	Trade	25.90	0.00	0.00%	$0.00	6	$8.80	$10,247.51	193.62%	$15,540.00	Edit
MDRHP	Trade	12.90	0.90	7.50%	-$10.24	3	$12.90	-$10.24	-0.26%	$3,870.00	Edit
NOVGR	Trade	26.28	1.78	7.27%	$890.00	5	$11.40	$7,428.26	130.05%	$13,140.00	Edit
NOVHS	Trade	22.50	2.00	9 76%	$400.00	2	$13.00	$1,890.51	72.45%	$4,500.00	Edit
NOVHT	Trade	17.90	1.42	8.62%	$426.00	3	$12.70	$1,549.76	40.57%	$5,370.00	Edit
PCPGB	Trade	23.00	0.00	0.00%	$0.00	6	$8.10	$8,919.52	182.76%	$13,800.00	Edit
PCPHC	Trade	19.00	0.00	0.00%	$0.00	4	$12.40	$2,629.01	52.89%	$7,600.00	Edit

Continued from previous page . . .

PCUGP	Trade	30.80	0.00	0.00%	$0.00	5	$13.30	$8,738.26	131.17%	$15,400.00	Edit
PCUHQ	Trade	25.10	0.00	0.00%	$0.00	4	$8.50	$6,629.01	194.34%	$10,040.00	Edit
QAAGT	Trade	40.50	2.48	6.52%	$992.00	4	$13.00	$10,989.01	210.88%	$16,200.00	Edit
QAAHB	Trade	31.30	2.90	10.21%	$1,160.00	4	$14.20	$6,829.01	120.00%	$12,520.00	Edit
RFYHT	Trade	37.90	4.90	14.85%	$2,940.00	6	$22.50	$9,227.51	68.29%	$22,740.00	Edit
RIGGR	Trade	16.30	0.00	0.00%	$0.00	5	$11.20	$2,538.26	45.23%	$8,150.00	Edit
RIGHS	Trade	14.80	1.20	8.82%	$480.00	4	$13.00	$709.01	13.61%	$5,920.00	Edit
▣ UFBGR	Trade	27.50	0.00	0.00%	$0.00	4	$15.00	$4,989.01	83.00%	$11,000.00	Edit
UFBHS	Trade	25.00	0.00	0.00%	$0.00	3	$14.00	$3,289.76	78.14%	$7,500.00	Edit
XTQGI	Trade	9.00	0.00	0.00%	$0.00	14	$4.90	$5,726.76	83.32%	$12,600.00	Edit
XTQHI	Trade	9.50	0.00	0.00%	$0.00	6	$5.75	$2,239.76	64.73%	$5,700.00	Edit
Cash					4,327.00					$4,327.00	
				Totals	$11,968.76		$163,838.44	$155,361.56	94.83%	$323,527.00	

LEGEND: ▣ collapsed (click to expand) ▣ expanded (click to collapse)

Real-time quotes

Option Strategy   Profits $315,756.53   Average Return 87.6%

E✳TRADE FINANCIAL

✳ Open An Account   ● Help Cent

Enter Symbol or Name | QUOTES | Enter Question or Keywords | SEARCH |

| Accounts | Trading & Portfolios | Quotes & Research | Mutual Funds, ETFs & Bonds | Advice & Retirement | Banking & Credit Cards |

Mortgages & Home Equity

| Trade Portfolios View Orders | Balances | Transaction History | IPO Center | Account Records | Active Trading | Global Trading

Portfolios

⚡ Alerts | ▶▶ Transfer Money | ▶▶ Bill Pay | ● Hel

| Portfolios | Performance & Value | Positions | Gains & Losses | Risk Analyzer | Portfolio Analyzer | Income Estimator |

Account/Watch List: 559 Defined Benefit Plan ▓ Create / Edit List   View: Performance   ▓ Customize

Market Value: $678,220.28 ($315,756.53 / 87.64%)   DJIA 13,970.17 ▲ +62.92 Nasdaq 2,708.73 ▲ +1.73

| REFRESH 🔄 | | STREAMING QUOTES | | EXPORT TO EXCEL ⬇ | Results per Page: 200

☐ Symbol		Current Price	Change $	Change %	Day's Gain	Qty	Price Paid	Total Gain $	Total Gain %	Market Val	Edit
BGCGL	Trade	22.30	0.00	0.00%	$0.00	10	$8.20	$14,084.51	171.44%	$22,300.00	Edit
BGCGM	Trade	16.70	0.00	0.00%	$-0.00	-10	$7.20	-$9,515.49	-131.88%	-$16,700.00	Edit
BGCHL	Trade	22.30	0.00	0.00%	$0.00	5	$17.00	$2,638.26	31.00%	$11,150.00	Edit
☐ BGCHN	Trade	14.40	1.10	8.27%	$990.00	9	$10.79	$3,227.27	33.16%	$12,960.00	Edit
☐ COPGN	Trade	18.10	-2.30	-11.27%	-$3,220.00	14	$8.5429	$13,353.52	111.40%	$25,340.00	Edit
☐ DEGB	Trade	19.00	0.00	0.00%	$0.00	12	$10.90	$9,695.02	73.98%	$22,800.00	Edit
EMCHQ	Trade	3.40	0.00	0.00%	$0.00	22	$3.50	-$244.49	-3.17%	$7,480.00	Edit
☐ FCXGM	Trade	25.90	0.00	0.00%	$0.00	10	$12.12	$13,748.53	113.14%	$25,900.00	Edit
FCXHQ	Trade	19.60	-0.30	-1.51%	-$210.00	7	$11.00	$6,006.76	77.88%	$13,720.00	Edit
☐ FLRGS	Trade	25.41	0.00	0.00%	$0.00	12	$10.00	$18,467.02	153.57%	$30,492.00	Edit
☐ FLRHT	Trade	20.82	0.00	0.00%	$0.00	6	$5.00	$9,479.51	314.67%	$12,492.00	Edit
GOPHO	Trade	61.50	4.00	6.96%	$1,600.00	4	$49.60	$4,749.01	23.92%	$24,600.00	Edit
IHHHJ	Trade	25.50	4.00	18.60%	$1,600.00	4	$23.50	$789.01	8.38%	$10,200.00	Edit
☐ JECGJ	Trade	13.50	0.00	0.00%	$0.00	18	$3.75	$17,535.26	259.22%	$24,300.00	Edit
☐ JECHJ	Trade	15.10	0.00	0.00%	$0.00	8	$9.00	$4,866.01	67.45%	$12,080.00	Edit
JECHK	Trade	9.80	-0.75	-7.11%	-$675.00	9	$5.70	$3,675.26	71.44%	$8,820.00	Edit
☐ MALGG	Trade	39.00	0.00	0.00%	$0.00	9	$12.43	$23,887.27	213.04%	$35,100.00	Edit

Continued from previous page . . .

Symbol		Price	Change	%	$ Change	Qty	Paid	Value	%	Market Value	
▣ MALHJ	Trade	24.30	1.60	7.05%	$480.00	3	$17.40	$2,059.76	39.38%	$7,290.00	Edi
▣ MDRGN	Trade	17.07	0.00	0.00%	$0.00	13	$9.6231	$9,655.27	77.02%	$22,191.00	Edi
▣ MDRHN	Trade	23.65	1.15	5.11%	$690.00	6	$13.60	$6,017.51	73.63%	$14,190.00	Edi
▣ NOVGQ	Trade	22.70	0.00	0.00%	$0.00	10	$12.12	$10,548.53	86.81%	$22,700.00	Edi
▣ NOVHS	Trade	18.10	0.00	0.00%	$0.00	6	$13.50	$2,747.51	33.87%	$10,860.00	Edi
▣ PCPGC	Trade	16.64	0.44	2.72%	$792.00	18	$6.65	$17,952.52	149.61%	$29,952.00	Edi
PCPHB	Trade	17.70	0.00	0.00%	$0.00	10	$9.00	$8,684.51	96.33%	$17,700.00	Edi
▣ PCUGP	Trade	30.10	0.00	0.00%	$0.00	9	$13.20	$15,195.26	127.75%	$27,090.00	Edi
PCUHQ	Trade	24.00	0.00	0.00%	$0.00	10	$10.00	$13,984.51	139.63%	$24,000.00	Edi
▣ QAAGA	Trade	34.30	1.60	4.89%	$1,440.00	9	$14.88	$17,457.27	130.15%	$30,870.00	Edi
QAAHB	Trade	29.90	1.27	4.44%	$889.00	7	$14.20	$10,976.76	110.28%	$20,930.00	Edi
▣ RFYHT	Trade	32.99	2.39	7.81%	$3,346.00	14	$22.41	$14,779.52	47.06%	$46,186.00	Edi
▣ RIGGR	Trade	19.10	0.00	0.00%	$0.00	11	$11.38	$8,465.77	67.49%	$21,010.00	Edit
RIGHR	Trade	18.70	-0.80	-4.10%	-$480.00	6	$13.70	$2,987.51	36.29%	$11,220.00	Edit
▣ UFBGR	Trade	29.80	0.00	0.00%	$0.00	8	$12.89	$13,508.02	130.74%	$23,840.00	Edit
UFBHS	Trade	26.90	0.00	0.00%	$0.00	6	$14.00	$7,727.51	91.86%	$16,140.00	Edit
▣ UVAHH	Trade	7.40	0.90	13.85%	$1,260.00	14	$6.80	$821.51	8.61%	$10,360.00	Edit
▣ XTQGI	Trade	9.16	0.66	7.76%	$1,716.00	26	$4.8077	$11,290.27	90.14%	$23,816.00	Edit
▣ XTQHI	Trade	9.04	-0.06	-0.66%	-$84.00	14	$5.8429	$4,454.77	54.32%	$12,656.00	Edit
Cash							2,185.28			$2,185.28	
					Totals	$10,134.00		$360,278.47	$315,756.53	87.64%	$678,220.28

LEGEND: ▣ collapsed (click to expand) ▣ expanded (click to collapse)

Real-time quotes

Option Strategy   Profits $109,021.20   Average Return 91.7%

Account Reports: Profit/Loss Report

PRINT   Account: 900

Give your accountant a break. View profits/losses for all trades executed on one specific date or during a range of dates. Track by position, whether it's closed, or still opened. Download to a spreadsheet for easy manipulation, processing and tax reporting.

Trade date: « [   ] » SELECT DATE
Trade date: « [   ] » SELECT DATE
Symbol: [   ] SUBMIT   ☐ **Show detailed unrealized positions**

* To see all transactions within specified date range leave symbol blank

Guide to the Profit/Loss Report

Click here to download data

Realized P&L on Closed Positions

Symbol	Date Bought	Date Sold	Shares	Cost Basis	Sales Price	Gain-loss
+MROGK	6/18/2007 11:59:59 PM	7/12/2007 2:39:34 PM	10	$0.00	$8,274.85	$8,274.85
+MROGK	6/19/2007 11:59:59 PM	7/12/2007 2:39:34 PM	10	$0.00	$8,274.85	$8,274.85
+MROGL	7/12/2007 2:39:01 PM	6/18/2007 11:59:59 PM	10	$3,625.00	$0.00	-$3,625.00
+MROGL	7/12/2007 2:39:01 PM	6/19/2007 11:59:59 PM	10	$3,625.00	$0.00	-$3,625.00

Total Realized Gain-Loss: $9,299.70

Unrealized P&L on Open Positions

Symbol	Description	Position	Avg Price	Cost Basis	Market Value	Type	Unrealized Val.
+CLFGP	Cleveland Cliffs Inc Jul 2007 80.00 Call	10	$10.5350	$10,535.00	$6,000.00	Stock Option	-$4,535.00
+DEGB	Deere & Co Jul 2007 110.00 Call	10	$12.2350	$12,235.00	$20,600.00	Stock Option	$8,365.00
+FCXGO	Freeport-Mcmoran Copper & Gold Jul 2007 75.00 Call	10	$7.5350	$7,535.00	$17,900.00	Stock Option	$10,365.00
+FLRGT	Fluor Corp New Jul 2007 100.00 Call	10	$8.0350	$8,035.00	$18,700.00	Stock Option	$10,665.00
+GOPHV	Google Inc Cl A Aug 2007 520.00 Call	1	$36.9150	$3,691.50	$4,090.00	Stock Option	$398.50
+IHHHK	Intercontinentalexchange Inc Aug 2007 155.00 Call	5	$17.8550	$8,927.50	$7,500.00	Stock Option	-$1,427.50
+JECGJ	Jacobs Engr Group Inc Del Jul 2007 50.00 Call	10	$6.5350	$6,535.00	$15,900.00	Stock Option	$9,365.00
+MALGI	Mastercard Inc Cl A Jul 2007 145.00 Call	10	$10.8950	$10,895.00	$23,400.00	Stock Option	$12,505.00
+NOVGS	National Oilwell Varco Inc Jul 2007 95.00 Call	10	$12.3350	$12,335.00	$20,200.00	Stock Option	$7,865.00
+QAAGB	Apple Computer Inc Jul 2007 110.00 Call	10	$11.6350	$11,635.00	$28,000.00	Stock Option	$16,365.00
+RFYHT	Research In Motion Ltd Aug 2007 200.00 Call	4	$22.2650	$8,906.00	$13,120.00	Stock Option	$4,214.00
+UFBGR	Foster Wheeler Ltd Shs New Jul 2007 90.00 Call	9	$11.4372	$10,293.50	$26,370.00	Stock Option	$16,076.50
+XTQGI	Express Scripts Inc Jul 2007 45.00 Call	10	$0.0000	$0.00	$9,500.00	Stock Option	$9,500.00

Total Unrealized Gain-Loss: $99,721.50

Option Strategy   Profits $105,901.03   Average Return 70.7%

Account Reports: Profit/Loss Report   🖨 PRINT   Account: 927

Realized P&L on Closed Positions

Symbol	Date Bought	Date Sold	Shares	Cost Basis	Sales Price	Gain-loss
+FCXGN	6/4/2007 1:52:30 PM	7/9/2007 3:56:27 PM	1	$986.50	$1,911.96	$925.46
+FCXGN	6/4/2007 1:52:30 PM	7/9/2007 3:56:37 PM	2	$1,973.00	$3,825.93	$1,852.93
+FCXGN	6/4/2007 1:52:30 PM	7/9/2007 3:56:54 PM	1	$986.50	$1,913.96	$927.46
+FCXGN	6/4/2007 1:52:30 PM	7/9/2007 3:57:06 PM	1	$986.50	$1,914.96	$928.46
+FCXGN	6/4/2007 1:52:30 PM	7/9/2007 3:57:23 PM	2	$1,973.00	$3,806.93	$1,833.93
+FCXGN	6/4/2007 1:52:30 PM	7/11/2007 2:34:22 PM	3	$2,959.50	$6,308.89	$3,349.39
+FCXGP	7/9/2007 3:54:49 PM	6/4/2007 1:52:53 PM	1	$937.00	$353.49	-$583.51
+FCXGP	7/9/2007 3:55:01 PM	6/4/2007 1:52:53 PM	2	$1,826.00	$706.98	-$1,119.02
+FCXGP	7/9/2007 3:55:13 PM	6/4/2007 1:52:53 PM	2	$1,828.00	$706.98	-$1,121.02
+FCXGP	7/9/2007 3:55:36 PM	6/4/2007 1:52:53 PM	2	$1,830.00	$706.98	-$1,123.02
+FCXGP	7/11/2007 2:33:58 PM	6/4/2007 1:52:53 PM	3	$3,363.00	$1,060.48	-$2,302.52
+MROGY	6/18/2007 11:59:59 PM	7/12/2007 2:38:09 PM	5	$0.00	$2,929.94	$2,929.94
+MROGY	6/19/2007 11:59:59 PM	7/12/2007 2:38:09 PM	3	$0.00	$1,757.96	$1,757.96
+MROGY	6/19/2007 11:59:59 PM	7/12/2007 2:38:18 PM	2	$0.00	$1,176.97	$1,176.97
+MROHK	6/20/2007 11:06:46 AM	7/12/2007 2:37:37 PM	2	$1,823.00	$1,756.97	-$66.04
+MROHK	6/20/2007 11:06:46 AM	7/12/2007 2:37:37 PM	2	$1,803.00	$1,756.97	-$46.04
+MROHK	6/20/2007 11:06:47 AM	7/12/2007 2:37:46 PM	1	$901.50	$858.47	-$43.03
+XTQGI	6/22/2007 11:59:59 PM	7/9/2007 1:04:05 PM	5	$0.00	$3,832.43	$3,832.43
+XTQGI	6/25/2007 11:59:59 PM	7/9/2007 1:04:05 PM	5	$0.00	$3,832.43	$3,832.43

Total Realized Gain-Loss: **$16,943.18**

Unrealized P&L on Open Positions

Symbol	Description	Position	Avg Price	Cost Basis	Market Value	Type	Unrealized Val.
+BGCHN	General Cable Corp Del New Aug 2007 70.00 Call	4	$12.6650	$5,066.00	$5,600.00	Stock Option	$534.00
+FCXHP	Freeport-Mcmoran Copper & Gold Cl B Aug 2007 80.00 Call	5	$12.3550	$6,177.50	$6,550.00	Stock Option	$372.50
+FLRGS	Fluor Corp New Jul 2007 95.00 Call	10	$8.1350	$8,135.00	$24,600.00	Stock Option	$16,465.00
+GOPHO	Google Inc Cl A Aug 2007 500.00 Call	1	$50.2150	$5,021.50	$6,070.00	Stock Option	$1,048.50
+GOPHV	Google Inc Cl A Aug 2007 520.00 Call	1	$36.9150	$3,691.50	$4,430.00	Stock Option	$738.50
+IHHHK	Intercontinentalexchange Inc Aug 2007 155.00 Call	7	$17.8436	$12,490.50	$12,600.00	Stock Option	$109.50
+JECGJ	Jacobs Engr Group Inc Del Jul 2007 50.00 Call	10	$6.4350	$6,435.00	$15,300.00	Stock Option	$8,865.00
+MALGH	Mastercard Inc Cl A Jul 2007 140.00 Call	5	$13.1550	$6,577.50	$14,600.00	Stock Option	$8,022.50
+MALHK		5	$17.6550	$8,827.50	$9,500.00	Stock Option	$672.50
+MDRHP	Mcdermott Intl Inc Aug 2007 80.00 Call	5	$11.6550	$5,827.50	$6,350.00	Stock Option	$522.50
+NOVGR	National Oilwell Varco Inc Jul 2007 90.00 Call	5	$13.5550	$6,777.50	$11,100.00	Stock Option	$4,322.50
+NOVHS	National Oilwell Varco Inc Aug 2007 95.00 Call	5	$12.5550	$6,277.50	$9,250.00	Stock Option	$2,972.50
+PCPHD	Precision Castparts Corp Aug 2007 120.00 Call	5	$10.6550	$5,327.50	$7,450.00	Stock Option	$2,122.50
+PCUHR	Southern Copper Corp Aug 2007 90.00 Call	5	$12.6750	$6,337.50	$10,200.00	Stock Option	$3,862.50
+QAAHB	Apple Inc Aug 2007 110.00 Call	10	$14.2350	$14,235.00	$29,700.00	Stock Option	$15,465.00
+RFYHT	Research In Motion Ltd Aug 2007 200.00 Call	5	$22.2350	$11,117.50	$16,350.00	Stock Option	$5,232.50
+RIGGA	Transocean Inc Ord Jul 2007 105.00 Call	-10	-$2.3549	$2,354.94	-$1,850.00	Stock Option	$504.94
+RIGGS	Transocean Inc Ord Jul 2007 95.00 Call	10	$7.8550	$7,855.00	$10,800.00	Stock Option	$2,945.00
+UFBGB	Foster Wheeler Ltd Shs New Jul 2007 110.00 Call	-10	-$3.9949	$3,994.91	-$7,500.00	Stock Option	-$3,505.09
+UFBGT	Foster Wheeler Ltd Shs New Jul 2007 100.00 Call	10	$9.2150	$9,215.00	$17,400.00	Stock Option	$8,185.00
+XTQGW	Express Scripts Inc Jul 2007 47.50 Call	20	$0.0000	$0.00	$13,200.00	Stock Option	$13,200.00
+XTQGX	Express Scripts Inc Jul 2007 52.50 Call	-20	$0.0000	$0.00	-$3,700.00	Stock Option	-$3,700.00

Total Unrealized Gain-Loss: **$88,957.85**

Option Strategy   Profits $135,765.00   Average Return 64.2%

Account Reports: Profit/Loss Report   🖶 PRINT

Give your accountant a break. View profits/losses for all trades executed on one specific date or during a range of dates. Track by position, whether it's closed, or still opened. Download to a spreadsheet for easy manipulation, processing and tax reporting.

Trade date: [«]   [»] [SELECT DATE]
Trade date: [«]   [»] [SELECT DATE]
Symbol: [SUBMIT]   ☐ Show detailed unrealized positions

* To see all transactions within specified date range leave symbol blank   Guide to the Profit/Loss Report

Unrealized P&L on Open Positions on 9/25/2007

Symbol	Description	Position	Avg Price	Cost Basis	Market Value	Type	Unrealized Val.
+FCXAO	Freeport-Mcmoran Copper & Gold Jan 2008 75.00 Call	15	$19.2983	$28,947.50	$48,600.00	Stock Option	$19,652.50
+FLRJB	Fluor Corp New Oct 2007 110.00 Call	15	$18.3583	$27,537.50	$49,200.00	Stock Option	$21,662.50
+GQRJA	Garmin Ltd Ord Oct 2007 90.00 Call	15	$16.6117	$24,917.50	$43,800.00	Stock Option	$18,882.50
+NOVKT	National Oilwell Varco Inc Nov 2007 100.00 Call	15	$25.3717	$38,057.50	$64,950.00	Stock Option	$26,892.50
+QAAJD	Apple Inc Oct 2007 120.00 Call	15	$18.5650	$27,847.50	$50,550.00	Stock Option	$22,702.50
+RFYAN	Research In Motion Ltd Jan 2008 70.00 Call	15	$18.7250	$28,087.50	$44,850.00	Stock Option	$16,762.50
+RIGAR	Transocean Inc Ord Jan 2008 90.00 Call	15	$18.0317	$27,047.50	$36,450.00	Stock Option	$9,402.50
+ZQNJR	Amazon Com Inc Oct 2007 90.00 Call	15	$6.0283	$9,042.50	$8,850.00	Stock Option	-$192.50

Total Unrealized Gain-Loss: $135,765.00

SCHEDULE D (Form 1040)
Dept. of the Treasury
Internal Revenue Service

Capital Gains and Losses
and Reconciliation of Forms 1099-B

Attach to Form 1040.   See instructions for Sch. D (Form 1040).

OMB No. 1545-0074

1985

12

Name(s) as shown on Form 1040	Your social security number
Charles and Catherine Hughes	

Part I Summary of Forms 1099-B for Sales of Stocks, Bonds, Etc.

1a Report here and on line 37, Part VII, page 2, total sales of stocks, bonds, etc., reported for 1985 by your broker to you on Form(s) 1099-B or an equivalent substitute statement(s), such as a broker's confirmation statement . . . . **1a** | 33,204

Note: Also complete Part VII if you received one or more Form(s) 1099-B or equivalent statement(s) for 1985, for bartering income.

Part II Short-term Capital Gains and Losses-Assets Held Six Months or Less(one year or less if acquired before 6/23/84)

(a) Description of Property (Example, 100 shares 7% preferred of "Z" Co.)	(b) Date acquired (Mo., day, yr.)	(c) Date sold (Mo., day, yr.)	(d) Gross sales price	(e) Cost or other basis (see	(f) LOSS If column (e) is more	(g) GAIN If column (d) is more than (e) subtract (e) from (d)
1b						
From Form 6781 Option Trading						27,612
EAL stock	01/01/85	03/25/8				1,085
GDBD	08/22/84	02/10/8				
WDBJ	12/05/84	02/05/8				

Copies of Tax Returns from my first two years of trading showing $460,164 in option profits

2 Short-term gain from sale or exchange of a principal residence from Form 2119, lines 6 or 12	**2**		
3 Short-term gain from installment sales from Form 6252, lines 22 or 30	**3**		
4 Net short-term gain or (loss) from partnerships, S corporations, and fiduciaries .	**4**		
5 Add lines 1b through 4 in columns (f) and (g) **5**	(726)		28,697
6 Combine columns (f) and (g) of line 5 and enter the net gain or (loss)	**6**		27,971
7 Short-term capital loss carryover from years beginning after 1969	**7**		
8 Net short-term gain or (loss), combine lines 6 and 7	**8**		27,971

Part III Long-term Capital Gains and Losses-Assets Held More Than Six Months (more than one year if acquired before 6/23/84)

9						
From Form 6781 Option Trading						41,418
20th Century Funds 10/21/83	01/01/85	28,299	33,327	5,028		

10 Long-term gain from sale or exchange of principal residence from Form 2119, lines 6, 8 or 12	**10**		
11 Long-term gain from installment sales from Form 6252, lines 22 or 30	**11**		
12 Net long-term gain or (loss) from partnerships, S corporations, and fiduciaries .	**12**		
13 Add lines 9 through 12 in columns (f) and (g) **13**	(5,028)		41,418
14 Combine columns (f) and (g) of line 13 and enter the net gain or (loss) . . .	**14**		36,390
15 Capital gain distributions	**15**		115
16 Enter gain from Form 4797, lines 6 or 8b	**16**		
17 Combine lines 14 through 16	**17**		36,505
18 Long-term capital loss carryover from years beginning after 1969	**18**		
19 Net short-term gain or (loss), combine lines 6 and 7	**19**		36,505

Note: *Complete the back of this form. However, if you have capital loss carryovers from years beginning before 1970, do not complete Parts IV or V. See Form 4798 instead.*

For Paperwork Reduction Act Notice, see Form 1040 instructions.

Schedule D (Form 1040) 1985

SCHEDULE D
(Form 1040)
Dept. of the Treasury
Internal Revenue Service

Capital Gains and Losses
and Reconciliation of Forms 1099-B
Attach to Form 1040.   See instructions for Sch. D (Form 1040).
For Paperwork Reduction Act Notice, see Form 1040 instructions

OMB No. 1545-0074

1986
12

Name(s) as shown on Form 1040	Your social security number
Charles and Catherine Hughes	

1 Report here total sales of stocks, bonds, etc., reported for 1986 by your broker to you on Form(s) 1099-B or an equivalent substitute statement(s) . . . . **1** | 9,245

If this amount differs from the total of lines 2b and 9b, column (d), attach a statement explaining the difference. See the instructions for line 1, Schedule D (Form 1040) for examples.

Part I Short-term Capital Gains and Losses —Assets Held Six Months or Less

(a) Description of Property (Example, 100 shares 7% preferred of "Z" Co.)	(b) Date acquired (Mo., day, yr.)	(c) Date sold (Mo., day, yr.)	(d) Sales price (see instructions)	(e) Cost or other basis (see Instructions)	(f) LOSS If (e) is more than (d) subtract (d) from (e)	(g) GAIN If (d) is more than (e) subtract (e) from (d)
2a Form 1099-B Transactions (Sales of Stocks...)						
From Form 6781 Option Trading						156,454

Copies of Tax Returns from my first two years of trading showing $460,164 in option profits

2b Total (add column (d))						
2c Other Transactions:						

3 Short-term gain from sale or exchange of a principal residence from Form 2119, lines 6 or 12 — **3**
4 Short-term gain from installment sales from Form 6252, lines 22 or 30 . . . — **4**
5 Net short-term gain or (loss) from partnerships, S corporations, and fiduciaries . — **5**
6 Short-term capital loss carryover from years beginning after 1969 . . . . — **6**
7 Add all of the transactions on lines 2a and 2c and lines 3 through 6 in columns (f) and (g) — **7**
8 Net short-term gain or (loss), combine columns (f) and (g) of line 7 . . . . **8** | 156,454

Part II Long-term Capital Gains and Losses — Assets Held More Than Six Months

9a Form 1099-B Transactions (Sales of Stocks, Bonds, etc.):						
From Form 6781 Option Trading						234,680
50 Nuveen Fund	11/03/81	09/25/86	6,331	5,101		1,230
Lindner Fund	12/05/84	05/12/86	2,914	2,327		587
9b Total (add column (d)) . . . . →						
9c Other Transactions:						

10 Long-term gain from sale or exchange of principal residence from Form 2119, lines 6, 8 or 12 — **10**
11 Long-term gain from installment sales from Form 6252, lines 22 or 30 . . . — **11**
12 Net long-term gain or (loss) from partnerships, S corporations, and fiduciaries . — **12**
13 Capital gain distributions . . . . — **13**
14 Enter gain from Form 4797, lines 6 or 8b . . . . — **14**
15 Combine lines 14 through 16 . . . . — **15**
16 Long-term capital loss carryover from years beginning after 1969 . . . . . — **16**
17 Net short-term gain or (loss), combine lines 6 and 7 . . . . **17** | 236,497

Schedule D (Form 1040) 1986

Chapter 4

I'm Retired But I Still Collect a Weekly Paycheck

"It was the best of times, it was the worst of times."

- Charles Dickens

I would like to take this opportunity to introduce you to one of the most profitable and low-risk income strategies I have encountered in my 27 year investing career. This income strategy produced consistent returns during the recent financial crisis and the severe 2008 - 2009 bear market.

During the recent recession, US corporations have been slashing their dividends at the fastest pace in over 50 years. The table below lists a few examples of the painful dividend cuts imposed by major corporations.

Company	Dividend Cut
JP Morgan	87%
Pfizer	50%
Wells Fargo	85%
Dow Chemical	64%

These type of dividend cuts are rare for blue chip companies. For example, until recently Pfizer increased its dividend regularly for more than 40 years. And Dow Chemical went almost 100 years without cutting its dividend.

At the same time these blue chip companies were slashing dividends, a little known option income strategy was actually increasing cash pay outs to investors due to rich option premiums. So while it was the worst of times for corporate dividend payouts, it was the best of times for investors who sell option premium to generate cash income.

Most investors are not familiar with the concept of selling option premium to generate cash income. Selling option premium is a very simple but lucrative income strategy.

When you sell an option, cash equal to the option price or premium is immediately credited to your brokerage account. Unlike a traditional stock dividend you don't have to own the stock on the dividend date to receive the quarterly dividend and you don't have to wait a year to receive a 3% or 4% annual dividend yield.

When you sell option premium, you can get paid up to a 20% to 30% cash payment up front when the option is sold. You get to keep this cash payment regardless of the price movement of the underlying stock.

Ideal Strategy for Today's Volatile Markets

Selling option premium to generate immediate cash income is the ideal strategy for today's volatile markets and uncertain economy. We will look at an actual trade example shortly that allowed me to purchase Morgan Stanley stock at a 30% discount to its current price. When you buy stock at a 30% discount you can profit if the stock price increases, remains flat or even declines 20% to 25% resulting in a much higher probability that the trade will be profitable. This gives the option income strategy a huge advantage over a stock purchase strategy and allows you to profit in any type of market condition.

Added Dimension

This gives the option income strategy a huge advantage over a stock purchase strategy and allows you to profit in any type of market. The option income strategy works just as well with bearish trades which allow you to profit in bear markets when stocks and ETFs are declining in price. Bearish income trades not only reduce portfolio risk but can dramatically increase profit opportunities and provide a whole new dimension to income investing.

Over 7.4 Million Dollars in Cash Income Over the Past 5 Years

Due to the versatility of the option income strategy and its ability to profit in up, down or flat markets, I have been very active generating option premium income during the recent severe bear market and the recent volatile markets. Copies of my brokerage account trade confirmations in the Appendix show that I collected $7,485,348.68 in gross option premium income over the last five years. This averages out to more than $124,000 in cash income per month. Brokerage confirmations list the call and put options I sold and the amount of cash that was credited to my brokerage account for each option sale. I have been trading the option income strategy for many years. During the 1990s I generated over 11 million dollars of gross option income. Copies of my brokerage account statements documenting this option income are presented in my *Guaranteed Real Income Program* manual.

The key to selling option premium to generate cash income is to make sure the option you sell is 'covered'. There are two ways to implement the option income strategy with limited risk:

Bullish Option Income Trades

- **Buy 100 shares of a stock and sell a related call option also known as a 'buy write' or 'covered call' or**

- **Purchase a call option and sell a call option with a higher strike price to create an option debit spread**

Bearish Option Income Trades

- **Purchase 100 shares of a bearish ETF and sell a related call option also known as a 'buy write' or 'covered call' or**

- **Purchase a put option and sell a put option with a lower strike price to create an option debit spread**

For bullish trades the short option is 'covered' by owning the stock or owning a call option. And for bearish trades the short option is 'covered' by owning the bearish ETF or owning a put option. Because the short option is 'covered' this is a limited risk strategy. Selling 'covered' option premium incurs considerably less risk than investing in stocks. Selling option premium enables me to profit if the market goes up, down or remains flat and has given me the edge in producing consistent returns during any type of market condition.

Selling 'Covered' Option Premium

- **Buy 100 Shares of a Stock and Sell a Call Option or**

- **Buy Call Option and Sell Call Option with Higher Strike Price to Create a Debit Spread**

Selling 'Covered' Options is a Limited Risk Strategy

Let's look at an example of an option sale and the resulting amount of cash that was credited to my brokerage account. The brokerage confirmation that follows shows that I 'sold to open' 10 of the National Oilwell Jan 25-strike call options symbol YMPA25 at 12.72 points. Options cover one hundred shares of stock so a 12.72 point option is worth $1,272 ($12.72 x 100 = $1,272). Selling 10 options at 12.72 points resulted in $12,720 cash being credited to my brokerage account ($1,272 x 10 = $12,720). I get to keep this $12,720 cash payment ($12,708 after commission) regardless of the price movement of National Oilwell stock.

Sale of 10 Options at 12.72 Points Results in

$12,720 Cash Dividend Credited to Brokerage Account

$1,272 x 10 Contracts = $12,720

TRADE CONFIRMATION

TRADE DATE	SETL DATE	MKT/ CPT	SYMBOL/ CUSIP	BUY/ SELL	QUANTITY	PRICE	ACCT TYPE		
03/26/09	03/27/09	5 1	YMPA25	SELL	10	$12.72	Margin	PRINCIPAL	$12,720.00
CALL NATL OILWELL JAN 025								COMMISSION	$11.49
01/16/2010 EXPIRATION DATE								FEE	$0.08
OPEN CONTRACT								NET AMOUNT	$12,708.43

Let's look at an example of the first type of option income trade that is initiated by purchasing stock and selling a related call option (we will look at the second type of option income trade in Chapter 6). This is also known as a buy write or covered call trade. My brokerage confirmation below shows that I bought 600 shares of Morgan Stanley stock at 24.22 and sold to open 6 Morgan Stanley July 20-Strike call options at 7.27. These options expire in 4 months.

Buy Morgan Stanley Stock at 24.22 and Sell 20-Strike Call at 7.27

TRADE CONFIRMATION

TRADE DATE	SETL DATE	MKT/ CPT	SYMBOL/ CUSIP	BUY/ SELL	QUANTITY	PRICE	ACCT TYPE		
03/18/09	03/23/09	1 3	MS	BUY	600	$24.22	Margin	PRINCIPAL	$14,532.00
MORGAN STANLEY								COMMISSION	$7.99
								NET AMOUNT	$14,539.99
03/18/09	03/19/09	6 1	MSG20	SELL	6	$7.27	Margin	PRINCIPAL	$4,362.00
CALL MORGAN STANL JUL 020 ****								COMMISSION	$12.49
07/18/2009 EXPIRATION DATE								FEE	$0.03
OPEN CONTRACT								NET AMOUNT	$4,349.48

Selling to open the 20-strike call option at 7.27 points resulted in $727 in cash per contract being credited to my brokerage account or a total of $4,362 ($4,349 after commission) for 6 contracts.

Purchasing the stock at 24.22 points and receiving 7.27 points in cash resulted in a 30% cash payment I received up front on the day I initiated the trade. I get to keep this 30% cash payment regardless of the price movement of Morgan Stanley stock.

Buy Stock at 24.22 Points and Sell Option at 7.27 Points

Equals 30% Cash Dividend Over a Four Month Period

7.27 Divided by 24.22 = 30%

When this option expires in 4 months I can sell another option and collect another cash payment. This is called a 'rollover'. If I rollover this option a second time I would receive a total of 3 cash payment over the course of one year. This has the potential of producing up to a 90% cash payment over the course of one year which could almost pay for the initial cost of the stock and dramatically lower risk.

Up to 90% Cash Dividend Potential

Over the Course of One Year

By 'Rolling Over' Option

Buying Morgan Stanley stock at a 30% discount reduces risk considerably. This trade will profit if Morgan Stanley stock increases, remains flat or even declines 20% to 25% resulting in a much higher probability that the trade will be profitable. This can result in a high percentage of winning trades even if your market timing is not very accurate. This gives the option income strategy a big advantage over a stock purchase strategy which requires a stock price increase to be profitable.

The brokerage account Profit/Loss Report that follows shows my current option income trades for one of my trading accounts. This account had a $311,800 starting balance when I initiated the current trades. There are currently $118,546.86 in net profits after commissions for this portfolio.

49% Cash Income by Rolling Over Trades
I normally reinvest the cash income I receive from option income trades in additional option income trades allowing me to compound my trading results. I received a total of $152,900 in cash income for the current trades resulting in an average cash payment of 49% for the portfolio.

This portfolio is widely diversified across different industry groups. All of the trades in this portfolio are currently showing a net profit for the spread demonstrating the ability of the option income strategy to produce a high percentage of winning trades. Even if the underlying stocks in this portfolio decline moderately I can still realize a good return for the portfolio.

I normally take profits when an option income trade reaches 90% of its profit potential. This enabled me to take profits on trades well before option expiration and initiate new option income trades allowing me to compound the cash income I receive.

Note: I trade a large number of option contracts in this account. Trading one option contract would require a smaller trading account.

Option Income Trades

Realized P&L on Closed Positions

Symbol	Date Bought	Date Sold	Shares	Cost Basis	Sales Price	Gain-loss
+FCXEG	3/26/2009 11:59:59 PM	3/17/2009 12:46:27 PM	10	$0.00	$5,164.89	$5,164.89
+FCXEG	3/26/2009 11:59:59 PM	3/18/2009 3:18:38 PM	5	$0.00	$3,022.44	$3,022.44
+FPAEG	4/30/2009 10:18:36 AM	3/26/2009 11:59:59 PM	15	$11,697.59	$0.00	-$11,697.59
+GSGM	3/25/2009 3:40:27 PM	5/6/2009 10:00:37 AM	15	$72,027.59	$109,244.57	$37,216.98
+GSGS	5/6/2009 10:00:37 AM	3/25/2009 3:40:27 PM	15	$65,832.59	$38,492.16	-$27,340.43
+NOVEF	5/4/2009 11:59:59 PM	3/17/2009 12:49:34 PM	10	$3,218.39	$3,564.89	$346.50
+NOVEF	5/4/2009 11:59:59 PM	3/18/2009 3:36:31 PM	5	$1,609.20	$1,722.45	$113.25
+YCPAU	5/8/2009 11:59:59 PM	5/1/2009 12:36:20 PM	15	$0.00	$9,422.13	$9,422.13
+YFQAW	5/8/2009 11:59:59 PM	5/6/2009 3:17:12 PM	15	$0.00	$10,307.11	$10,307.11
+YHBAE	5/8/2009 11:59:59 PM	5/1/2009 1:41:20 PM	15	$0.00	$7,322.19	$7,322.19
FCX	3/17/2009 12:45:32 PM	4/30/2009 10:20:38 AM	800	$29,052.72	$33,960.39	$4,907.67
FCX	3/17/2009 12:45:32 PM	4/30/2009 10:20:38 AM	200	$7,282.20	$8,490.10	$1,207.90
FCX	3/18/2009 3:17:41 PM	4/30/2009 10:20:38 AM	300	$11,353.77	$12,735.15	$1,381.38
FCX	3/18/2009 3:17:41 PM	4/30/2009 10:20:38 AM	100	$3,784.60	$4,245.05	$460.45
FCX	3/18/2009 3:17:41 PM	4/30/2009 10:20:38 AM	100	$3,804.58	$4,245.05	$440.47
NOV	3/17/2009 12:48:27 PM	5/4/2009 10:13:50 AM	100	$2,987.60	$3,271.87	$284.27
NOV	3/17/2009 12:48:27 PM	5/4/2009 10:13:50 AM	200	$5,995.20	$6,543.75	$548.55
NOV	3/17/2009 12:48:27 PM	5/4/2009 10:13:50 AM	500	$14,938.00	$16,359.37	$1,421.37
NOV	3/17/2009 12:48:27 PM	5/4/2009 10:13:50 AM	200	$5,975.20	$6,543.75	$568.55
NOV	3/18/2009 3:35:49 PM	5/4/2009 10:13:50 AM	500	$14,898.00	$16,359.37	$1,461.37

Total Realized Gain-Loss: $46,559.45

Unrealized P&L on Open Positions

Symbol	Description	Position	Avg Price	Cost Basis	Market Value	Type	Unrealized Val.
+AASAH	Allegheny Technologies Inc Jan 2010 40.00 Call	-15	$0.0000	$0.00	$0.00	Stock Option	$0.00
+CLFAA	Cliffs Natural Resources Inc Jan 2010 20.00 Call	-15	$0.0000	$0.00	$0.00	Stock Option	$0.00
+CLFGD	Cliffs Natural Resources Inc Jul 2009 20.00 Call	-15	-$3.5715	$5,357.31	-$17,550.00	Stock Option	-$12,192.69
+CXJHD	Caterpillar Inc Del Aug 2009 30.00 Call	-15	-$3.3516	$5,027.35	-$16,200.00	Stock Option	-$11,172.65
+HBUAE	Bucyrus Intl Inc New Jan 2010 25.00 Call	-15	$0.0000	$0.00	$0.00	Stock Option	$0.00
+HBUGD	Bucyrus Intl Inc New Jul 2009 20.00 Call	-15	-$2.5615	$3,842.28	-$11,700.00	Stock Option	-$7,857.72
+MDRHC	Mcdermott Intl Inc Aug 2009 15.00 Call	-15	-$2.6249	$3,937.35	-$6,600.00	Stock Option	-$2,662.65
+MOSFH	Mosaic Co Jun 2009 40.00 Call	-15	-$7.8582	$11,787.30	-$10,500.00	Stock Option	$1,287.30
+MSGD	Morgan Stanley New Jul 2009 20.00 Call	-15	-$6.4249	$9,637.30	-$12,750.00	Stock Option	-$3,112.70
+PBRGY	Petroleo Brasileiro Sa Petrobr Sponsored Adr Jul 2009 27.50 Call	-15	-$5.7915	$8,687.31	-$18,900.00	Stock Option	-$10,212.69
+SIIGY	Smith Intl Inc Jul 2009 27.50 Call	-10	-$3.3649	$3,364.88	-$5,600.00	Stock Option	-$2,235.12
+STTHF	State Str Corp Aug 2009 32.00 Call	-15	-$7.8915	$11,837.31	-$20,550.00	Stock Option	-$8,712.69
+UNEAR	United States Natl Gas Fund Lp Unit Jan 2010 18.00 Call	-30	-$2.1715	$6,514.58	-$8,550.00	Stock Option	-$2,035.42
+WFCGT	Wells Fargo & Co New Jul 2009 17.50 Call	-15	-$3.5716	$5,357.34	-$16,200.00	Stock Option	-$10,842.66
+YNMAE	Foster Wheeler Ag Jan 2010 25.00 Call	-15	-$4.5715	$6,857.20	-$7,800.00	Stock Option	-$942.80
ATI	Allegheny Technologies Inc	1500	$38.0293	$57,044.00	$57,390.00	Equities	$346.00
BUCY	Bucyrus Intl Inc New	3000	$21.3533	$64,060.00	$83,430.00	Equities	$19,370.00
CAT	Caterpillar Inc Del	1500	$28.7083	$43,062.50	$59,460.00	Equities	$16,397.50
CLF	Cliffs Natural Resources Inc	3000	$21.9788	$65,936.50	$93,060.00	Equities	$27,123.50
FWLT	Foster Wheeler Ag	1500	$23.5293	$35,294.00	$37,470.00	Equities	$2,176.00
MDR	Mcdermott Intl Inc	1500	$14.4960	$21,744.00	$27,615.00	Equities	$5,871.00
MOS	Mosaic Co	1500	$42.0493	$63,073.90	$68,175.00	Equities	$5,101.10
MS	Morgan Stanley New	1500	$23.1305	$34,695.80	$42,300.00	Equities	$7,604.20
PBR	Petroleo Brasileiro Sa Petrobr Sponsored Adr	1500	$30.2159	$45,323.90	$60,000.00	Equities	$14,676.10
SII	Smith Intl Inc	1000	$25.7360	$25,736.00	$31,720.00	Equities	$5,984.00
STT	State Str Corp	1500	$32.7483	$49,122.50	$65,625.00	Equities	$16,502.50
UNG	United States Natl Gas Fund Lp Unit	3000	$15.3793	$46,138.00	$50,790.00	Equities	$4,652.00
WFC	Wells Fargo & Co New	1500	$16.9293	$25,394.00	$42,270.00	Equities	$16,876.00

Total Unrealized Gain-Loss: $71,987.41

Bearish Option Income Trade Example

Bearish option income trades can also established by purchasing a bearish ETF and selling the related call option. I trade bearish option income trades when a market is on a *Prime Trade Select* 'sell' signal. My brokerage confirmation below shows that I purchased 300 shares of the bearish Emerging Market ETF symbol EEV at 96.80 and sold to open 3 of the EEV December 120-Strike call options symbol EEVLD at 20.00 points. The bearish Emerging Market ETF increases in value as the price of the Emerging Market ETF declines. These options expire in about 3 months.

Selling to open the 120-strike call option at 20.00 points resulted in $2,000 in cash per contract being credited to my brokerage account or a total of $6,000 (before commission) for 3 contracts.

USD - US DOLLAR

Trades

Trade Date	Settlement Date	Trade Time	Action	Quantity	Symbol	Price
08/26/2008	08/29/2008	2:32:13 pm	Buy	300	EFU	107.790000
08/26/2008	08/29/2008	2:39:36 pm	Buy	100	EEV	96.800000
08/26/2008	08/29/2008	2:39:36 pm	Buy	100	EEV	96.800000
08/26/2008	08/29/2008	2:39:36 pm	Buy	100	EEV	96.800000
08/26/2008	08/27/2008	3:51:00 pm	Buy to Open	5	+RSXWX	13.000000

USD - US DOLLAR

Trades

Trade Date	Settlement Date	Trade Time	Action	Quantity	Symbol	Price
09/11/2008	09/12/2008	9:59:01 am	Sell to Open	-3	+EEVLD	20.000000

Profiting in Down Markets

The Buy Write Analysis below displays the profit/loss potential for buying the bearish Emerging Market ETF symbol EEV at 96.80 and selling the EEV December 120-Strike call for 20.0 points. The Analysis displays potential profit results for various price changes for the EEV ETF at option expiration from a 25% increase to a 10% decrease in price. The cost of this buy write 76.80 points and is calculated by subtracting the 20.0 points I received from the sale of the 120-Strike call from the 96.80 cost of the EEV purchase.

Wealth Creation Alliance
Buy Write Analysis

Stock Symbol	Current Stock Price	Call Strike	Call Price
EEV	96.80	120	20.00

Break Even 76.80

[Calculate] [New Analysis] [Print]

% Change	25.0%	20.0%	15.0%	10.0%	0.0%	-5.0%	-10.0%
Stock Price	$121.00	$116.16	$111.32	$106.48	$96.80	$91.96	$87.12
Stock Prof/Loss	$2,420.00	$1,936.00	$1,452.00	$968.00	$0.00	$-484.00	$-968.00
Call Value	$1.00	$0.00	$0.00	$0.00	$0.00	$0.00	$0.00
Call Profit/Loss	$1,900.00	$2,000.00	$2,000.00	$2,000.00	$2,000.00	$2,000.00	$2,000.00
Net Profit/Loss	$4,320.00	$3,936.00	$3,452.00	$2,968.00	$2,000.00	$1,516.00	$1,032.00
% Return	56.3%	51.3%	44.9%	38.6%	26.0%	19.7%	13.4%

The Buy Write Analysis reveals that if the EEV ETF price remains flat at 96.80 at option expiration a 26% return will be realized (circled). A 25% increase in price for the EEV ETF to 121.00 results in a 56.3% return and a 10% decrease in price to 87.12 results in a 13.4% return (circled). The return calculations for this bearish option income trade demonstrate the ability of the option income strategy to provide excellent profit opportunities during down markets.

$1633 Stock Loss = $3,553 Covered Call Profit

Let's take a look at an example of how a buy write trade can be profitable even if the underlying stock declines in price. My brokerage confirmation below shows that I purchased 1,500 shares of Mosaic stock at an average price of 42.0 and sold to open 15 of the Mosaic 40-strike call options at an average price of 7.90 points. I received $11,850 in cash income for this option sale which provides substantial downside protection if Mosaic stock declines in price.

USD - US DOLLAR

Trades

Trade Date	Settlement Date	Trade Time	Action	Quantity	Symbol	Price
03/17/2009	03/20/2009	12:50:25 pm	Buy	1,000	MOS	42.059900
03/18/2009	03/23/2009	3:30:49 pm	Buy	500	MOS	41.900000
03/17/2009	03/18/2009	1:04:43 pm	Sell to Open	-10	+MOSFH	8.000000
03/18/2009	03/19/2009	3:33:00 pm	Sell to Open	-5	+MOSFH	7.700000

Mosaic stock price declined after I initiated this trade. Below is a snapshot of my Mosaic buy write trade in my online brokerage account. Even though I currently have a $1,633 loss in Mosaic stock I have a $5,187 gain in the short Mosaic options giving me an overall net profit of $3,553 for this covered call trade.

$3,553 Net Profit Even Though Stock Declined in Price

Positions	Open Orders	Activity	Summary	Trade Journal	Balances
Type	Sy...	Last	Change	Qty	Avg Price	Profit/Loss
2	MOS	$40.96	$2.75	1500	42.0493	$-1633.95
2	+MOSFH	$4.20	$1.10	-15	7.8582	$5187.30

Option Income Strategy Incurs

Less Risk than Owning Stock

160

Generating Weekly Income with Covered Calls

I have been very active selling option premium with weekly covered calls. Weekly covered calls are initiated by buying 100 shares of stock and selling 1 weekly call option. As noted previously, when you sell an option cash equal to the option premium sold is immediately credited to your brokerage account. If you sell a weekly option with a 1.5 point premium, $150 in cash is credited to your brokerage account. This cash credit reduces the cost basis of the stock and reduces the overall risk of the trade.

The great advantage to selling weekly calls is that **you get to sell 52 options every year!** This has allowed me to compound my returns very quickly.

Options consist of time value and intrinsic value. At-the-money and out-of-the-money calls consist of only time value. At option expiration options lose all time value. *If you are short an option, the time value of that option becomes profit at expiration regardless of the price movement of the underlying stock.*

Time Value = Profit When You Are Short an Option

Let's look at a weekly covered call trade I took this week so that you can understand this important concept. I own 1,800 shares of the small cap ETF symbol TNA. I have been selling weekly covered calls against my TNA ETF. My brokerage account spread order below shows that I closed out 18 of the May 25 weekly calls and sold to open 18 of the TNA Jun 1st 49-Strike calls. The TNA ETF was trading at 48.43.

My brokerage account confirmation below shows that I sold the 18 TNA Jun 01 49-Strike weekly calls at 1.47 points. After the commission, $2,628.31 in cash was credited to my brokerage account for the sale of the 18 options.

Transaction History				Alerts | Transfer Money | Bill Pay | ? Help

Transactions	Check Summary	Deposit Summary	Categories	Reports

Account: DBP - 918

Date	Type	View Description	Categories (hide)	Amount ($)
05/25/12	Sold Short	18 TNA Jun 01 '12 $49 Call w(TNA) @ $1.47		2,628.31

Time Value = Profit When You Are Short an Option

With TNA trading at 48.43 the 49-Strike call is an out-of-the-money call consisting of only time value. At option expiration in one week, the time value of these options becomes profit regardless of the price movement of TNA.

162% Cash on Cash Return

Purchasing 100 shares of the TNA ETF at the current price of 48.43 and selling the 49-Strike call at 1.47 would cost $4,696 to initiate this covered call trade (48.43-1.47 = 46.96 x 100 = $4,696 cost basis). If you were to rollover this trade weekly and receive a similar premium you have the potential to collect $7,644 in cash over the next year. Receiving $7,644 in cash over the next year would result in a 162% 'cash on cash' return ($7,644 cash income / by original $4,696 investment cost = 162%).

If you receive a 162% cash on cash return a lot can go wrong and you could still profit from the trade. The underlying stock/ETF could decline substantially and you could still profit. If you had bad timing on entering the trade you could still profit. And there could be volatile price swings in the underlying stock/ETF and you could still profit. This gives the weekly covered call strategy a huge advantage over stock and option directional trades that require the stock or ETF price to move in the right direction to profit. Also many times directional trades can get 'stopped' out during volatile price swings if you employ a portfolio money management system.

162% Cash on Cash Return Can Profit

- If you have bad timing when entering a trade

- During volatile price swings

- Even if the underlying stock/ETF price declines substantially

Time Value = Profit When You Are Short an Option

With the TNA ETF trading at 48.43, the 49-Strike call option consists of only time value at option expiration. When you are short an option the time value portion of an option becomes profit as the time value decays to zero at expiration.

If the TNA ETF remains flat at 48.43 at weekly option expiration the 1.47 points of time value in the 49-Strike call becomes profit as the value of the option goes to zero.

If the TNA ETF increases in price at option expiration I still collect a 1.47 point time premium profit at expiration. The short option may show a loss if the TNA ETF increases in price above the 49 strike price but this loss is offset by an increase in the ETF price and I still wind up with a 1.47 point profit.

If the TNA ETF declines in price at expiration I collect a 1.47 point profit as the value of the short option goes to zero. This 1.47 point profit could be offset by a loss in the ETF price depending on how far the TNA ETF declines in price.

- If TNA remains flat at option expiration = $147 time value profit

- If TNA increases in price at option expiration = $147 time value profit

- If TNA decreases in price at option expiration = $147 time value profit (could be offset by loss in ETF value)

162% Return Potential Increases When I Rollover Options

I normally rollover my weekly options using an option spread order similar to the spread order just displayed for the TNA ETF. If you receive a cash income of $147 each week and a total income of $7.644 over the course of a year, this income will allow you to purchase additional shares of the TNA ETF and make additional covered call trades. This would allow you to compound your returns and increase the 162% cash on cash return.

The weekly option covered call strategy offers very attractive returns and very low risk making this one of the best overall strategies for the average investor.

Selling Weekly Option Premium

My brokerage account Transaction History below shows that I have been active selling weekly option premium. I sold $16,053.53 in option premium recently over a one week period. The right hand column of the Report shows the amount of cash that was credited to my account for each option sale. These covered call trades were in my retirement accounts.

$16,053.53 Weekly Paycheck

Transaction History   Alerts | Transfer Money | Bill Pay | ? Help

| Transactions | Check Summary | Deposit Summary | Categories | Reports |

Date	Type	View	Description	Categories (hide)	Amount ($)
04/13/12	Sold Short		10 HD Apr 21 '12 $50 Call(HD) @ $1.00		984.38
04/12/12	Sold Short		10 SSO Apr 21 '12 $57 Call(SSO) @ $0.70		684.41
04/12/12	Sold Short		1 MA Apr 21 '12 $435 Call(MA) @ $5.10		501.23
04/12/12	Sold Short		2 AAPL Apr 21 '12 $630 Call(AAPL) @ $9.00		1,790.44
04/12/12	Sold Short		1 PCLN Apr 21 '12 $740 Call(PCLN) @ $14.40		1,431.21
04/12/12	Sold Short		8 QQQ Apr 21 '12 $67 Call(QQQ) @ $0.70		545.93
04/12/12	Sold Short		15 WFC Apr 21 '12 $34 Call(WFC) @ $0.61		899.56
04/12/12	Sold Short		1 CMG Apr 21 '12 $435 Call(CMG) @ $8.37		832.23
04/12/12	Sold Short		12 JPM Apr 21 '12 $45 Call(JPM) @ $0.75		886.88
04/12/12	Sold Short		8 AIG Apr 21 '12 $34 Call(AIG) @ $0.45		345.94
04/12/12	Sold Short		8 AIG Apr 21 '12 $33 Call(AIG) @ $0.72		561.93
04/11/12	Sold Short		1 ISRG Apr 21 '12 $550 Call(ISRG) @ $12.43		1,234.22
04/12/12	Sold Short		1 MA Apr 21 '12 $435 Call(MA) @ $4.90		481.23
04/12/12	Sold Short		1 AAPL Apr 21 '12 $630 Call(AAPL) @ $9.00		891.22
04/12/12	Sold Short		1 PCLN Apr 21 '12 $740 Call(PCLN) @ $14.38		1,433.21
04/12/12	Sold Short		4 QQQ Apr 21 '12 $67 Call(QQQ) @ $0.71		272.97
04/12/12	Sold Short		8 WFC Apr 21 '12 $34 Call(WFC) @ $0.55		429.94
04/12/12	Sold Short		1 CMG Apr 21 '12 $435 Call(CMG) @ $9.56		951.22
04/12/12	Sold Short		6 JPM Apr 21 '12 $45 Call(JPM) @ $0.77		453.44
04/12/12	Sold Short		4 AIG Apr 21 '12 $34 Call(AIG) @ $0.44		164.97
04/12/12	Sold Short		4 AIG Apr 21 '12 $33 Call(AIG) @ $0.72		276.97

Selling Weekly Option Premium

And the brokerage account Transaction History below shows that I have been increasing my weekly covered call trades. I sold $28,454.92 in weekly option premium over this one week period. The right hand column of the Report shows the amount of cash that was credited to my account for each option sale. These covered call trades were in my retirement accounts.

$28,454.92 Weekly Paycheck

Transaction History: Reports

Alerts | Transfer Money | Bill Pay | Help

| Transactions | Check Summary | Deposit Summary | Categories | Reports |

Type	Date	Category	Subcategory	Description	Amount
Sold Short					
	05/16/12	Unassigned		1 MA May 19 '12 $410 Call(MA) MASTERCARD INC CL A SHORT...	$482.23
	05/16/12	Unassigned		2 AAPL May 19 '12 $550 Call(AAPL) APPLE INC COM SHORT...	$1,172.46
	05/16/12	Unassigned		50 USO May 19 '12 $35 Call(USO) UNITED STATES OIL FUND,...	$2,304.05
	05/16/12	Unassigned		38 EEM May 19 '12 $38 Call(EEM) ISHARES MSCI EMERGING M...	$1,977.16
	05/16/12	Unassigned		51 FXI May 19 '12 $34 Call(FXI) ISHARES FTSE CHINA 25 L...	$2,299.29
	05/16/12	Unassigned		18 EWZ May 19 '12 $53 Call(EWZ) ISHARES MSCI BRAZIL IND...	$1,130.28
	05/16/12	Unassigned		13 HD May 19 '12 $49 Call(HD) HOME DEPOT INC COM SHORT...	$502.14
	05/15/12	Unassigned		18 XLE May 19 '12 $66 Call(XLE) ENERGY SELECT SECTOR SP...	$878.34
	05/15/12	Unassigned		10 EFA May 19 '12 $50 Call(EFA) ISHARES MSCI EAFE INDEX...	$524.37
	05/15/12	Unassigned		23 FXI May 19 '12 $35 Call(FXI) ISHARES FTSE CHINA 25 L...	$802.56
	05/15/12	Unassigned		15 EWZ May 19 '12 $54 Call(EWZ) ISHARES MSCI BRAZIL IND...	$1,090.61
	05/14/12	Unassigned		14 EFA May 19 '12 $50 Call(EFA) ISHARES MSCI EAFE INDEX...	$1,105.31
	05/14/12	Unassigned		21 FXI May 19 '12 $35 Call(FXI) ISHARES FTSE CHINA 25 L...	$757.07
	05/14/12	Unassigned		21 EWZ May 19 '12 $55 Call(EWZ) ISHARES MSCI BRAZIL IND...	$1,261.06
	05/11/12	Unassigned		15 WFC May 19 '12 $33 Call(WFC) WELLS FARGO & CO NEW CO...	$944.61
	05/11/12	Unassigned		2 AAPL May 19 '12 $570 Call(AAPL) APPLE INC COM SHORT...	$1,330.46
	05/11/12	Unassigned		12 USO May 19 '12 $36 Call(USO) UNITED STATES OIL FUND,...	$796.89
	05/11/12	Unassigned		9 EFA May 19 '12 $51 Call(EFA) ISHARES MSCI EAFE INDEX...	$759.15
	05/11/12	Unassigned		12 FXI May 19 '12 $35 Call(FXI) ISHARES FTSE CHINA 25 L...	$882.88
	05/11/12	Unassigned		8 EWZ May 19 '12 $57 Call(EWZ) ISHARES MSCI BRAZIL INDE...	$561.89
	05/10/12	Unassigned		1 MA May 19 '12 $425 Call(MA) MASTERCARD INC CL A SHORT...	$601.23
	05/10/12	Unassigned		20 USO May 19 '12 $37 Call(USO) UNITED STATES OIL FUND,...	$796.83
	05/10/12	Unassigned		13 HD May 19 '12 $50 Call(HD) HOME DEPOT INC COM SHORT...	$1,607.10
	05/10/12	Unassigned		14 EFA May 19 '12 $52 Call(EFA) ISHARES MSCI EAFE INDEX...	$751.36
	05/10/12	Unassigned		21 FXI May 19 '12 $36 Call(FXI) ISHARES FTSE CHINA 25 L...	$900.06
	05/10/12	Unassigned		13 EWZ May 19 '12 $57 Call(EWZ) ISHARES MSCI BRAZIL IND...	$1,347.12
	05/10/12	Unassigned		1 CMG May 19 '12 $410 Call(CMG) CHIPOTLE MEXICAN GRILL...	$496.23
	05/10/12	Unassigned		9 WMB May 19 '12 $33 Call(WMB) WILLIAMS COS INC DEL COM...	$390.18
				Total Sold Short	**$28,454.92**

Double Dipping

When trading covered calls, if the underlying stock/ETF declines in price I like to close the short call if the value of the short call declines 75% to 85% from the sale price. For example, If I sell a weekly call option at 1.00 points I will enter a GTC (Good Until Cancelled) limit order to buy to close the call at .25 or .15. If the call declines to .25 or .15 it will be closed out. I can then sell another call option and collect two premiums in one week.

The first brokerage account Transaction History Report below shows short calls that I closed out when the value of the call declined 75% to 85% from the sale price. The second brokerage account Transaction History Report shows additional calls I sold that allowed me to collect an additional $6,618.22 in premium within a one week period.

Bought Back Short Calls

Transaction History

Alerts | Transfer Money | Bill Pay | Help

| Transactions | Check Summary | Deposit Summary | Categories | Reports |

Date	Type	View	Description	Categories (hide)	Amount ($)
04/16/12	Bought To Cover		2 AAPL Apr 21 '12 $630 Call(AAPL) @ $0.76		-161.51
04/16/12	Bought To Cover		1 PCLN Apr 21 '12 $740 Call(PCLN) @ $2.90		-298.75
04/16/12	Bought To Cover		8 QQQ Apr 21 '12 $67 Call(QQQ) @ $0.12		-110.05
04/16/12	Bought To Cover		1 AAPL Apr 21 '12 $630 Call(AAPL) @ $0.78		-86.75
04/16/12	Bought To Cover		1 PCLN Apr 21 '12 $740 Call(PCLN) @ $3.30		-338.75
04/16/12	Bought To Cover		4 QQQ Apr 21 '12 $67 Call(QQQ) @ $0.12		-59.03

And Sold an Additional $6,618.22 in Premium

Transaction History

Alerts | Transfer Money | Bill Pay | Help

| Transactions | Check Summary | Deposit Summary | Categories | Reports |

Date	Type	View	Description	Categories (hide)	Amount ($)
04/17/12	Sold Short		1 PCLN Apr 21 '12 $720 Call(PCLN) @ $9.60		951.22
04/17/12	Sold Short		2 AAPL Apr 21 '12 $600 Call(AAPL) @ $10.00		1,990.44
04/17/12	Sold Short		8 QQQ Apr 21 '12 $66 Call(QQQ) @ $0.60		465.93
04/17/12	Sold Short		1 PCLN Apr 21 '12 $720 Call(PCLN) @ $10.00		991.22
04/17/12	Sold Short		2 AAPL Apr 21 '12 $600 Call(AAPL) @ $10.00		1,990.44
04/17/12	Sold Short		4 QQQ Apr 21 '12 $66 Call(QQQ) @ $0.60		228.97

Covered Call Trade Examples

The weekly covered call trade examples that follow include my brokerage confirmations that show the purchase price of the stock and the strike price and option premium for the call option sold. The Covered Call Calculator shows the annualized profit potential for the covered call trade.

Buy ISRG at 541.225, Sell Apr 21 550 call @ 12.43

View Orders											

Open | **Executed** | Cancelled | Individual Fills | Expired | Rejected | All | 2-Second Execution Guarantee | Bond Quotes

Orders   † = Share-weighted Average   * = Execution Guarantee Eligible

Date	Order #	Type	Order Type	Quantity (Exec / Entered)	Symbol	Price Type	Term	Price	Price Executed	Status	Related Links
04/11/12	2942	Option	Buy Sell Open	100 1	ISRG ISRG Apr 21 '12 $550 Call	Net Debit	Day	528.80	541.225 12.43	Executed	Portfolios

Covered Calls

Stock	Entry Date	Option Expiration	Stock Price	Call Strike	Call Price	Cost	Net Profit Potential	Percent Return	Annualized Return
ISRG	4/11/2012	4/21/2012	541.22	550.0	12.43	528.79	$2,121	4.0%	146.4%

Buy AIG at 33.25, Sell Apr 21 34 call @ .45

View Orders											

Open | **Executed** | Cancelled | Individual Fills | Expired | Rejected | All | 2-Second Execution Guarantee | Bond Quotes

Orders   † = Share-weighted Average   * = Execution Guarantee Eligible

Date	Order #	Type	Order Type	Quantity (Exec / Entered)	Symbol	Price Type	Term	Price	Price Executed	Status	Related Links
04/12/12	2972	Option	Buy Sell Open	800 8	AIG AIG Apr 21 '12 $34 Call	Net Debit	Day	32.80	33.25 0.45	Executed	Portfolios

Covered Calls

Stock	Entry Date	Option Expiration	Stock Price	Call Strike	Call Price	Cost	Net Profit Potential	Percent Return	Annualized Return
AIG	4/12/2012	4/21/2012	33.25	34.0	0.45	32.80	$120	3.7%	148.4%

Rolling Over Expiring Options

I like to rollover my weekly covered call trades using option spread orders. Option spread orders help reduce commission costs and can help you to save on the 'bid/ask' spread costs associated with buying and selling options if you use a limit spread order that is mid-way between the bid/ask prices. I normally can get filled on spread orders at a limit price that is mid-way between the bid/ask prices.

Examples of option spread orders used to rollover my expiring weekly covered call trades follow.

Spread Orders Used to Rollover Weekly Covered Calls

Enter Order: Options

| Stocks | Options | Mutual Funds | Bonds | Conditional |

Account: DBP ▼   Positions ▼   Orders ▼   Alerts ▼   LEVEL❹

[+] Purchasing Power

| Basic | Spreads | Buy-Writes | Butterfly ▼ | Condor ▼ |

Symbol 🔍

hd   GO   OPTIONS CHAIN

EXAMPLE: IBM, SPY

HOME DEPOT INC COM (HD)   ↻ Refresh

| 46.89 -0.05 (-0.12%) | Bid: 46.89 | Ask: 46.9 | Vol: 6,849,518 |

2/24/12 2:10:00 PM ET

Order Type	Contracts	Type	Expiration	Strike		Last	Bid (Size)	Ask (size)	Volume
Buy Close ▼	10	Call ▼	Feb 24 '12w ▼	47.0 ▼		0.10*	0.01 (257)	0.04 (353)	2,345
Sell Open ▼	10	Call ▼	Mar 2 '12w ▼	47.0 ▼		0.41**	0.36 (157)	0.39 (103)	536
						[?] Net: 0.38 [?]		0.32 [?]	

Price Type	Price	Term	
Net Credit ▼	.35	Good For The Day ▼	☐ All-or-none

[?] MIDPOINT: $0.35

*2/24/12 1:24:00 PM ET   **2/24/12 2:03:00 PM ET

Real Time   ↻ Refresh

Buy Close 10 HD Feb 24 '12 $47 Call w **and Sell Open 10** HD Mar 02 '12 $47 Call w **at $.35 Net Credit**

PREVIEW ORDER

Spread Orders Used to Rollover Weekly Covered Calls

Enter Order: Options

| Stocks | Options | Mutual Funds | Bonds | Conditional |

Account: DBP ▼   Positions ▼   Orders ▼   Alerts ▼   LEVEL ❹ 🎓 ❓

⊞ Purchasing Power

| Basic | Spreads | Buy-Writes | NEW Butterfly ▼ | NEW Condor ▼ |

Symbol 🔍 | **APPLE INC COM (AAPL)** | ↻ Refresh

| aapl | GO ⊠ OPTIONS CHAIN | **521.62** +5.23 (+1.01%) | Bid: **521.59** | Ask: **521.63** | Vol: **10,394,424** |
EXAMPLE: IBM, SPY | | | 2/24/12 2:18:00 PM ET

Order Type	Contracts	Type	Expiration	Strike		Last	Bid (Size)	Ask (size)	Volume
Buy Close ▼	1	Call ▼	Feb 24 '12w ▼	505.0 ▼		16.94*	16.55 (1)	16.70 (54)	2,508
Sell Open ▼	1	Call ▼	Mar 2 '12w ▼	525.0 ▼		5.14**	5.05 (7)	5.15 (34)	7,974

Price Type	Price	Term		
Net Debit ▼	11.55	Good For The Day ▼	☐ All-or-none	

| ❓ Net: | 11.40 | ❓ | 11.65 | ❓ |
*2/24/12 2:15:00 PM ET   **2/24/12 2:17:00 PM ET

❓ MIDPOINT: $11.53

Real Time   ↻ Refresh

Buy Close 1 AAPL Feb 24 '12 $505 Call w **and Sell Open 1** AAPL Mar 02 '12 $525 Call w **at $11.55 Net Debit**

PREVIEW ORDER

Enter Order: Options

| Stocks | Options | Mutual Funds | Bonds | Conditional |

Account: PSP ▼   Positions ▼   Orders ▼   Alerts ▼   LEVEL ❹ 🎓 ❓

⊞ Purchasing Power

| Basic | Spreads | Buy-Writes | NEW Butterfly ▼ | NEW Condor ▼ |

Symbol 🔍 | **ISHARES MSCI EMERGING MARKETS INDEX FUND (EEM)** | ↻ Refresh

| eem | GO ⊠ OPTIONS CHAIN | **44.13** +0.38 (+0.87%) | Bid: **44.12** | Ask: **44.13** | Vol: **22,405,040** |
EXAMPLE: IBM, SPY | | | 2/24/12 2:23:00 PM ET

Order Type	Contracts	Type	Expiration	Strike		Last	Bid (Size)	Ask (size)	Volume
Buy Close ▼	5	Call ▼	Feb 24 '12w ▼	44.0 ▼		0.16*	0.15 (67)	0.17 (603)	1,348
Sell Open ▼	5	Call ▼	Mar 2 '12w ▼	44.0 ▼		0.59**	0.55 (730)	0.58 (616)	419

Price Type	Price	Term		
Net Credit ▼	.41	Good For The Day ▼	☐ All-or-none	

| ❓ Net: | 0.43 | ❓ | 0.38 | ❓ |
*2/24/12 2:22:00 PM ET   **2/24/12 2:05:00 PM ET

❓ MIDPOINT: $0.41

Real Time   ↻ Refresh

Buy Close 5 EEM Feb 24 '12 $44 Call w **and Sell Open 5** EEM Mar 02 '12 $44 Call w **at $.41 Net Credit**

PREVIEW ORDER

Weekly Options Provide Up to Six Times More Premium Than Monthly Options

The option chain below displays option prices for the Mastercard May 04 weekly options and the MA July monthly options. Mastercard stock is trading at 457.58 and the at-the-money 460-Strike weekly call is trading at 11.90. The July 460-Strike monthly option is trading at 23.50 and expires in about 12 weeks.

Selling 12 of the MA weekly calls at 11.90 can provide up to 142 points ($14,280) of premium versus the 23.50 points of premium available for the July option over the same period of time. This demonstrates the substantial additional premium available from selling weekly options versus monthly options.

12 Weeklys Provide 142.8 Points of Premium versus 23.5 Points of Premium for Monthly

MASTERCARD INC CL A | S&P Capital IQ Options Report What's

Symbol	Bid	Ask	Last	Change	Change %	B/A Size	High	L
MA	458.00	458.00	457.58	3.60	0.79	700X100	462.3399	4

Calls and Puts | Learn more

| MA Apr 27 2012 | -1 Days to Expiration (Weeklys) |

| MA May 4 2012 | 4 Days to Expiration (Weeklys) |

Calls

Calls	Bid	Ask	Last	Change	Vol	Op Int	Strike
445.0 Call	19.75	21.50	20.50	1.99	0	88	445.00
450.0 Call	17.25	18.30	17.96	2.36	0	198	450.00
455.0 Call	14.15	15.50	15.09	2.13	0	143	455.00
460.0 Call	11.90	12.75	12.00	1.38	0	130	460.00
465.0 Call	9.65	10.65	10.15	1.58	0	82	465.00
470.0 Call	7.95	8.80	8.63	1.83	0	107	470.00

Color Indicates options that are in-the-money Indicates non-standard option

MA May 19 2012	19 Days to Expiration
MA Jun 16 2012	47 Days to Expiration
MA Jul 21 2012	82 Days to Expiration

Calls

Calls	Bid	Ask	Last	Change	Vol	Op Int	Strike
445.0 Call	31.75	32.30	30.40	1.03	0	126	445.00
450.0 Call	28.85	29.40	29.65	3.05	0	364	450.00
455.0 Call	26.15	26.55	26.60	2.76	0	361	455.00
460.0 Call	23.50	23.90	24.06	2.83	0	339	460.00
465.0 Call	21.05	21.55	22.03	2.97	0	282	465.00

Below is another example of the substantial option premium available from selling weekly options. The option chain below displays option prices for the AIG May 04 weekly options and the AIG Aug monthly options. AIG stock is trading at 34.46 and the 35-Strike weekly call is trading at .71. The Aug 35-Strike monthly option is trading at 2.39 and expires in about 16 weeks.

If you sold 16 weekly calls at .71 you would collect about 11.36 points of premium versus the 2.39 points of premium available for the Aug option over the same period of time. This again demonstrates the additional premium available from selling weekly options versus monthly options.

16 Weeklys Provide 11.36 Points of Premium versus 2.39 Points of Premium for Monthly

AMERICAN INTL GROUP INC COM NEW | S&P Capital IQ Options

Symbol	Bid	Ask	Last	Change	Change %	B/A Size	High	Low
AIG	34.48	34.50	34.46	0.75	2.18	100X1500	34.91	33.41

Calls and Puts | Learn more

AIG Apr 27 2012 — -1 Days to Expiration (Weeklys)

AIG May 4 2012 — 4 Days to Expiration (Weeklys)

Calls	Bid	Ask	Last	Change	Vol	Op Int	Strike
32.0 Call	2.53	2.77	2.83	0.80	0	101	32.00
33.0 Call	1.81	1.85	1.85	0.51	0	997	33.00
34.0 Call	1.17	1.22	1.25	0.42	0	842	34.00
35.0 Call	0.71	0.72	0.74	0.27	0	1,686	35.00
36.0 Call	0.39	0.43	0.40	0.15	0	233	36.00
37.0 Call	0.20	0.23	0.21	0.08	0	29	37.00

Color Indicates options that are in-the-money **NS** Indicates non-standard option

AIG May 19 2012 — 19 Days to Expiration

AIG Jun 16 2012 — 47 Days to Expiration

AIG Aug 18 2012 — 110 Days to Expiration

Calls	Bid	Ask	Last	Change	Vol	Op Int	Strike
32.0 Call	4.05	4.20	4.16	0.56	0	12,755	32.00
33.0 Call	3.45	3.55	3.50	0.47	0	6,762	33.00
34.0 Call	2.89	2.95	2.93	0.42	0	2,873	34.00
35.0 Call	2.39	2.45	2.54	0.48	0	43,121	35.00
36.0 Call	1.95	2.00	2.03	0.37	0	5,646	36.00

Real Time Covered Call Results
$332,597.96 in Profits and 36.9% Average Return

Copies of my two brokerage account Profit/Loss statements that follow show I currently have $332,597.96 in profits and an average return of 36.9%. Most of the trades in these two portfolios are weekly Covered Calls. Both of these accounts are retirement accounts.

Portfolios   Alerts | Transfer Money | Bill Pay | Help

| Portfolios | Performance & Value | Positions | Gains & Losses | Risk Analyzer | Portfolio Analyzer | Income Estimator |

Account/Watch List: 919 PSP ▾   Create / Edit List   View: Performance ▾   Customize /

Market Value: $422,13 .12 $116,935.13   DJIA 13,199.55 ▼ -64.94 (-0.49%) Nasdaq 3,113.57 ▼ -6.13 (-0.20%)

REFRESH ↻   STREAMING QUOTES   EXPORT TO EXCEL* ⬇   Results per Page: 200 ▾

Symbol	Buy / Sell / Trade	Last Trade	Change $	Change %	Day's Gain	Qty	Price Paid	Total Gain $	Total Gain %	Market Val	Edit
⊞ AAPL	Buy / Sell	629.32	10.69	1.73%	$3,207.00	300	$400.34	$68,0 1. 6	7. 5%	$188,796.00	Edit
⊞ CMG	Buy / Sell	422.26	3.86	0.92%	$675.50	175	$417.37	$831.53	1.14%	$73,895.50	Edit
⊞ HD	Buy / Sell	50.00	0.01	0.02%	$10.00	1,000	$45.07	$4,909.66	10.89%	$50,000.00	Edit
⊞ JPM	Buy / Sell	45.42	-0.41	-0.89%	-$492.00	1,200	$38.92	$7,790.02	16.68%	$54,504.00	Edit
⊞ PCLN	Buy / Sell	743.62	23.65	3.28%	$3,547.50	150	$719.69	$3,574.02	3.31%	$111,543.00	Edit
⊞ QQQ	Buy / Sell	68.23	-0.02	-0.03%	-$16.00	800	$61.19	$5,601.04	11.43%	$54,584.00	Edit
⊞ SSO	Buy / Sell	58.80	-0.41	-0.69%	-$410.00	1,000	$54.94	$3,844.02	6.99%	$58,800.00	Edit
⊞ TJX	Buy / Sell	39.61	-0.26	-0.65%	-$624.00	2,400	$31.28	$19,964.05	26.58%	$95,064.00	Edit
⊞ WFC	Buy / Sell	34.48	-0.03	-0.09%	-$48.00	1,600	$31.43	$4,864.02	9.67%	$55,168.00	Edit
⊞ AAPL Apr 05 '12 $615 Call w	Trade	15.45	7.05	83.93%	-$705.00	-1	$6.10	-$939.77	-152.87%	-$1,545.00	Edit
⊞ CMG Apr 05 '12 $420 Call w	Trade	4.00	1.50	60.00%	-$150.00	-1	$3.10	-$94.76	-30.10%	-$400.00	Edit
⊞ HD Apr 05 '12 $50 Call w	Trade	0.22	-0.08	-26.67%	$40.00	-5	$0.31	$37.20	22.85%	-$110.00	Edit
⊞ JPM Apr 05 '12 $46 Call w	Trade	0.16	-0.14	-46.67%	$84.00	-6	$0.32	$87.44	43.60%	-$96.00	Edit
⊞ PCLN Apr 05 '12 $715 Call w	Trade	28.90	18.90	189.00%	-$1,890.00	-1	$12.04	-$1,690.77	-139.88%	-$2,890.00	Edit
⊞ QQQ Apr 05 '12 $68 Call w	Trade	0.50	0.02	4.17%	-$4.00*	-4	$0.30	-$83.04*	-65.36%*	-$196.00*	Edit
⊞ SSO Apr 05 '12 $58 Call w	Trade	0.95	-0.39	-29.10%	$205.00*	-5	$0.53	-$217.80	-79.84%	-$475.00	Edit
⊞ WFC Apr 05 '12 $34 Call w	Trade	0.55	-0.06	-9.84%	$48.00	-8	$0.33	-$186.09	-67.89%	-$440.00	Edit
					Totals $3,478.00			$116,935.13		$422,133.12	

172

Portfolios

Alerts | Transfer Money | Bill Pay | Help

| Portfolios | Performance & Value | Positions | Gains & Losses | Risk Analyzer | Portfolio Analyzer | Income Estimator |

Account/Watch List: 918 DBP ▼ Create / Edit List   **View:** Performance ▼ Customize /

Market Value: $820,939.7? **$215,662.83**   DJIA 13,199.55 ▼ -64.94 (-0.49%) **Nasdaq** 3,113.57 ▼ -6.13 (-0.20%)

REFRESH ⟳   STREAMING QUOTES   EXPORT TO EXCEL* ⬇   Results per Page: 200 ▼

Symbol		Last Trade	Change $	Change %	Day's Gain	Qty	Price Paid	Total Gain $	Total Gain %	Market Val	Edit
⊞ AAPL	Buy / Sell	629.32	10.69	1.73%	$4,276.00	400	$400.36	$91,527.17	57.13%	$251,728.00	Edit
⊞ AGNC	Buy / Sell	30.06	0.15	0.50%	$1,003.65	6,691	$26.37	$24,684.60	13.99%	$201,131.46	Edit
⊞ CMG	Buy / Sell	422.26	3.86	0.92%	$579.00	150	$417.05	$765.52	1.22%	$63,339.00	Edit
⊞ HD	Buy / Sell	50.00	0.01	0.02%	$20.00	2,000	$46.17	$7,636.11	8.27%	$100,000.00	Edit
⊞ JPM	Buy / Sell	45.42	-0.41	-0.89%	-$984.00	2,400	$39.65	$13,811.04	14.51%	$109,008.00	Edit
⊞ MLPL	Buy / Sell	42.07	0.49	1.18%	$2,505.97	5,114.22958	$36.30	$29,445.19	15.86%	$215,155.64	Edit
⊞ PCLN	Buy / Sell	743.62	23.65	3.28%	$3,547.50	150	$719.98	$3,529.52	3.27%	$111,543.00	Edit
⊞ QQQ	Buy / Sell	68.23	-0.02	-0.03%	-$30.00	1,500	$60.99	$10,831.53	11.84%	$102,345.00	Edit
⊞ SSO	Buy / Sell	58.80	-0.41	-0.69%	-$820.00	2,000	$55.67	$6,229.53	5.59%	$117,600.00	Edit
⊞ TJX	Buy / Sell	39.61	-0.26	-0.65%	-$780.00	3,000	$30.82	$26,336.03	28.47%	$118,830.00	Edit
⊞ WFC	Buy / Sell	34.48	-0.03	-0.09%	-$90.00	3,000	$31.35	$9,376.27	9.97%	$103,440.00	Edit
⊞ AAPL Apr 05 '12 $615 Call w	Trade	15.45	7.05	83.93%	-$1,410.00	-2	$6.53	-$1,789.54	-136.45%	-$3,090.00	Edit
⊞ CMG Apr 05 '12 $420 Call w	Trade	4.00	1.50	60.00%	-$150.00	-1	$3.46	-$58.76	-16.75%	-$400.00	Edit
⊞ HD Apr 05 '12 $50 Call w	Trade	0.22	-0.08	-26.67%	$80.00	-10	$0.33	$98.39	28.80%	-$220.00	Edit
⊞ JPM Apr 05 '12 $46 Call w	Trade	0.16	-0.14	-46.67%	$168.00	-12	$0.34	$202.86	48.17%	-$192.00	Edit
⊞ PCLN Apr 05 '12 $715 Call w	Trade	28.90	18.90	189.00%	-$1,890.00	-1	$11.97	-$1,697.78	-141.27%	-$2,890.00	Edit
⊞ QQQ Apr 05 '12 $68 Call w	Trade	0.50	0.02	4.17%	-$8.00*	-8	$0.32	-$146.09*	-54.90%*	-$392.00*	Edit
⊞ SSO Apr 05 '12 $58 Call w	Trade	0.95	-0.39	-29.10%	$410.00*	-10	$0.54	-$421.61	-76.43%	-$950.00	Edit
⊞ TJX Jan 19 '13 $28.75 Call	Trade	11.30	11.30	—	$70.00*	-7	$5.05	-$4,381.73	-123.72%	-$7,910.00	Edit
⊞ WFC Apr 05 '12 $34 Call w	Trade	0.55	-0.06	-9.84%	$90.00	-15	$0.35	-$315.42	-58.37%	-$825.00	Edit

2011 Weekly Covered Calls   Profits $323,069.44   Avg Return 54.8%

My brokerage account Profit/Loss Report below shows $323,069.44 in profits and an average return of 54.8% from weekly covered call trades that I took about 13 months ago. These covered calls were traded in my retirement account.

Portfolios

Alerts | Transfer Money | Bill Pay | Help

Portfolios   Performance & Value   Positions   Gains & Losses   Risk Analyzer   Portfolio Analyzer   Income Estimator

Account/Watch List: QQP   Create / Edit List   View: Performance   Customize /

Market Value: $912,396.29 $323,069.44   DJIA 12,391.25 ▲ +73.11 (+0.59%) Nasdaq 2,833.95 ▲ +2.37 (+0.08%)

REFRESH   STREAMING QUOTES   EXPORT TO EXCEL   Results per Page: 200

Symbol		Last Trade	Change $	Change %	Day's Gain	Qty	Price Paid	Total Gain $	Total Gain %	Market Val	Edit
AAPL	Buy / Sell	350.56	-7.74	-2.16%	-$3,870.00	500	$273.62	$38,431.65	28.08%	$175,280.00	Edit
BIDU	Buy / Sell	126.80	-1.74	-1.35%	-$2,436.00	1,400	$84.47	$59,216.38	50.05%	$177,520.00	Edit
DIG	Buy / Sell	58.68	0.58	1.00%	$1,740.00	3,000	$49.38	$27,890.02	18.83%	$176,040.00	✕
FAS	Buy / Sell	34.26	0.18	0.53%	$1,080.00	6,000	$29.55	$28,182.17	15.89%	$205,560.00	✕
NOV	Buy / Sell	80.18	-1.22	-1.50%	-$2,440.00	2,000	$63.05	$34,208.41	27.12%	$160,360.00	Edit
QLD	Buy / Sell	94.44	-0.39	-0.41%	-$1,404.00	3,600	$70.25	$87,003.57	34.39%	$339,984.00	Edit
SSO	Buy / Sell	54.78	0.22	0.40%	$660.00	3,000	$50.61	$12,482.02	8.22%	$164,340.00	✕
UWM	Buy / Sell	48.34	0.12	0.25%	$456.00	3,800	$44.19	$15,748.05	9.38%	$183,692.00	✕
UYM	Buy / Sell	54.75	-1.32	-2.35%	-$4,208.00	3,200	$48.69	$19,336.13	12.41%	$175,200.00	Edit
BIDU Mar 19 '11 $130 Call	Trade	2.96	-0.89	-23.12%	$890.00	-10	$4.737	$1,761.28	37.06%	-$2,960.00	Edit
DIG Mar 19 '11 $58 Call	Trade	2.55	0.00	0.00%	$-0.00	-12	$1.72	-$1,009.19	-48.58%	-$3,060.00	Edit
DIG Mar 19 '11 $59 Call	Trade	2.05	0.05	2.50%	-$45.00	-9	$1.37	-$622.89	-50.08%	-$1,845.00	Edit
FAS Mar 19 '11 $36 Call	Trade	0.97	-0.05	-4.90%	$210.00	-42	$1.00	$89.86	2.12%	-$4,074.00	Edit
NOV Mar 19 '11 $85 Call	Trade	1.18	-0.47	-28.48%	$658.00	-14	$1.47	$391.28	18.88%	-$1,652.00	Edit
QLD Mar 19 '11 $96 Call	Trade	2.15	-0.51	-19.17%	$735.00*	-15	$2.49	$464.49*	12.38%*	-$3,255.00*	Edit
QLD Mar 19 '11 $97 Call	Trade	1.80	-0.36	-16.67%	$396.00	-11	$2.1827	$404.57	16.74%	-$1,980.00	Edit
SSO Mar 19 '11 $55 Call	Trade	1.38	0.02	1.47%	-$63.00*	-21	$1.24	-$335.07*	-12.77%*	-$2,919.00*	Edit
UWM Mar 19 '11 $49 Call	Trade	1.65	-0.08	-4.62%	$224.00	-28	$1.25	-$1,117.44	-31.45%	-$4,620.00	Edit
UYM Mar 19 '11 $57 Call	Trade	1.45	-0.63	-30.29%	$1,197.00	-19	$1.68	$418.44	13.03%	-$2,755.00	Edit
					Totals -$6,070.00			$323,069.44		$912,396.29	

Snapshot of My 2009 Trading Contest Account

My brokerage account Profit/Loss Report below is a snapshot of my 2009 real money trading contest account. I traded monthly covered calls in this contest account. I placed first in the competition with an Annual Return of 122%. The contest results are audited and posted on the World Cup website so the results are an accurate representation of your performance.

I traded monthly covered calls and rolled over the options which allowed me to compound my returns. Covered calls produced a great annual return in this account with low risk.

Realized P&L on Closed Positions

Symbol	Date Bought	Date Sold	Shares	Cost Basis	Sales Price	Gain-loss
+FCXEG	3/26/2009 11:59:59 PM	3/17/2009 12:46:27 PM	10	$0.00	$5,164.89	$5,164.89
+FCXEG	3/26/2009 11:59:59 PM	3/18/2009 3:18:38 PM	5	$0.00	$3,022.44	$3,022.44
+FPAEG	4/30/2009 10:18:36 AM	3/26/2009 11:59:59 PM	15	$11,697.59	$0.00	-$11,697.59
+GSGM	3/25/2009 3:40:27 PM	5/6/2009 10:00:37 AM	15	$72,027.59	$109,244.57	$37,216.98
+GSGS	5/6/2009 10:00:37 AM	3/25/2009 3:40:27 PM	15	$65,832.59	$38,492.16	-$27,340.43
+NOVEF	5/4/2009 11:59:59 PM	3/17/2009 12:49:34 PM	10	$3,218.39	$3,564.89	$346.50
+NOVEF	5/4/2009 11:59:59 PM	3/18/2009 3:36:31 PM	5	$1,609.20	$1,722.45	$113.25
+YCPAU	5/8/2009 11:59:59 PM	5/1/2009 12:36:20 PM	15	$0.00	$9,422.13	$9,422.13
+YFQAW	5/8/2009 11:59:59 PM	5/6/2009 3:17:12 PM	15	$0.00	$10,307.11	$10,307.11
+YHBAE	5/8/2009 11:59:59 PM	5/1/2009 1:41:20 PM	15	$0.00	$7,322.19	$7,322.19
FCX	3/17/2009 12:45:32 PM	4/30/2009 10:20:38 AM	800	$29,052.72	$33,960.39	$4,907.67
FCX	3/17/2009 12:45:32 PM	4/30/2009 10:20:38 AM	200	$7,282.20	$8,490.10	$1,207.90
FCX	3/18/2009 3:17:41 PM	4/30/2009 10:20:38 AM	300	$11,353.77	$12,735.15	$1,381.38
FCX	3/18/2009 3:17:41 PM	4/30/2009 10:20:38 AM	100	$3,784.60	$4,245.05	$460.45
FCX	3/18/2009 3:17:41 PM	4/30/2009 10:20:38 AM	100	$3,804.58	$4,245.05	$440.47
NOV	3/17/2009 12:48:27 PM	5/4/2009 10:13:50 AM	100	$2,987.60	$3,271.87	$284.27
NOV	3/17/2009 12:48:27 PM	5/4/2009 10:13:50 AM	200	$5,995.20	$6,543.75	$548.55
NOV	3/17/2009 12:48:27 PM	5/4/2009 10:13:50 AM	500	$14,938.00	$16,359.37	$1,421.37
NOV	3/17/2009 12:48:27 PM	5/4/2009 10:13:50 AM	200	$5,975.20	$6,543.75	$568.55
NOV	3/18/2009 3:35:49 PM	5/4/2009 10:13:50 AM	500	$14,898.00	$16,359.37	$1,461.37

Total Realized Gain-Loss: $46,559.45

Unrealized P&L on Open Positions

Symbol	Description	Position	Avg Price	Cost Basis	Market Value	Type	Unrealized Val.
+AASAH	Allegheny Technologies Inc Jan 2010 40.00 Call	-15	$0.0000	$0.00	$0.00	Stock Option	$0.00
+CLFAA	Cliffs Natural Resources Inc Jan 2010 20.00 Call	-15	$0.0000	$0.00	$0.00	Stock Option	$0.00
+CLFGD	Cliffs Natural Resources Inc Jul 2009 20.00 Call	-15	-$3.5715	$5,357.31	-$17,550.00	Stock Option	-$12,192.69
+CXJHD	Caterpillar Inc Del Aug 2009 30.00 Call	-15	-$3.3516	$5,027.35	-$16,200.00	Stock Option	-$11,172.65
+HBUAE	Bucyrus Intl Inc New Jan 2010 25.00 Call	-15	$0.0000	$0.00	$0.00	Stock Option	$0.00
+HBUGD	Bucyrus Intl Inc New Jul 2009 20.00 Call	-15	-$2.5615	$3,842.28	-$11,700.00	Stock Option	-$7,857.72
+MDRHC	Mcdermott Intl Inc Aug 2009 15.00 Call	-15	-$2.6249	$3,937.35	-$6,600.00	Stock Option	-$2,662.65
+MOSFH	Mosaic Co Jun 2009 40.00 Call	-15	-$7.8582	$11,787.30	-$10,500.00	Stock Option	$1,287.30
+MSGD	Morgan Stanley New Jul 2009 20.00 Call	-15	-$6.4249	$9,637.30	-$12,750.00	Stock Option	-$3,112.70
+PBRGY	Petroleo Brasileiro Sa Petrobr Sponsored Adr Jul 2009 27.50 Call	-15	-$5.7915	$8,687.31	-$18,900.00	Stock Option	-$10,212.69
+SIIGY	Smith Intl Inc Jul 2009 27.50 Call	-10	-$3.3649	$3,364.88	-$5,600.00	Stock Option	-$2,235.12
+STTHF	State Str Corp Aug 2009 32.00 Call	-15	-$7.8915	$11,837.31	-$20,550.00	Stock Option	-$8,712.69
+UNEAR	United States Natl Gas Fund Lp Unit Jan 2010 18.00 Call	-30	-$2.1715	$6,514.58	-$8,550.00	Stock Option	-$2,035.42
+WFCGT	Wells Fargo & Co New Jul 2009 17.50 Call	-15	-$3.5716	$5,357.34	-$16,200.00	Stock Option	-$10,842.66
+YNMAE	Foster Wheeler Ag Jan 2010 25.00 Call	-15	-$4.5715	$6,857.20	-$7,800.00	Stock Option	-$942.80
ATI	Allegheny Technologies Inc	1500	$38.0293	$57,044.00	$57,390.00	Equities	$346.00
BUCY	Bucyrus Intl Inc New	3000	$21.3533	$64,060.00	$83,430.00	Equities	$19,370.00
CAT	Caterpillar Inc Del	1500	$28.7083	$43,062.50	$59,460.00	Equities	$16,397.50
CLF	Cliffs Natural Resources Inc	3000	$21.9788	$65,936.50	$93,060.00	Equities	$27,123.50
FWLT	Foster Wheeler Ag	1500	$23.5293	$35,294.00	$37,470.00	Equities	$2,176.00
MDR	Mcdermott Intl Inc	1500	$14.4960	$21,744.00	$27,615.00	Equities	$5,871.00
MOS	Mosaic Co	1500	$42.0493	$63,073.90	$68,175.00	Equities	$5,101.10
MS	Morgan Stanley New	1500	$23.1305	$34,695.80	$42,300.00	Equities	$7,604.20
PBR	Petroleo Brasileiro Sa Petrobr Sponsored Adr	1500	$30.2159	$45,323.90	$60,000.00	Equities	$14,676.10
SII	Smith Intl Inc	1000	$25.7360	$25,736.00	$31,720.00	Equities	$5,984.00
STT	State Str Corp	1500	$32.7483	$49,122.50	$65,625.00	Equities	$16,502.50
UNG	United States Natl Gas Fund Lp Unit	3000	$15.3793	$46,138.00	$50,790.00	Equities	$4,652.00
WFC	Wells Fargo & Co New	1500	$16.9293	$25,394.00	$42,270.00	Equities	$16,876.00

Total Unrealized Gain-Loss: $71,987.41

Investment Required to Generate $50,000 of Yearly Income
$6,756,756 versus $150,000 Investment

Let's now compare income returns for bank CDs versus weekly covered calls. Let's also assume you want to generate $50,000 a year in income.

According to the *Bank Rate Monitor* the average annual yield for 1 Year CDs is .34% and the average annual yield for a 5 Year CD is 1.14%. If you split your funds evenly between 1 and 5 Year CDs it would take *an investment of $6,756,756* to generate a yearly income of $50,000! Of course your return is guaranteed but who has $6.7 million to invest?

My 2009 trading contest account had an annual return of 122% trading monthly covered calls. My 2011 weekly covered call trading account had an 54.8% average return and my 2012 weekly covered call trading account has an average return of 36.9% return so far this year.

Based on these real time results I think it is reasonable to assume a 33.3% annual return for weekly covered calls. A 33.3% annual return would require a $150,000 investment to generate a $50,000 yearly income. And a 50% yearly return requires a $100,000 investment to generate a $50,000 yearly income demonstrating the ability of the covered call strategy to deliver excellent income returns compared to fixed income investments.

Comparing Income Returns

- It would take an investment of $6,756,756 in 1 and 5 Year CDs to generate a yearly income of $50,000

- A 33.3% yearly return for selling weekly options would require a $150,000 investment to generate a $50,000 yearly income

- And a 50% yearly return for selling weekly options requires a $100,000 investment to generate a $50,000 yearly income

Covered Calls Produce $1,048,701.89 Real Time Profit

My retirement accounts Profit/Loss Reports that follow show $1,048,701.89 in real time profits for covered call trades over the past three years with an average return of 36.7% ($847,744.65 of this total were weekly covered calls). There were 77 winning trades and no losing trades. These real time profit results demonstrate the ability of the covered call strategy to deliver excellent returns with very low risk.

Covered Calls Produce $1,048,701.89 Real Time Profit

Covered Calls   Profits $116,935.13   Average Return 38.3%

Portfolios   ⚡ Alerts | ≫ Transfer Money | ≫ Bill Pay | ❓ Help

| Portfolios | Performance & Value | Positions | Gains & Losses | Risk Analyzer | Portfolio Analyzer | Income Estimator |

Account/Watch List: 919 PSP ▼ Create / Edit List   View: Performance ▼ Customize /

Market Value: $422,133.12 $116,935.13   DJIA 13,199.55 ▼ -64.94 (-0.49%)   Nasdaq 3,113.57 ▼ -6.13 (-0.20%)

[REFRESH 🔄] [STREAMING QUOTES] [EXPORT TO EXCEL ⬇]   Results per Page: 200 ▼

Symbol		Last Trade	Change $	Change %	Day's Gain	Qty	Price Paid	Total Gain $	Total Gain %	Market Val	Edit
⊞ AAPL	Buy / Sell	629.32	10.69	1.73%	$3,207.00	300	$400.34	$68,014.36	57.15%	$188,796.00	Edit
⊞ CMG	Buy / Sell	422.26	3.86	0.92%	$675.50	175	$417.37	$831.53	1.14%	$73,895.50	Edit
⊞ HD	Buy / Sell	50.00	0.01	0.02%	$10.00	1,000	$45.07	$4,909.66	10.89%	$50,000.00	Edit
⊞ JPM	Buy / Sell	45.42	-0.41	-0.89%	-$492.00	1,200	$38.92	$7,790.02	16.68%	$54,504.00	Edit
⊞ PCLN	Buy / Sell	743.62	23.65	3.28%	$3,547.50	150	$719.69	$3,574.02	3.31%	$111,543.00	Edit
⊞ QQQ	Buy / Sell	68.23	-0.02	-0.03%	-$16.00	800	$61.19	$5,601.04	11.43%	$54,584.00	Edit
⊞ SSO	Buy / Sell	58.80	-0.41	-0.69%	-$410.00	1,000	$54.94	$3,844.02	6.99%	$58,800.00	Edit
⊞ TJX	Buy / Sell	39.61	-0.26	-0.65%	-$624.00	2,400	$31.28	$19,964.05	26.58%	$95,064.00	Edit
⊞ WFC	Buy / Sell	34.48	-0.03	-0.09%	-$48.00	1,600	$31.43	$4,864.02	9.67%	$55,168.00	Edit
⊞ AAPL Apr 05 '12 $615 Call w	Trade	15.45	7.05	83.93%	-$705.00	-1	$6.10	-$939.77	-152.87%	-$1,545.00	Edit
⊞ CMG Apr 05 '12 $420 Call w	Trade	4.00	1.50	60.00%	-$150.00	-1	$3.10	-$94.76	-30.10%	-$400.00	Edit
⊞ HD Apr 05 '12 $50 Call w	Trade	0.22	-0.08	-26.67%	$40.00	-5	$0.31	$37.20	22.85%	-$110.00	Edit
⊞ JPM Apr 05 '12 $46 Call w	Trade	0.16	-0.14	-46.67%	$84.00	-6	$0.32	$87.44	43.60%	-$96.00	Edit
⊞ PCLN Apr 05 '12 $715 Call w	Trade	28.90	18.90	189.00%	-$1,890.00	-1	$12.04	-$1,690.77	-139.88%	-$2,890.00	Edit
⊞ QQQ Apr 05 '12 $68 Call w	Trade	0.50	0.02	4.17%	-$4.00*	-4	$0.30	-$83.04*	-65.36%*	-$196.00*	Edit
⊞ SSO Apr 05 '12 $58 Call w	Trade	0.95	-0.39	-29.10%	$205.00*	-5	$0.53	-$217.80	-79.84%	-$475.00	Edit
⊞ WFC Apr 05 '12 $34 Call w	Trade	0.55	-0.06	-9.84%	$48.00	-8	$0.33	$186.09	-67.89%	-$440.00	Edit
	Totals				$3,478.00			$116,935.13	%	$422,133.12	

Covered Calls   Profits $192,077.25   Average Return 71.6%

Portfolios

Alerts | Transfer Money | Bill Pay | Help

Portfolios   Performance & Value   Positions   Gains & Losses   Risk Analyzer   Portfolio Analyzer   Income Estimator

Account/Watch List: P&P   Create / Edit List   View: | Performance   Customize /

Market Value: $460,307.49 $192,077.25   DJIA 12,391.25 ▲ +73.11 (+0.59%) Nasdaq 2,833.95 ▲ +2.37 (+0.08%)

REFRESH ⟳   STREAMING QUOTES   EXPORT TO EXCEL* ⬇   Results per Page: | 200 |

Symbol		Last Trade	Change $	Change %	Day's Gain	Qty	Price Paid	Total Gain $	Total Gain %	Market Val	Edit
AAPL	Buy/ Sell	350.56	-7.74	-2.16%	-$2,089.80	270	$292.81	$15,630.56	19.78%	$94,651.20	Edit
BIDU	Buy/ Sell	126.80	-1.74	-1.35%	-$1,392.00	800	$77.52	$39,413.38	63.54%	$101,440.00	Edit
DIG	Buy/ Sell	58.68	0.58	1.00%	$986.00	1,700	$51.09	$12,872.08	14.82%	$99,756.00	✗
FAS	Buy/ Sell	34.26	0.18	0.53%	$684.00	3,800	$29.88	$16,573.47	14.59%	$130,188.00	✗
NOV	Buy/ Sell	80.18	-1.22	-1.50%	-$1,586.00	1,300	$62.40	$23,063.84	28.41%	$104,234.00	Edit
QLD	Buy/ Sell	94.44	-0.39	-0.41%	-$819.00	2,100	$66.49	$58,658.14	42.00%	$198,324.00	Edit
UWM	Buy/ Sell	48.34	0.12	0.25%	$240.00	2,000	$42.00	$12,667.44	15.08%	$96,680.00	Edit
UYM	Buy/ Sell	54.75	-1.32	-2.35%	-$2,367.00	1,800	$47.91	$12,286.13	14.24%	$98,550.00	Edit
BIDU Mar 19 '11 $130 Call	Trade	2.96	-0.89	-23.12%	$534.00	-6	$4.47	$897.38	33.35%	-$1,776.00	Edit
DIG Mar 19 '11 $58 Call	Trade	2.55	0.00	0.00%	$-0.00	-9	$1.78	-$703.89	-43.64%	-$2,295.00	Edit
DIG Mar 19 '11 $60 Call	Trade	1.52	-0.08	-5.00%	$24.00	-3	$1.43	-$37.29	-8.49%	-$456.00	Edit
FAS Mar 19 '11 $36 Call	Trade	0.97	-0.05	-4.90%	$135.00	-27	$1.03	$137.34	4.90%	-$2,619.00	Edit
NOV Mar 19 '11 $85 Call	Trade	1.18	-0.47	-28.48%	$423.00	-9	$1.45	$232.11	17.64%	-$1,062.00	Edit
QLD Mar 19 '11 $96 Call	Trade	2.15	-0.51	-19.17%	$735.00*	-15	$2.50	$479.49*	12.73%*	-$3,255.00*	Edit
UWM Mar 19 '11 $49 Call	Trade	1.65	-0.08	-4.62%	$104.00	-13	$1.37	-$377.95	-21.06%	-$2,145.00	Edit
UYM Mar 19 '11 $57 Call	Trade	1.45	-0.63	-30.29%	$819.00	-13	$1.68	$285.04	12.97%	-$1,885.00	Edit
				Totals	-$3,569.80			$192,077.25		$460,307.49	

LEGEND: ⊞ collapsed (click to expand) ▣ expanded (click to collapse)
- Lot edited by firm   + - Lot edited by customer

Real-time quotes

178

Covered Calls   Profits $323,069.44   Average Return 54.8%

Portfolios

Portfolios   Performance & Value   Positions   Gains & Losses   Risk Analyzer   Portfolio Analyzer   Income Estimator

Account/Watch List: OBP   Create / Edit List   View: Performance   Customize /

Market Value: $912,396.29 $323,069.44   DJIA 12,391.25 ▲ +73.11 (+0.59%)   Nasdaq 2,833.95 ▲ +2.37 (+0.08%)

REFRESH ⟳   STREAMING QUOTES   EXPORT TO EXCEL ⬇   Results per Page: 200

Symbol		Last Trade	Change $	Change %	Day's Gain	Qty	Price Paid	Total Gain $	Total Gain %	Market Val	Edit
AAPL	Buy / Sell	350.56	-7.74	-2.16%	-$3,870.00	500	$273.62	$38,431.65	28.08%	$175,280.00	Edit
BIDU	Buy / Sell	126.80	-1.74	-1.35%	-$2,436.00	1,400	$84.47	$59,216.38	50.05%	$177,520.00	Edit
DIG	Buy / Sell	58.68	0.58	1.00%	$1,740.00	3,000	$49.38	$27,890.02	18.83%	$176,040.00	✕
FAS	Buy / Sell	34.26	0.18	0.53%	$1,080.00	6,000	$29.55	$28,182.17	15.89%	$205,560.00	✕
NOV	Buy / Sell	80.18	-1.22	-1.50%	-$2,440.00	2,000	$63.05	$34,208.41	27.12%	$160,360.00	Edit
QLD	Buy / Sell	94.44	-0.39	-0.41%	-$1,404.00	3,600	$70.28	$87,003.57	34.39%	$339,984.00	Edit
SSO	Buy / Sell	54.78	0.22	0.40%	$660.00	3,000	$50.61	$12,482.02	8.22%	$164,340.00	✕
UWM	Buy / Sell	48.34	0.12	0.25%	$456.00	3,800	$44.19	$15,748.06	9.38%	$183,692.00	✕
UYM	Buy / Sell	54.75	-1.32	-2.35%	-$4,208.00	3,200	$48.69	$19,336.13	12.41%	$175,200.00	Edit
BIDU Mar 19 '11 $130 Call	Trade	2.96	-0.89	-23.12%	$890.00	-10	$4.737	$1,761.28	37.06%	-$2,960.00	Edit
DIG Mar 19 '11 $58 Call	Trade	2.55	0.00	0.00%	$-0.00	-12	$1.72	-$1,009.19	-48.58%	-$3,060.00	Edit
DIG Mar 19 '11 $59 Call	Trade	2.05	0.05	2.50%	-$45.00	-9	$1.37	-$622.89	-50.08%	-$1,845.00	Edit
FAS Mar 19 '11 $36 Call	Trade	0.97	-0.05	-4.90%	$210.00	-42	$1.00	$89.86	2.12%	-$4,074.00	Edit
NOV Mar 19 '11 $85 Call	Trade	1.18	-0.47	-28.48%	$658.00	-14	$1.47	$391.28	18.88%	-$1,652.00	Edit
QLD Mar 19 '11 $96 Call	Trade	2.15	-0.51	-19.17%	$735.00*	-15	$2.49	$464.49*	12.38%*	-$3,255.00*	Edit
QLD Mar 19 '11 $97 Call	Trade	1.80	-0.36	-16.67%	$396.00	-11	$2.1827	$404.57	16.74%	-$1,980.00	Edit
SSO Mar 19 '11 $55 Call	Trade	1.38	0.02	1.47%	-$63.00*	-21	$1.24	-$335.07*	-12.77%*	-$2,919.00*	Edit
UWM Mar 19 '11 $49 Call	Trade	1.65	-0.08	-4.62%	$224.00	-28	$1.26	-$1,117.44	-31.45%	-$4,620.00	Edit
UYM Mar 19 '11 $57 Call	Trade	1.45	-0.63	-30.29%	$1,197.00	-19	$1.68	-$418.44	13.03%	-$2,755.00	Edit
Totals					-$6,070.00			$323,069.44		$912,396.29	

Covered Calls   Profits $71,987.41   Average Return 14.5%

Unrealized P&L on Open Positions

Symbol	Description	Position	Avg Price	Cost Basis	Market Value	Type	Unrealized Val.
+AASAH	Allegheny Technologies Inc Jan 2010 40.00 Call	-15	$0.0000	$0.00	$0.00	Stock Option	$0.00
+CLFAA	Cliffs Natural Resources Inc Jan 2010 20.00 Call	-15	$0.0000	$0.00	$0.00	Stock Option	$0.00
+CLFGD	Cliffs Natural Resources Inc Jul 2009 20.00 Call	-15	-$3.5715	$5,357.31	-$17,550.00	Stock Option	-$12,192.69
+CXJHD	Caterpillar Inc Del Aug 2009 30.00 Call	-15	-$3.3516	$5,027.35	-$16,200.00	Stock Option	-$11,172.65
+HBUAE	Bucyrus Intl Inc New Jan 2010 25.00 Call	-15	$0.0000	$0.00	$0.00	Stock Option	$0.00
+HBUGD	Bucyrus Intl Inc New Jul 2009 20.00 Call	-15	-$2.5615	$3,842.28	-$11,700.00	Stock Option	-$7,857.72
+MDRHC	Mcdermott Intl Inc Aug 2009 15.00 Call	-15	-$2.6249	$3,937.35	-$6,600.00	Stock Option	-$2,662.65
+MOSFH	Mosaic Co Jun 2009 40.00 Call	-15	-$7.8582	$11,787.30	-$10,500.00	Stock Option	$1,287.30
+MSGD	Morgan Stanley New Jul 2009 20.00 Call	-15	-$6.4249	$9,637.30	-$12,750.00	Stock Option	-$3,112.70
+PBRGY	Petroleo Brasileiro Sa Petrobr Sponsored Adr Jul 2009 27.50 Call	-15	-$5.7915	$8,687.31	-$18,900.00	Stock Option	-$10,212.69
+SIIGY	Smith Intl Inc Jul 2009 27.50 Call	-10	-$3.3649	$3,364.88	-$5,600.00	Stock Option	-$2,235.12
+STTHF	State Str Corp Aug 2009 32.00 Call	-15	-$7.8915	$11,837.31	-$20,550.00	Stock Option	-$8,712.69
+UNEAR	United States Natl Gas Fund Lp Unit Jan 2010 18.00 Call	-30	-$2.1715	$6,514.58	-$8,550.00	Stock Option	-$2,035.42
+WFCGT	Wells Fargo & Co New Jul 2009 17.50 Call	-15	-$3.5716	$5,357.34	-$16,200.00	Stock Option	-$10,842.66
+YNMAE	Foster Wheeler Ag Jan 2010 25.00 Call	-15	-$4.5715	$6,857.20	-$7,800.00	Stock Option	-$942.80
ATI	Allegheny Technologies Inc	1500	$38.0293	$57,044.00	$57,390.00	Equities	$346.00
BUCY	Bucyrus Intl Inc New	3000	$21.3533	$64,060.00	$83,430.00	Equities	$19,370.00
CAT	Caterpillar Inc Del	1500	$28.7083	$43,062.50	$59,460.00	Equities	$16,397.50
CLF	Cliffs Natural Resources Inc	3000	$21.9788	$65,936.50	$93,060.00	Equities	$27,123.50
FWLT	Foster Wheeler Ag	1500	$23.5293	$35,294.00	$37,470.00	Equities	$2,176.00
MDR	Mcdermott Intl Inc	1500	$14.4960	$21,744.00	$27,615.00	Equities	$5,871.00
MOS	Mosaic Co	1500	$42.0493	$63,073.90	$68,175.00	Equities	$5,101.10
MS	Morgan Stanley New	1500	$23.1305	$34,695.80	$42,300.00	Equities	$7,604.20
PBR	Petroleo Brasileiro Sa Petrobr Sponsored Adr	1500	$30.2159	$45,323.90	$60,000.00	Equities	$14,676.10
SII	Smith Intl Inc	1000	$25.7360	$25,736.00	$31,720.00	Equities	$5,984.00
STT	State Str Corp	1500	$32.7483	$49,122.50	$65,625.00	Equities	$16,502.50
UNG	United States Natl Gas Fund Lp Unit	3000	$15.3793	$46,138.00	$50,790.00	Equities	$4,652.00
WFC	Wells Fargo & Co New	1500	$16.9293	$25,394.00	$42,270.00	Equities	$16,876.00

Total Unrealized Gain-Loss: $71,987.41

Covered Calls   Profits $323,069.44   Average Return 54.8%

Portfolios

Alerts | Transfer Money | Bill Pay | Help

| Portfolios | Performance & Value | Positions | Gains & Losses | Risk Analyzer | Portfolio Analyzer | Income Estimator |

Account/Watch List: 918 DBP ▼ Create / Edit List   View: Performance ▼ Customize /

Market Value: $820,939.71 $215,662.83   DJIA 13,199.55 ▼ -64.94 (-0.49%) Nasdaq 3,113.57 ▼ -6.13 (-0.20%)

REFRESH | STREAMING QUOTES | EXPORT TO EXCEL*   Results per Page: 200 ▼

Symbol		Last Trade	Change $	Change %	Day's Gain	Qty	Price Paid	Total Gain $	Total Gain %	Market Val	Edit
AAPL	Buy / Sell	629.32	10.69	1.73%	$4,276.00	400	$400.36	$91,527.17	57.13%	$251,728.00	Edit
AGNC	Buy / Sell	30.06	0.15	0.50%	$1,003.65	6,691	$26.37	$24,684.60	13.99%	$201,131.46	Edit
CMG	Buy / Sell	422.26	3.86	0.92%	$579.00	150	$417.05	$765.52	1.22%	$63,339.00	Edit
HD	Buy / Sell	50.00	0.01	0.02%	$20.00	2,000	$46.17	$7,636.11	8.27%	$100,000.00	Edit
JPM	Buy / Sell	45.42	-0.41	-0.89%	-$984.00	2,400	$39.65	$13,811.04	14.51%	$109,008.00	Edit
MLPL	Buy / Sell	42.07	0.49	1.18%	$2,505.97	5,114.22958	$36.30	$29,445.19	15.86%	$215,155.64	Edit
PCLN	Buy / Sell	743.62	23.65	3.28%	$3,547.50	150	$719.98	$3,529.52	3.27%	$111,543.00	Edit
QQQ	Buy / Sell	68.23	-0.02	-0.03%	-$30.00	1,500	$60.99	$10,831.53	11.84%	$102,345.00	Edit
SSO	Buy / Sell	58.80	-0.41	-0.69%	-$820.00	2,000	$55.67	$6,229.53	5.59%	$117,600.00	Edit
TJX	Buy / Sell	39.61	-0.26	-0.65%	-$780.00	3,000	$30.82	$26,336.03	28.47%	$118,830.00	Edit
WFC	Buy / Sell	34.48	-0.03	-0.09%	-$90.00	3,000	$31.35	$9,376.27	9.97%	$103,440.00	Edit
AAPL Apr 05 '12 $615 Call w	Trade	15.45	7.05	83.93%	-$1,410.00	-2	$6.53	-$1,789.54	-136.45%	-$3,090.00	Edit
CMG Apr 05 '12 $420 Call w	Trade	4.00	1.50	60.00%	-$150.00	-1	$3.46	-$58.76	-16.75%	-$400.00	Edit
HD Apr 05 '12 $50 Call w	Trade	0.22	-0.08	-26.67%	$80.00	-10	$0.33	$98.39	28.80%	-$220.00	Edit
JPM Apr 05 '12 $46 Call w	Trade	0.16	-0.14	-46.67%	$168.00	-12	$0.34	$202.86	48.17%	-$192.00	Edit
PCLN Apr 05 '12 $715 Call w	Trade	28.90	18.90	189.00%	-$1,890.00	-1	$11.97	-$1,697.78	-141.27%	-$2,890.00	Edit
QQQ Apr 05 '12 $68 Call w	Trade	0.50	0.02	4.17%	-$8.00*	-8	$0.32	-$146.09*	-54.90%*	-$392.00*	Edit
SSO Apr 05 '12 $58 Call w	Trade	0.95	-0.39	-29.10%	$410.00*	-10	$0.54	-$421.61	-76.43%	-$950.00	Edit
TJX Jan 19 '13 $28.75 Call	Trade	11.30	11.30	—	$70.00*	-7	$5.05	-$4,381.73	-123.72%	-$7,910.00	Edit
WFC Apr 05 '12 $34 Call w	Trade	0.55	-0.06	-9.84%	$90.00	-15	$0.35	-$315.42	-58.37%	-$825.00	Edit

Covered Calls   Profits $62,431.83   Average Return 24.2%

Portfolios

| Portfolios | Performance & Value | Positions | Gains & Losses | Risk Analyzer | Portfolio Analyzer | Income Estimator |

Account/Watch List: [ ] Create / Edit List   View: Performance [ ] Customize /

Market Value: $319,767.28 $62,431.83   DJIA 8,704.55 ▲ +204.22 (+2.40%)   Nasdaq 1,822.52 ▲ +48.19 (+2.72%)

[REFRESH]   [STREAMING QUOTES]   [EXPORT TO EXCEL]   Results per Page: [200]

Symbol		Last Trade	Change $	Change %	Day's Gain	Qty	Price Paid	Total Gain $	Total Gain %	Market Val	Edit
⊞ BUCY	Buy / Sell	30.256	1.58	5.50%	$3,467.20	2,200	$19.02	$24,677.26	58.92%	$66,563.20	Edit
⊞ CHK	Buy / Sell	24.05	1.39	6.13%	$1,946.00	1,400	$20.40	$5,081.36	17.77%	$33,670.00	Edit
⊞ CLF	Buy / Sell	29.13	1.88	6.90%	$4,136.00	2,200	$20.64	$18,641.06	41.02%	$64,086.00	Edit
⊞ FCX	Buy / Sell	58.57	4.14	7.61%	$4,140.00	1,000	$43.90	$14,632.05	33.30%	$58,570.00	Edit
⊞ FWLT	Buy / Sell	28.20	1.68	6.33%	$2,520.00	1,500	$24.07	$6,176.03	17.10%	$42,300.00	Edit
⊞ JPM	Buy / Sell	37.48	0.58	1.57%	$696.00	1,200	$33.24	$5,052.05	12.65%	$44,976.00	Edit
⊞ MDR	Buy / Sell	22.80	0.83	3.78%	$2,158.00	2,600	$15.58	$18,732.08	46.20%	$59,280.00	Edit
⊞ MOS	Buy / Sell	56.06	1.36	2.49%	$544.00	400	$45.60	$4,170.02	22.84%	$22,424.00	Edit
⊞ MS	Buy / Sell	30.64	0.32	1.06%	$256.00	800	$23.50	$5,696.02	30.27%	$24,512.00	Edit
⊞ NOV	Buy / Sell	40.28	1.66	4.30%	$2,324.00	1,400	$32.19	$11,279.06	25.00%	$56,392.00	Edit
⊞ NYX	Buy / Sell	31.60	1.60	5.33%	$1,440.00	900	$28.57	$2,706.03	10.52%	$28,440.00	Edit
⊞ PBR	Buy / Sell	45.585	1.56	3.53%	$1,244.00	800	$34.80	$8,594.04	30.83%	$36,468.00	Edit
⊞ SQM	Buy / Sell	37.38	1.02	2.81%	$612.00	600	$35.89	$878.32	4.08%	$22,428.00	Edit
⊞ STT	Buy / Sell	47.23	0.78	1.68%	$936.00	1,200	$32.68	$17,428.04	44.40%	$56,676.00	Edit

Continued . . .   Profits $62,431.83   Average Return 24.2%

⊞ MDRHC	Trade	6.70	0.00	0.00%	-$700.00*	-10	$2.935	-$4,988.50*	-168.62%*	-$7,900.00*	Edit
⊞ MDRHW	Trade	6.00	0.90	17.65%	-$240.00	-3	$2.70	-$1,000.26	-121.94%	-$1,800.00	Edit
⊞ MSAD	Trade	12.30	0.50	4.24%	-$200.00	-4	$8.59	-$1,495.01	-43.37%	-$4,920.00	Edit
⊞ MSAX	Trade	9.15	0.00	0.00%	-$200.00*	-4	$7.20	-$1,171.01*	-40.51%*	-$4,040.00*	Edit
⊞ NONHF	Trade	8.00	1.10	15.94%	-$240.00*	-2	$4.70	-$689.51*	-72.62%*	-$1,620.00*	Edit
⊞ NOVHF	Trade	11.25	1.65	17.19%	-$775.00*	-5	$6.784	-$2,252.75	-66.03%	-$5,625.00*	Edit
⊞ PBRAF	Trade	17.20	1.92	12.57%	-$384.00	-2	$7.50	-$1,949.50	-129.15%	-$3,440.00	Edit
⊞ PBRAG	Trade	11.20	0.00	0.00%	-$220.00*	-2	$7.03	-$1,123.50*	-79.37%*	-$2,520.00*	Edit
⊞ PBRAW	Trade	10.00	0.00	0.00%	-$180.00*	-2	$5.78	-$1,033.52*	-88.67%*	-$2,180.00*	Edit
⊞ PBRGH	Trade	9.40	0.00	0.00%	-$160.00*	-2	$3.52	-$1,245.51*	-174.56%*	-$1,940.00*	Edit
⊞ STTHX	Trade	17.00	0.00	0.00%	-$420.00*	-6	$9.095	-$5,183.51*	-94.63%*	-$10,620.00*	Edit
⊞ WJPAG	Trade	7.39	0.86	13.17%	-$272.00*	-8	$6.205	-$978.10	-19.59%	-$5,912.00	Edit
⊞ WRHAX	Trade	19.50	1.70	9.55%	-$600.00*	-6	$11.32	-$4,931.52	-72.42%	-$11,700.00	Edit
⊞ YAEAW	Trade	7.10	1.18	19.93%	-$240.00*	-3	$4.00	-$940.27	-77.69%	-$2,130.00	Edit
⊞ YAEAZ	Trade	9.00	1.07	13.49%	-$1,000.00*	-10	$4.245	-$4,778.50	-111.95%	-$9,000.00	Edit
⊞ YMPAF	Trade	13.60	2.00	17.24%	-$850.00*	-5	$8.894	-$2,222.75*	-49.76%*	-$6,650.00*	Edit
⊞ YMPAG	Trade	9.72	0.92	10.45%	-$184.00	-2	$6.73	-$607.52	-44.82%	-$1,944.00	Edit
⊞ YNMAE	Trade	6.90	0.80	13.11%	-$1,350.00*	-15	$5.0333	-$2,835.41	-37.38%	-$10,350.00	Edit
⊞ YPXAH	Trade	22.40	4.05	22.07%	-$1,520.00*	-4	$11.68	-$4,307.01	-91.81%	-$8,960.00	Edit
⊞ YPXAK	Trade	13.59	3.74	37.97%	-$327.55*	-2	$12.00	-$327.55	-13.59%	-$2,718.00	Edit
⊞ YVXAU	Trade	5.40	0.98	22.17%	$75.13*	-9	$5.50	$75.13	1.51%	-$4,860.00	Edit
				Totals	$6,583.78			$381,636.37	$62,431.83		$319,767.28	

LEGEND: ⊞ collapsed (click to expand) ⊟ expanded (click to collapse)   Real-time quotes

183

Covered Calls   Profits $66,537.95   Average Return 18.5%

	Account Equity	DTBP	ONBP	Non-Margin BP
	424,773.03	1,179,102.12	345,974.06	172,987.03
	Open P/L	Closed P/L	Commission	Total P/L
	66,537.95 +	--- −	--- =	66,537.95

Positions | Open Orders | Activity | Summary | Trade Journal | Balances

Type	Sy...	Last	Change	Qty	Avg Price	Profit/Loss
2	+CLFGD	$11.87	$1.30	-15	3.5715	$-12492.75
2	+CXJHD	$10.90	$1.35	-15	3.3516	$-11322.60
2	+HBUGD	$8.15	$2.05	-15	2.5615	$-9207.75
2	+MDRHC	$4.40	$0.40	-15	2.6249	$-2962.65
2	+MOSFH	$7.00	$-0.23	-15	7.8582	$1137.30
2	+MSGD	$8.60	$0.70	-15	6.4249	$-3562.65
2	+PBRGY	$12.90	$1.78	-15	5.7915	$-11112.75
2	+SIIGY	$5.70	$1.30	-10	3.3649	$-2435.10
2	+STTHF	$10.10	---	-15	7.8915	$-9012.75
2	+UNEAR	$2.85	$0.25	-30	2.1715	$-2785.50
2	+WFCGT	$10.77	$2.46	-15	3.5716	$-11142.60
2	+YCPAU	---	---	-15	6.2814	---
2	+YFQAW	---	---	-15	6.8714	---
2	+YHBAE	---	---	-15	4.8815	---
2	+YNMAE	$5.29	$1.28	-15	4.5715	$-1242.75
2	ATI	$38.26	$0.98	1500	38.0293	$346.05
2	BUCY	$27.81	$2.73	3000	21.3533	$19370.10
2	CAT	$39.64	$1.72	1500	28.7083	$16397.55
2	CLF	$31.02	$1.01	3000	21.9788	$27123.60
2	FWLT	$24.98	$1.96	1500	23.5293	$2176.05
2	MDR	$18.41	$0.63	1500	14.496	$5871.00
2	MOS	$45.45	$-0.08	1500	42.0493	$5101.05
2	MS	$28.20	$1.06	1500	23.1305	$7604.25
2	PBR	$40.00	$1.68	1500	30.2159	$14676.15
2	SII	$31.72	$1.91	1000	25.736	$5984.00
2	STT	$43.75	$5.92	1500	32.7483	$16502.55
2	UNG	$16.93	$0.71	3000	15.3793	$4652.10
2	WFC	$28.18	$3.42	1500	16.9293	$16876.05

Put Selling

Put selling also known as being short a put is a bullish option income strategy. Selling or writing a put option entails the obligation to buy the underlying stock/ETF at the strike price from the owner of the long put upon exercise. When you are short a naked put, the risk can be high if you use leverage and put selling requires a margin account.

If a trading account has cash that covers the value of the short put and leverage is not used, then the risk is equivalent to owning the underlying security. An example of cash covering a put would be to have $5,000 in cash in your account to sell a 50-Strike put.

The risk in a put selling strategy develops if the underlying stock/ETF declines below the strike price of the short put by more than the amount of option premium received. At this point, the premium no longer protects you from losses and you incur risk if the underlying stock continues to decline in price.

The profit potential for naked put writing is limited to the premium received for selling the put option. For example, if you sell a put for 1.00 points your profit potential is limited to $100. Selling naked puts is a strategy that is implemented if you are bullish on the underlying stock/ETF and you expect the underlying security to close at or above the strike price of the short put at option expiration. If the underlying security closes at or above the strike price of the short put then the put expires worthless and you realize the full profit potential of the trade.

Let's take a look at a recent example of a put selling trade. The daily price graph that follows shows Home Depot in a price up trend with the 50-Day EMA above the 100-Day EMA.

The price up trend is confirmed with an up sloping On Balance Volume line and HD is making a series of new 52-Week highs.

Confirmed Price Up Trend for Home Depot:

- 50-Day EMA above 100-Day EMA = Buy

- HD making a series of new 52-Week highs

- On Balance Volume line is sloping up

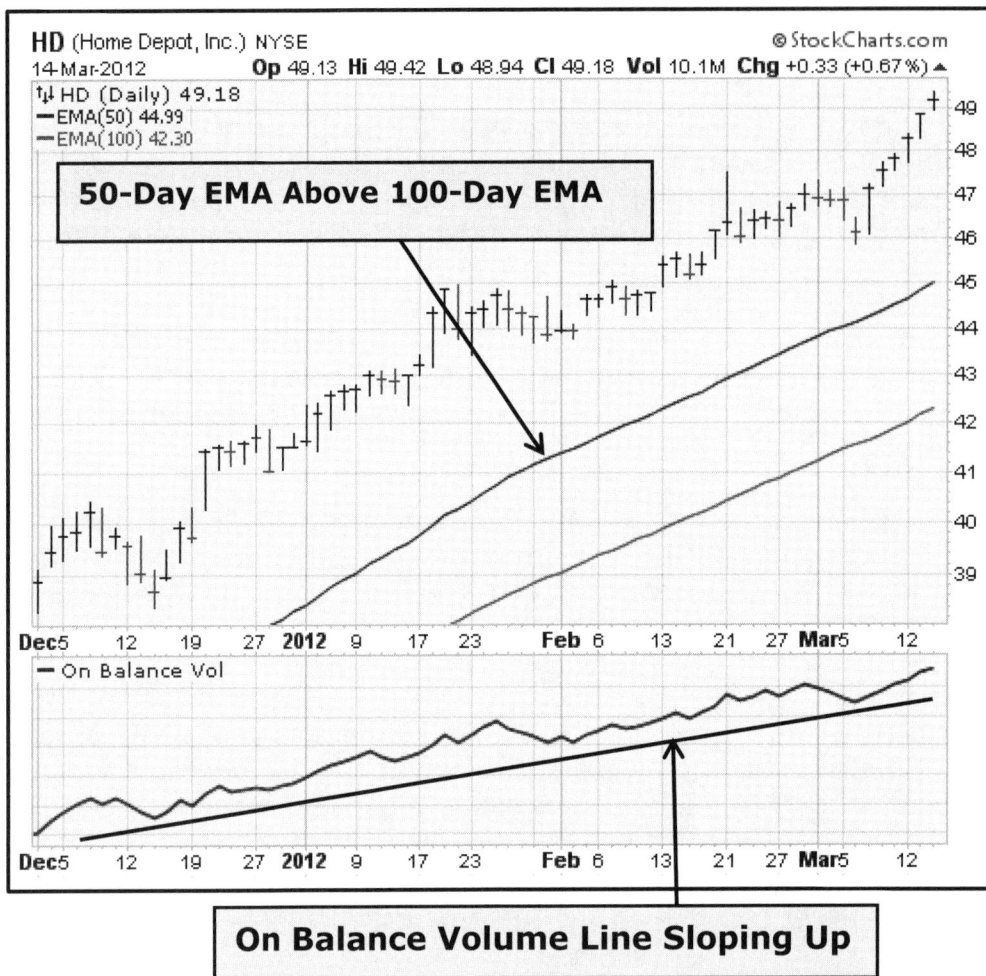

HD (Home Depot, Inc.) NYSE   © StockCharts.com
14-Mar-2012   Op 49.13 Hi 49.42 Lo 48.94 Cl 49.18 Vol 10.1M Chg +0.33 (+0.67%) ▲

50-Day EMA Above 100-Day EMA

On Balance Volume Line Sloping Up

With Home Depot in a confirmed up trend I sold HD put options. My brokerage account Confirmation below shows that I sold 4 of the HD Mar 02 47-Strike weekly put options at .45 points or $45.

History & Statements

| Transactions | Statements | Confirmations |

✉ Search results for 2/23/2012 to 2/23/2012

Date	Transaction	Action (Buy, Sell)	Symbol	Quantity	Price
☐ 02/23/2012	08136895406	Sold	HD Mar 02 2012 47.0 Put	4	0.45

The profit potential for short put options is limited so I like to enter a GTC (Good Until Cancelled) order to close out a short put if the trade reaches about 90% of the profit potential. I like to lock in a profit in case the underlying stock/ETF starts to decline in price which can lead to a loss for a short put. I entered a GTC order to 'buy to close' this short put at .05 points which was about 90% of the .45 point profit potential.

My brokerage account Confirmation below shows that one week later I closed out the 4 HD Mar 02 47-Strike weekly put options at .05 points resulting in a .40 point or $40 profit for each contract.

History & Statements

| Transactions | Statements | Confirmations |

✉ Search results for 3/1/2012 to 3/1/2012

Date	Transaction	Action (Buy, Sell)	Symbol	Quantity	Price
03/01/2012	08166795922	Bought	HD Mar 02 2012 47.0 Put	4	0.05

Recent Profit Results

My brokerage account Realized Gain/Loss Report below shows that I realized an average return of 452.8% for this portfolio of weekly put options.

Average Portfolio Return of 452.8% for Weekly Put Options

| Home | Accounts | Trade | Research & Ideas | Trading Tools | Planning & Retirement | Education | Client Services |

Balances & Positions | Portfolio Planner | Gain/Loss | Watch Lists | History & Statements | Tax Center | Deposit/Withdraw | Online Cash Services

Sunday, March 11, 2012 02:30:29 PM EST   Export data | Printer-friendly page

| Realized Gain/Loss ⚙ | Unrealized Gain/Loss ⚙ | Unsettled Closed Positions ⚙ | Expand All   Edit your GainsKeeper cost basis

Security ▾	Trans type	Qty	Open date	Adj cost per share	Adj cost	Close date	Adj proceeds per share	Adj proceeds	Adj gain ($)	Adj gain (%)	Term
HD Feb 18 2012 46.0 Put	Buy to Close.FIFO	800	02/14/12	0.05	40.10	02/17/12	0.48	386.89	346.79	864.81	Short-term ▶
IWM Feb 18 2012 82.0 Put	Buy to Close.FIFO	500	02/14/12	0.10	50.81	02/17/12	0.78	389.18	338.37	665.95	Short-term ▶
WFC Feb 18 2012 31.0 Put	Buy to Close.FIFO	1,000	02/14/12	0.21	214.62	02/17/12	0.69	685.36	470.74	219.34	Short-term ▶
XLF Feb 18 2012 15.0 Put	Buy to Close.FIFO	2,000	02/14/12	0.24	482.24	02/17/12	0.39	777.74	295.50	61.28	Short-term ▶

| Enter symbol | QUOTE ▾ | Options: Enter underlying symbol and click Chain | Index: use "$" (e.g. $DJI) | | CHAIN $? ☐ ⊡ |

SnapTicket™   New cost-basis rules will change our tax reporting. | Symbol lookup | Quote disclaimer | Price Lock: On | Off   Streaming quotes: On | Of

And my brokerage account Realized Gain/Loss Report below shows that I realized an average return of 542.8% for this portfolio of weekly put options.

Average Portfolio Return of 542.8% for Weekly Put Options

Security ▾	Trans type	Qty	Open date	Adj cost per share	Adj cost	Close date	Adj proceeds per share	Adj proceeds	Adj gain ($)	Adj gain (%)	Term
EEM Mar 02 2012 44.0 Put	Buy to Close.FIFO	500	02/24/12	0.05	25.06	03/01/12	0.44	219.18	194.12	774.62	Short-term
HD Mar 02 2012 47.0 Put	Buy to Close.FIFO	400	02/23/12	0.05	20.05	03/01/12	0.42	169.94	149.89	747.58	Short-term
IWM Mar 02 2012 83.0 Put	Buy to Close.FIFO	300	02/23/12	1.53	459.29	03/01/12	1.12	335.70	-123.59	-26.91	Short-term
QQQ Mar 02 2012 64.0 Put	Buy to Close.FIFO	400	02/23/12	0.10	38.05	03/01/12	0.72	289.94	251.89	662.00	Short-term
WFC Mar 02 2012 31.0 Put	Buy to Close.FIFO	400	02/23/12	0.10	38.05	02/29/12	0.62	249.94	211.89	556.87	Short-term

Chapter 5

The Super Portfolio

The *Super Portfolio* is a spread strategy that buys the strongest performing stocks on a *Prime Trade Select* 'buy' signal and sells weekly call options on ETFs in weak sectors. This is similar to a covered call strategy except that the weekly ETF call option that is sold is 'naked' as the underlying stock is not owned. This type of spread trade requires a margin account and incurs more risk than a covered call trade.

The goal of the *Super Portfolio* is to profit from the best performing stocks and at the same time profit from selling weekly call options for ETFs in weak sectors.

With current market conditions, the stocks that I purchase in the *Super Portfolio* are typically stocks in sectors that are performing well despite the financial crisis in Europe and the slow growing US economy. And with current market conditions the typical weak sectors that I use to sell call options are the Europe and China equity ETFs and the energy and commodity ETFs.

The typical stocks that are purchased and the call options that are sold will change from time to time depending on market conditions. By the time you read this Chapter these typical strong/weak sectors could change.

Let's look at a couple of current examples of *Super Portfolio* spread trades. As noted in Chapter 4, covered call trades place a limit on the profit potential of a trade but the *Super Portfolio* spread strategy does not cap your upside potential if a stock moves up in price. For example, I currently have a 37% profit on *Super Portfolio* stock TJX and at the same time I have been profiting from selling call option premium on Europe, China and energy ETFs.

Selling ETF option premium against TJX stock has not capped my upside profit potential. The *Super Portfolio* spread trades have been working well in the current volatile market environment.

My brokerage account Profit/Loss Reports below show I currently have $61,636.08 in open trade profits in two of my trading accounts for *Super Portfolio* stock TJX Companies.

$61,636.08 in Open Trade Profits for TJX

Portfolios									Alerts | Transfer Money | Bill Pay | Help		
Portfolios	Performance & Value	Positions	Gains & Losses	Risk Analyzer	Portfolio Analyzer	Income Estimator					

⊞ Symbol ⊟		Last Trade	Change $	%	Day's Gain	Qty	Price Paid	Total Gain $	%	Market Val	Edit
⊞ TJX	Buy / Sell	42.45	2.75	6.93%	$8,250.00	3,000	$30.82	$34,856.03	37.68%	$127,350.00	Edit

Portfolios									Alerts | Transfer Money | Bill Pay | Help		
Portfolios	Performance & Value	Positions	Gains & Losses	Risk Analyzer	Portfolio Analyzer	Income Estimator					

⊞ Symbol ⊟		Last Trade	Change $	%	Day's Gain	Qty	Price Paid	Total Gain $	%	Market Val	Edit
⊞ TJX	Buy / Sell	42.45	2.75	6.93%	$6,600.00	2,400	$31.28	$26,780.05	35.66%	$101,880.00	Edit

Common Characteristics of Super Portfolio Stocks in Current Market Environment:

- Are in a confirmed price up trend

- Have little or no correlation to European economies and debt

- Are not dependent on the price of oil or commodities

- Have strong growth rates in a slow growing US economy

- Are in leading industries

TJX in a Confirmed Price Up Trend:

- 50 Day EMA above 100 Day EMA

- OBV Line sloping up

- TJX making a series of new 52-Week highs

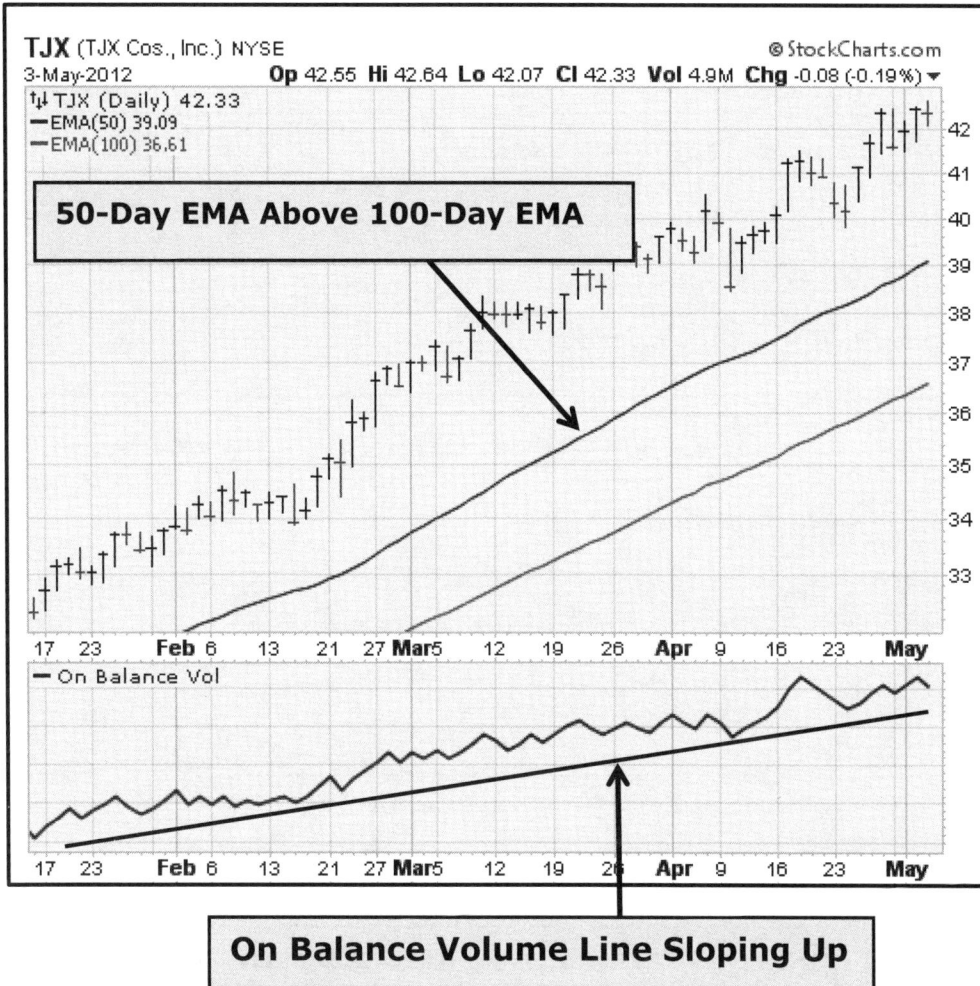

On Balance Volume Line Sloping Up

Super Portfolio Stock TJX

- TJX is in a confirmed price up trend

- Has little correlation to European debt crisis

- TJX is not dependent on the price of oil or commodities

- TJX has strong equity and retained earnings growth rates in a slow growing US Economy

- TJX is in a leading industry . . . retail

I have been selling Brazil ETF (EWZ) call options against my TJX stock.

Confirmed Price Down Trend for EWZ

- 50 Day EMA below 100 Day EMA

- OBV Line sloping down

- EWZ making new 52-Week lows

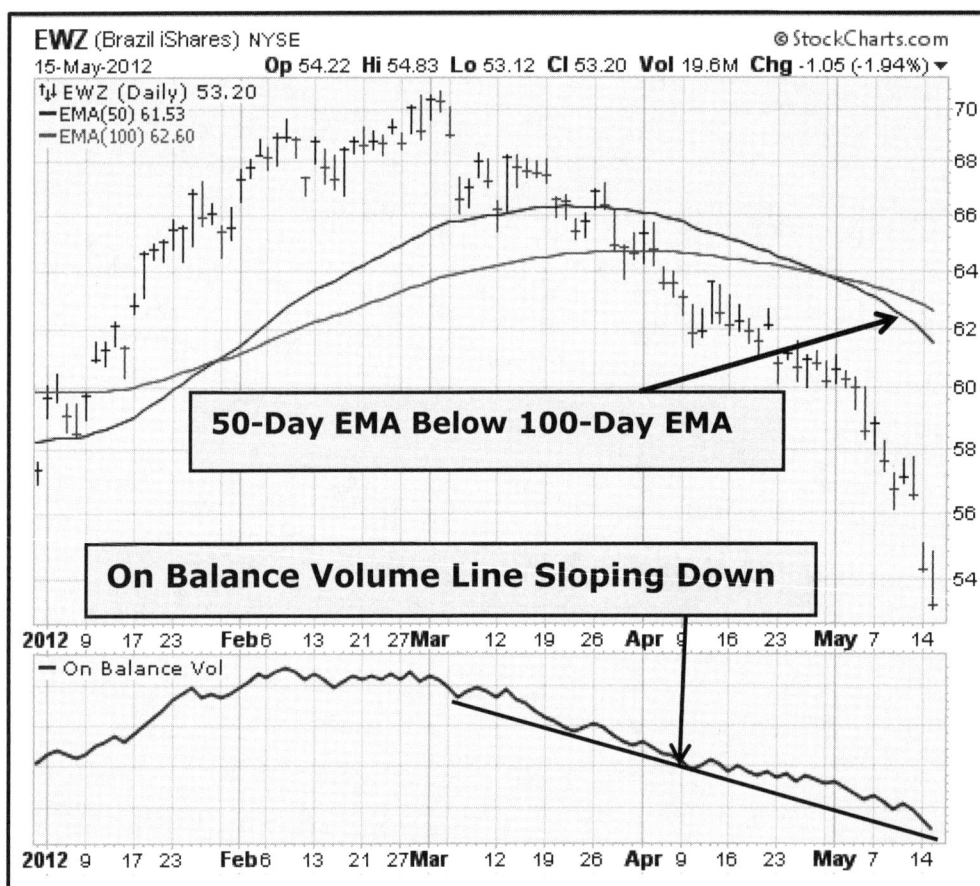

With EWZ in a confirmed price down trend, I sold EWZ call options against my *Super Portfolio* stock TJX. My brokerage account Transaction Report below shows that I sold 21 of the Brazil ETF 57-Strike weekly call options and collected $1,909.01 in cash income for the option sales.

Sold 21 EWZ 57-Strike Weekly Calls
Collected $1,909.01 in Cash Income

Transaction History   Alerts | Transfer Money | Bill Pay | Help

Date	Type	View	Description	Categories (hide)	Amount ($)
05/10/12	Sold Short		13 EWZ May 19 '12 $57 Call(EWZ) @ $1.05		1,347.12
05/11/12	Sold Short		8 EWZ May 19 '12 $57 Call(EWZ) @ $0.72		561.89

After selling the 57-Strike calls, the EWZ ETF continued to decline in price. My brokerage account Transaction Reports below show that I bought to close the 21 57-strike calls at .13 points. I then sold an additional 21 55-Strike calls and collected an additional $1,261.06 in premium for a total of $2,877.16 in premium in 1 week.

Bought to Close 21 EWZ 57-Strike Calls at .13

Transaction History   Alerts | Transfer Money | Bill Pay | Help

Date	Type	View	Description	Categories (hide)	Amount ($)
05/14/12	Bought To Cover		21 EWZ May 19 '12 $57 Call(EWZ) @ $0.13		-292.91

Sold to Open an Additional 21 EWZ 55-Strike Calls and Collected $1,261.06 in Additional Premium for a Total of $2,877.16 in premium in 1 week

Transaction History   Alerts | Transfer Money | Bill Pay | Help

Date	Type	View	Description	Categories (hide)	Amount ($)
05/14/12	Sold Short		21 EWZ May 19 '12 $55 Call(EWZ) @ $0.61		1,261.06

Time Value = Profit When You Are Short an Option

As we learned in the previous TNA covered call example, if you are short an option the time value of the option becomes profit at option expiration as the time value decays to zero.

My brokerage account Transaction Report below shows that I sold 13 of the EWZ 57-Strike weekly options at 1.05 points. After the commission, $1,347.12 in cash was credited to my brokerage account for the sale of the 13 options. With the EWZ ETF trading at 56.95 this was an at-the-money call consisting of only time value. This $1,347.12 premium becomes profit at option expiration.

Transaction History			Alerts | Transfer Money | Bill Pay | Help

Transactions	Check Summary	Deposit Summary	Categories	Reports

Date	Type	View	Description	Categories (hide)	Amount ($)
05/10/12	Sold Short		13 EWZ May 19 '12 $57 Call(EWZ) @ $1.05		1,347.12

Potential Cash on Cash Return of 94.5%

With weekly options I get to sell calls against my TJX stock 52 times per year. I purchase *Super Portfolio* stock that is equivalent in value to the short ETF options. For example, if I sold the EWZ 57-Strike call option I would own $5,700 of a *Super Portfolio* stock or $2,850 of two *Super Portfolio* stocks to create the spread.

In this example, I sold 13 57-strike calls which covered approximately $74,100 of TJX stock (5,700 x 13 = $74,100). If I sell a similar premium each week I have the potential to collect about $70,044 in premium over the next year ($ 1,347 premium X 52 weeks = $70,044). If I divide this total premium by the $74,100 investment in TJX stock I have the potential to receive about a 94.5% cash on cash yearly return ($70,044 total premium divided by $74,100 TJX stock investment = 94.5% return).

As mentioned previously, unlike a covered call trade, the short call options in the *Super Portfolio* spreads do not limit the price appreciation of the stocks in the portfolio. This 94.5% potential cash on cash return does not include any potential return for an increase in TJX stock price.

Let's take a look at another *Super Portfolio* spread I have been trading. My brokerage account Profit/Loss Report below shows I currently have $38,556.80 in open trade profits for *Super Portfolio* stock American Capital (AGNC). American Capital has the added benefit of paying a 16% annual dividend.

Portfolios											
Symbol		Last Trade	Change $	Change %	Day's Gain	Qty	Price Paid	Total Gain $	Total Gain %	Market Val	Edit
AGNC	Buy / Sell	32.105	0.36	1.15%	$2,525.90	6,920.26111	$26.53	$38,556.80	21.00%	$222,174.98	Edit

AGNC in a Confirmed Price Up Trend:

- 50 Day EMA above 100 Day EMA

- OBV Line sloping up

- AGNC making a series of new 52-Week highs

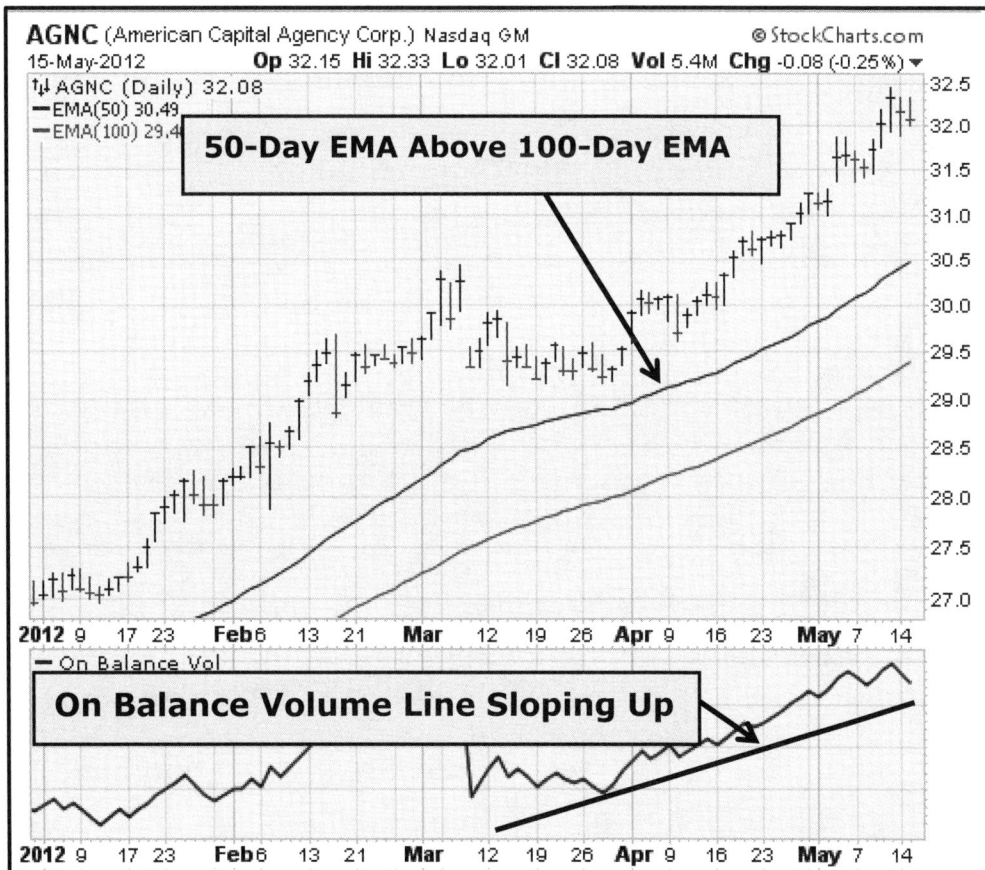

American Agency stock shares the common characteristics of *Super Portfolio* stocks.

- AGNC is in a confirmed price up trend

- Has no correlation to European debt crisis

- AGNC is not dependent on the price of oil or commodities

- AGNC has a strong equity growth rate in a slow growing US economy

- AGNC is in a leading industry . . . mortgage REIT

I have been selling China ETF (FXI) call options against my AGNC stock.

Confirmed Price Down Trend for FXI

- 50 Day EMA below 100 Day EMA

- OBV Line sloping down

- FXI making new 52-Week lows

With FXI in a confirmed price down trend, I sold FXI call options against my *Super Portfolio* stock AGNC. My brokerage account Transaction Report below shows that on May 10th and 11th I sold a total of 33 of the China ETF 36-Strike and 35-Strike weekly call options and collected $1,782.94 in cash income for the option sales.

FXI continued to decline in price so on May 14th I closed 21 of the short 36-Strike calls and sold an additional 21 of the 35-Strike calls collecting an additional $757.07 in premium. On May 15th I sold another 23 of the 35-Strike calls collecting another $802.56 in premium. FXI continued to decline and on May 16th I closed the 35-Strike calls and sold the 34-Strike calls collecting another $2,299.29 in premium.

After accounting for the $819.35 cost to close out the short FXI calls, I collected a total of $4,822.51 in premium over this one week period.

Collected $4,822.51 in FXI Premium during a One Week Period

Transaction History   🔔 Alerts | ≫ Transfer Money | ≫ Bill Pay | ⑦ Help

Transactions	Check Summary	Deposit Summary	Categories	Reports		

Date	Type	View	Description	Categories (hide)	Amount ($)
05/10/12	Sold Short		21 FXI May 19 '12 $36 Call(FXI) @ $0.44		900.06
05/11/12	Sold Short		12 FXI May 19 '12 $35 Call(FXI) @ $0.75		882.88
05/14/12	Sold Short		21 FXI May 19 '12 $35 Call(FXI) @ $0.37		757.07
05/14/12	Bought To Cover		21 FXI May 19 '12 $36 Call(FXI) @ $0.09		-208.91
05/15/12	Sold Short		23 FXI May 19 '12 $35 Call(FXI) @ $0.36		802.56
05/16/12	Bought To Cover		56 FXI May 19 '12 $35 Call(FXI) @ $0.10		-610.44
05/16/12	Sold Short		51 FXI May 19 '12 $34 Call(FXI) @ $0.46		2,299.29

Smaller Accounts

As noted earlier, I purchase a dollar amount of *Super Portfolio* stock that is equivalent in value to the short ETF options. If you sold the FXI 34-Strike call option in a smaller account, you could invest $3,400 in a *Super Portfolio* stock or $1,700 in two *Super Portfolio* stocks to create a spread. A margin account is required to trade this type of uncovered option spread.

- Invest $3,400 in 1 or 2 Super Portfolio stocks

- Sell 1 FXI 34–strike call

- Need margin account to sell uncovered ETF calls

$24,077 In Net Profits Over Past Two Weeks

My brokerage account Gain/Losses Reports that follow show all of the close-outs of my *Super Portfolio* short ETF call option trades over the past two weeks. There were a total of $24,077 in net profits after commissions over the two week period.

Despite the severe sell off in global markets over this two week period, my *Super Portfolio* stocks, on average, actually had a **positive** ¾ of 1% return over this same period demonstrating the ability of the *Super Portfolio Strategy* to generate substantial profits despite very difficult market conditions.

Portfolios: Gains & Losses

| Portfolios | Performance & Value | Positions | Gains & Losses | Risk Analyzer | Portfolio Analyzer | Income Estimator |

Realized Gains/Losses | Unrealized Gains/Losses

Positions: # - Lot edited by firm   + - Lot edited by customer

Symbol	Quantity	Opening Transaction			Order	Closing Transaction			Gain (Loss)	Term	Action
		Date	Price	Net Amount		Date	Price	Net Amount			
EEM May 19 '12 $38 Call	-38	05/16/2012	0.53	-1977.03	BC	05/18/2012	0.10	-416.93	1560	Short	Edit
EFA May 19 '12 $50 Call	-14	05/14/2012	0.80	-1105.32	BC	05/17/2012	0.09	-141.32	964	Short	Edit
EFA May 19 '12 $50 Call	-10	05/15/2012	0.54	-524.38	BC	05/17/2012	0.09	-100.94	423	Short	Edit
EFA May 19 '12 $51 Call	-9	05/11/2012	0.86	-759.14	BC	05/16/2012	0.10	-104.84	654	Short	Edit
EFA May 19 '12 $52 Call	-14	05/10/2012	0.55	-751.33	BC	05/14/2012	0.13	-196.65	555	Short	Edit
EFA May 25 '12 $49 Call w	-35	05/17/2012	0.73	-2520.30	BC	05/23/2012	0.17	-629.64	1891	Short	Edit
EWZ May 19 '12 $53 Call	-18	05/16/2012	0.64	-1130.28	BC	05/17/2012	0.14	-269.70	861	Short	Edit
EWZ May 19 '12 $54 Call	-15	05/15/2012	0.74	-1090.56	BC	05/17/2012	0.10	-169.41	921	Short	Edit
EWZ May 19 '12 $55 Call	-21	05/14/2012	0.61	-1260.99	BC	05/16/2012	0.13	-296.98	964	Short	Edit
EWZ May 19 '12 $57 Call	-13	05/10/2012	1.05	-1347.08	BC	05/14/2012	0.13	-181.37	1166	Short	Edit
EWZ May 19 '12 $57 Call	-8	05/11/2012	0.72	-561.91	BC	05/14/2012	0.13	-111.61	450	Short	Edit
EWZ May 25 '12 $52 Call w	-15	05/17/2012	1.11	-1645.55	BC	05/23/2012	0.22	-345.05	1300	Short	Edit
EWZ May 25 '12 $52 Call w	-18	05/17/2012	1.14	-2034.26	BC	05/23/2012	0.22	-414.07	1620	Short	Edit

Closed trades continued . . .

Portfolios: Gains & Losses

| Portfolios | Performance & Value | Positions | Gains & Losses | Risk Analyzer | Portfolio Analyzer | Income Estimator |

Realized Gains/Losses | Unrealized Gains/Losses

Positions: # - Lot edited by firm   + - Lot edited by customer

| Symbol | Quantity | Opening Transaction | | | Closing Transaction | | | | Gain (Loss) | Term | Action |
		Date	Price	Net Amount	Order	Date	Price	Net Amount			
FXI May 19 '12 $34 Call	-51	05/16/2012	0.46	-2299.12	BC	05/17/2012	0.11	-603.83	1695	Short	Edit
FXI May 19 '12 $35 Call	-12	05/11/2012	0.75	-882.85	BC	05/16/2012	0.10	-130.85	752	Short	Edit
FXI May 19 '12 $35 Call	-21	05/14/2012	0.37	-757.00	BC	05/16/2012	0.10	-228.99	528	Short	Edit
FXI May 19 '12 $35 Call	-23	05/15/2012	0.36	-802.48	BC	05/16/2012	0.10	-250.80	552	Short	Edit
FXI May 19 '12 $36 Call	-21	05/10/2012	0.44	-900.00	BC	05/14/2012	0.09	-208.98	691	Short	Edit
FXI May 25 '12 $34 Call w	-51	05/17/2012	0.39	-1946.13	BC	05/23/2012	0.08	-454.83	1491	Short	Edit
USO May 19 '12 $35 Call	-50	05/16/2012	0.47	-2303.88	BC	05/17/2012	0.29	-1492.06	812	Short	Edit
USO May 19 '12 $36 Call	-12	05/11/2012	0.68	-798.85	BC	05/16/2012	0.12	-161.13	638	Short	Edit
USO May 19 '12 $37 Call	-20	05/10/2012	0.41	-796.76	BC	05/15/2012	0.06	-143.22	654	Short	Edit
USO May 25 '12 $35 Call w	-50	05/17/2012	0.60	-2957.87	BC	05/23/2012	0.12	-646.06	2312	Short	Edit
XLE May 19 '12 $66 Call	-18	05/15/2012	0.50	-878.28	BC	05/17/2012	0.13	-255.70	623	Short	Edit

Super Portfolio Stocks versus Global ETFs

The portfolio snap shots that follow show the year to date returns for the *Super Portfolio* stocks and YTD results for a sampling of weak global and energy ETFs. As previously noted, the *Super Portfolio* stocks and the ETFs used in the *Super Portfolio* spread strategy can change over time depending on market conditions. The snap shots were taken over different time periods and demonstrate the ability of the *Super Portfolio* stocks to outperform the weak ETFs. Although the *Super Portfolio* stocks normally outperform the weaker ETFs there can be days when the reverse occurs and the ETFs outperform the *Super Portfolio* stocks.

Index 2012 Performan... ▼   Edit · Reorder · Download · Set alerts · Add/edit holdings |

| Basic | DayWatch | Performance | MLPL | Portfolio YTD | Real-Time | Fundan |

"Company or symbol"   ➕ Add Symbol   Customize current view

SYMBOL	TIME & PRICE		CHANGE	SHARES	DAY'S VAL CHG & %		PRICE PAID	GAIN & % GAIN	
EEM	12:53PM	38.15	↓0.03	263.5	↓$7.90	↓0.09%	37.94	↑$51.38	↑0.55%
XLB	12:52PM	33.79	↑0.06	299.7	↑$17.98	↑0.19%	33.37	↑$131.87	↑1.26%
EFA	12:53PM	49.35	↑0.18	201.9	↑$36.34	↑0.37%	49.53	↓$38.56	↓0.36%
XLE	12:53PM	65.56	↑0.15	145.2	↑$21.78	↑0.23%	68.86	↓$477.71	↓4.79%
USO	12:53PM	34.63	↓0.52	262.4	↓$136.45	↓1.48%	38.11	↓$913.15	↓9.13%
EWZ	12:53PM	52.04	↓0.57	168.3	↓$95.93	↓1.08%	57.39	↓$908.82	↓9.32%
IWM	12:53PM	76.53	↑0.08	136	↑$10.88	↑0.10%	73.52	↑$409.35	↑4.09%
FXI	12:52PM	33.79	↓0.07	286.7	↓$20.07	↓0.21%	34.87	↓$309.64	↓3.10%
Total					↓$173.37	↓0.22%		↓$2,055.28	↓2.58%

Super Portfolio ▼   Edit · Reorder · Download · Set alerts · Add/edit holdings | Create new · Manage all

| Basic | DayWatch | Performance | MLPL | Portfolio YTD | Real-Time | Fundamentals | Det |

"Company or symbol"   ➕ Add Symbol   Customize current view

SYMBOL	TIME & PRICE		CHG & % CHG		VOLUME	DAY'S VAL CHG & %		PRICE PAID	GAIN & % GAIN	
	12:48pm EDT	15.14	0.30	+2.02%	2,043,811	↑$252.60	↑2.02%	11.87	↑$2,753.34	↑27.55%
	12:54pm EDT	30.21	0.20	+0.67%	3,323,023	↑$80.44	↑0.67%	24.86	↑$2,151.77	↑21.52%
	12:54pm EDT	40.90	0.57	+1.41%	2,250,687	↑$177.04	↑1.41%	32.19	↑$2,705.33	↑27.06%
	12:54pm EDT	98.52	1.63	+1.68%	418,926	↑$196.09	↑1.68%	83.11	↑$1,853.82	↑18.54%
	12:54pm EDT	119.70	0.88	+0.74%	523,501	↑$98.91	↑0.74%	88.92	↑$3,459.67	↑34.62%
	12:53pm EDT	54.43	0.98	+1.83%	214,841	↑$267.25	↑1.83%	36.66	↑$4,845.88	↑48.47%
	12:54pm EDT	100.03	0.49	+0.49%	371,792	↑$59.04	↑0.49%	82.96	↑$2,056.93	↑20.58%
Total						↑$1,131.37	↑1.28%		↑$19,826.74	↑28.33%

Index 2012 Performan... ▼   Edit · Reorder · Download · Set alerts · Add/edit holdings

Basic	DayWatch	**Performance**	MLPL	Portfolio YTD	Real-Time	Funda

"Company or symbol"   ➕ Add Symbol   Customize current view

SYMBOL	TIME & PRICE		CHANGE	SHARES	DAY'S VAL CHG & %		PRICE PAID	GAIN & % GAIN	
EEM	May 24	37.33	↓0.19	263.5	↓$50.06	↓0.51%	37.94	↓$160.73	↓1.61%
XLB	May 24	34.13	↑0.21	299.7	↑$62.94	↑0.62%	33.37	↑$227.77	↑2.28%
EFA	May 24	48.27	↓0.32	201.9	↓$64.61	↓0.66%	49.53	↓$254.39	↓2.54%
XLE	May 24	65.44	↓0.05	145.2	↓$7.26	↓0.08%	68.86	↓$496.58	↓4.97%
USO	May 24	34.26	↑0.17	262.4	↑$44.61	↑0.50%	38.11	↓$1,010.24	↓10.10%
EWZ	May 24	51.12	↓0.10	168.3	↓$16.83	↓0.20%	57.39	↓$1,055.24	↓10.93%
IWM	May 24	76.64	↑0.16	136	↑$21.76	↑0.21%	73.52	↑$424.32	↑4.24%
FXI	May 24	32.74	↓0.51	286.7	↓$146.22	↓1.53%	34.87	↓$610.67	↓6.11%
Total					↓$155.67	↓0.20%		↓$2,935.77	↓3.69%

Super Portfolio ▼   Edit · Reorder · Download · Set alerts · Add/edit holdings | Create new · Manage all

Basic	DayWatch	Performance	MLPL	Portfolio YTD	Real-Time	Fundamentals

"Company or symbol"   ➕ Add Symbol   Customize current view

SYMBOL	TIME & PRICE		CHG & % CHG		VOLUME	DAY'S VAL CHG & %		PRICE PAID	GAIN & % GAIN	
	May 24	15.55	↑0.19	↑1.24%	1,462,360	↑$159.98	↑1.24%	11.87	↑$3,098.56	↑31.00%
	May 24	30.26	↑0.12	↑0.40%	3,568,403	↑$48.26	↑0.40%	24.86	↑$2,171.88	↑21.72%
	May 24	40.90	↑0.23	↑0.57%	4,384,767	↑$71.44	↑0.57%	32.19	↑$2,705.33	↑27.06%
	May 24	101.71	↑2.38	↑2.40%	1,080,983	↑$286.31	↑2.40%	83.11	↑$2,237.58	↑22.38%
	May 24	125.33	↑1.03	↑0.83%	1,825,365	↑$115.77	↑0.83%	88.92	↑$4,092.48	↑40.95%
	May 24	55.04	↑0.70	↑1.29%	487,829	↑$190.89	↑1.29%	36.66	↑$5,012.23	↑50.14%
	May 24	104.20	↑3.40	↑3.37%	2,030,240	↑$409.70	↑3.37%	82.96	↑$2,559.42	↑25.60%
Total						↑$1,282.36	↑1.42%		↑$21,877.48	↑31.26%

Index 2012 Performan... ▼   Edit · Reorder · Download · Set alerts · Add/edit holdings | Create

| Basic | DayWatch | Performance | MLPL | Portfolio YTD | Real-Time | Fundamentals |

"Company or symbol"   ➕ Add Symbol   Customize current view

SYMBOL	TIME & PRICE		CHANGE	SHARES	DAY'S VAL CHG & %		PRICE PAID	GAIN & % GAIN	
EEM	04:00pm EDT	38.16	0.78	263.5	↑ $204.21	↑ 2.07%	37.94	↑ $57.97	↑ 0.58%
XLB	04:00pm EDT	34.57	0.63	299.7	↑ $188.81	↑ 1.86%	33.37	↑ $359.64	↑ 3.60%
EFA	04:00pm EDT	48.84	0.80	201.9	↑ $161.52	↑ 1.67%	49.53	↓ $139.31	↓ 1.39%
XLE	04:00pm EDT	64.52	0.90	145.2	↑ $130.68	↑ 1.41%	68.86	↓ $630.17	↓ 6.30%
USO	04:00pm EDT	31.415	0.72	262.4	↑ $187.88	↑ 2.33%	38.11	↓ $1,756.77	↓ 17.57%
EWZ	04:00pm EDT	51.57	0.75	168.3	↑ $126.22	↑ 1.48%	57.39	↓ $979.51	↓ 10.14%
IWM	04:00pm EDT	76.22	0.95	136	↑ $129.20	↑ 1.26%	73.52	↑ $367.20	↑ 3.67%
FXI	04:00pm EDT	33.52	0.73	286.7	↑ $209.29	↑ 2.23%	34.87	↓ $387.04	↓ 3.87%
Total					↑ $1,337.82	↑ 1.78%		↓ $3,107.99	↓ 3.90%

Super Portfolio ▼   Edit · Reorder · Download · Set alerts · Add/edit holdings | Create new · Manage all

| Basic | DayWatch | Performance | MLPL | Portfolio YTD | Real-Time | Fundamentals | D |

"Company or symbol"   ➕ Add Symbol   Customize current view

SYMBOL	TIME & PRICE		CHG & % CHG		VOLUME	DAY'S VAL CHG & %		PRICE PAID	GAIN & % GAIN	
	04:00pm EDT	33.27	0.37	+1.12%	6,069,347	↑ $137.27	↑ 1.12%	26.95	↑ $2,344.72	↑ 23.45%
	04:00pm EDT	44.91	0.55	+1.24%	5,010	↑ $154.00	↑ 1.24%	35.69	↑ $2,581.60	↑ 25.83%
	04:00pm EDT	14.68	0.17	+1.17%	1,696,932	↑ $143.14	↑ 1.17%	11.87	↑ $2,366.02	↑ 23.67%
	04:00pm EDT	41.70	0.45	+1.09%	5,035,011	↑ $139.77	↑ 1.09%	32.19	↑ $2,953.81	↑ 29.54%
	04:00pm EDT	133.01	2.80	+2.15%	1,463,285	↑ $314.72	↑ 2.15%	88.92	↑ $4,955.72	↑ 49.58%
	04:00pm EDT	53.76	0.38	+0.71%	337,552	↑ $103.63	↑ 0.71%	36.66	↑ $4,663.17	↑ 46.64%
Total						↑ $992.52	↑ 1.26%		↑ $19,865.03	↑ 33.12%

Chapter 6

Profiting in Any Type of Market

Let's now look at another type of option income strategy using option spreads. Debit option spreads are implemented using only options by purchasing a call option and selling a call option with a higher strike price. Because the short option is 'covered' with the option purchase this would be a limited risk trade. The brokerage confirmation below shows that I bought 6 of the Goldman Sachs (GS) July 65-strike calls symbol GSG65 at 50.63 points and sold to open 6 Goldman Sachs July 95-Strike call options GSG95 at 27.93. These options expire in about 4 months.

Buy GS 65-Strike Call at 50.63, Sell GS 95-Strike Call at 27.93

TRADE CONFIRMATION

TRADE DATE	SETL DATE	MKT/ CPT	SYMBOL/ CUSIP	BUY/ SELL	QUANTITY	PRICE	ACCT TYPE		
03/26/09	03/27/09	5 1	GSG65	BUY	6	$50.63	Margin	PRINCIPAL	$30,378.00
CALL GOLDMAN SACH JUL 065 ****								COMMISSION	$8.49
07/18/2009 EXPIRATION DATE								NET AMOUNT	$30,386.49
OPEN CONTRACT									
03/26/09	03/27/09	5 1	GSG95	SELL	6	$27.93	Margin	PRINCIPAL	$16,758.00
CALL GOLDMAN SACH JUL 095 ****								COMMISSION	$8.49
07/18/2009 EXPIRATION DATE								FEE	$0.10
OPEN CONTRACT								NET AMOUNT	$16,749.41

Selling to open the 95-strike call at 27.93 points resulted in a $2,793 cash payment per contract being credited to my brokerage account or a total of $16,750 for 6 contracts. So purchasing the 65-strike call at 50.63 points and receiving 27.93 points in cash for the sale of the 95-strike call resulted in a 55% cash payment I received up front when I initiated the trade. I get to keep this 55% cash payment regardless of the price movement of Goldman Sachs stock. Goldman Sachs stock was trading at 112.10 when I initiated this trade.

Buy 65-Strike Call at 50.63 Points, Sell 95-Strike Call at 27.93 Points

Equals 55% Cash Dividend Over a Four Month Period

27.93 Divided by 50.63 = 55%

When this option spread expires in 4 months I can create another option spread and collect another cash payment. This is called a 'rollover'. If I rollover this option spread a second time I would receive a total of 3 cash payments over the course of one year. Collecting a similar option premium on rollovers has the potential of producing up to a 165% cash dividend over the course of one year.

Up to 165% Cash Dividend Potential

Over the Course of One Year

By 'Rolling Over' Option Spread

Buying the GS 65-strike call option at a 55% discount reduces risk considerably and provides considerable downside protection in the event Goldman Sachs stock declines in price. Goldman Sachs stock moved up in price and is currently trading at 140.32.

We can see from the Call Option Spread Analysis below that Goldman Sachs stock could drop 30% from its current price to 98.22 and I would still realize a 32.2% return for this spread trade (circled). This spread trade profits if Goldman Sachs stock increases in price, remains flat or decreases 30% in price demonstrating the versatility of the option income spread strategy in producing profits under various market conditions. This gives the option income spread strategy a big advantage over an option purchase strategy which requires a stock price increase in the underlying stock to be profitable.

Wealth Creation Alliance

Call Option Spread Analysis

Stock Symbol	Current Stock Price	Buy Strike	Buy Price	Sell Strike	Sell Price
GS July	140.32	65	50.63	95	27.93

Cost
$22.70

[Calculate] [New Analysis] [Print]

% Change	5.0%	0.0%	-10.0%	-15.0%	-20.0%	-25.0%	-30.0%
Stock Price	$147.34	$140.32	$126.29	$119.27	$112.26	$105.24	$98.22
Call Buy Value	$82.34	$75.32	$61.29	$54.27	$47.26	$40.24	$33.22
Call Sell Value	$-52.34	$-45.32	$-31.29	$-24.27	$-17.26	$-10.24	$-3.22
Spread Value	$30.00	$30.00	$30.00	$30.00	$30.00	$30.00	$30.00
Spread Cost	$22.70	$22.70	$22.70	$22.70	$22.70	$22.70	$22.70
Spread Profit	$7.30	$7.30	$7.30	$7.30	$7.30	$7.30	$7.30
Spread % Ret	32.2%	32.2%	32.2%	32.2%	32.2%	32.2%	32.2%

Bearish Option Income Spread Trade Example

Bearish option income spread trades can be established by purchasing a put option and selling a put option with a lower strike price. Because the short put is covered with the put option purchase this would be a limited risk trade. My brokerage confirmation below shows that I bought 7 of the Intuitive Surgical April 400-strike puts symbol IJAP400 at 70.02 points and sold to open 7 Intuitive Surgical April 370-Strike put options at 45.02. These options expire in about 3 weeks.

Buy Intuitive Surgical 400-Strike Put at 70.02

Sell Intuitive Surgical 370-Strike Put at 45.02

TRADE CONFIRMATION

TRADE DATE	SETL DATE	MKT/ CPT	SYMBOL/ CUSIP	BUY/ SELL	QUANTITY	PRICE	ACCT TYPE		
04/01/08	04/02/08	5 1	IJAP400	BUY	7	$70.02	Margin	PRINCIPAL	$49,014.00
								COMMISSION	$9.24
PUT INTUITIVE SU APR 400 ****								NET AMOUNT	$49,023.24
04/19/2008 EXPIRATION DATE									
OPEN CONTRACT									
04/01/08	04/02/08	5 1	IJAP370	SELL	7	$45.02	Margin	PRINCIPAL	$31,514.00
								COMMISSION	$9.24
PUT INTUITIVE SU APR 370 ****								FEE	$0.18
04/19/2008 EXPIRATION DATE								NET AMOUNT	$31,504.58
OPEN CONTRACT									

Selling to open the 370-strike put at 45.02 points resulted in a $4,500 cash payment per contract being credited to my brokerage account or a total of $31,500 for 7 contracts. So purchasing the 400-strike put at 70.02 points and receiving 45.02 points in cash for the sale of the 370-strike put resulted in a 64% cash payment I received up front when I initiated the trade. I get to keep this 64% cash payment regardless of the price movement of Intuitive Surgical stock. This option spread trade can profit if ISRG stock increases in price, remains flat or decreases in price.

Buy 400-Strike Put at 70.02 Points

Sell 370-Strike Put at 45.02 Points

Equals 64% Cash Dividend

45.02 Divided by 70.02 = 64%

Legging Into an Option Spread

The two option spread examples just presented for GS and ISRG are examples of creating a debit spread with the simultaneous purchase and sale of an option. You can also 'Leg In' to an option spread by purchasing an option and then leg in to a spread by selling an option at a later date. Legging into a spread has many advantages especially during volatile markets.

Let's take a look at an example of legging into a spread using Google options. You can see from my brokerage confirmations below that I purchased 18 Google 570-Strike call options at an average price of 37.35. Two weeks later I then sold to open 18 Google 640-Strike call options at an average price of 28.65 which resulted in $2,865 cash income per contract being credited to my brokerage account.

Buy to Open 18 GOOG 570 Calls at an Average Price of 37.35
Sell to Open 18 GOOG 640 Calls at an Average Price of 28.65

Daily Account Activity

Trade Date	Settlement Date	Activity	Quantity	Trade #	Currency	Price
				PURCHASES AND SALES		
+GOPKQ:		Google Inc Cl A Nov 2007 570.00 Call				
10/04/2007	10/05/2007	Buy to Open	3.0000	47958637	USD	31.000000
10/04/2007	10/05/2007	Buy to Open	3.0000	47958639	USD	31.000000
10/04/2007	10/05/2007	Buy to Open	1.0000	47958641	USD	30.800000
10/05/2007	10/09/2007	Buy to Open	7.0000	48019599	USD	40.500000
10/08/2007	10/09/2007	Buy to Open	4.0000	48073360	USD	43.000000
+GOOKH:		Google Inc Cl A Nov 2007 640.00 Call				
10/18/2007	10/19/2007	Sell to Open	-1.0000	48631362	USD	28.800000
10/18/2007	10/19/2007	Sell to Open	-1.0000	48631364	USD	28.800000
10/18/2007	10/19/2007	Sell to Open	-2.0000	48631366	USD	28.800000
10/18/2007	10/19/2007	Sell to Open	-1.0000	48631368	USD	28.800000
10/18/2007	10/19/2007	Sell to Open	-5.0000	48632035	USD	28.600000
10/18/2007	10/19/2007	Sell to Open	-5.0000	48632037	USD	28.600000
10/18/2007	10/19/2007	Sell to Open	-2.0000	48632039	USD	28.600000
10/18/2007	10/19/2007	Sell to Open	-1.0000	48632041	USD	28.600000

The short sale of the 640-Strike call option was 'covered' by the purchase of the 570-Strike call option thereby limiting my risk to the cost of the spread. The cost of the spread is calculated by subtracting the sale price from the buy price and in this example is 8.70 points or $870.

Buy Price of 37.35 Minus Sale Price of 28.65 = Maximum Risk of $870

At the time I sold the 640-Strike call option Google stock was trading at 639. The 640-Strike call option was an 'out-of-the-money' option as the strike price was greater than the stock price.

Strike Price of 640 and Stock Price of 639 = 'Out-of-the-Money' Option

Out-of-the-money options consist of only time value and no intrinsic value. Shorting an out-of-the-money option that consists of only time value takes full advantage of the 'time decay' characteristics of options. In this example the out-of-the-money 640-Strike call that I sold for 28.65 points is all time value which will decay to zero and will result in a 28.65 point ($2,865) profit at option expiration regardless of the price movement of Google stock.

Selling an Option at 28.65 and Later Buying Back at Zero = 28.65 Point Profit

Short 28.65 Points of Time Value = 28.65 Points of Profit at Option Expiration

The full profit potential for this spread will be realized if Google stock closes at or above the strike price of the option that was sold at option expiration. In this example if Google stock closes at or above 640 the full profit potential of 61.30 points ($6,130) will be realized.

The profit potential is calculated by subtracting the 8.70 point cost of the spread from the difference between the strike price of the option sold (640) and the strike price of the option purchased (570).

640 Sell Strike – 570 Buy Strike – 8.70 Cost = 61.30 Profit Potential

The *Call Option Spread Analysis* below displays the profit/loss potential for buying the Google 570-Strike call for 37.35 points and selling the Google 640-Strike call for 28.65 points. The table displays profit results for various price changes for Google stock at option expiration from a 10% increase to a 5% decline. Google stock is currently trading at 639.

Wealth Creation Alliance

Call Option Spread Analysis

Stock Symbol	Current Stock Price	Buy Strike	Buy Price	Sell Strike	Sell Price
GOOG	639	570	37.35	640	28.65

Cost: $8.70

[Calculate] [New Analysis] [Print]

% Change	10.0%	7.5%	5.0%	2.5%	0.0%	-2.5%	-5.0%
Stock Price	$702.90	$686.93	$670.95	$654.98	$639.00	$623.03	$607.05
Call Buy Value	$132.90	$116.93	$100.95	$84.98	$69.00	$53.03	$37.05
Call Sell Value	$-62.90	$-46.93	$-30.95	$-14.98	$0.00	$0.00	$0.00
Spread Value	$70.00	$70.00	$70.00	$70.00	$69.00	$53.03	$37.05
Spread Cost	$8.70	$8.70	$8.70	$8.70	$8.70	$8.70	$8.70
Spread Profit	$61.30	$61.30	$61.30	$61.30	$60.30	$44.33	$28.35
Spread % Ret	704.6%	704.6%	704.6%	704.6%	693.1%	509.5%	325.9%

The analysis reveals that if Google stock increases 2.5% at option expiration to 654.98 a 704.6% return will be realized (circled). If Google is trading at 654.98 at option expiration, the option we purchased would increase in value to 84.98 and the option sold would incur a 14.98 point loss, resulting in a 70.0 point net spread value (84.98 – 14.98 = 70.0). A 70.0 point spread value would result in a 61.30 point profit with a 8.70 point cost. With an 8.70 cost, a 61.30 profit represents a 704% return.

Google Stock Increases 2.5% = 704% Option Return

The *Call Option Spread Analysis* below for the Google option spread trade shows that if Google stock remains flat at 639 at option expiration then a 693% return will be realized (circled). And if Google stock declines 5% to 607.05 a 325% return will be realized (circled). Profiting on a call option trade when the underlying stock declines in price is only possible because of the sale of the 640-strike call. This option trade can be closed out any time prior to option expiration by selling the 570-strike call to close and buying back to close the 640-strike call. I will normally close out and take profits on a spread if the spread reaches 90 to 95% of its profit potential.

Google Stock Flat = 693% Option Return

Google Stock Decreases 5.0% = 325% Option Return

Wealth Creation Alliance

Call Option Spread Analysis

Stock Symbol	Current Stock Price	Buy Strike	Buy Price	Sell Strike	Sell Price
GOOG	639	570	37.35	640	28.65

Cost: $8.70

[Calculate] [New Analysis] [Print]

% Change	10.0%	7.5%	5.0%	2.5%	0.0%	-2.5%	-5.0%
Stock Price	$702.90	$686.93	$670.95	$654.98	$639.00	$623.03	$607.05
Call Buy Value	$132.90	$116.93	$100.95	$84.98	$69.00	$53.03	$37.05
Call Sell Value	$-62.90	$-46.93	$-30.95	$-14.98	$0.00	$0.00	$0.00
Spread Value	$70.00	$70.00	$70.00	$70.00	$69.00	$53.03	$37.05
Spread Cost	$8.70	$8.70	$8.70	$8.70	$8.70	$8.70	$8.70
Spread Profit	$61.30	$61.30	$61.30	$61.30	$60.30	$44.33	$28.35
Spread % Ret	704.6%	704.6%	704.6%	704.6%	693.1%	509.5%	325.9%

The *Call Option Spread Analysis* for the Google spread trade demonstrates the attractive profit potential with limited risk for option spreads.

- **Profit Potential of $110,340 ($6,130 Per Option X 18 Options)**

- **704% Option Return if Google Stock is Up 2.5% at Option Expiration**

- **693% Option Return if Google Stock is Flat at Option Expiration**

- **325% Option Return if Google Stock is Down 5% at Option Expiration**

- **Maximum Risk of $870 Per Option**

Advantages of Option Spreads
versus Option Purchases

1) Increased Profit Potential

A limited risk call option spread is created by purchasing a call option and selling a call option with a higher strike price. If you have an existing profit for a call option purchase and leg into an option spread, the spread can typically increase the existing profit of an option purchase by 50% to 100% or more. In the GOOG spread example just presented, the profit potential of the existing GOOG option purchase was increased by 85% with the creation of the spread.

2) The Option Sale Provides Downside Protection

The sale of a call option results in cash being credited to your brokerage account. This reduces the cost basis of the option purchase and provides downside protection in the event the price of the underlying stock declines in price.

3) Reduces Risk

In the GOOG spread trade just presented, the sale of the 640-Strike call reduced the risk of the 570 call purchase from $3,735 per contract to $870 per contract.

$$\begin{array}{ll} & 37.35 \text{ Cost of 570-Strike call purchase} \\ - & \underline{28.65 \text{ Sale of 640-Strike call}} \\ = & 8.70 \text{ Cost of spread and maximum risk} \end{array}$$

4) Allows You to Maintain Positions During Volatile Markets

The downside protection provided by the sale of a call option to create a spread can help you maintain your spread trade during volatile markets. If you traded option purchases only, volatile price swings in the underlying stock may force you to sell an option to prevent large losses.

5) Spreads Can Be Profitable If a Stock Goes Up or Down

Depending on the strike price, option spreads can be profitable if the underlying stock price increases, decreases or remains flat at option expiration.

Trading Weekly Option Spreads

Option spreads can be traded using weekly options. Purchasing a weekly call option and selling a weekly call option with a higher strike price creates a bullish debit spread. Weekly option spreads share the same characteristics as monthly option spreads.

The sale of the call option reduces the cost basis of the option purchase and reduces the overall risk of the option purchase. The sale of a call options results in a cash credit to your brokerage account for the amount of the premium. The short call option profits as the underlying stock decreases in price providing downside protection.

Depending on the strike prices, weekly option spreads can be profitable if the underlying stock price increases, decreases or remains flat at option expiration.

Let's now take a look at several weekly option spread trade examples. My brokerage account Confirmation below shows that I purchased the Apple Mar 02 515-Strike weekly call at 10.52 and sold the Mar 02 520-Strike weekly call at 7.32. This created a bullish debit spread that cost 3.20 points or $320 which was my maximum risk for this trade. Five days later I closed out this spread at a 4.8 point debit which resulted in a 50.6% weekly return.

Buy AAPL Mar 02 515-strike weekly call @ 10.52, Sell 520-strike call @ 7.32

History & Statements					
Transactions	Statements	**Confirmations**			
Date	Transaction	Action (Buy, Sell)	Symbol	Quantity	Price
02/24/2012	08141800646	Bought	AAPL Mar 02 2012 515.0 Call	1	10.52
02/24/2012	08141800594	Sold	AAPL Mar 02 2012 520.0 Call	1	7.32
Enter symbol	QUOTE ▼	Options: Enter underlying symbol and click Chain	Index: use "$" (e.g. $DJI)		

Sell to close Mar 02 515-strike call @ 28.34, Buy to close 520-strike weekly call @ 23.52

50.6% Weekly Return

History & Statements					
Transactions	Statements	**Confirmations**			
Date	Transaction	Action (Buy, Sell)	Symbol	Quantity	Price
02/29/2012	08152474084	Bought	AAPL Mar 02 2012 520.0 Call	1	23.52
02/29/2012	08152473935	Sold	AAPL Mar 02 2012 515.0 Call	1	28.34
Enter symbol	QUOTE ▼	Options: Enter underlying symbol and click Chain	Index: use "$" (e.g. $DJI)		

In the example below, my brokerage account Confirmation below shows that I purchased 5 of the S&P 500 Index ETF Mar 02 54-Strike weekly calls at 1.26 points and sold 5 of the Mar 02 55-Strike weekly calls at .62 points. This created a bullish debit spread that cost .64 points or $64 per contract which was my maximum risk for this trade. One week later I closed out this spread at a .91 point debit which resulted in a 42.2% weekly return.

Buy SSO Mar 02 54-strike weekly call @ 1.26
Sell SSO Mar 02 55-strike weekly call @ .62

History & Statements

| Transactions | Statements | Confirmations | | | |

Date	Transaction	Action (Buy, Sell)	Symbol	Quantity	Price
02/24/2012	08141797692	Sold	SSO Mar 02 2012 55.0 Call	5	0.62
02/24/2012	08141797673	Bought	SSO Mar 02 2012 54.0 Call	5	1.26

Enter symbol QUOTE ▼ Options: Enter underlying symbol and click Chain | Index: use "$" (e.g. $DJI)

Sell to close SSO Mar 02 54-strike weekly call @ 1.18
Buy to close SSO Mar 02 55-strike weekly call @ .27

42.2% Weekly Return

History & Statements

| Transactions | Statements | Confirmations | | | |

Date	Transaction	Action (Buy, Sell)	Symbol	Quantity	Price
03/02/2012	08173306996	Bought	SSO Mar 02 2012 55.0 Call	5	0.27
03/02/2012	08173306926	Sold	SSO Mar 02 2012 54.0 Call	5	1.18

Enter symbol QUOTE ▼ Options: Enter underlying symbol and click Chain | Index: use "$" (e.g. $DJI)

And in the example below, my brokerage account Confirmation below shows that I purchased 5 of the Nasdaq QQQ ETF Mar 02 63-Strike weekly calls at 1.13 points and sold 5 of the Mar 02 64-Strike weekly calls at .44 points. This created a bullish debit spread that cost .69 points or $69 per contract which was my maximum risk for this trade. One week later I closed out this spread at a .97 point debit which resulted in a 40.5% weekly return.

Buy QQQ Mar 02 63-strike weekly call @ 1.13
Sell QQQ Mar 02 64-strike weekly call @   .44

History & Statements

| Transactions | Statements | Confirmations |

Date	Transaction	Action (Buy, Sell)	Symbol	Quantity	Price
☐ 02/24/2012	08141791429	Bought	QQQ Mar 02 2012 63.0 Call	5	1.13
☐ 02/24/2012	08141791425	Sold	QQQ Mar 02 2012 64.0 Call	5	0.44

Enter symbol   **QUOTE** ▾   Options: Enter underlying symbol and click Chain | Index: use "$" (e.g. $DJI)

Sell to close QQQ Mar 02 63-strike weekly call @ 1.96
Buy to close QQQ Mar 02 64-strike weekly call @   .99

40.5% Weekly Return

History & Statements

| Transactions | Statements | Confirmations |

Date	Transaction	Action (Buy, Sell)	Symbol	Quantity	Price
☐ 03/01/2012	08167855027	Bought	QQQ Mar 02 2012 64.0 Call	5	0.99
☐ 03/01/2012	08167855025	Sold	QQQ Mar 02 2012 63.0 Call	5	1.96

Enter symbol   **QUOTE** ▾   Options: Enter underlying symbol and click Chain | Index: use "$" (e.g. $DJI)

$919,318.52 in Real Time Option Spread Profits

My brokerage account Profit/Loss Reports that follow show $919,318.52 in profits for the option spread strategy over the past 5 years with an average return of 58.2%. There were 130 winning trades and 11 losing trades resulting in 92.2% accuracy.

Note: The profit/loss for option spread trades is calculated by 'netting out' the profit or loss for the long position and the short position. For example, the CAMAM/CAMJR option spread trade circled below shows a $27,657.78 profit for the 11 long CAMAM options and a -$10,026.24 loss for the 11 short CAMJR options resulting in a net profit of $17,631.54 for the spread trade.

Market Value: $296,226.28 ($118,514.37 / 99.69%)

		Last Trade	Change $	Change %	Day's Gain	Qty	Price Paid	Total Gain $	Total Gain %	Market Val	Edit
⊞ CAMAM	Trade	30.70	0.00	0.00%	$2,860.00*	11	$16.73	$27,657.78*	150.05%*	$46,090.00*	Edit
⊞ CAMJR	Trade	15.70	2.10	15.44%	-$2,750.00*	-11	$7.00	-$10,026.24*	-129.94%*	-$17,710.00*	Edit
⊞ DEAD	Trade	33.30	0.00	0.00%	$1,260.00*	9	$20.93	$15,959.28*	84.57%*	$34,830.00*	Edit
⊞ DEJH	Trade	16.48	1.18	7.71%	-$1,080.00*	-9	$6.50	-$9,014.74*	-153.71%*	-$14,850.00*	Edit
⊞ FCXAO	Trade	45.15	2.80	6.61%	$720.00*	9	$20.60	$21,479.28*	115.66%*	$40,050.00*	Edit
⊞ FCXJT	Trade	17.25	-0.30	-1.71%	-$315.00*	-9	$6.6667	-$10,132.73*	-168.24%*	-$16,110.00*	Edit

Option Spreads   Profits $175,467.53   Average Return 95.7%

Market Value: $445,284.87 ($175,467.53 / 95.71%)   DJIA 14,143.72 ▲ +65.03   Nasdaq 2,825.96 ▲ +14.35

REFRESH ⟳   STREAMING QUOTES   EXPORT TO EXCEL' ⬇   Results per Page: 200 ▾

⊞⊟ Symbol		Last Trade	Change $	Change %	Day's Gain	Qty	Price Paid	Total Gain $	Total Gain %	Market Val	Edit
⊞ APVJK	Trade	15.35	2.75	21.83%	-$3,420.00*	-12	$5.0667	-$12,494.47	-204.34%*	-$18,540.00*	Edit
⊞ CAMAM	Trade	30.70	0.00	0.00%	$5,200.00*	20	$16.45	$50,853.04*	154.35%*	$83,800.00*	Edit
⊞ CAMJR	Trade	15.70	2.10	15.44%	-$5,200.00*	-20	$3.875	-$24,680.98*	-317.20%*	-$32,400.00*	Edit
⊞ DEAD	Trade	33.30	0.00	0.00%	$1,680.00*	12	$19.70	$22,759.04*	96.11%*	$46,440.00*	Edit
⊞ DEJH	Trade	16.48	1.18	7.71%	-$1,440.00*	-12	$5.30	-$13,464.98*	-210.89%*	-$19,800.00*	Edit
⊞ FCXAO	Trade	45.15	2.80	6.61%	$1,280.00*	16	$19.38	$40,156.04*	129.35%*	$71,200.00*	Edit
⊞ FCXJT	Trade	17.25	-0.30	-1.71%	-$640.00*	-16	$6.225	-$18,787.98*	-188.11%*	-$28,720.00*	Edit
⊞ FLRAA	Trade	52.30	0.00	0.00%	$1,080.00*	12	$25.62	$35,809.04*	116.30%*	$66,600.00*	Edit
⊞ FLRJH	Trade	20.50	2.50	13.89%	-$1,920.00*	-12	$7.00	-$15,496.99*	-184.12%*	-$23,880.00*	Edit
⊞ GOPAY	Trade	105.00	11.90	12.78%	$2,380.00	2	$60.50	$8,882.52	73.30%	$21,000.00	Edit
⊞ NOVJU	Trade	11.90	1.67	16.32%	-$4,008.00	-24	$4.0625	-$18,834.98	-192.69%	-$28,560.00	Edit
⊞ NOVKJ	Trade	26.20	0.00	0.00%	$4,320.00*	24	$12.08	$41,539.04*	143.13%*	$70,560.00*	Edit
⊞ QAAAD	Trade	52.66	2.96	5.96%	$3,552.00	12	$23.52	$34,921.04	123.52%	$63,192.00	Edit
⊞ RFYAN	Trade	47.80	-0.45	-0.93%	-$840.00*	12	$19.00	$34,219.04*	149.81%*	$57,060.00*	Edit
⊞ RIGAR	Trade	24.00	0.00	0.00%	$1,560.00*	12	$17.92	$11,089.04*	51.45%*	$32,640.00*	Edit
⊞ RIGJB	Trade	6.20	1.20	24.00%	-$1,440.00	-12	$7.00	$943.01	11.20%	-$7,440.00	Edit
⊞ RULJT	Trade	16.35	-0.70	-4.11%	$900.00*	-12	$7.20	-$10,936.99*	-126.34%*	-$19,560.00*	Edit
⊞ SDBJT	Trade	10.30	1.30	14.44%	-$1,680.00*	-12	$5.875	-$5,334.98	-75.41%	-$12,360.00	Edit
⊞ SLBAP	Trade	31.30	1.30	4.33%	$1,680.00*	12	$19.32	$14,329.04	61.68%	$37,560.00	Edit
Cash					86,492.87					$86,492.87	
				Totals	$3,044.00		$183,324.47	$175,467.53	95.71%	$445,284.87	

LEGEND: ⊞ collapsed (click to expand)   ⊟ expanded (click to collapse)   Real-time quotes

Option Spreads   Profits $118,514.37   Average Return 99.7%

Market Value: $296,226.28   ($118,514.37 / 99.69%)   DJIA 14,143.48 ▲ +64.79   Nasdaq 2,825.87 ▲ +14.26

| REFRESH ⟳ | STREAMING QUOTES | EXPORT TO EXCEL' ⬇ | | | | | | | Results per Page: 200 ▼ | |

⊞ ⊟ Symbol		Last Trade	Change $	%	Day's Gain	Qty	Price Paid	Total Gain $	%	Market Val	Edit
⊞ CAMAM	Trade	30.70	0.00	0.00%	$2,860.00*	11	$16.73	$27,657.78*	150.05%*	$46,090.00*	Edit
⊞ CAMJR	Trade	15.70	2.10	15.44%	-$2,750.00*	-11	$7.00	-$10,026.24*	-129.94%*	-$17,710.00*	Edit
⊞ DEAD	Trade	33.30	0.00	0.00%	$1,260.00*	9	$20.93	$15,959.28*	84.57%*	$34,830.00*	Edit
⊞ DEJH	Trade	16.48	1.18	7.71%	-$1,080.00*	-9	$6.50	-$9,014.74*	-153.71%*	-$14,850.00*	Edit
⊞ FCXAO	Trade	45.15	2.80	6.61%	$720.00*	9	$20.60	$21,479.28*	115.66%*	$40,050.00*	Edit
⊞ FCXJT	Trade	17.25	-0.30	-1.71%	-$315.00*	-9	$6.6667	-$10,132.73*	-168.24%*	-$16,110.00*	Edit
⊞ FLRAA	Trade	52.30	0.00	0.00%	$540.00*	6	$27.00	$17,071.53*	105.19%*	$33,300.00*	Edit
⊞ FLRJH	Trade	20.50	2.50	13.89%	-$900.00*	-6	$7.00	-$7,692.49*	-182.61%*	-$11,880.00*	Edit
⊞ GOPAY	Trade	105.00	11.90	12.78%	$2,380.00	2	$60.75	$8,832.52	72.59%	$21,000.00	Edit
⊞ NOVJU	Trade	11.90	1.67	16.32%	-$3,006.00	-18	$4.25	-$13,792.73	-179.76%	-$21,420.00	Edit
⊞ NOVKJ	Trade	26.20	0.00	0.00%	$3,240.00*	18	$12.62	$30,179.28*	132.71%*	$52,920.00*	Edit
⊞ QAAAD	Trade	52.66	2.96	5.96%	$1,776.00	6	$24.47	$16,887.53	114.82%	$31,596.00	Edit
⊞ RFYAN	Trade	47.80	-0.45	-0.93%	-$630.00*	9	$19.83	$24,914.28*	139.34%*	$42,795.00*	Edit
⊞ RIGAR	Trade	24.00	0.00	0.00%	$1,170.00*	9	$18.13	$8,129.28*	49.72%*	$24,480.00*	Edit
⊞ RIGJB	Trade	6.20	1.20	24.00%	-$1,080.00	-9	$7.00	$705.26	11.17%	-$5,580.00	Edit
⊞ RULJT	Trade	16.35	-0.70	-4.11%	$630.00	-9	$7.20	-$8,249.74	-127.02%	-$14,715.00	Edit
⊞ SDBJT	Trade	10.30	1.30	14.44%	-$840.00*	-6	$5.50	-$2,892.49	-87.32%	-$6,180.00	Edit
⊞ SLBAP	Trade	31.30	1.30	4.33%	$840.00*	6	$17.10	$8,499.52	82.68%	$18,780.00	Edit
Cash					58,830.28					$58,830.28	
				Totals	$4,815.00		$118,881.63	$118,514.37	99.69%	$296,226.28	

LEGEND: ⊞ collapsed (click to expand)   ⊟ expanded (click to collapse)   Real-time quotes

Option Spreads   Profits $92,326.65   Average Return 33.7%

E✳TRADE FINANCIAL

✳ Open An Account   ❓ Help Center

Enter Symbol or Name   QUOTES   Enter Question or Keywords   SEARCH   LOG OFF

| Accounts | Trading & Portfolios | Quotes & Research | Mutual Funds, ETFs & Bonds | Advice & Retirement | Banking & Credit Cards |

Mortgages & Home Equity

Trade Portfolios View Orders | Balances | Transaction History | IPO Center | Account Records | Active Trading | Global Trading

Portfolios

⚡ Alerts | ≫Transfer Money | ≫Bill Pay | ⑦ Help

Portfolios   Performance & Value   Positions   Gains & Losses   Risk Analyzer   Portfolio Analyzer   Income Estimator

Account/Watch List: 061   Create / Edit List   View: Performance   Customize

Market Value: $369,869.37 ($92,326.65 / 33.74%)   DJIA 13,649.66 ▼ -18.45 Nasdaq 2,611.13 ▼ -2.79

REFRESH 🔄 | STREAMING QUOTES | EXPORT TO EXCEL ⬇   Results per Page: 200

		Price	$	%	Gain			$	%		
AGEFN	Trade	18.20	0.00	0.00%	$0.00	10	$5.90	$12,284.51	207.67%	$18,200.00	Edit
AGEFO	Trade	13.00	-0.50	-3.70%	$500.00	-10	$13.10	$84.51	0.64%	-$13,000.00	Edit
BGCGL	Trade	11.00	0.50	4.76%	$500.00	10	$8.20	$2,784.51	33.89%	$11,000.00	Edit
BGCGM	Trade	6.70	-0.10	-1.47%	$100.00	-10	$7.20	$484.51	6.71%	-$6,700.00	Edit
⊞ CATFN	Trade	8.15	-0.10	-1.21%	-$100.00	10	$5.00	$3,134.51	62.50%	$8,150.00	Edit
⊞ CATFO	Trade	3.45	-0.15	-4.17%	$150.00	-10	$3.00	-$465.49	-15.44%	-$3,450.00	Edit
CATGN	Trade	8.70	0.00	0.00%	$0.00	8	$8.20	$386.01	5.87%	$6,960.00	Edit
CIFK	Trade	15.36	1.36	9.71%	$1,360.00	10	$9.38	$5,968.51	63.55%	$15,360.00	Edit
CIFM	Trade	4.90	-0.20	-3.92%	$200.00	-10	$3.08	-$1,831.49	-59.24%	-$4,900.00	Edit
CLFFM	Trade	23.20	-1.10	-4.53%	-$1,100.00	10	$9.82	$13,368.51	135.98%	$23,200.00	Edit
CLFFO	Trade	13.10	-1.52	-10.40%	$1,520.00	-10	$3.02	-$10,091.49	-332.89%	-$13,100.00	Edit
⊞ CLFGP	Trade	10.20	-1.70	-14.29%	-$1,700.00	10	$10.00	$184.51	1.84%	$10,200.00	Edit
COPGN	Trade	10.50	0.80	8.25%	$640.00	8	$8.80	$1,346.01	19.08%	$8,400.00	Edit
CVXFO	Trade	8.20	0.80	10.81%	$800.00	10	$5.30	$2,884.51	54.27%	$8,200.00	Edit
⊞ CVXFP	Trade	3.60	0.85	30.91%	-$850.00	-10	$3.30	-$315.49	-9.52%	-$3,600.00	Edit
DEGB	Trade	11.00	-0.30	-2.65%	-$180.00	6	$12.60	-$972.49	-12.84%	$6,600.00	Edit
⊞ ETNFQ	Trade	7.14	0.00	0.00%	$0.00	10	$7.30	-$175.49	-2.40%	$7,140.00	Edit

217

Continued from previous page . . .

FCXFL	Trade	18.70	-0.50	-2.60%	-$500.00	10	$9.81	$6,878.51	90.40%	$18,700.00	Edit
FCXFN	Trade	8.70	-0.90	-9.38%	$900.00	-10	$3.01	-$5,701.49	-188.70%	-$8,700.00	Edit
FCXGM	Trade	14.80	0.00	0.00%	$0.00	6	$11.20	$2,147.51	31.90%	$8,880.00	Edit
FLRFT	Trade	5.20	-0.30	-5.45%	-$300.00	10	$4.80	$384.51	7.98%	$5,200.00	Edit
FLRGS	Trade	10.90	0.00	0.00%	$0.00	7	$10.00	$616.76	8.79%	$7,630.00	Edit
GPYFD	Trade	10.80	-1.50	-12.20%	-$1,500.00	10	$13.50	-$2,711.49	-20.07%	$10,800.00	Edit
GPYFF	Trade	4.30	-0.93	-17.78%	$930.00	-10	$7.00	$2,688.51	38.34%	-$4,300.00	Edit
GPYGD	Trade	14.50	-1.20	-7.64%	-$480.00	4	$17.10	-$1,050.99	-15.34%	$5,800.00	Edit
⊞ GQOFD	Trade	4.20	0.20	5.00%	$200.00	10	$3.00	$1,184.51	39.28%	$4,200.00	Edit
⊞ HALGS	Trade	4.30	0.50	13.16%	$700.00	14	$5.00	-$998.49	-14.23%	$6,020.00	Edit
JCIFA	Trade	5.01	-0.09	-1.76%	-$90.00	10	$5.80	-$805.49	-13.85%	$5,010.00	Edit
JECFJ	Trade	7.60	0.00	0.00%	$0.00	10	$5.10	$2,484.51	48.57%	$7,600.00	Edit
⊞ JECFK	Trade	4.30	0.40	10.26%	-$400.00	-10	$2.60	-$1,715.49	-65.59%	-$4,300.00	Edit
JECGJ	Trade	7.80	0.00	0.00%	$0.00	9	$7.40	$345.26	5.17%	$7,020.00	Edit
MAFF	Trade	21.00	-0.40	-1.87%	-$400.00	10	$12.05	$8,938.51	74.11%	$21,000.00	Edit
MALFH	Trade	11.30	-0.50	-4.24%	$500.00	-10	$5.75	-$5,561.49	-96.53%	-$11,300.00	Edit
MALGG	Trade	18.40	0.00	0.00%	$0.00	6	$11.00	$4,427.51	66.96%	$11,040.00	Edit
MDRFJ	Trade	29.52	8.62	41.24%	$7,758.00	9	$8.81	$18,627.51	234.59%	$26,568.00	Edit
MDRFL	Trade	19.62	3.42	21.11%	-$3,078.00	-9	$1.81	-$16,040.49	-977.79%	-$17,658.00	Edit
MDRGN	Trade	10.20	0.00	0.00%	$0.00	8	$9.70	$386.01	4.97%	$8,160.00	Edit
MROFA	Trade	23.14	1.39	6.39%	-$1,251.00	-9	$4.70	-$16,611.49	-391.27%	-$20,826.00	Edit
MROFT	Trade	28.04	1.54	5.81%	$1,386.00	9	$6.70	$19,190.51	317.44%	$25,236.00	Edit
MROGD	Trade	11.00	1.20	12.24%	$840.00	7	$7.80	$2,226.76	40.68%	$7,700.00	Edit
NBRFF	Trade	5.70	0.29	5.36%	$290.00	10	$4.50	$1,184.51	26.23%	$5,700.00	Edit
NOVFQ	Trade	12.10	1.30	12.04%	$1,300.00	10	$9.03	$3,058.51	33.83%	$12,100.00	Edit
NOVFS	Trade	3.40	0.60	21.43%	-$600.00	-10	$2.53	-$881.49	-34.68%	-$3,400.00	Edit
NOVGQ	Trade	12.40	0.00	0.00%	$0.00	6	$11.00	$827.51	12.51%	$7,440.00	Edit
OIHFJ	Trade	23.65	3.65	18.25%	$3,650.00	10	$12.65	$10,988.51	86.79%	$23,650.00	Edit
OIHFL	Trade	13.70	3.40	33.01%	-$3,400.00	-10	$5.95	-$7,761.49	-130.19%	-$13,700.00	Edit
PCPFB	Trade	9.00	0.90	11.11%	-$900.00	-10	$4.81	-$4,201.49	-87.14%	-$9,000.00	Edit

Continued from previous page . . .

Symbol		Price	Chg	%Chg	$Chg	Qty	Cost	Gain/Loss	%G/L	Value	
PCPFT	Trade	18.30	-0.70	-3.68%	-$700.00	10	$11.01	$7,278.51	66.04%	$18,300.00	Edit
PCPGC	Trade	7.00	0.30	4.48%	$270.00	9	$8.10	-$1,004.74	-13.75%	$6,300.00	Edit
PCUFP	Trade	12.70	-0.40	-3.05%	-$400.00	10	$10.20	$2,484.51	24.32%	$12,700.00	Edit
QAAFA	Trade	15.60	1.60	11.43%	-$1,600.00	-10	$2.50	-$13,115.49	-521.39%	-$15,600.00	Edit
⊞ QAAFS	Trade	24.91	1.11	4.66%	$1,110.00	10	$7.50	$17,394.51	231.45%	$24,910.00	Edit
QAAGA	Trade	16.70	1.50	9.87%	$750.00	5	$12.70	$1,988.26	31.25%	$8,350.00	Edit
⊞ RIGFR	Trade	10.50	1.30	14.13%	$1,300.00	10	$6.10	$4,384.51	71.70%	$10,500.00	Edit
RSFK	Trade	7.50	-0.08	-1.06%	-$80.00	10	$9.17	-$1,681.49	-18.31%	$7,500.00	Edit
RSFM	Trade	0.50	-0.20	-28.57%	$200.00	-10	$2.37	$1,858.51	78.04%	-$500.00	Edit
⊞ TEXFO	Trade	11.20	0.00	0.00%	$0.00	10	$8.30	$2,884.51	34.69%	$11,200.00	Edit
TEXGP	Trade	8.20	-0.10	-1.20%	-$100.00	10	$7.70	$484.51	6.28%	$8,200.00	Edit
TIFFI	Trade	7.10	0.00	0.00%	$0.00	10	$5.60	$1,484.51	26.44%	$7,100.00	Edit
TSOFK	Trade	9.50	0.70	7.95%	$1,400.00	20	$5.40	$8,188.51	75.74%	$19,000.00	Edit
TSOFL	Trade	4.74	0.24	5.33%	-$480.00	-20	$2.20	-$5,091.49	-115.41%	-$9,480.00	Edit
UFBFQ	Trade	20.60	0.30	1.48%	$300.00	10	$10.53	$10,058.51	95.42%	$20,600.00	Edit
UFBFS	Trade	11.00	-0.50	-4.35%	$500.00	-10	$4.03	-$6,981.49	-172.75%	-$11,000.00	Edit
UFBGR	Trade	16.40	-0.20	-1.20%	-$100.00	5	$10.60	$2,888.26	54.38%	$8,200.00	Edit
XTQFR	Trade	12.53	0.00	0.00%	$0.00	10	$8.40	$4,114.51	48.89%	$12,530.00	Edit
ZPYGN	Trade	7.80	0.40	5.41%	$320.00	8	$6.40	$1,106.01	21.54%	$6,240.00	Edit
Cash					3,889.37					$3,889.37	
				Totals	$10,085.00		$273,653.35	$92,326.65	33.74%	$369,869.37	

LEGEND: ⊞ collapsed (click to expand)   ⊟ expanded (click to collapse)

Real-time quotes

Option Spreads   Profits $94,959.71   Average Return 45.5%

Account Reports: Profit/Loss Report   🖨 PRINT

Give your accountant a break. View profits/losses for all trades executed on one specific date or during a range of dates. Track by position, whether it's closed, or still opened. Download to a spreadsheet for easy manipulation, processing and tax reporting.

Realized P&L on Closed Positions

Symbol	Date Bought	Date Sold	Shares	Cost Basis	Sales Price	Gain-loss
+FCXJQ	9/5/2007 3:52:39 PM	10/9/2007 3:36:33 PM	9	$7,551.00	$25,434.94	$17,883.94
+FCXJQ	9/5/2007 3:52:50 PM	10/9/2007 3:36:33 PM	1	$839.00	$2,826.10	$1,987.10
+FCXJQ	9/11/2007 11:42:41 AM	10/9/2007 3:36:33 PM	10	$8,918.50	$28,261.05	$19,342.55
+FCXJS	10/9/2007 3:36:33 PM	9/5/2007 3:53:05 PM	9	$16,558.65	$3,123.93	-$13,434.72
+FCXJS	10/9/2007 3:36:33 PM	9/5/2007 3:53:17 PM	1	$1,839.85	$346.98	-$1,492.87
+FCXJS	10/9/2007 3:36:33 PM	9/11/2007 11:42:41 AM	10	$18,398.50	$3,581.42	-$14,817.08
+RFYJT	9/6/2007 2:17:32 PM	10/5/2007 3:03:03 PM	10	$11,969.00	$38,730.88	$26,761.88
+RFYJT	9/11/2007 11:42:41 AM	10/5/2007 3:03:03 PM	10	$11,438.50	$38,380.89	$26,942.39
+RFYJX	10/5/2007 3:03:03 PM	9/6/2007 2:17:50 PM	10	$28,868.50	$6,131.88	-$22,736.62
+RFYJX	10/5/2007 3:03:03 PM	9/11/2007 11:42:41 AM	10	$28,518.50	$5,531.39	-$22,987.11

Total Realized Gain-Loss: $17,449.46

Unrealized P&L on Open Positions

Symbol	Description	Position	Avg Price	Cost Basis	Market Value	Type	Unrealized Val.
+APVKJ	Apple Inc Nov 2007 150.00 Call	30	$13.6707	$41,012.00	$64,350.00	Stock Option	$23,338.00
+APVKL	Apple Inc Nov 2007 160.00 Call	-30	-$8.1659	$24,497.56	-$45,000.00	Stock Option	-$20,502.44
+CAMJP	Cameron International Corp Oct 2007 80.00 Call	20	$10.2745	$20,549.00	$46,800.00	Stock Option	$26,251.00
+CAMJS	Cameron International Corp Oct 2007 95.00 Call	-20	-$3.9814	$7,962.82	-$17,600.00	Stock Option	-$9,637.18
+DEJF	Deere & Co Oct 2007 130.00 Call	20	$11.0038	$22,007.50	$49,800.00	Stock Option	$27,792.50
+DEJH	Deere & Co Oct 2007 140.00 Call	-20	-$5.1766	$10,353.29	-$30,200.00	Stock Option	-$19,846.71
+FLRJE	Fluor Corp New Oct 2007 125.00 Call	20	$10.7338	$21,467.50	$66,000.00	Stock Option	$44,532.50
+FLRJG	Fluor Corp New Oct 2007 135.00 Call	-20	-$4.9967	$9,993.30	-$46,200.00	Stock Option	-$36,206.70
+GOOKP	Google Inc Cl A Nov 2007 580.00 Call	-30	-$25.3589	$76,076.76	-$168,600.00	Stock Option	-$92,523.24
+GOPKQ	Google Inc Cl A Nov 2007 570.00 Call	30	$31.1673	$93,502.00	$192,600.00	Stock Option	$99,098.00
+MALKK	Mastercard Inc Cl A Nov 2007 155.00 Call	30	$14.9965	$44,989.50	$46,800.00	Stock Option	$1,810.50
+MALKM	Mastercard Inc Cl A Nov 2007 165.00 Call	-30	-$9.2633	$27,790.01	-$30,300.00	Stock Option	-$2,509.99
+MDRKK	Mcdermott Intl Inc Nov 2007 55.00 Call	30	$5.3465	$16,039.50	$20,700.00	Stock Option	$4,660.50
+MDRKL	Mcdermott Intl Inc Nov 2007 60.00 Call	-30	-$2.5133	$7,540.02	-$10,800.00	Stock Option	-$3,259.98
+NOVJU	National Oilwell Varco Inc Oct 2007 67.50 Call	-40	$0.0000	$0.00	-$40,000.00	Stock Option	-$40,000.00
+NOVJZ	National Oilwell Varco Inc Oct 2007 62.50 Call	40	$0.0000	$0.00	$59,600.00	Stock Option	$59,600.00
+OIIKN	Oceaneering Intl Inc Nov 2007 70.00 Call	30	$8.6307	$25,892.00	$37,800.00	Stock Option	$11,908.00
+OIIKP	Oceaneering Intl Inc Nov 2007 80.00 Call	-30	-$2.7693	$8,307.81	-$16,500.00	Stock Option	-$8,192.19
+RIGJT	Transocean Inc Ord Oct 2007 100.00 Call	20	$12.4805	$24,961.00	$28,600.00	Stock Option	$3,639.00
+RULKB	Research In Motion Ltd Nov 2007 110.00 Call	30	$10.3165	$30,949.50	$35,400.00	Stock Option	$4,450.50
+RULKD	Research In Motion Ltd Nov 2007 120.00 Call	-30	-$5.4834	$16,450.18	-$19,800.00	Stock Option	-$3,349.82
+SDBKB	Schlumberger Ltd Nov 2007 110.00 Call	-30	-$3.7893	$11,367.75	-$12,900.00	Stock Option	-$1,532.25
+SDBKT	Schlumberger Ltd Nov 2007 100.00 Call	30	$9.5307	$28,592.00	$31,500.00	Stock Option	$2,908.00
+ZQNJP	Amazon Com Inc Oct 2007 80.00 Call	15	$11.3618	$17,042.75	$22,125.00	Stock Option	$5,082.25

Total Unrealized Gain-Loss: $77,510.25

Option Spreads   Profits $111,648.05   Average Return 41.7%

Portfolios

| Portfolios | Performance & Value | Positions | Gains & Losses | Risk Analyzer | Portfolio Analyzer [NEW] | Income Estimator [BETA] |

Account/Watch List: [   ] Create / Edit List   View: Performance   Customize

Market Value: $381,595.74 ($111,648.05 / 41.77%)   DJIA 13,846.93 ▲ +107.54   Nasdaq 2,677.55 ▲ +25.89

[REFRESH ↻] [STREAMING QUOTES] [EXPORT TO EXCEL* ⬇]   Results per Page: 200 ▾

Symbol		Current Price	Change $	Change %	Day's Gain	Qty	Price Paid	Total Gain $	Total Gain %	Market Val	Edit
⊞ APVJH	Trade	8.00	1.10	15.94%	-$990.00	-9	$7.00	-$914.74	-14.49%	-$7,200.00	Edit
⊞ CAMAM	Trade	27.20	0.00	0.00%	$0.00	20	$16.45	$21,453.04	65.11%	$54,400.00	Edit
⊞ CAMJR	Trade	5.20	1.10	26.83%	-$1,650.00	-15	$3.50	-$2,569.24	-48.76%	-$7,800.00	Edit
⊞ DEAD	Trade	30.64	1.44	4.93%	$1,728.00	12	$19.70	$13,087.04	55.26%	$36,768.00	Edit
⊞ DEJH	Trade	9.10	0.70	8.33%	-$630.00	-9	$4.90	-$3,794.74	-85.76%	-$8,190.00	Edit
⊞ FCXAO	Trade	35.40	4.80	15.69%	$7,680.00	16	$19.38	$25,596.04	82.45%	$56,640.00	Edit
⊞ FCXJT	Trade	10.50	3.20	43.84%	-$3,840.00	-12	$5.30	-$6,256.99	-98.12%	-$12,600.00	Edit
⊞ FLRAA	Trade	36.70	0.00	0.00%	$0.00	12	$25.62	$13,249.04	43.03%	$44,040.00	Edit
⊞ GQRAA	Trade	25.30	0.80	3.27%	$960.00	12	$21.24	$4,821.05	18.88%	$30,360.00	Edit
⊞ MHSAN	Trade	21.50	0.00	0.00%	$0.00	12	$18.02	$4,129.04	19.05%	$25,800.00	Edit
⊞ NOVJG	Trade	8.31	1.01	13.84%	-$909.00	-9	$7.00	-$1,193.74	-18.90%	-$7,479.00	Edit
⊞ NOVKT	Trade	37.50	0.70	1.90%	$840.00	12	$24.15	$15,979.04	55.06%	$45,000.00	Edit
⊞ PCPJG	Trade	7.70	0.00	0.00%	$-0.00	-9	$5.50	-$1,994.74	-40.18%	-$6,930.00	Edit
⊞ PCPLD	Trade	24.00	0.00	0.00%	$0.00	9	$22.03	$1,739.28	8.76%	$21,600.00	Edit
⊞ QAAAD	Trade	29.48	1.20	4.24%	$1,440.00	12	$23.52	$7,105.04	25.13%	$35,376.00	Edit
⊞ RFYAN	Trade	26.80	2.30	9.39%	$2,760.00	12	$19.00	$9,319.04	40.80%	$32,160.00	Edit
⊞ RFYJR	Trade	7.80	1.56	25.00%	-$1,404.00	-9	$5.30	-$2,264.74	-47.33%	-$7,020.00	Edit
⊞ RIGAR	Trade	23.20	1.90	8.92%	$2,280.00	12	$17.92	$6,289.04	29.18%	$27,840.00	Edit
⊞ SDBJT	Trade	8.26	0.86	11.62%	-$774.00	-9	$5.50	-$2,498.74	-50.33%	-$7,434.00	Edit
⊞ SLBAP	Trade	28.00	1.10	4.09%	$1,320.00	12	$19.32	$10,369.04	44.63%	$33,600.00	Edit
Cash					2,664.74					$2,664.74	
				Totals	$8,811.00		$267,282.96	$111,648.05	41.77%	$381,595.74	

LEGEND: ⊞ collapsed (click to expand) ⊟ expanded (click to collapse)   Real-time quotes

Option Spreads   Profits $115,311.95   Average Return 38.0%

Account Reports: Profit/Loss Report   🖨 PRINT

Realized P&L on Closed Positions

Symbol	Date Bought	Date Sold	Shares	Cost Basis	Sales Price	Gain-loss
+APVJF	8/31/2007 3:36:37 PM	10/5/2007 3:18:21 PM	15	$21,026.25	$45,418.52	$24,392.2?
+APVJH	10/5/2007 3:03:03 PM	8/31/2007 3:37:38 PM	5	$10,260.25	$4,126.17	-$6,134.08
+APVJH	10/5/2007 3:03:03 PM	8/31/2007 3:38:04 PM	10	$20,520.50	$8,242.35	-$12,278.15
+APVJI	10/5/2007 3:18:21 PM	10/5/2007 3:03:03 PM	15	$45,480.75	$45,418.52	-$62.23
+CAMJN	8/28/2007 2:57:53 PM	10/3/2007 12:16:53 PM	12	$10,097.50	$32,266.88	$22,169.38
+CAMJN	8/28/2007 2:58:07 PM	10/3/2007 12:16:53 PM	3	$2,543.50	$8,066.72	$5,523.22
+CAMJP	10/3/2007 12:16:53 PM	8/28/2007 2:58:23 PM	12	$20,544.60	$2,982.42	-$17,562.18
+CAMJP	10/3/2007 12:16:53 PM	8/28/2007 2:58:31 PM	3	$5,136.15	$738.47	-$4,397.68
+DEJE	8/28/2007 2:33:35 PM	10/10/2007 12:13:09 PM	15	$13,460.00	$42,268.57	$28,808.57
+DEJG	10/10/2007 12:13:09 PM	8/28/2007 2:34:29 PM	15	$27,630.75	$5,889.87	-$21,740.88
+FCXJO	8/28/2007 2:48:16 PM	10/4/2007 12:08:35 PM	12	$13,097.50	$38,206.58	$25,109.08
+FCXJO	8/28/2007 2:48:28 PM	10/4/2007 12:08:35 PM	3	$3,266.50	$9,551.65	$6,285.15
+FCXJQ	10/4/2007 12:07:59 PM	8/28/2007 2:49:51 PM	12	$26,496.80	$5,982.37	-$20,514.43
+FCXJQ	10/4/2007 12:07:59 PM	8/28/2007 2:50:07 PM	3	$6,624.20	$1,461.46	-$5,162.74
+FLRJC	8/28/2007 2:35:06 PM	10/8/2007 2:07:13 PM	6	$6,653.68	$22,359.45	$15,705.77
+FLRJC	8/28/2007 2:35:17 PM	10/8/2007 2:07:13 PM	6	$6,629.66	$22,359.45	$15,729.79
+FLRJC	8/28/2007 2:35:26 PM	10/8/2007 2:07:13 PM	1	$1,086.89	$3,726.57	$2,639.69
+FLRJC	8/28/2007 2:35:26 PM	10/9/2007 11:43:02 AM	2	$2,173.77	$7,659.87	$5,486.10
+FLRJE	10/8/2007 2:07:13 PM	8/28/2007 2:35:47 PM	6	$16,448.19	$3,330.24	-$13,117.95
+FLRJE	10/8/2007 2:07:13 PM	8/28/2007 2:36:01 PM	6	$16,448.19	$3,306.26	-$13,141.93
+FLRJE	10/8/2007 2:07:13 PM	8/28/2007 2:36:09 PM	1	$2,741.37	$530.10	-$2,211.27
+FLRJE	10/9/2007 11:43:02 AM	8/28/2007 2:36:09 PM	2	$5,680.00	$1,060.20	-$4,619.80
+GQRJC	8/28/2007 2:28:17 PM	10/3/2007 12:16:53 PM	10	$9,397.50	$7,629.36	-$1,768.14
+GQRJC	8/28/2007 2:28:28 PM	10/3/2007 12:16:53 PM	5	$4,752.50	$3,814.68	-$937.82
+MDRJI	9/10/2007 11:59:59 PM	10/3/2007 12:16:53 PM	15	$0.00	$17,389.95	$17,389.95
+MDRJI	9/11/2007 11:59:59 PM	10/3/2007 12:16:53 PM	15	$0.00	$17,389.95	$17,389.95
+MDRJJ	10/3/2007 12:16:53 PM	9/10/2007 11:59:59 PM	15	$10,239.75	$0.00	-$10,239.75
+MDRJJ	10/3/2007 12:16:53 PM	9/11/2007 11:59:59 PM	15	$10,239.75	$0.00	-$10,239.75
+NOVJY	9/28/2007 11:59:59 PM	10/5/2007 3:03:03 PM	10	$0.00	$19,133.18	$19,133.18
+NOVJY	9/28/2007 11:59:59 PM	10/5/2007 3:03:03 PM	5	$0.00	$9,591.59	$9,591.59
+NOVJY	10/1/2007 11:59:59 PM	10/5/2007 3:03:03 PM	5	$0.00	$9,591.59	$9,591.59
+NOVJY	10/1/2007 11:59:59 PM	10/5/2007 3:03:03 PM	10	$0.00	$19,203.18	$19,203.18
+NOVJZ	10/5/2007 3:03:03 PM	9/28/2007 11:59:59 PM	10	$14,266.50	$0.00	-$14,266.50
+NOVJZ	10/5/2007 3:03:03 PM	9/28/2007 11:59:59 PM	5	$7,158.25	$0.00	-$7,158.25
+NOVJZ	10/5/2007 3:03:03 PM	10/1/2007 11:59:59 PM	5	$7,158.25	$0.00	-$7,158.25
+NOVJZ	10/5/2007 3:03:03 PM	10/1/2007 11:59:59 PM	10	$14,336.50	$0.00	-$14,336.50
+RFYJN	8/28/2007 2:55:50 PM	10/5/2007 2:28:57 PM	15	$17,435.00	$65,833.21	$48,398.21
+RFYJP	10/5/2007 2:28:57 PM	8/28/2007 2:56:05 PM	15	$51,075.75	$8,514.83	-$42,560.92
+RIGJA	10/10/2007	8/28/2007 2:31:02 PM	12	$11,520.60	$3,918.40	-$7,602.20
+RIGJA	10/10/2007	8/28/2007 2:31:35 PM	3	$2,880.15	$1,065.47	-$1,814.68
+RIGJS	8/28/2007 2:30:28 PM	10/10/2007	12	$11,033.50	$23,231.02	$12,197.52
+RIGJS	8/28/2007 2:30:38 PM	10/10/2007	3	$2,855.50	$5,807.75	$2,952.25
+RZJJA	10/3/2007 12:16:53 PM	8/28/2007 2:29:02 PM	10	$3,140.50	$4,662.40	$1,521.90
+RZJJA	10/3/2007 12:16:53 PM	8/28/2007 2:29:20 PM	5	$1,570.25	$2,367.45	$797.20

Total Realized Gain-Loss: **$70,989.45**

Unrealized P&L on Open Positions

Symbol	Description	Position	Avg Price	Cost Basis	Market Value	Type	Unrealized Val.
+APVKK	Apple Inc Nov 2007 155.00 Call	30	$12.5564	$37,669.20	$54,000.00	Stock Option	$16,330.80
+APVKM	Apple Inc Nov 2007 165.00 Call	-30	-$7.5234	$22,570.09	-$36,900.00	Stock Option	-$14,329.91
+AXVJF	Intuitive Surgical Inc New Oct 2007 230.00 Call	-15	-$13.1291	$19,693.66	-$48,450.00	Stock Option	-$28,756.34
+AXVJW	Intuitive Surgical Inc New Oct 2007 220.00 Call	15	$18.3707	$27,556.00	$60,900.00	Stock Option	$33,344.00
+CAMKR	Cameron International Corp Nov 2007 90.00 Call	30	$8.8265	$26,479.50	$44,400.00	Stock Option	$17,920.50
+CAMKX	Cameron International Corp Nov 2007 100.00 Call	-30	-$3.3034	$9,910.28	-$21,600.00	Stock Option	-$11,689.72
+FCXKB	Freeport-Mcmoran Copper & Gold Nov 2007 110.00 Call	-30	-$6.7234	$20,170.13	-$35,550.00	Stock Option	-$15,379.87
+FCXKT	Freeport-Mcmoran Copper & Gold Nov 2007 100.00 Call	30	$12.4565	$37,369.50	$58,350.00	Stock Option	$20,980.50
+FLRKK	Fluor Corp New Nov 2007 155.00 Call	30	$10.0865	$30,259.50	$30,600.00	Stock Option	$340.50
+FLRKM	Fluor Corp New Nov 2007 165.00 Call	-30	-$5.0534	$15,160.20	-$15,900.00	Stock Option	-$739.80
+GOOKP	Google Inc Cl A Nov 2007 580.00 Call	30	$28.6965	$86,089.50	$168,600.00	Stock Option	$82,510.50
+GOOKR	Google Inc Cl A Nov 2007 590.00 Call	-30	-$23.3631	$70,089.36	-$146,100.00	Stock Option	-$76,010.64
+MALKK	Mastercard Inc Cl A Nov 2007 155.00 Call	30	$14.7665	$44,299.50	$46,800.00	Stock Option	$2,500.50
+MALKM	Mastercard Inc Cl A Nov 2007 165.00 Call	-30	-$9.1333	$27,400.02	-$30,300.00	Stock Option	-$2,899.98
+MHSJP	Medco Health Solutions Inc Oct 2007 80.00 Call	15	$8.0633	$12,095.00	$18,450.00	Stock Option	$6,355.00
+MHSJR	Medco Health Solutions Inc Oct 2007 90.00 Call	-15	-$2.1166	$3,174.92	-$4,500.00	Stock Option	-$1,325.08
+NOVKN	National Oilwell Varco Inc Nov 2007 70.00 Call	30	$9.3032	$27,909.50	$28,500.00	Stock Option	$590.50
+NOVKP	National Oilwell Varco Inc Nov 2007 80.00 Call	-30	-$3.3701	$10,110.27	-$10,500.00	Stock Option	-$389.73
+PCPJE	Precision Castparts Corp Oct 2007 125.00 Call	15	$12.9733	$19,460.00	$33,600.00	Stock Option	$14,140.00
+PCPJG	Precision Castparts Corp Oct 2007 135.00 Call	-15	-$7.3265	$10,989.49	-$19,500.00	Stock Option	-$8,510.20
+RULKB	Research In Motion Ltd Nov 2007 110.00 Call	30	$10.3165	$30,949.50	$35,400.00	Stock Option	$4,450.50
+RULKD	Research In Motion Ltd Nov 2007 120.00 Call	-30	-$5.4834	$16,450.18	-$19,800.00	Stock Option	-$3,349.82
+SDBJT	Schlumberger Ltd Oct 2007 100.00 Call	-15	-$3.5824	$5,373.63	-$13,050.00	Stock Option	-$7,676.37
+SLBJR	Schlumberger Ltd Oct 2007 90.00 Call	15	$9.7275	$14,591.25	$27,300.00	Stock Option	$12,708.75
+ZQNJQ	Amazon Com Inc Oct 2007 85.00 Call	15	$7.8507	$11,776.00	$14,850.00	Stock Option	$3,074.00
+ZQNJT	Amazon Com Inc Oct 2007 95.00 Call	-15	-$2.3093	$3,463.91	-$3,330.00	Stock Option	-$133.91

Total Unrealized Gain-Loss: **$44,322.50**

Option Spreads Profits $64,044.20 Average Return 36.5%

Portfolios

| Portfolios | Performance & Value | Positions | Gains & Losses | Risk Analyzer | new Portfolio Analyzer | BETA Income Estimator |

Account/Watch List: [ ] Create / Edit List   View: Performance [ ] Customize

Market Value: $244,337.41 ($64,044.20 / 36.51%)   DJIA 13,840.59 ▲ +101.20 Nasdaq 2,674.40 ▲ +22.74

[REFRESH] [STREAMING QUOTES] [EXPORT TO EXCEL]   Results per Page: 200

⊞⊟ Symbol		Current Price	Change $	Change %	Day's Gain	Qty	Price Paid	Total Gain $	Total Gain %	Market Val	Edit
⊞ APVJH	Trade	7.80	0.90	13.04%	-$360.00	-4	$6.90	-$370.99	-13.39%	-$3,120.00	Edit
⊞ CAMAM	Trade	27.20	0.00	0.00%	$0.00	11	$16.73	$11,487.78	62.32%	$29,920.00	Edit
⊞ CAMJR	Trade	5.20	1.10	26.83%	-$880.00	-8	$3.50	-$1,373.99	-48.83%	-$4,160.00	Edit
⊞ DEAD	Trade	29.83	0.63	2.16%	$567.00	9	$20.93	$7,976.28	42.27%	$26,847.00	Edit
⊞ DEJH	Trade	9.10	0.70	8.33%	-$420.00	-6	$4.90	-$2,532.49	-85.77%	-$5,460.00	Edit
⊞ FCXAO	Trade	35.40	4.80	15.69%	$4,320.00	9	$20.60	$13,289.28	71.56%	$31,860.00	Edit
⊞ FCXJT	Trade	9.90	2.60	35.62%	-$1,560.00	-6	$5.50	-$2,652.49	-80.08%	-$5,940.00	Edit
⊞ FLRAA	Trade	36.70	0.00	0.00%	$0.00	6	$27.00	$5,791.53	35.69%	$22,020.00	Edit
⊞ GQRAA	Trade	25.00	0.50	2.04%	$450.00	9	$21.77	$2,879.28	14.67%	$22,500.00	Edit
⊞ MHSAN	Trade	21.50	0.00	0.00%	$0.00	9	$18.90	$2,309.28	13.55%	$19,350.00	Edit
⊞ MHSJR	Trade	2.95	0.25	9.26%	-$125.00	-5	$3.00	$13.26	0.88%	-$1,475.00	Edit
⊞ NOVJG	Trade	8.00	0.70	9.59%	-$420.00	-6	$7.00	-$612.49	-14.54%	-$4,800.00	Edit
⊞ NOVKT	Trade	37.50	0.70	1.90%	$630.00	9	$25.23	$11,009.28	48.41%	$33,750.00	Edit
⊞ PCPJG	Trade	7.70	0.00	0.00%	$-0.00	-4	$5.50	-$890.99	-40.30%	-$3,080.00	Edit
⊞ PCPLD	Trade	24.00	0.00	0.00%	$0.00	6	$22.63	$791.53	5.82%	$14,400.00	Edit
⊞ QAAAD	Trade	29.48	1.20	4.24%	$720.00	6	$24.47	$2,979.53	20.26%	$17,688.00	Edit
⊞ RFYAN	Trade	26.80	2.30	9.39%	$2,070.00	9	$19.83	$6,239.28	34.89%	$24,120.00	Edit
⊞ RFYJR	Trade	7.70	1.46	23.40%	-$876.00	-6	$5.30	-$1,452.49	-45.50%	-$4,620.00	Edit
⊞ RIGAR	Trade	23.00	1.70	7.98%	$1,530.00	9	$18.13	$4,349.28	26.60%	$20,700.00	Edit
⊞ RZJJB	Trade	5.20	0.40	8.33%	-$240.00	-6	$4.80	-$252.49	-8.73%	-$3,120.00	Edit
⊞ SDBJT	Trade	7.90	0.50	6.76%	-$300.00	-6	$5.50	-$1,452.49	-43.85%	-$4,740.00	Edit
⊞ SLBAP	Trade	28.00	1.10	4.09%	$660.00	6	$17.10	$6,519.52	63.42%	$16,800.00	Edit
Cash					4,897.41					$4,897.41	
Totals					$5,766.00		$175,395.80	$64,044.20	36.51%	$244,337.41	

LEGEND: ⊞ collapsed (click to expand) ⊟ expanded (click to collapse)   Real-time quotes

Option Spreads   **Profits $147,046.06**   **Average Return 74.4%**

Portfolios

Portfolios	Performance & Value	Positions	Gains & Losses	Risk Analyzer	Portfolio Analyzer `new`	Income Estimator `BETA`

Account/Watch List: [▼] Create / Edit List   View: [Performance ▼] Customize

Market Value: $415,549.47   ($147,046.06 / 74.42%)   DJIA 13,864.65 ▲ +86.00   Nasdaq 2,708.15 ▲ +24.70

[REFRESH ⟳]   [STREAMING QUOTES]   [EXPORT TO EXCEL ⬇]   Results per Page: [200 ▼]

⊞⊟ Symbol		Current Price	Change $	Change %	Day's Gain	Qty	Price Paid	Total Gain $	Total Gain %	Market Val	Edit
⊞ APVJK	Trade	5.10	0.10	2.00%	-$14.47	-14	$5.1143	-$14.47	-0.20%	-$7,140.00	Edit
⊞ CAMAM	Trade	27.20	0.00	0.00%	$0.00	20	$16.45	$21,453.04	65.11%	$54,400.00	Edit
⊞ CAMJR	Trade	4.00	-0.55	-12.09%	$1,313.26	-20	$3.875	-$280.98	-3.61%	-$8,000.00	Edit
⊞ DEAD	Trade	28.80	3.80	15.20%	$4,560.00	12	$19.70	$10,879.04	45.94%	$34,560.00	Edit
⊞ DEJH	Trade	8.00	1.90	31.15%	-$2,170.24	-12	$5.30	-$3,264.98	-51.14%	-$9,600.00	Edit
⊞ FCXAO	Trade	31.10	-1.10	-3.42%	-$1,760.00	16	$19.38	$18,716.04	60.29%	$49,760.00	Edit
⊞ FCXJT	Trade	6.60	-1.20	-15.38%	$2,389.01	-16	$6.225	-$627.98	-6.29%	-$10,560.00	Edit
⊞ FLRAA	Trade	41.20	3.00	7.85%	$3,600.00	12	$25.62	$18,649.04	60.57%	$49,440.00	Edit
⊞ FLRJH	Trade	7.20	0.90	14.29%	-$256.99	-12	$7.00	-$256.99	-3.05%	-$8,640.00	Edit
⊞ GQRAA	Trade	30.00	-3.00	-9.09%	-$3,600.00	12	$21.24	$10,461.05	40.96%	$36,000.00	Edit
⊞ NOVJG	Trade	10.20	-0.80	-7.27%	$1,099.76	-12	$8.125	-$2,514.98	-25.73%	-$12,240.00	Edit
⊞ NOVKT	Trade	43.41	0.00	0.00%	$0.00	12	$24.15	$23,071.04	79.50%	$52,092.00	Edit
⊞ QAAAD	Trade	36.90	-1.20	-3.15%	-$1,440.00	12	$23.52	$16,009.04	56.63%	$44,280.00	Edit
⊞ RFYAN	Trade	32.20	2.20	7.33%	$2,640.00	12	$19.00	$15,799.04	69.17%	$38,640.00	Edit
⊞ RIGAR	Trade	24.20	0.00	0.00%	$0.00	12	$17.92	$7,489.04	34.75%	$29,040.00	Edit
⊞ RULJT	Trade	7.00	1.60	29.63%	$223.01	-12	$7.20	$223.01	2.58%	-$8,400.00	Edit
⊞ RZJJD	Trade	4.40	-1.20	-21.43%	$1,183.01	-12	$5.40	$1,183.01	18.21%	-$5,280.00	Edit
⊞ SDBJT	Trade	5.00	-1.80	-26.47%	$2,209.76	-12	$5.875	$1,025.02	14.49%	-$6,000.00	Edit
⊞ SLBAP	Trade	26.90	0.00	0.00%	$0.00	12	$19.32	$9,049.04	38.95%	$32,280.00	Edit
Cash					70,917.47					$70,917.47	
			Totals	$9,976.10			$197,585.94	$147,046.06	74.42%	$415,549.47	

LEGEND: ⊞ collapsed (click to expand)   ⊟ expanded (click to collapse)   Real-time quotes

Summary

WOW! I can't believe this project is over. What started out to be a small book developed into quite a significant manual. When I get excited about something I can go on forever! For me this is one of the most exciting and significant revelations of my entire trading career! I see my job as a code cracker. I work endlessly to break the code and gain profits. The code has been broken.

With my Weekly Option Winners strategies you can profit in the most difficult markets regardless of their nature. You can sleep at night knowing the code has been broken and that your money is working for you! This is for me the most important breakthrough in my 27 year trading career. Yes, it is the ultimate investing tool. It is the ultimate income generator, and yes, it is an experience I will never forget.

My team and myself will continue to use these methods and reap our rewards, over and over again. And yes, this is a WOW! But not a WOW moment, for all of us here at Legacy Publishing, WOW is now the cornerstone of our trading. It is what we stand behind and allows us to trade, live and win! Come join us. Your WOW moments are ready to go! Are you?

Wishing You the Best in Investment Success,

Chuck Hughes

Appendix

$7,485,348.68 in Option Premium Income
Over the Past Five Years

Copies of my brokerage account trade confirmations that follow show that I collected $7,485,348.68 in gross option premium income over the last five years. This averages out to more than $124,000 in option premium income per month. Brokerage confirmations list the options I sold and the amount of cash that was credited to my brokerage account for each option sale.

Transaction History: Reports

| Transactions | Check Summary | Deposit Summary | Categories | **Reports** |

Type	Date	Category	Subcategory	Description	Amount
Sold Short					
	04/27/12	Unassigned		1 ISRG May 19 '12 $585 Call(ISRG) INTUITIVE SURGICAL IN...	$1,115.22
	04/27/12	Unassigned		15 WFC May 04 '12 $34 Call w(WFC) WELLS FARGO & CO NEW ...	$284.63
	04/27/12	Unassigned		9 SSO May 04 '12 $58 Call w(SSO) PROSHARES ULTRA S&P 50...	$673.17
	04/27/12	Unassigned		9 SBUX May 04 '12 $57.50 Call w(SBUX) STARBUCKS CORP CO...	$777.15
	04/27/12	Unassigned		8 QQQ May 04 '12 $67 Call w(QQQ) POWERSHARES QQQ TRUST,...	$565.93
	04/27/12	Unassigned		1 MA May 04 '12 $460 Call w(MA) MASTERCARD INC CL A SHO...	$1,247.22
	04/27/12	Unassigned		12 JPM May 04 '12 $44 Call w(JPM) JPMORGAN CHASE & CO C...	$262.90
	04/27/12	Unassigned		1 CMG May 04 '12 $420 Call w(CMG) CHIPOTLE MEXICAN GRIL...	$545.23
	04/27/12	Unassigned		15 AIG May 04 '12 $35 Call w(AIG) AMERICAN INTL GROUP I...	$1,289.61
	04/27/12	Unassigned		2 AAPL May 04 '12 $605 Call w(AAPL) APPLE INC COM SHORT...	$1,428.45
	04/25/12	Unassigned		5 WFC Apr 27 '12 $33 Call w(WFC) WELLS FARGO & CO NEW C...	$238.21
	04/25/12	Unassigned		5 SSO Apr 27 '12 $57 Call w(SSO) PROSHARES ULTRA S&P 50...	$153.21
	04/25/12	Unassigned		2 SSO Apr 27 '12 $57 Call w(SSO) PROSHARES ULTRA S&P 50...	$82.47
	04/25/12	Unassigned		2 SSO Apr 27 '12 $57 Call w(SSO) PROSHARES ULTRA S&P 50...	$72.48
	04/25/12	Unassigned		3 SBUX Apr 27 '12 $60 Call w(SBUX) STARBUCKS CORP COM S...	$309.72
	04/25/12	Unassigned		3 SBUX Apr 27 '12 $60 Call w(SBUX) STARBUCKS CORP COM S...	$294.72
	04/25/12	Unassigned		2 SBUX Apr 27 '12 $60 Call w(SBUX) STARBUCKS CORP COM S...	$196.48
	04/25/12	Unassigned		2 SBUX Apr 27 '12 $60 Call w(SBUX) STARBUCKS CORP COM S...	$186.48
	04/25/12	Unassigned		1 MA Apr 27 '12 $435 Call w(MA) MASTERCARD INC CL A SHO...	$491.23
	04/25/12	Unassigned		1 ISRG Apr 27 '12 $565 Call w(ISRG) INTUITIVE SURGICAL ...	$591.23
	04/25/12	Unassigned		1 CMG Apr 27 '12 $410 Call w(CMG) CHIPOTLE MEXICAN GRIL...	$491.23
	04/24/12	Unassigned		4 JPM Apr 27 '12 $43 Call w(JPM) JPMORGAN CHASE & CO CO...	$188.96
	04/24/12	Unassigned		13 HD Apr 27 '12 $50 Call w(HD) HOME DEPOT INC COM SHOR...	$1,932.09
	04/23/12	Unassigned		2 QQQ Apr 27 '12 $65 Call w(QQQ) POWERSHARES QQQ TRUST,...	$130.48
	04/23/12	Unassigned		4 AIG Apr 27 '12 $32 Call w(AIG) AMERICAN INTL GROUP IN...	$188.96
	04/20/12	Unassigned		15 WFC Apr 27 '12 $33 Call w(WFC) WELLS FARGO & CO NEW ...	$520.62
	04/20/12	Unassigned		8 QQQ Apr 27 '12 $66 Call w(QQQ) POWERSHARES QQQ TRUST,...	$557.90
	04/20/12	Unassigned		1 PCLN Apr 27 '12 $710 Call w(PCLN) PRICELINE COM INC C...	$1,271.22
	04/20/12	Unassigned		1 MA Apr 27 '12 $440 Call w(MA) MASTERCARD INC CL A SHO...	$562.23
	04/20/12	Unassigned		12 JPM Apr 27 '12 $43 Call w(JPM) JPMORGAN CHASE & CO C...	$618.89
	04/20/12	Unassigned		1 ISRG Apr 27 '12 $575 Call w(ISRG) INTUITIVE SURGICAL ...	$627.23
	04/20/12	Unassigned		1 CMG Apr 27 '12 $420 Call w(CMG) CHIPOTLE MEXICAN GRIL...	$802.23
	04/20/12	Unassigned		12 AIG Apr 27 '12 $32 Call w(AIG) AMERICAN INTL GROUP I...	$654.88
	04/20/12	Unassigned		2 AAPL Apr 27 '12 $590 Call w(AAPL) APPLE INC COM SHORT...	$3,242.41
	04/17/12	Unassigned		1 PCLN Apr 21 '12 $720 Call(PCLN) PRICELINE COM INC COM...	$951.22
	04/17/12	Unassigned		2 AAPL Apr 21 '12 $600 Call(AAPL) APPLE INC COM SHORT...	$1,990.44
	04/17/12	Unassigned		8 QQQ Apr 21 '12 $66 Call(QQQ) POWERSHARES QQQ TRUST, S...	$465.93
	04/13/12	Unassigned		10 HD Apr 21 '12 $50 Call(HD) HOME DEPOT INC COM SHORT...	$984.38
	04/12/12	Unassigned		10 SSO Apr 21 '12 $57 Call(SSO) PROSHARES ULTRA S&P 500...	$684.41
	04/12/12	Unassigned		1 MA Apr 21 '12 $435 Call(MA) MASTERCARD INC CL A SHORT...	$501.23
	04/12/12	Unassigned		2 AAPL Apr 21 '12 $630 Call(AAPL) APPLE INC COM SHORT...	$1,790.44
	04/12/12	Unassigned		1 PCLN Apr 21 '12 $740 Call(PCLN) PRICELINE COM INC COM...	$1,431.21
	04/12/12	Unassigned		8 QQQ Apr 21 '12 $67 Call(QQQ) POWERSHARES QQQ TRUST, S...	$545.93
	04/12/12	Unassigned		15 WFC Apr 21 '12 $34 Call(WFC) WELLS FARGO & CO NEW CO...	$899.56
	04/12/12	Unassigned		1 CMG Apr 21 '12 $435 Call(CMG) CHIPOTLE MEXICAN GRILL ...	$832.23
	04/12/12	Unassigned		12 JPM Apr 21 '12 $45 Call(JPM) JPMORGAN CHASE & CO COM...	$886.88

Transaction History: Reports

| Transactions | Check Summary | Deposit Summary | Categories | Reports |

Type	Date	Category	Subcategory	Description	Amount
Sold Short					
	04/12/12	Unassigned		8 AIG Apr 21 '12 $34 Call(AIG) AMERICAN INTL GROUP INC ...	$345.94
	04/12/12	Unassigned		8 AIG Apr 21 '12 $33 Call(AIG) AMERICAN INTL GROUP INC ...	$561.93
	04/11/12	Unassigned		1 ISRG Apr 21 '12 $550 Call(ISRG) INTUITIVE SURGICAL IN...	$1,234.22
	04/05/12	Unassigned		15 WFC Apr 13 '12 $34 Call w(WFC) WELLS FARGO & CO NEW ...	$734.62
	04/05/12	Unassigned		10 SSO Apr 13 '12 $58 Call w(SSO) PROSHARES ULTRA S&P 5...	$548.38
	04/05/12	Unassigned		8 QQQ Apr 13 '12 $68 Call w(QQQ) POWERSHARES QQQ TRUST,...	$341.91
	04/05/12	Unassigned		1 PCLN Apr 13 '12 $755 Call w(PCLN) PRICELINE COM INC C...	$1,137.22
	04/05/12	Unassigned		1 MA Apr 13 '12 $440 Call w(MA) MASTERCARD INC CL A SHO...	$576.23
	04/05/12	Unassigned		12 JPM Apr 13 '12 $45 Call w(JPM) JPMORGAN CHASE & CO C...	$586.89
	04/05/12	Unassigned		10 HD Apr 13 '12 $50 Call w(HD) HOME DEPOT INC COM SHOR...	$808.41
	04/05/12	Unassigned		1 CMG Apr 13 '12 $425 Call w(CMG) CHIPOTLE MEXICAN GRIL...	$425.24
	04/05/12	Unassigned		2 AAPL Apr 13 '12 $635 Call w(AAPL) APPLE INC COM SHORT...	$1,596.45
	03/29/12	Unassigned		15 WFC Apr 05 '12 $34 Call w(WFC) WELLS FARGO & CO NEW ...	$509.63
	03/29/12	Unassigned		10 SSO Apr 05 '12 $58 Call w(SSO) PROSHARES ULTRA S&P 5...	$528.39
	03/29/12	Unassigned		8 QQQ Apr 05 '12 $68 Call w(QQQ) POWERSHARES QQQ TRUST,...	$245.94
	03/29/12	Unassigned		1 PCLN Apr 05 '12 $715 Call w(PCLN) PRICELINE COM INC C...	$1,192.22
	03/29/12	Unassigned		12 JPM Apr 05 '12 $46 Call w(JPM) JPMORGAN CHASE & CO C...	$394.90
	03/29/12	Unassigned		10 HD Apr 05 '12 $50 Call w(HD) HOME DEPOT INC COM SHOR...	$318.42
	03/29/12	Unassigned		1 CMG Apr 05 '12 $420 Call w(CMG) CHIPOTLE MEXICAN GRIL...	$341.24
	03/29/12	Unassigned		2 AAPL Apr 05 '12 $615 Call w(AAPL) APPLE INC COM SHORT...	$1,300.46
	03/23/12	Unassigned		8 QQQ Mar 30 '12 $67 Call w(QQQ) POWERSHARES QQQ TRUST,...	$349.91
	03/23/12	Unassigned		1 PCLN Mar 30 '12 $715 Call w(PCLN) PRICELINE COM INC C...	$1,084.23
	03/23/12	Unassigned		12 JPM Mar 30 '12 $45 Call w(JPM) JPMORGAN CHASE & CO C...	$730.89
	03/23/12	Unassigned		10 HD Mar 30 '12 $49 Call w(HD) HOME DEPOT INC COM SHOR...	$708.41
	03/23/12	Unassigned		1 CMG Mar 30 '12 $415 Call w(CMG) CHIPOTLE MEXICAN GRIL...	$429.24
	03/23/12	Unassigned		1 AAPL Mar 30 '12 $600 Call w(AAPL) APPLE INC COM SHORT...	$715.23
	03/23/12	Unassigned		1 AAPL Mar 30 '12 $600 Call w(AAPL) APPLE INC COM SHORT...	$991.23
	03/22/12	Unassigned		15 WFC Mar 30 '12 $34 Call w(WFC) WELLS FARGO & CO NEW ...	$344.63
	03/22/12	Unassigned		10 SSO Mar 30 '12 $58 Call w(SSO) PROSHARES ULTRA S&P 5...	$458.42
	03/20/12	Unassigned		1 AAPL Mar 23 '12 $605 Call w(AAPL) APPLE INC COM SHORT...	$791.23
	03/16/12	Unassigned		10 HD Mar 23 '12 $49 Call w(HD) HOME DEPOT INC COM SHOR...	$498.42
	03/16/12	Unassigned		10 EEM Mar 23 '12 $44 Call w(EEM) ISHARES MSCI EMERGING...	$558.38
	03/16/12	Unassigned		1 AAPL Mar 23 '12 $590 Call w(AAPL) APPLE INC COM SHORT...	$1,034.23
	03/15/12	Unassigned		15 WFC Mar 23 '12 $34 Call w(WFC) WELLS FARGO & CO NEW ...	$644.62
	03/15/12	Unassigned		5 SSO Mar 23 '12 $58 Call w(SSO) PROSHARES ULTRA S&P 50...	$342.19
	03/15/12	Unassigned		5 SSO Mar 23 '12 $58 Call w(SSO) PROSHARES ULTRA S&P 50...	$357.19
	03/15/12	Unassigned		8 QQQ Mar 23 '12 $67 Call w(QQQ) POWERSHARES QQQ TRUST,...	$261.94
	03/15/12	Unassigned		12 JPM Mar 23 '12 $45 Call w(JPM) JPMORGAN CHASE & CO C...	$802.89
	03/13/12	Unassigned		5 SSO Mar 17 '12 $57 Call(SSO) PROSHARES ULTRA S&P 500 ...	$138.21
	03/13/12	Unassigned		5 EEM Mar 17 '12 $44 Call(EEM) ISHARES MSCI EMERGING MA...	$193.21
	03/08/12	Unassigned		15 WFC Mar 17 '12 $31 Call(WFC) WELLS FARGO & CO NEW CO...	$730.60
	03/08/12	Unassigned		5 SSO Mar 17 '12 $55 Call(SSO) PROSHARES ULTRA S&P 500 ...	$363.21
	03/08/12	Unassigned		8 QQQ Mar 17 '12 $64 Call(QQQ) POWERSHARES QQQ TRUST, S...	$785.93
	03/08/12	Unassigned		12 JPM Mar 17 '12 $41 Call(JPM) JPMORGAN CHASE & CO COM...	$442.90
	03/08/12	Unassigned		10 HD Mar 17 '12 $48 Call(HD) HOME DEPOT INC COM SHORT...	$428.42
	03/08/12	Unassigned		18 AIG Mar 17 '12 $29 Call(AIG) AMERICAN INTL GROUP INC...	$680.32
	03/08/12	Unassigned		5 EEM Mar 17 '12 $44 Call(EEM) ISHARES MSCI EMERGING MA...	$238.21

4

Transaction History: Reports

| Transactions | Check Summary | Deposit Summary | Categories | Reports |

Type	Date	Category	Subcategory	Description	Amount
Sold Short					
	03/07/12	Unassigned		1 AAPL Mar 17 '12 $530 Call(AAPL) APPLE INC COM SHORT...	$991.23
	03/02/12	Unassigned		6 JPM Mar 09 '12 $41 Call w(JPM) JPMORGAN CHASE & CO CO...	$261.45
	03/02/12	Unassigned		10 HD Mar 09 '12 $47 Call w(HD) HOME DEPOT INC COM SHOR...	$508.42
	03/02/12	Unassigned		1 AAPL Mar 09 '12 $550 Call w(AAPL) APPLE INC COM SHORT...	$666.23
	03/01/12	Unassigned		5 SSO Mar 09 '12 $56 Call w(SSO) PROSHARES ULTRA S&P 50...	$267.21
	03/01/12	Unassigned		7 QQQ Mar 09 '12 $65 Call w(QQQ) POWERSHARES QQQ TRUST,...	$319.69
	03/01/12	Unassigned		6 JPM Mar 09 '12 $41 Call w(JPM) JPMORGAN CHASE & CO CO...	$161.45
	03/01/12	Unassigned		5 EEM Mar 09 '12 $45 Call w(EEM) ISHARES MSCI EMERGING ...	$187.21
	03/01/12	Unassigned		8 AIG Mar 09 '12 $30 Call w(AIG) AMERICAN INTL GROUP IN...	$229.94
	03/01/12	Unassigned		1 AIG Mar 09 '12 $30 Call w(AIG) AMERICAN INTL GROUP IN...	$24.24
	03/01/12	Unassigned		9 AIG Mar 09 '12 $30 Call w(AIG) AMERICAN INTL GROUP IN...	$363.18
	02/28/12	Unassigned		9 AIG Mar 02 '12 $29 Call w(AIG) AMERICAN INTL GROUP IN...	$237.18
	02/24/12	Unassigned		7 QQQ Mar 02 '12 $64 Call w(QQQ) POWERSHARES QQQ TRUST,...	$326.69
	02/24/12	Unassigned		10 HD Mar 02 '12 $47 Call w(HD) HOME DEPOT INC COM SHOR...	$344.40
	02/24/12	Unassigned		1 AAPL Mar 02 '12 $525 Call w(AAPL) APPLE INC COM SHORT...	$503.24
	02/23/12	Unassigned		5 SSO Mar 02 '12 $55 Call w(SSO) PROSHARES ULTRA S&P 50...	$297.21
	02/23/12	Unassigned		25 MS Mar 02 '12 $19 Call w(MS) MORGAN STANLEY COM NEW ...	$877.04
	02/23/12	Unassigned		6 JPM Mar 02 '12 $38 Call w(JPM) JPMORGAN CHASE & CO CO...	$407.44
	02/23/12	Unassigned		6 IWM Mar 02 '12 $83 Call w(IWM) ISHARES RUSSELL 2000 I...	$467.44
	02/23/12	Unassigned		5 EEM Mar 02 '12 $44 Call w(EEM) ISHARES MSCI EMERGING ...	$212.21
	02/21/12	Unassigned		3 SSO Feb 24 '12 $55 Call w(SSO) PROSHARES ULTRA S&P 50...	$162.72
	02/21/12	Unassigned		2 SSO Feb 24 '12 $55 Call w(SSO) PROSHARES ULTRA S&P 50...	$98.48
	02/21/12	Unassigned		6 JPM Feb 24 '12 $39 Call w(JPM) JPMORGAN CHASE & CO CO...	$185.45
	02/21/12	Unassigned		5 EEM Feb 24 '12 $44 Call w(EEM) ISHARES MSCI EMERGING ...	$178.21
	02/17/12	Unassigned		7 QQQ Feb 24 '12 $63 Call w(QQQ) POWERSHARES QQQ TRUST,...	$567.66
	02/17/12	Unassigned		25 MS Feb 24 '12 $19 Call w(MS) MORGAN STANLEY COM NEW ...	$1,098.03
	02/17/12	Unassigned		6 IWM Feb 24 '12 $83 Call w(IWM) ISHARES RUSSELL 2000 I...	$467.45
	02/17/12	Unassigned		10 HD Feb 24 '12 $47 Call w(HD) HOME DEPOT INC COM SHOR...	$554.39
	02/17/12	Unassigned		1 AAPL Feb 24 '12 $505 Call w(AAPL) APPLE INC COM SHORT...	$711.23
	02/14/12	Unassigned		3 AAPL Feb 18 '12 $500 Call(AAPL) APPLE INC COM SHORT...	$2,299.69
	02/14/12	Unassigned		60 XLF Feb 18 '12 $14 Call(XLF) FINANCIAL SELECT SECTOR...	$2,946.47
	02/14/12	Unassigned		3 XLF Feb 18 '12 $14 Call(XLF) FINANCIAL SELECT SECTOR ...	$145.73
	02/14/12	Unassigned		15 QQQ Feb 18 '12 $63 Call(QQQ) POWERSHARES QQQ TRUST, ...	$580.57
	02/14/12	Unassigned		7 HUM Feb 18 '12 $87.50 Call(HUM) HUMANA INC COM SHORT...	$686.66
	02/14/12	Unassigned		11 IWM Feb 18 '12 $82 Call(IWM) ISHARES RUSSELL 2000 IN...	$533.65
	02/14/12	Unassigned		10 HD Feb 18 '12 $46 Call(HD) HOME DEPOT INC COM SHORT...	$384.42
				Total Sold Short	**$82,645.77**

Transaction History: Reports

| | Transactions | Check Summary | Deposit Summary | Categories | Reports | |

Type	Date	Category	Subcategory	Description	Amount
Sold Short					
	04/27/12	Unassigned		8 WFC May 04 '12 $34 Call w(WFC) WELLS FARGO & CO NEW C...	$149.90
	04/27/12	Unassigned		5 SSO May 04 '12 $58 Call w(SSO) PROSHARES ULTRA S&P 50...	$382.19
	04/27/12	Unassigned		4 SBUX May 04 '12 $57.50 Call w(SBUX) STARBUCKS CORP CO...	$348.96
	04/27/12	Unassigned		4 QQQ May 04 '12 $67 Call w(QQQ) POWERSHARES QQQ TRUST,...	$280.97
	04/27/12	Unassigned		1 MA May 04 '12 $460 Call w(MA) MASTERCARD INC CL A SHO...	$1,292.22
	04/27/12	Unassigned		1 CMG May 04 '12 $420 Call w(CMG) CHIPOTLE MEXICAN GRIL...	$603.23
	04/27/12	Unassigned		8 AIG May 04 '12 $35 Call w(AIG) AMERICAN INTL GROUP IN...	$637.93
	04/27/12	Unassigned		2 AAPL May 04 '12 $610 Call w(AAPL) APPLE INC COM SHORT...	$1,148.46
	04/25/12	Unassigned		2 WFC Apr 27 '12 $33 Call w(WFC) WELLS FARGO & CO NEW C...	$70.48
	04/25/12	Unassigned		3 SSO Apr 27 '12 $57 Call w(SSO) PROSHARES ULTRA S&P 50...	$109.73
	04/25/12	Unassigned		1 SSO Apr 27 '12 $57 Call w(SSO) PROSHARES ULTRA S&P 50...	$32.23
	04/25/12	Unassigned		1 SSO Apr 27 '12 $57 Call w(SSO) PROSHARES ULTRA S&P 50...	$23.24
	04/25/12	Unassigned		1 SBUX Apr 27 '12 $60 Call w(SBUX) STARBUCKS CORP COM S...	$101.23
	04/25/12	Unassigned		1 SBUX Apr 27 '12 $60 Call w(SBUX) STARBUCKS CORP COM S...	$92.24
	04/25/12	Unassigned		1 SBUX Apr 27 '12 $60 Call w(SBUX) STARBUCKS CORP COM S...	$98.23
	04/25/12	Unassigned		1 SBUX Apr 27 '12 $60 Call w(SBUX) STARBUCKS CORP COM S...	$89.24
	04/25/12	Unassigned		1 QQQ Apr 27 '12 $66 Call w(QQQ) POWERSHARES QQQ TRUST,...	$59.24
	04/25/12	Unassigned		1 MA Apr 27 '12 $435 Call w(MA) MASTERCARD INC CL A SHO...	$591.23
	04/25/12	Unassigned		1 CMG Apr 27 '12 $410 Call w(CMG) CHIPOTLE MEXICAN GRIL...	$491.23
	04/24/12	Unassigned		2 JPM Apr 27 '12 $43 Call w(JPM) JPMORGAN CHASE & CO CO...	$82.48
	04/24/12	Unassigned		6 HD Apr 27 '12 $50 Call w(HD) HOME DEPOT INC COM SHORT...	$887.42
	04/23/12	Unassigned		2 AIG Apr 27 '12 $32 Call w(AIG) AMERICAN INTL GROUP IN...	$90.48
	04/20/12	Unassigned		8 WFC Apr 27 '12 $33 Call w(WFC) WELLS FARGO & CO NEW C...	$281.91
	04/20/12	Unassigned		4 QQQ Apr 27 '12 $66 Call w(QQQ) POWERSHARES QQQ TRUST,...	$264.96
	04/20/12	Unassigned		1 PCLN Apr 27 '12 $710 Call w(PCLN) PRICELINE COM INC C...	$1,294.22
	04/20/12	Unassigned		1 MA Apr 27 '12 $440 Call w(MA) MASTERCARD INC CL A SHO...	$502.23
	04/20/12	Unassigned		6 JPM Apr 27 '12 $43 Call w(JPM) JPMORGAN CHASE & CO CO...	$257.45
	04/20/12	Unassigned		1 CMG Apr 27 '12 $420 Call w(CMG) CHIPOTLE MEXICAN GRIL...	$627.23
	04/20/12	Unassigned		6 AIG Apr 27 '12 $32 Call w(AIG) AMERICAN INTL GROUP IN...	$311.44
	04/20/12	Unassigned		1 AAPL Apr 27 '12 $590 Call w(AAPL) APPLE INC COM SHORT...	$1,597.21
	04/20/12	Unassigned		1 AAPL Apr 27 '12 $590 Call w(AAPL) APPLE INC COM SHORT...	$1,602.20
	04/17/12	Unassigned		1 PCLN Apr 21 '12 $720 Call(PCLN) PRICELINE COM INC COM...	$991.22
	04/17/12	Unassigned		2 AAPL Apr 21 '12 $600 Call(AAPL) APPLE INC COM SHORT...	$1,990.44
	04/17/12	Unassigned		4 QQQ Apr 21 '12 $66 Call(QQQ) POWERSHARES QQQ TRUST, S...	$228.97
	04/12/12	Unassigned		1 MA Apr 21 '12 $435 Call(MA) MASTERCARD INC CL A SHORT...	$481.23
	04/12/12	Unassigned		1 AAPL Apr 21 '12 $630 Call(AAPL) APPLE INC COM SHORT...	$891.22
	04/12/12	Unassigned		1 PCLN Apr 21 '12 $740 Call(PCLN) PRICELINE COM INC COM...	$1,433.21
	04/12/12	Unassigned		4 QQQ Apr 21 '12 $67 Call(QQQ) POWERSHARES QQQ TRUST, S...	$272.97
	04/12/12	Unassigned		8 WFC Apr 21 '12 $34 Call(WFC) WELLS FARGO & CO NEW COM...	$429.94
	04/12/12	Unassigned		1 CMG Apr 21 '12 $435 Call(CMG) CHIPOTLE MEXICAN GRILL ...	$951.22
	04/12/12	Unassigned		6 JPM Apr 21 '12 $45 Call(JPM) JPMORGAN CHASE & CO COM ...	$453.44
	04/12/12	Unassigned		4 AIG Apr 21 '12 $34 Call(AIG) AMERICAN INTL GROUP INC ...	$164.97
	04/12/12	Unassigned		4 AIG Apr 21 '12 $33 Call(AIG) AMERICAN INTL GROUP INC ...	$276.97
	04/05/12	Unassigned		8 WFC Apr 13 '12 $34 Call w(WFC) WELLS FARGO & CO NEW C...	$389.91
	04/05/12	Unassigned		5 SSO Apr 13 '12 $58 Call w(SSO) PROSHARES ULTRA S&P 50...	$262.19
	04/05/12	Unassigned		4 QQQ Apr 13 '12 $68 Call w(QQQ) POWERSHARES QQQ TRUST,...	$148.96
	04/05/12	Unassigned		1 PCLN Apr 13 '12 $755 Call w(PCLN) PRICELINE COM INC C...	$1,148.22

Transaction History: Reports

⚡ Alerts | ≫ Transfer Money | ≫ Bill Pay | ⑦ Help

Transactions	Check Summary	Deposit Summary	Categories	Reports

Type	Date	Category	Subcategory	Description	Amount
Sold Short					
	04/05/12	Unassigned		1 MA Apr 13 '12 $440 Call w(MA) MASTERCARD INC CL A SHO...	$573.23
	04/05/12	Unassigned		6 JPM Apr 13 '12 $45 Call w(JPM) JPMORGAN CHASE & CO CO...	$279.45
	04/05/12	Unassigned		5 HD Apr 13 '12 $50 Call w(HD) HOME DEPOT INC COM SHORT...	$377.21
	04/05/12	Unassigned		1 CMG Apr 13 '12 $425 Call w(CMG) CHIPOTLE MEXICAN GRIL...	$434.24
	04/05/12	Unassigned		1 AAPL Apr 13 '12 $630 Call w(AAPL) APPLE INC COM SHORT...	$1,033.22
	03/29/12	Unassigned		8 WFC Apr 05 '12 $34 Call w(WFC) WELLS FARGO & CO NEW C...	$253.91
	03/29/12	Unassigned		5 SSO Apr 05 '12 $58 Call w(SSO) PROSHARES ULTRA S&P 50...	$257.21
	03/29/12	Unassigned		4 QQQ Apr 05 '12 $68 Call w(QQQ) POWERSHARES QQQ TRUST,...	$112.96
	03/29/12	Unassigned		1 PCLN Apr 05 '12 $715 Call w(PCLN) PRICELINE COM INC C...	$1,199.22
	03/29/12	Unassigned		6 JPM Apr 05 '12 $46 Call w(JPM) JPMORGAN CHASE & CO CO...	$183.45
	03/29/12	Unassigned		5 HD Apr 05 '12 $50 Call w(HD) HOME DEPOT INC COM SHORT...	$147.21
	03/29/12	Unassigned		1 CMG Apr 05 '12 $420 Call w(CMG) CHIPOTLE MEXICAN GRIL...	$305.24
	03/29/12	Unassigned		1 AAPL Apr 05 '12 $615 Call w(AAPL) APPLE INC COM SHORT...	$605.23
	03/23/12	Unassigned		4 QQQ Mar 30 '12 $67 Call w(QQQ) POWERSHARES QQQ TRUST,...	$180.96
	03/23/12	Unassigned		1 PCLN Mar 30 '12 $715 Call w(PCLN) PRICELINE COM INC C...	$1,061.23
	03/23/12	Unassigned		6 JPM Mar 30 '12 $45 Call w(JPM) JPMORGAN CHASE & CO CO...	$339.45
	03/23/12	Unassigned		5 HD Mar 30 '12 $49 Call w(HD) HOME DEPOT INC COM SHORT...	$352.21
	03/23/12	Unassigned		1 CMG Mar 30 '12 $415 Call w(CMG) CHIPOTLE MEXICAN GRIL...	$421.24
	03/23/12	Unassigned		1 AAPL Mar 30 '12 $600 Call w(AAPL) APPLE INC COM SHORT...	$991.23
	03/22/12	Unassigned		8 WFC Mar 30 '12 $34 Call w(WFC) WELLS FARGO & CO NEW C...	$165.94
	03/22/12	Unassigned		5 SSO Mar 30 '12 $58 Call w(SSO) PROSHARES ULTRA S&P 50...	$222.19
	03/20/12	Unassigned		1 AAPL Mar 23 '12 $605 Call w(AAPL) APPLE INC COM SHORT...	$791.23
	03/16/12	Unassigned		5 HD Mar 23 '12 $49 Call w(HD) HOME DEPOT INC COM SHORT...	$242.21
	03/16/12	Unassigned		6 EEM Mar 23 '12 $44 Call w(EEM) ISHARES MSCI EMERGING ...	$333.45
	03/15/12	Unassigned		8 WFC Mar 23 '12 $34 Call w(WFC) WELLS FARGO & CO NEW C...	$349.94
	03/15/12	Unassigned		5 SSO Mar 23 '12 $58 Call w(SSO) PROSHARES ULTRA S&P 50...	$337.19
	03/15/12	Unassigned		4 QQQ Mar 23 '12 $67 Call w(QQQ) POWERSHARES QQQ TRUST,...	$128.96
	03/15/12	Unassigned		6 JPM Mar 23 '12 $45 Call w(JPM) JPMORGAN CHASE & CO CO...	$363.45
	03/08/12	Unassigned		8 WFC Mar 17 '12 $31 Call(WFC) WELLS FARGO & CO NEW COM...	$465.92
	03/08/12	Unassigned		5 SSO Mar 17 '12 $55 Call(SSO) PROSHARES ULTRA S&P 500 ...	$363.21
	03/08/12	Unassigned		4 QQQ Mar 17 '12 $64 Call(QQQ) POWERSHARES QQQ TRUST, S...	$388.97
	03/08/12	Unassigned		6 JPM Mar 17 '12 $41 Call(JPM) JPMORGAN CHASE & CO COM ...	$213.45
	03/08/12	Unassigned		5 HD Mar 17 '12 $48 Call(HD) HOME DEPOT INC COM SHORT...	$208.21
	03/08/12	Unassigned		9 AIG Mar 17 '12 $29 Call(AIG) AMERICAN INTL GROUP INC ...	$327.18
	03/08/12	Unassigned		6 EEM Mar 17 '12 $44 Call(EEM) ISHARES MSCI EMERGING MA...	$287.45
	03/02/12	Unassigned		5 SSO Mar 09 '12 $55 Call w(SSO) PROSHARES ULTRA S&P 50...	$417.21
	03/02/12	Unassigned		4 QQQ Mar 09 '12 $65 Call w(QQQ) POWERSHARES QQQ TRUST,...	$152.97
	03/02/12	Unassigned		6 JPM Mar 09 '12 $41 Call w(JPM) JPMORGAN CHASE & CO CO...	$249.45
	03/02/12	Unassigned		5 EEM Mar 09 '12 $45 Call w(EEM) ISHARES MSCI EMERGING ...	$142.21
	03/02/12	Unassigned		9 AIG Mar 09 '12 $30 Call w(AIG) AMERICAN INTL GROUP IN...	$322.18
	03/01/12	Unassigned		4 WFC Mar 09 '12 $32 Call w(WFC) WELLS FARGO & CO NEW C...	$84.97
	02/28/12	Unassigned		5 MS Mar 02 '12 $19 Call w(MS) MORGAN STANLEY COM NEW S...	$113.21
	02/28/12	Unassigned		5 AIG Mar 02 '12 $29 Call w(AIG) AMERICAN INTL GROUP IN...	$151.20
	02/28/12	Unassigned		4 AIG Mar 02 '12 $29 Call w(AIG) AMERICAN INTL GROUP IN...	$108.97
	02/24/12	Unassigned		5 SSO Mar 02 '12 $55 Call w(SSO) PROSHARES ULTRA S&P 50...	$297.21
	02/24/12	Unassigned		4 QQQ Mar 02 '12 $64 Call w(QQQ) POWERSHARES QQQ TRUST,...	$164.97

| Transactions | Check Summary | Deposit Summary | Categories | Reports |

Type	Date	Category	Subcategory	Description	Amount
Sold Short					
	02/24/12	Unassigned		5 HD Mar 02 '12 $47 Call w(HD) HOME DEPOT INC COM SHORT...	$167.21
	02/24/12	Unassigned		5 EEM Mar 02 '12 $44 Call w(EEM) ISHARES MSCI EMERGING ...	$257.21
	02/23/12	Unassigned		6 JPM Mar 02 '12 $38 Call w(JPM) JPMORGAN CHASE & CO CO...	$407.44
	02/23/12	Unassigned		3 IWM Mar 02 '12 $83 Call w(IWM) ISHARES RUSSELL 2000 I...	$229.72
	02/21/12	Unassigned		5 SSO Feb 24 '12 $55 Call w(SSO) PROSHARES ULTRA S&P 50...	$248.21
	02/21/12	Unassigned		6 JPM Feb 24 '12 $39 Call w(JPM) JPMORGAN CHASE & CO CO...	$185.45
	02/21/12	Unassigned		5 EEM Feb 24 '12 $44 Call w(EEM) ISHARES MSCI EMERGING ...	$193.21
	02/17/12	Unassigned		4 QQQ Feb 24 '12 $63 Call w(QQQ) POWERSHARES QQQ TRUST,...	$304.96
	02/17/12	Unassigned		13 MS Feb 24 '12 $19 Call w(MS) MORGAN STANLEY COM NEW ...	$580.14
	02/17/12	Unassigned		3 IWM Feb 24 '12 $83 Call w(IWM) ISHARES RUSSELL 2000 I...	$217.72
	02/17/12	Unassigned		3 HD Feb 24 '12 $47 Call w(HD) HOME DEPOT INC COM SHORT...	$177.72
	02/17/12	Unassigned		2 HD Feb 24 '12 $47 Call w(HD) HOME DEPOT INC COM SHORT...	$108.48
	02/14/12	Unassigned		2 AAPL Feb 18 '12 $500 Call(AAPL) APPLE INC COM SHORT...	$1,530.46
	02/14/12	Unassigned		32 XLF Feb 18 '12 $14 Call(XLF) FINANCIAL SELECT SECTOR...	$1,567.62
	02/14/12	Unassigned		7 QQQ Feb 18 '12 $63 Call(QQQ) POWERSHARES QQQ TRUST, S...	$266.68
	02/14/12	Unassigned		6 HUM Feb 18 '12 $87.50 Call(HUM) HUMANA INC COM SHORT...	$587.42
	02/14/12	Unassigned		5 IWM Feb 18 '12 $82 Call(IWM) ISHARES RUSSELL 2000 IND...	$288.21
				Total Sold Short	**$48,735.95**

| Transactions | Check Summary | Deposit Summary | Categories | Reports |

Type	Date	Category	Subcategory	Description	Amount
Sold Short					
	12/09/11	Unassigned		1 GOOG Jan 19 '13 $510 Call(GOOG) GOOGLE INC CL A SHORT...	$14,990.96
	12/09/11	Unassigned		7 TJX Jan 19 '13 $57.50 Call(TJX) TJX COS INC NEW COM S...	$7,056.56
	12/09/11	Unassigned		1 NOV Jan 19 '13 $50 Call(NOV) NATIONAL OILWELL VARCO I...	$2,661.19
	12/09/11	Unassigned		1 HUM Jan 19 '13 $60 Call(HUM) HUMANA INC COM SHORT...	$2,911.19
	11/22/11	Unassigned		1 AAPL Jan 19 '13 $270 Call(AAPL) APPLE INC COM SHORT...	$12,920.00
	11/21/11	Unassigned		1 MA Jan 19 '13 $260 Call(MA) MASTERCARD INC CL A SHORT...	$11,511.02
	11/21/11	Unassigned		5 NOV Jan 19 '13 $50 Call(NOV) NATIONAL OILWELL VARCO I...	$11,537.97
	11/21/11	Unassigned		4 HUM Jan 19 '13 $60 Call(HUM) HUMANA INC COM SHORT...	$10,988.74
	09/23/11	Unassigned		8 QQQ Sep 30 '11 $54 Call w(QQQ) POWERSHARES QQQ TRUST,...	$1,001.93
	09/23/11	Unassigned		1 AAPL Sep 30 '11 $405 Call w(AAPL) APPLE INC COM SHORT...	$812.23
	09/20/11	Unassigned		3 BIDU Sep 23 '11 $150 Call w(BIDU) BAIDU INC SPON ADR ...	$889.71
	09/16/11	Unassigned		10 EEM Sep 23 '11 $41 Call w(EEM) ISHARES MSCI EMERGING...	$454.38
	09/16/11	Unassigned		1 AAPL Sep 23 '11 $400 Call w(AAPL) APPLE INC COM SHORT...	$551.23
	09/16/11	Unassigned		7 XLE Sep 23 '11 $67 Call w(XLE) ENERGY SELECT SECTOR S...	$840.68
	09/16/11	Unassigned		8 QQQ Sep 23 '11 $57 Call w(QQQ) POWERSHARES QQQ TRUST,...	$505.94
	09/16/11	Unassigned		7 GLD Sep 23 '11 $177 Call w(GLD) SPDR GOLD SHARES SHOR...	$1,568.66
	09/16/11	Unassigned		2 GLD Sep 23 '11 $177 Call w(GLD) SPDR GOLD SHARES SHOR...	$450.47
	09/16/11	Unassigned		2 GLD Sep 23 '11 $177 Call w(GLD) SPDR GOLD SHARES SHOR...	$450.47
	09/16/11	Unassigned		2 GLD Sep 23 '11 $177 Call w(GLD) SPDR GOLD SHARES SHOR...	$450.47
	09/09/11	Unassigned		3 BIDU Sep 17 '11 $145 Call(BIDU) BAIDU INC SPON ADR RE...	$1,099.70
	09/09/11	Unassigned		7 XLE Sep 17 '11 $65 Call(XLE) ENERGY SELECT SECTOR SPD...	$973.66

Transaction History: Reports

Alerts | Transfer Money | Bill Pay | Help

| Transactions | Check Summary | Deposit Summary | Categories | **Reports** |

Type	Date	Category	Subcategory	Description	Amount
Sold Short					
	09/09/11	Unassigned		8 QQQ Sep 17 '11 $53 Call(QQQ) POWERSHARES QQQ TRUST, S...	$929.93
	09/09/11	Unassigned		1 AAPL Sep 17 '11 $380 Call(AAPL) APPLE INC COM SHORT...	$566.23
	09/09/11	Unassigned		10 EEM Sep 17 '11 $40 Call(EEM) ISHARES MSCI EMERGING M...	$1,124.40
	08/07/11	Unassigned		10 UGL Sep 17 '11 $100 Call(UGL) PROSHARES ULTRA GOLD S...	$6,284.30
	05/20/11	Unassigned		4 BIDU Jun 18 '11 $135 Call(BIDU) BAIDU INC SPON ADR RE...	$2,248.91
	05/20/11	Unassigned		11 UWM Jun 18 '11 $48 Call(UWM) PROSHARES ULTRA RUSSELL...	$1,908.63
	05/20/11	Unassigned		7 UGL Jun 18 '11 $79 Call(UGL) PROSHARES ULTRA GOLD SHO...	$1,701.66
	05/20/11	Unassigned		9 QLD Jun 18 '11 $92 Call(QLD) PROSHARES ULTRA QQQ SHOR...	$2,235.11
	05/20/11	Unassigned		10 SSO Jun 18 '11 $55 Call(SSO) PROSHARES ULTRA S&P 500...	$1,144.36
	05/20/11	Unassigned		9 DIG Jun 18 '11 $55 Call(DIG) PROSHARES ULTRA OIL & GA...	$1,974.15
	05/05/11	Unassigned		1 AAPL Jan 19 '13 $320 Call(AAPL) APPLE INC COM SHORT...	$7,671.10
	04/27/11	Unassigned		10 SSO May 21 '11 $54 Call(SSO) PROSHARES ULTRA S&P 500...	$2,484.31
	04/27/11	Unassigned		9 QLD May 21 '11 $92 Call(QLD) PROSHARES ULTRA QQQ SHOR...	$4,485.04
	04/26/11	Unassigned		4 BIDU May 21 '11 $150 Call(BIDU) BAIDU INC SPON ADR RE...	$3,988.87
	04/25/11	Unassigned		2 EDC Jan 19 '13 $39.35 Call(EDC) DIREXION DAILY EMERGI...	$3,112.42
	04/21/11	Unassigned		6 EDC Jan 19 '13 $39.35 Call(EDC) DIREXION DAILY EMERGI...	$9,755.23
	04/20/11	Unassigned		2 UGL Oct 22 '11 $72 Call(UGL) PROSHARES ULTRA GOLD SHO...	$1,990.44
	04/20/11	Unassigned		5 EEM Jan 19 '13 $48 Call(EEM) ISHARES MSCI EMERGING MA...	$3,598.12
	04/19/11	Unassigned		4 BIDU May 21 '11 $145 Call(BIDU) BAIDU INC SPON ADR RE...	$3,988.87
	04/19/11	Unassigned		5 EEM Jan 19 '13 $46 Call(EEM) ISHARES MSCI EMERGING MA...	$3,838.11
	04/18/11	Unassigned		4 UGL Oct 22 '11 $70 Call(UGL) PROSHARES ULTRA GOLD SHO...	$4,312.86
	04/15/11	Unassigned		4 UGL Oct 22 '11 $70 Call(UGL) PROSHARES ULTRA GOLD SHO...	$3,988.87
	04/14/11	Unassigned		4 UGL Oct 22 '11 $68 Call(UGL) PROSHARES ULTRA GOLD SHO...	$4,124.87
	04/13/11	Unassigned		10 EEM Jan 19 '13 $46 Call(EEM) ISHARES MSCI EMERGING M...	$7,994.20
	03/31/11	Unassigned		10 UYM Jan 19 '13 $45 Call(UYM) PROSHARES ULTRA BASIC M...	$18,488.00
	03/25/11	Unassigned		1 NOV Jan 19 '13 $70 Call(NOV) NATIONAL OILWELL VARCO I...	$2,078.21
	03/23/11	Unassigned		12 NOV Jan 19 '13 $70 Call(NOV) NATIONAL OILWELL VARCO ...	$24,826.36
	03/23/11	Unassigned		10 UYM Jan 19 '13 $40 Call(UYM) PROSHARES ULTRA BASIC M...	$19,383.98
	03/23/11	Unassigned		1 NOV Jan 19 '13 $65 Call(NOV) NATIONAL OILWELL VARCO I...	$2,355.20
	03/21/11	Unassigned		3 AAPL Jan 19 '13 $300 Call(AAPL) APPLE INC COM SHORT...	$25,979.22
	03/21/11	Unassigned		18 QLD Jan 19 '13 $67 Call(QLD) PROSHARES ULTRA QQQ SHO...	$49,391.30
	03/21/11	Unassigned		17 SSO Jan 19 '13 $42 Call(SSO) PROSHARES ULTRA S&P 500...	$24,122.54
	03/21/11	Unassigned		3 SSO Jan 19 '13 $42 Call(SSO) PROSHARES ULTRA S&P 500 ...	$4,223.63
	03/21/11	Unassigned		16 DIG Jan 19 '13 $42 Call(DIG) PROSHARES ULTRA OIL & G...	$33,503.13
	03/21/11	Unassigned		2 DIG Jan 19 '13 $42 Call(DIG) PROSHARES ULTRA OIL & GA...	$4,214.39
	03/21/11	Unassigned		8 BIDU Jan 19 '13 $105 Call(BIDU) BAIDU INC SPON ADR RE...	$30,349.30
	03/21/11	Unassigned		5 UYM Jan 19 '13 $40 Call(UYM) PROSHARES ULTRA BASIC MA...	$9,298.01
	03/21/11	Unassigned		5 UYM Jan 19 '13 $40 Call(UYM) PROSHARES ULTRA BASIC MA...	$9,353.01
	03/21/11	Unassigned		5 CAT Jan 19 '13 $95 Call(CAT) CATERPILLAR INC DEL COM ...	$11,312.97
	03/18/11	Unassigned		2 QLD Jan 21 '12 $65 Call(QLD) PROSHARES ULTRA QQQ SHOR...	$4,750.38
	03/18/11	Unassigned		3 SSO Jan 21 '12 $41 Call(SSO) PROSHARES ULTRA S&P 500 ...	$3,724.64
	03/18/11	Unassigned		3 UWM Jan 21 '12 $36 Call(UWM) PROSHARES ULTRA RUSSELL ...	$3,610.65
	03/18/11	Unassigned		1 DIG Jan 21 '12 $44 Call(DIG) PROSHARES ULTRA OIL & GA...	$1,641.21
	03/18/11	Unassigned		1 DIG Jan 21 '12 $44 Call(DIG) PROSHARES ULTRA OIL & GA...	$1,632.21
	03/17/11	Unassigned		12 NOV Jan 21 '12 $60 Call(NOV) NATIONAL OILWELL VARCO ...	$26,382.33
	03/17/11	Unassigned		20 QLD Jan 21 '12 $65 Call(QLD) PROSHARES ULTRA QQQ SHO...	$47,975.79
	03/17/11	Unassigned		17 SSO Jan 21 '12 $40 Call(SSO) PROSHARES ULTRA S&P 500...	$21,228.60

| Transactions | Check Summary | Deposit Summary | Categories | Reports |

Type	Date	Category	Subcategory	Description	Amount
Sold Short					
	03/17/11	Unassigned		5 CAT Jan 21 '12 $90 Call(CAT) CATERPILLAR INC DEL COM ...	$9,633.00
	03/17/11	Unassigned		20 UWM Jan 21 '12 $35 Call(UWM) PROSHARES ULTRA RUSSELL...	$24,976.24
	03/17/11	Unassigned		8 BIDU Jan 21 '12 $100 Call(BIDU) BAIDU INC SPON ADR RE...	$26,385.38
	03/17/11	Unassigned		16 DIG Jan 21 '12 $43 Call(DIG) PROSHARES ULTRA OIL & G...	$25,579.28
	03/17/11	Unassigned		3 AAPL Jan 21 '12 $270 Call(AAPL) APPLE INC COM SHORT...	$25,639.22
	03/03/11	Unassigned		3 UYM Mar 19 '11 $54 Call(UYM) PROSHARES ULTRA BASIC MA...	$322.71
	03/03/11	Unassigned		1 UWM Mar 19 '11 $49 Call(UWM) PROSHARES ULTRA RUSSELL ...	$81.24
	03/03/11	Unassigned		1 QLD Mar 19 '11 $94 Call(QLD) PROSHARES ULTRA QQQ SHOR...	$164.24
	03/02/11	Unassigned		1 BIDU Mar 19 '11 $125 Call(BIDU) BAIDU INC SPON ADR RE...	$159.24
	03/02/11	Unassigned		4 SSO Mar 19 '11 $54 Call(SSO) PROSHARES ULTRA S&P 500 ...	$260.94
	03/02/11	Unassigned		3 NOV Mar 19 '11 $80 Call(NOV) NATIONAL OILWELL VARCO I...	$601.70
	03/02/11	Unassigned		1 DIG Mar 19 '11 $60 Call(DIG) PROSHARES ULTRA OIL & GA...	$159.24
	02/17/11	Unassigned		3 UYM Mar 19 '11 $58 Call(UYM) PROSHARES ULTRA BASIC MA...	$482.71
	02/17/11	Unassigned		1 BIDU Mar 19 '11 $130 Call(BIDU) BAIDU INC SPON ADR RE...	$412.24
	02/17/11	Unassigned		9 QLD Mar 19 '11 $97 Call(QLD) PROSHARES ULTRA QQQ SHOR...	$1,960.09
	02/17/11	Unassigned		2 QLD Mar 19 '11 $97 Call(QLD) PROSHARES ULTRA QQQ SHOR...	$424.47
	02/16/11	Unassigned		19 UYM Mar 19 '11 $57 Call(UYM) PROSHARES ULTRA BASIC M...	$3,173.41
	02/16/11	Unassigned		15 QLD Mar 19 '11 $96 Call(QLD) PROSHARES ULTRA QQQ SHO...	$3,719.46
	02/16/11	Unassigned		14 NOV Mar 19 '11 $85 Call(NOV) NATIONAL OILWELL VARCO ...	$2,043.27
	02/16/11	Unassigned		42 FAS Mar 19 '11 $36 Call(FAS) DIREXION DAILY FINANCIA...	$4,163.81
	02/16/11	Unassigned		21 SSO Mar 19 '11 $55 Call(SSO) PROSHARES ULTRA S&P 500...	$2,583.91
	02/16/11	Unassigned		9 DIG Mar 19 '11 $59 Call(DIG) PROSHARES ULTRA OIL & GA...	$1,222.10
	02/14/11	Unassigned		28 UWM Mar 19 '11 $49 Call(UWM) PROSHARES ULTRA RUSSELL...	$3,502.53
	02/14/11	Unassigned		9 BIDU Mar 19 '11 $130 Call(BIDU) BAIDU INC SPON ADR RE...	$4,309.04
	02/14/11	Unassigned		12 DIG Mar 19 '11 $58 Call(DIG) PROSHARES ULTRA OIL & G...	$2,050.80
	02/03/11	Unassigned		2 UWM Feb 19 '11 $45 Call(UWM) PROSHARES ULTRA RUSSELL ...	$188.47
	02/03/11	Unassigned		3 QLD Feb 19 '11 $90 Call(QLD) PROSHARES ULTRA QQQ SHOR...	$520.70
	02/03/11	Unassigned		2 UYM Feb 19 '11 $54 Call(UYM) PROSHARES ULTRA BASIC MA...	$198.47
	02/02/11	Unassigned		13 UWM Feb 19 '11 $45 Call(UWM) PROSHARES ULTRA RUSSELL...	$1,438.04
	02/01/11	Unassigned		13 UWM Feb 19 '11 $45 Call(UWM) PROSHARES ULTRA RUSSELL...	$1,529.04
	01/26/11	Unassigned		2 UWM Feb 19 '11 $45 Call(UWM) PROSHARES ULTRA RUSSELL ...	$202.47
	01/26/11	Unassigned		2 SSO Feb 19 '11 $52 Call(SSO) PROSHARES ULTRA S&P 500 ...	$162.47
	01/26/11	Unassigned		1 BIDU Feb 19 '11 $110 Call(BIDU) BAIDU INC SPON ADR RE...	$408.24
	01/26/11	Unassigned		3 UYM Feb 19 '11 $52 Call(UYM) PROSHARES ULTRA BASIC MA...	$349.71
	01/24/11	Unassigned		20 SSO Feb 19 '11 $51 Call(SSO) PROSHARES ULTRA S&P 500...	$2,244.66
	01/24/11	Unassigned		2 SSO Feb 19 '11 $51 Call(SSO) PROSHARES ULTRA S&P 500 ...	$214.47
	01/24/11	Unassigned		22 DIG Feb 19 '11 $50 Call(DIG) PROSHARES ULTRA OIL & G...	$2,593.13
	01/20/11	Unassigned		9 NOV Feb 19 '11 $70 Call(NOV) NATIONAL OILWELL VARCO I...	$1,645.09
	01/20/11	Unassigned		6 NOV Feb 19 '11 $70 Call(NOV) NATIONAL OILWELL VARCO I...	$1,101.39
	01/20/11	Unassigned		15 XME Feb 19 '11 $68 Call(XME) SPDR S&P METALS & MININ...	$2,830.48
	01/20/11	Unassigned		16 UWM Feb 19 '11 $43 Call(UWM) PROSHARES ULTRA RUSSELL...	$2,879.72
	01/20/11	Unassigned		9 UWM Feb 19 '11 $43 Call(UWM) PROSHARES ULTRA RUSSELL ...	$1,650.09
	01/20/11	Unassigned		9 QLD Feb 19 '11 $88 Call(QLD) PROSHARES ULTRA QQQ SHOR...	$2,212.08
	01/20/11	Unassigned		15 QLD Feb 19 '11 $87 Call(QLD) PROSHARES ULTRA QQQ SHO...	$3,899.46
	01/20/11	Unassigned		50 FAS Feb 19 '11 $30 Call(FAS) DIREXION DAILY FINANCIA...	$7,953.62
	01/20/11	Unassigned		35 EDC Feb 19 '11 $40 Call(EDC) DIREXION DAILY EMERGING...	$7,525.10
	01/20/11	Unassigned		3 EDC Feb 19 '11 $40 Call(EDC) DIREXION DAILY EMERGING ...	$649.70

Transaction History: Reports

Alerts | Transfer Money | Bill Pay | Help

	Transactions	Check Summary	Deposit Summary	Categories	Reports	

Type	Date	Category	Subcategory	Description	Amount
Sold Short					
	01/20/11	Unassigned		8 BIDU Feb 19 '11 $105 Call(BIDU) BAIDU INC SPON ADR RE...	$4,261.80
	01/20/11	Unassigned		1 BIDU Feb 19 '11 $105 Call(BIDU) BAIDU INC SPON ADR RE...	$521.23
	01/20/11	Unassigned		11 UYM Feb 19 '11 $49 Call(UYM) PROSHARES ULTRA BASIC M...	$2,297.55
	01/20/11	Unassigned		8 UYM Feb 19 '11 $49 Call(UYM) PROSHARES ULTRA BASIC MA...	$1,665.85
	01/12/11	Unassigned		6 XME Jan 22 '11 $70 Call(XME) SPDR S&P METALS & MINING...	$1,253.39
	01/12/11	Unassigned		9 UWM Jan 22 '11 $44 Call(UWM) PROSHARES ULTRA RUSSELL2...	$1,335.10
	01/11/11	Unassigned		9 FAS Jan 22 '11 $30 Call(FAS) DIREXION DAILY FINANCIAL...	$768.11
	01/07/11	Unassigned		9 FAS Jan 22 '11 $30 Call(FAS) DIREXION DAILY FINANCIAL...	$804.11
	01/07/11	Unassigned		6 NOV Jan 22 '11 $65 Call(NOV) NATIONAL OILWELL VARCO I...	$1,187.39
	01/05/11	Unassigned		9 FAS Jan 22 '11 $30 Call(FAS) DIREXION DAILY FINANCIAL...	$1,290.10
	01/05/11	Unassigned		8 BIDU Jan 22 '11 $102 Call(BIDU) BAIDU INC SPON ADR RE...	$3,185.83
	01/05/11	Unassigned		2 QLD Jan 22 '11 $83 Call(QLD) PROSHARES ULTRA QQQ SHOR...	$690.46
	01/04/11	Unassigned		9 FAS Jan 22 '11 $30 Call(FAS) DIREXION DAILY FINANCIAL...	$966.11
	01/03/11	Unassigned		13 QLD Jan 22 '11 $83 Call(QLD) PROSHARES ULTRA QQQ SHO...	$4,531.99
	01/03/11	Unassigned		3 AGQ Jan 22 '11 $160 Call(AGQ) PROSHARES ULTRA SILVER ...	$2,932.67
				Total Sold Short	**$764,001.77**

Transaction History: Reports

Alerts | Transfer Money | Bill Pay | Help

	Transactions	Check Summary	Deposit Summary	Categories	Reports	

Type	Date	Category	Subcategory	Description	Amount
Sold Short					
	12/09/11	Unassigned		1 MA Jan 19 '13 $290 Call(MA) MASTERCARD INC CL A SHORT...	$10,941.03
	12/09/11	Unassigned		4 TJX Jan 19 '13 $57.50 Call(TJX) TJX COS INC NEW COM S...	$4,028.90
	12/09/11	Unassigned		1 NOV Jan 19 '13 $50 Call(NOV) NATIONAL OILWELL VARCO I...	$2,661.19
	12/09/11	Unassigned		1 HUM Jan 19 '13 $60 Call(HUM) HUMANA INC COM SHORT...	$2,911.19
	11/22/11	Unassigned		1 AAPL Jan 19 '13 $270 Call(AAPL) APPLE INC COM SHORT...	$12,959.00
	11/21/11	Unassigned		3 NOV Jan 19 '13 $50 Call(NOV) NATIONAL OILWELL VARCO I...	$6,949.59
	11/21/11	Unassigned		2 HUM Jan 19 '13 $60 Call(HUM) HUMANA INC COM SHORT...	$5,490.38
	09/23/11	Unassigned		1 AAPL Sep 30 '11 $405 Call w(AAPL) APPLE INC COM SHORT...	$815.23
	09/16/11	Unassigned		7 EEM Sep 23 '11 $40 Call w(EEM) ISHARES MSCI EMERGING ...	$676.68
	09/16/11	Unassigned		2 BIDU Sep 23 '11 $150 Call w(BIDU) BAIDU INC SPON ADR ...	$428.48
	09/16/11	Unassigned		1 AAPL Sep 23 '11 $400 Call w(AAPL) APPLE INC COM SHORT...	$528.23
	09/16/11	Unassigned		4 XLE Sep 23 '11 $67 Call w(XLE) ENERGY SELECT SECTOR S...	$448.97
	09/16/11	Unassigned		5 QQQ Sep 23 '11 $57 Call w(QQQ) POWERSHARES QQQ TRUST,...	$258.21
	09/16/11	Unassigned		7 GLD Sep 23 '11 $176 Call w(GLD) SPDR GOLD SHARES SHOR...	$1,806.66
	09/09/11	Unassigned		2 BIDU Sep 17 '11 $145 Call(BIDU) BAIDU INC SPON ADR RE...	$700.47
	09/09/11	Unassigned		4 XLE Sep 17 '11 $65 Call(XLE) ENERGY SELECT SECTOR SPD...	$548.95
	09/09/11	Unassigned		5 QQQ Sep 17 '11 $53 Call(QQQ) POWERSHARES QQQ TRUST, S...	$548.18
	09/09/11	Unassigned		1 AAPL Sep 17 '11 $380 Call(AAPL) APPLE INC COM SHORT...	$561.23
	09/09/11	Unassigned		7 EEM Sep 17 '11 $40 Call(EEM) ISHARES MSCI EMERGING MA...	$756.66
	08/07/11	Unassigned		5 UGL Sep 17 '11 $100 Call(UGL) PROSHARES ULTRA GOLD SH...	$3,188.15
	05/20/11	Unassigned		2 BIDU Jun 18 '11 $135 Call(BIDU) BAIDU INC SPON ADR RE...	$1,110.46

Transaction History: Reports

Alerts | >> Transfer Money | >≡ Bill Pay | ? Help

| Transactions | Check Summary | Deposit Summary | Categories | Reports |

Type	Date	Category	Subcategory	Description	Amount
Sold Short					
	05/20/11	Unassigned		5 UWM Jun 18 '11 $48 Call(UWM) PROSHARES ULTRA RUSSELL ...	$888.20
	05/20/11	Unassigned		3 UGL Jun 18 '11 $79 Call(UGL) PROSHARES ULTRA GOLD SHO...	$694.71
	05/20/11	Unassigned		4 QLD Jun 18 '11 $92 Call(QLD) PROSHARES ULTRA QQQ SHOR...	$968.94
	05/20/11	Unassigned		4 SSO Jun 18 '11 $55 Call(SSO) PROSHARES ULTRA S&P 500 ...	$452.95
	05/20/11	Unassigned		4 DIG Jun 18 '11 $55 Call(DIG) PROSHARES ULTRA OIL & GA...	$928.96
	05/06/11	Unassigned		1 AAPL Jan 19 '13 $320 Call(AAPL) APPLE INC COM SHORT...	$7,661.10
	04/27/11	Unassigned		5 SSO May 21 '11 $54 Call(SSO) PROSHARES ULTRA S&P 500 ...	$1,238.16
	04/27/11	Unassigned		4 QLD May 21 '11 $92 Call(QLD) PROSHARES ULTRA QQQ SHOR...	$1,988.91
	04/26/11	Unassigned		2 BIDU May 21 '11 $150 Call(BIDU) BAIDU INC SPON ADR RE...	$1,990.44
	04/25/11	Unassigned		1 EDC Jan 19 '13 $39.35 Call(EDC) DIREXION DAILY EMERGI...	$1,562.21
	04/21/11	Unassigned		4 EDC Jan 19 '13 $39.35 Call(EDC) DIREXION DAILY EMERGI...	$6,512.82
	04/20/11	Unassigned		1 UGL Oct 22 '11 $72 Call(UGL) PROSHARES ULTRA GOLD SHO...	$991.23
	04/20/11	Unassigned		2 EEM Jan 19 '13 $48 Call(EEM) ISHARES MSCI EMERGING MA...	$1,434.45
	04/19/11	Unassigned		3 BIDU May 21 '11 $145 Call(BIDU) BAIDU INC SPON ADR RE...	$2,989.66
	04/19/11	Unassigned		3 EEM Jan 19 '13 $46 Call(EEM) ISHARES MSCI EMERGING MA...	$2,299.67
	04/18/11	Unassigned		2 UGL Oct 22 '11 $70 Call(UGL) PROSHARES ULTRA GOLD SHO...	$2,168.43
	04/15/11	Unassigned		2 UGL Oct 22 '11 $70 Call(UGL) PROSHARES ULTRA GOLD SHO...	$1,950.44
	04/14/11	Unassigned		2 UGL Oct 22 '11 $68 Call(UGL) PROSHARES ULTRA GOLD SHO...	$2,058.44
	04/13/11	Unassigned		5 EEM Jan 19 '13 $46 Call(EEM) ISHARES MSCI EMERGING MA...	$3,983.11
	03/23/11	Unassigned		3 UYM Jan 19 '13 $45 Call(UYM) PROSHARES ULTRA BASIC MA...	$5,149.62
	03/23/11	Unassigned		7 NOV Jan 19 '13 $65 Call(NOV) NATIONAL OILWELL VARCO I...	$16,216.34
	03/21/11	Unassigned		2 AAPL Jan 19 '13 $280 Call(AAPL) APPLE INC COM SHORT...	$19,284.10
	03/21/11	Unassigned		5 QLD Jan 19 '13 $67 Call(QLD) PROSHARES ULTRA QQQ SHOR...	$13,720.91
	03/21/11	Unassigned		4 QLD Jan 19 '13 $67 Call(QLD) PROSHARES ULTRA QQQ SHOR...	$11,032.73
	03/21/11	Unassigned		10 SSO Jan 19 '13 $42 Call(SSO) PROSHARES ULTRA S&P 500...	$14,088.08
	03/21/11	Unassigned		6 DIG Jan 19 '13 $42 Call(DIG) PROSHARES ULTRA OIL & GA...	$12,561.17
	03/21/11	Unassigned		3 DIG Jan 19 '13 $42 Call(DIG) PROSHARES ULTRA OIL & GA...	$6,338.59
	03/21/11	Unassigned		5 BIDU Jan 19 '13 $105 Call(BIDU) BAIDU INC SPON ADR RE...	$19,076.82
	03/21/11	Unassigned		4 UYM Jan 19 '13 $40 Call(UYM) PROSHARES ULTRA BASIC MA...	$7,432.80
	03/21/11	Unassigned		3 UYM Jan 19 '13 $40 Call(UYM) PROSHARES ULTRA BASIC MA...	$5,602.61
	03/18/11	Unassigned		7 NOV Jan 21 '12 $60 Call(NOV) NATIONAL OILWELL VARCO I...	$16,051.35
	03/18/11	Unassigned		11 QLD Jan 21 '12 $65 Call(QLD) PROSHARES ULTRA QQQ SHO...	$26,548.08
	03/18/11	Unassigned		10 SSO Jan 21 '12 $41 Call(SSO) PROSHARES ULTRA S&P 500...	$12,384.12
	03/18/11	Unassigned		11 UWM Jan 21 '12 $35 Call(UWM) PROSHARES ULTRA RUSSELL...	$13,513.34
	03/18/11	Unassigned		5 BIDU Jan 21 '12 $100 Call(BIDU) BAIDU INC SPON ADR RE...	$16,487.87
	03/18/11	Unassigned		1 DIG Jan 21 '12 $45 Call(DIG) PROSHARES ULTRA OIL & GA...	$1,561.21
	03/18/11	Unassigned		1 DIG Jan 21 '12 $45 Call(DIG) PROSHARES ULTRA OIL & GA...	$1,571.21
	03/18/11	Unassigned		1 DIG Jan 21 '12 $45 Call(DIG) PROSHARES ULTRA OIL & GA...	$1,591.21
	03/18/11	Unassigned		6 DIG Jan 21 '12 $43 Call(DIG) PROSHARES ULTRA OIL & GA...	$9,887.22
	03/18/11	Unassigned		2 AAPL Jan 21 '12 $320 Call(AAPL) APPLE INC COM SHORT...	$10,700.27
	03/03/11	Unassigned		1 UYM Mar 19 '11 $54 Call(UYM) PROSHARES ULTRA BASIC MA...	$102.24
	03/03/11	Unassigned		2 UWM Mar 19 '11 $49 Call(UWM) PROSHARES ULTRA RUSSELL ...	$170.47
	03/03/11	Unassigned		1 DIG Mar 19 '11 $62 Call(DIG) PROSHARES ULTRA OIL & GA...	$113.24
	02/17/11	Unassigned		3 DIG Mar 19 '11 $60 Call(DIG) PROSHARES ULTRA OIL & GA...	$418.71
	02/16/11	Unassigned		13 UYM Mar 19 '11 $57 Call(UYM) PROSHARES ULTRA BASIC M...	$2,170.02
	02/16/11	Unassigned		13 UWM Mar 19 '11 $49 Call(UWM) PROSHARES ULTRA RUSSELL...	$1,767.03
	02/16/11	Unassigned		6 BIDU Mar 19 '11 $130 Call(BIDU) BAIDU INC SPON ADR RE...	$2,673.36

| Transactions | Check Summary | Deposit Summary | Categories | Reports |

Type	Date	Category	Subcategory	Description	Amount
Sold Short					
	02/16/11	Unassigned		15 QLD Mar 19 '11 $96 Call(QLD) PROSHARES ULTRA QQQ SHO...	$3,734.46
	02/16/11	Unassigned		9 NOV Mar 19 '11 $85 Call(NOV) NATIONAL OILWELL VARCO I...	$1,294.10
	02/16/11	Unassigned		27 FAS Mar 19 '11 $36 Call(FAS) DIREXION DAILY FINANCIA...	$2,756.31
	02/14/11	Unassigned		9 DIG Mar 19 '11 $58 Call(DIG) PROSHARES ULTRA OIL & GA...	$1,591.09
	01/26/11	Unassigned		5 UYM Feb 19 '11 $49 Call(UYM) PROSHARES ULTRA BASIC MA...	$1,238.16
	01/24/11	Unassigned		13 SSO Feb 19 '11 $51 Call(SSO) PROSHARES ULTRA S&P 500...	$1,490.04
	01/24/11	Unassigned		13 DIG Feb 19 '11 $50 Call(DIG) PROSHARES ULTRA OIL & G...	$1,529.04
	01/20/11	Unassigned		6 NOV Feb 19 '11 $70 Call(NOV) NATIONAL OILWELL VARCO I...	$1,107.39
	01/20/11	Unassigned		3 NOV Feb 19 '11 $70 Call(NOV) NATIONAL OILWELL VARCO I...	$551.70
	01/20/11	Unassigned		13 UWM Feb 19 '11 $44 Call(UWM) PROSHARES ULTRA RUSSELL...	$1,663.03
	01/20/11	Unassigned		15 QLD Feb 19 '11 $89 Call(QLD) PROSHARES ULTRA QQQ SHO...	$3,059.48
	01/20/11	Unassigned		30 FAS Feb 19 '11 $30 Call(FAS) DIREXION DAILY FINANCIA...	$4,768.97
	01/20/11	Unassigned		24 EDC Feb 19 '11 $40 Call(EDC) DIREXION DAILY EMERGING...	$5,157.56
	01/20/11	Unassigned		6 BIDU Feb 19 '11 $105 Call(BIDU) BAIDU INC SPON ADR RE...	$3,339.35
	01/20/11	Unassigned		7 UYM Feb 19 '11 $49 Call(UYM) PROSHARES ULTRA BASIC MA...	$1,418.63
	01/20/11	Unassigned		1 UYM Feb 19 '11 $49 Call(UYM) PROSHARES ULTRA BASIC MA...	$206.24
	01/12/11	Unassigned		4 XME Jan 22 '11 $70 Call(XME) SPDR S&P METALS & MINING...	$832.93
	01/12/11	Unassigned		2 UWM Jan 22 '11 $44 Call(UWM) PROSHARES ULTRA RUSSELL2...	$290.47
	01/07/11	Unassigned		4 FAS Jan 22 '11 $30 Call(FAS) DIREXION DAILY FINANCIAL...	$352.94
	01/07/11	Unassigned		3 NOV Jan 22 '11 $65 Call(NOV) NATIONAL OILWELL VARCO I...	$589.70
	01/06/11	Unassigned		16 QLD Jan 22 '11 $85 Call(QLD) PROSHARES ULTRA QQQ SHO...	$3,979.71
	01/05/11	Unassigned		9 FAS Jan 22 '11 $30 Call(FAS) DIREXION DAILY FINANCIAL...	$1,281.10
	01/05/11	Unassigned		6 BIDU Jan 22 '11 $102 Call(BIDU) BAIDU INC SPON ADR RE...	$2,387.37
	01/04/11	Unassigned		9 FAS Jan 22 '11 $30 Call(FAS) DIREXION DAILY FINANCIAL...	$957.11
	01/03/11	Unassigned		2 EET Jan 22 '11 $110 Call(EET) PROSHARES ULTRA MSCI EM...	$990.46
	01/03/11	Unassigned		1 AGQ Jan 22 '11 $160 Call(AGQ) PROSHARES ULTRA SILVER ...	$999.23
				Total Sold Short	**$396,861.96**

Type	Date	Category	Subcategory	Description	Amount
Sold Short					
	12/30/10	Unassigned		13 UYM Jan 22 '11 $50 Call(UYM) PROSHARES ULTRA BASIC M...	$3,232.02
	12/29/10	Unassigned		6 EET Jan 22 '11 $105 Call(EET) PROSHARES ULTRA MSCI EM...	$3,107.37
	12/29/10	Unassigned		6 EET Jan 22 '11 $105 Call(EET) PROSHARES ULTRA MSCI EM...	$2,987.37
	12/20/10	Unassigned		8 XME Jan 22 '11 $67 Call(XME) SPDR S&P METALS & MINING...	$1,985.86
	12/20/10	Unassigned		9 NOV Jan 22 '11 $64 Call(NOV) NATIONAL OILWELL VARCO I...	$2,235.10
	12/20/10	Unassigned		11 UYM Jan 22 '11 $48 Call(UYM) PROSHARES ULTRA BASIC M...	$2,623.56
	12/20/10	Unassigned		9 UGL Jan 22 '11 $66 Call(UGL) PROSHARES ULTRA GOLD SHO...	$2,775.09
	12/17/10	Unassigned		3 FFIV Jan 22 '11 $140 Call(FFIV) F5 NETWORKS INC COM S...	$2,062.68
	12/17/10	Unassigned		3 CRM Jan 22 '11 $140 Call(CRM) SALESFORCE COM INC COM ...	$1,609.69
	12/17/10	Unassigned		16 UWM Jan 22 '11 $42 Call(UWM) PROSHARES ULTRA RUSSELL...	$3,099.73
	12/17/10	Unassigned		15 SLW Jan 22 '11 $37 Call(SLW) SILVER WHEATON CORP COM...	$3,730.49
	12/17/10	Unassigned		9 QLD Jan 22 '11 $82 Call(QLD) PROSHARES ULTRA QQQ SHOR...	$2,730.09
	09/21/10	Unassigned		49 SSO Oct 16 '10 $40 Call(SSO) PROSHARES ULTRA S&P 500...	$5,834.50
	09/16/10	Unassigned		4 AAPL Oct 16 '10 $270 Call(AAPL) APPLE INC COM SHORT...	$3,988.89
	09/15/10	Unassigned		3 AAPL Oct 16 '10 $270 Call(AAPL) APPLE INC COM SHORT...	$2,389.67
	09/14/10	Unassigned		25 UGL Oct 16 '10 $55 Call(UGL) PROSHARES ULTRA GOLD SH...	$6,222.81
	09/14/10	Unassigned		19 QLD Oct 16 '10 $64 Call(QLD) PROSHARES ULTRA QQQ SHO...	$3,458.44
	09/14/10	Unassigned		11 QLD Oct 16 '10 $64 Call(QLD) PROSHARES ULTRA QQQ SHO...	$1,949.56
	09/14/10	Unassigned		25 BIDU Oct 16 '10 $90 Call(BIDU) BAIDU INC SPON ADR RE...	$5,301.83
	08/20/10	Unassigned		1 SSO Sep 18 '10 $36 Call(SSO) PROSHARES ULTRA S&P 500 ...	$97.22
	08/20/10	Unassigned		10 BIDU Sep 18 '10 $84 Call(BIDU) BAIDU INC SPON ADR RE...	$2,618.32
	08/20/10	Unassigned		10 BIDU Sep 18 '10 $84 Call(BIDU) BAIDU INC SPON ADR RE...	$2,618.32
	08/20/10	Unassigned		1 BIDU Sep 18 '10 $84 Call(BIDU) BAIDU INC SPON ADR REP...	$251.22
	08/20/10	Unassigned		4 BIDU Sep 18 '10 $84 Call(BIDU) BAIDU INC SPON ADR REP...	$1,188.93
	08/20/10	Unassigned		1 CAT Sep 18 '10 $70 Call(CAT) CATERPILLAR INC DEL COM ...	$161.22
	08/19/10	Unassigned		48 SSO Sep 18 '10 $36 Call(SSO) PROSHARES ULTRA S&P 500...	$5,955.25
	08/17/10	Unassigned		1 SNDK Sep 18 '10 $45 Call(SNDK) SANDISK CORP COM SHORT...	$187.22
	08/17/10	Unassigned		30 QLD Sep 18 '10 $57 Call(QLD) PROSHARES ULTRA QQQ SHO...	$8,968.94
	08/17/10	Unassigned		1 EEM Sep 18 '10 $43 Call(EEM) ISHARES MSCI EMERGING MA...	$57.22
	08/16/10	Unassigned		1 MWE Sep 18 '10 $35 Call(MWE) MARKWEST ENERGY PARTNERS...	$91.22
	08/13/10	Unassigned		1 VMW Sep 18 '10 $80 Call(VMW) VMWARE INC CL A COM SHOR...	$226.22
	08/01/10	Unassigned		4 BIDU Aug 21 '10 $85 Call(BIDU) BAIDU INC SPON ADR REP...	$1,188.93
	07/26/10	Unassigned		7 SSO Aug 21 '10 $39 Call(SSO) PROSHARES ULTRA S&P 500 ...	$560.65
	07/26/10	Unassigned		1 SSO Aug 21 '10 $39 Call(SSO) PROSHARES ULTRA S&P 500 ...	$74.21
	07/26/10	Unassigned		6 QLD Aug 21 '10 $61 Call(QLD) PROSHARES ULTRA QQQ SHOR...	$983.41
	07/23/10	Unassigned		5 BIDU Aug 21 '10 $80 Call(BIDU) BAIDU INC SPON ADR REP...	$1,278.16
	07/22/10	Unassigned		1 VMW Aug 21 '10 $80 Call(VMW) VMWARE INC CL A COM SHOR...	$142.21
	07/22/10	Unassigned		9 SSO Aug 21 '10 $38 Call(SSO) PROSHARES ULTRA S&P 500 ...	$731.10
	07/22/10	Unassigned		1 SSO Aug 21 '10 $38 Call(SSO) PROSHARES ULTRA S&P 500 ...	$74.21
	07/22/10	Unassigned		6 QLD Aug 21 '10 $60 Call(QLD) PROSHARES ULTRA QQQ SHOR...	$1,037.41
	07/22/10	Unassigned		5 BIDU Aug 21 '10 $80 Call(BIDU) BAIDU INC SPON ADR REP...	$993.17
	07/15/10	Unassigned		1 CAT Aug 21 '10 $67.50 Call(CAT) CATERPILLAR INC DEL C...	$228.21
	07/14/10	Unassigned		10 SSO Aug 21 '10 $38 Call(SSO) PROSHARES ULTRA S&P 500...	$1,264.34
	07/14/10	Unassigned		6 QLD Aug 21 '10 $60 Call(QLD) PROSHARES ULTRA QQQ SHOR...	$1,367.40
	07/14/10	Unassigned		18 EEM Aug 21 '10 $41 Call(EEM) ISHARES MSCI EMERGING M...	$1,886.22
	07/13/10	Unassigned		12 QLD Aug 21 '10 $58 Call(QLD) PROSHARES ULTRA QQQ SHO...	$2,838.79
	07/13/10	Unassigned		3 AAPL Aug 21 '10 $260 Call(AAPL) APPLE INC COM SHORT...	$2,890.67

Transaction History: Reports

	Transactions	Check Summary	Deposit Summary	Categories	**Reports**	

Type	Date	Category	Subcategory	Description	Amount
Sold Short					
	07/09/10	Unassigned		10 BIDU Aug 21 '10 $72.50 Call(BIDU) BAIDU INC SPON ADR...	$4,644.29
	07/09/10	Unassigned		17 SSO Aug 21 '10 $36 Call(SSO) PROSHARES ULTRA S&P 500...	$2,825.96
	07/09/10	Unassigned		2 SSO Aug 21 '10 $36 Call(SSO) PROSHARES ULTRA S&P 500 ...	$318.46
	07/09/10	Unassigned		1 SSO Aug 21 '10 $36 Call(SSO) PROSHARES ULTRA S&P 500 ...	$157.21
	07/07/10	Unassigned		1 SNDK Aug 21 '10 $43 Call(SNDK) SANDISK CORP COM SHORT...	$354.21
	07/07/10	Unassigned		1 BIDU Aug 21 '10 $70 Call(BIDU) BAIDU INC SPON ADR REP...	$622.20
	07/02/10	Unassigned		1 SSO Aug 21 '10 $32 Call(SSO) PROSHARES ULTRA S&P 500 ...	$243.21
	07/02/10	Unassigned		1 SDS Aug 21 '10 $38 Call(SDS) PROSHARES ULTRASHORT S&P...	$315.21
	06/24/10	Unassigned		1 CPNO Jul 17 '10 $25 Call(CPNO) COPANO ENERGY L L C CO...	$91.21
	06/22/10	Unassigned		3 SM Nov 20 '10 $40 Call(SM) SM ENERGY CO COM SHORT...	$2,333.68
	06/18/10	Unassigned		2 GLD Dec 18 '10 $115 Call(GLD) SPDR GOLD SHARES SHORT...	$2,534.42
	06/18/10	Unassigned		2 AAPL Jan 22 '11 $230 Call(AAPL) APPLE INC COM SHORT...	$11,610.27
	06/15/10	Unassigned		2 SNDK Oct 16 '10 $43 Call(SNDK) SANDISK CORP COM SHORT...	$1,856.42
	06/15/10	Unassigned		1 SNDK Oct 16 '10 $43 Call(SNDK) SANDISK CORP COM SHORT...	$926.20
	06/15/10	Unassigned		1 TIE Sep 18 '10 $20 Call(TIE) TITANIUM METALS CORP COM...	$249.21
	06/15/10	Unassigned		3 ESRX Jan 22 '11 $50 Call(ESRX) EXPRESS SCRIPTS INC CO...	$2,273.68
	06/14/10	Unassigned		3 XRT Dec 18 '10 $40 Call(XRT) SPDR S&P RETAIL ETF SHOR...	$1,172.70
	06/03/10	Unassigned		2 BIDU Jan 22 '11 $60 Call(BIDU) BAIDU INC SPON ADR REP...	$4,594.39
	05/28/10	Unassigned		2 AAPL Oct 16 '10 $230 Call(AAPL) APPLE INC COM SHORT...	$8,424.32
	04/29/10	Unassigned		3 XRT Dec 18 '10 $43 Call(XRT) SPDR SERIES TRUST S&P RE...	$1,232.69
	04/29/10	Unassigned		2 UTX Nov 20 '10 $75 Call(UTX) UNITED TECHNOLOGIES CORP...	$1,056.45
	04/23/10	Unassigned		2 IOW Nov 20 '10 $72 Call(IWM) ISHARES TR INDEX RUSSELL...	$1,250.44
	04/23/10	Unassigned		2 AAPL Jan 22 '11 $300 Call(AAPL) APPLE INC COM SHORT...	$3,890.40
	04/14/10	Unassigned		3 CLF Jan 22 '11 $80 Call(CLF) CLIFFS NATURAL RESOURCES...	$3,208.66
	04/14/10	Unassigned		2 AAPL Oct 16 '10 $220 Call(AAPL) APPLE INC COM SHORT...	$7,386.34
	04/13/10	Unassigned		3 CLF Oct 16 '10 $65 Call(CLF) CLIFFS NATURAL RESOURCES...	$4,502.64
	04/13/10	Unassigned		2 GCZ Dec 18 '10 $108 Call(GLD) SPDR GOLD TRUST GOLD SH...	$2,050.43
	04/09/10	Unassigned		2 GPY Oct 16 '10 $165 Call(GS) GOLDMAN SACHS GROUP INC ...	$4,514.39
	04/09/10	Unassigned		2 VAA Jan 22 '11 $270 Call(AAPL) APPLE INC COM SHORT...	$3,500.41
	04/09/10	Unassigned		4 XQX Jan 22 '11 $80 Call(BUCY) BUCYRUS INTL INC NEW CO...	$3,080.89
	04/06/10	Unassigned		8 OYK Jan 22 '11 $65 Call(PRU) PRUDENTIAL FINL INC COM ...	$4,785.81
	04/05/10	Unassigned		4 ZJM Jan 22 '11 $50 Call(TCK) TECK RESOURCES LTD CL B ...	$1,892.91
	04/05/10	Unassigned		2 SOA Sep 18 '10 $20 Call(SOA) SOLUTIA INC COM NEW SHOR...	$180.46
	04/05/10	Unassigned		3 EEM Sep 18 '10 $44 Call(EEM) ISHARES TR INDEX MSCI EM...	$782.70
	04/05/10	Uatssigned		2 TSX Aug 21 '10 $45 Call(TCK) TECK RESOURCES LTD CL B ...	$1,000.45
	04/05/10	Unassigned		1 VAA Jan 22 '11 $270 Call(AAPL) APPLE INC COM SHORT...	$1,579.19
	04/05/10	Unassigned		1 VAA Jan 22 '11 $270 Call(AAPL) APPLE INC COM SHORT...	$1,586.18
	04/05/10	Unassigned		4 XQX Jan 22 '11 $80 Call(BUCY) BUCYRUS INTL INC NEW CO...	$2,880.90
	04/05/10	Unassigned		4 XQX Jan 22 '11 $80 Call(BUCY) BUCYRUS INTL INC NEW CO...	$2,988.89
	03/30/10	Unassigned		2 WLT Sep 18 '10 $80 Call(WLT) WALTER ENERGY INC COM SH...	$3,466.42
	03/29/10	Unassigned		2 VAA Jan 22 '11 $270 Call(AAPL) APPLE INC COM SHORT...	$2,770.43
	03/23/10	Unassigned		20 F Jan 22 '11 $15 Call(F) FORD MOTOR CO SHORT...	$3,696.68
	03/23/10	Unassigned		2 ISJ Sep 18 '10 $78 Call(IYT) ISHARES TRUST-DOW JONES ...	$1,012.45
	03/23/10	Unassigned		2 F Sep 18 '10 $15 Call(F) FORD MOTOR CO SHORT...	$240.46
	03/23/10	Unassigned		2 AJL Jul 17 '10 $210 Call(AAPL) APPLE INC SHORT...	$5,158.40

	Transactions	Check Summary	Deposit Summary	Categories	Reports	

Type	Date	Category	Subcategory	Description	Amount
Sold Short					
	03/23/10	Unassigned		8 OZL Jan 22 '11 $22.50 Call(MRVL) MARVELL TECHNOLOGY G...	$1,961.86
	03/23/10	Unassigned		1 OZL Jan 22 '11 $22.50 Call(MRVL) MARVELL TECHNOLOGY G...	$244.20
	03/23/10	Unassigned		1 OZL Jan 22 '11 $22.50 Call(MRVL) MARVELL TECHNOLOGY G...	$241.21
	03/23/10	Unassigned		2 VAA Jan 22 '11 $260 Call(AAPL) APPLE INC SHORT...	$2,652.43
	03/05/10	Unassigned		2 ZYL Jan 22 '11 $65 Call(EWZ) ISHARES INC MSCI BRAZIL ...	$2,434.43
	03/05/10	Unassigned		3 XQX Jan 22 '11 $55 Call(BUCY) BUCYRUS INTL INC NEW CO...	$5,321.65
	03/04/10	Unassigned		1 UVM May 22 '10 $20 Call(MRVL) MARVELL TECHNOLOGY GROU...	$137.21
	03/01/10	Unassigned		1 FWK Sep 18 '10 $150 Put(FXB) CURRENCYSHS BRIT POUND S...	$671.21
	03/01/10	Unassigned		3 OFA Jan 22 '11 $63 Call(IWM) ISHARES TR INDEX RUSSELL...	$1,781.69
	02/25/10	Unassigned		1 QGJ Apr 17 '10 $25 Call(LINE) LINN ENERGY LLC UNIT LT...	$151.21
	02/22/10	Unassigned		2 VSK Jan 22 '11 $80 Call(V) VISA INC COM CL A SHORT...	$2,520.43
	02/18/10	Unassigned		4 OQI Jan 22 '11 $70 Call(CREE) CREE INC COM SHORT...	$3,348.90
	02/18/10	Unassigned		6 ZJM Jan 22 '11 $40 Call(TCK) TECK RESOURCES LTD CL B ...	$3,389.38
	02/18/10	Unassigned		4 OQI Jan 22 '11 $55 Call(CREE) CREE INC COM SHORT...	$6,392.86
	02/18/10	Unassigned		4 VGB Jan 22 '11 $36 Call(XRT) SPDR SERIES TRUST S&P RE...	$1,444.93
	02/17/10	Unassigned		2 ZJM Jan 22 '11 $35 Call(TCK) TECK RESOURCES LTD CL B ...	$1,554.45
	02/17/10	Unassigned		6 ZJM Jan 22 '11 $40 Call(TCK) TECK RESOURCES LTD CL B ...	$3,311.38
	02/16/10	Unassigned		2 VAA Jan 22 '11 $170 Call(AAPL) APPLE INC COM SHORT...	$9,592.34
	02/16/10	Unassigned		4 OQI Jan 22 '11 $65 Call(CREE) CREE INC COM SHORT...	$3,788.90
				Total Sold Short	**$267,469.13**

Transaction History: Reports

🔔 Alerts | ⟩⟩ Transfer Money | ⟩▤ Bill Pay | ⑦ Help

	Transactions	Check Summary	Deposit Summary	Categories	Reports	

Type	Date	Category	Subcategory	Description	Amount
Sold Short					
	12/30/10	Unassigned		10 UYM Jan 22 '11 $50 Call(UYM) PROSHARES ULTRA BASIC M...	$2,484.32
	12/29/10	Unassigned		4 EET Jan 22 '11 $105 Call(EET) PROSHARES ULTRA MSCI EM...	$1,988.92
	12/28/10	Unassigned		8 SLW Jan 22 '11 $38 Call(SLW) SILVER WHEATON CORP COM ...	$1,585.87
	12/28/10	Unassigned		2 AGQ Jan 22 '11 $160 Call(AGQ) PROSHARES ULTRA SILVER ...	$1,486.45
	12/28/10	Unassigned		1 AGQ Jan 22 '11 $160 Call(AGQ) PROSHARES ULTRA SILVER ...	$720.21
	12/21/10	Unassigned		5 XME Jan 22 '11 $67 Call(XME) SPDR S&P METALS & MINING...	$1,338.16
	12/21/10	Unassigned		6 NOV Jan 22 '11 $64 Call(NOV) NATIONAL OILWELL VARCO I...	$1,787.39
	12/21/10	Unassigned		13 UWM Jan 22 '11 $42 Call(UWM) PROSHARES ULTRA RUSSELL...	$3,232.02
	12/21/10	Unassigned		2 UYM Jan 22 '11 $48 Call(UYM) PROSHARES ULTRA BASIC MA...	$490.47
	12/20/10	Unassigned		6 UYM Jan 22 '11 $48 Call(UYM) PROSHARES ULTRA BASIC MA...	$1,487.40
	12/20/10	Unassigned		8 UGL Jan 22 '11 $66 Call(UGL) PROSHARES ULTRA GOLD SHO...	$2,705.85
	12/17/10	Unassigned		3 FFIV Jan 22 '11 $140 Call(FFIV) F5 NETWORKS INC COM S...	$2,017.68
	12/17/10	Unassigned		3 CRM Jan 22 '11 $140 Call(CRM) SALESFORCE COM INC COM ...	$1,693.69
	09/14/10	Unassigned		15 UGL Oct 16 '10 $55 Call(UGL) PROSHARES ULTRA GOLD SH...	$3,730.49
	09/14/10	Unassigned		18 QLD Oct 16 '10 $64 Call(QLD) PROSHARES ULTRA QQQ SHO...	$3,168.21
	09/14/10	Unassigned		15 BIDU Oct 16 '10 $90 Call(BIDU) BAIDU INC SPON ADR RE...	$3,464.50
	09/13/10	Unassigned		18 EEM Oct 16 '10 $43 Call(EEM) ISHARES MSCI EMERGING M...	$2,318.23
	09/09/10	Unassigned		4 AAPL Sep 18 '10 $260 Call(AAPL) APPLE INC COM SHORT...	$3,188.90
	08/20/10	Unassigned		10 BIDU Sep 18 '10 $84 Call(BIDU) BAIDU INC SPON ADR RE...	$2,618.32
	08/20/10	Unassigned		5 BIDU Sep 18 '10 $84 Call(BIDU) BAIDU INC SPON ADR REP...	$1,307.16
	08/19/10	Unassigned		30 SSO Sep 18 '10 $36 Call(SSO) PROSHARES ULTRA S&P 500...	$3,689.03

	Transactions	Check Summary	Deposit Summary	Categories	**Reports**	

Type	Date	Category	Subcategory	Description	Amount
Sold Short					
	08/17/10	Unassigned		18 QLD Sep 18 '10 $57 Call(QLD) PROSHARES ULTRA QQQ SHO...	$5,378.17
	07/22/10	Unassigned		5 BIDU Aug 21 '10 $80 Call(BIDU) BAIDU INC SPON ADR REP...	$898.17
	07/14/10	Unassigned		6 SSO Aug 21 '10 $38 Call(SSO) PROSHARES ULTRA S&P 500 ...	$757.40
	07/14/10	Unassigned		2 SSO Aug 21 '10 $38 Call(SSO) PROSHARES ULTRA S&P 500 ...	$256.45
	07/14/10	Unassigned		1 SSO Aug 21 '10 $38 Call(SSO) PROSHARES ULTRA S&P 500 ...	$119.21
	07/14/10	Unassigned		1 SSO Aug 21 '10 $38 Call(SSO) PROSHARES ULTRA S&P 500 ...	$121.21
	07/14/10	Unassigned		6 QLD Aug 21 '10 $60 Call(QLD) PROSHARES ULTRA QQQ SHOR...	$1,367.40
	07/14/10	Unassigned		10 EEM Aug 21 '10 $41 Call(EEM) ISHARES MSCI EMERGING M...	$1,064.35
	07/14/10	Unassigned		8 EEM Aug 21 '10 $41 Call(EEM) ISHARES MSCI EMERGING MA...	$849.87
	07/13/10	Unassigned		12 QLD Aug 21 '10 $58 Call(QLD) PROSHARES ULTRA QQQ SHO...	$2,826.79
	07/13/10	Unassigned		3 AAPL Aug 21 '10 $260 Call(AAPL) APPLE INC COM SHORT...	$2,872.67
	07/09/10	Unassigned		10 BIDU Aug 21 '10 $72.50 Call(BIDU) BAIDU INC SPON ADR...	$4,644.29
	07/09/10	Unassigned		18 SSO Aug 21 '10 $36 Call(SSO) PROSHARES ULTRA S&P 500...	$2,992.19
	07/09/10	Unassigned		1 SSO Aug 21 '10 $36 Call(SSO) PROSHARES ULTRA S&P 500 ...	$157.21
	07/09/10	Unassigned		1 SSO Aug 21 '10 $36 Call(SSO) PROSHARES ULTRA S&P 500 ...	$155.21
	04/23/10	Unassigned		2 AAPL Jan 22 '11 $300 Call(AAPL) APPLE INC COM SHORT...	$3,888.40
	04/14/10	Unassigned		3 CLF Jan 22 '11 $80 Call(CLF) CLIFFS NATURAL RESOURCES...	$3,157.66
	04/13/10	Unassigned		3 CLF Jan 22 '11 $80 Call(CLF) CLIFFS NATURAL RESOURCES...	$2,989.66
	04/09/10	Unassigned		2 VAA Jan 22 '11 $270 Call(AAPL) APPLE INC COM SHORT...	$3,506.41
	04/06/10	Unassigned		8 OYK Jan 22 '11 $65 Call(PRU) PRUDENTIAL FINL INC COM ...	$4,785.81
	04/05/10	Unassigned		4 XQX Jan 22 '11 $75 Call(BUCY) BUCYRUS INTL INC NEW CO...	$3,596.88
	04/05/10	Unassigned		6 ZJM Jan 22 '11 $50 Call(TCK) TECK RESOURCES LTD CL B ...	$2,843.38
	04/05/10	Unassigned		2 VAA Jan 22 '11 $270 Call(AAPL) APPLE INC COM SHORT...	$3,164.41
	03/29/10	Unassigned		12 VBA Jan 22 '11 $20 Call(BAC) BANK OF AMERICA CORPORA...	$1,722.81
	03/29/10	Unassigned		4 OQI Jan 22 '11 $75 Call(CREE) CREE INC COM SHORT...	$3,748.90
	03/29/10	Unassigned		6 ZJM Jan 22 '11 $45 Call(TCK) TECK RESOURCES LTD CL B ...	$2,855.39
	03/29/10	Unassigned		2 VAA Jan 22 '11 $270 Call(AAPL) APPLE INC COM SHORT...	$2,770.43
	03/25/10	Unassigned		4 XQX Jan 22 '11 $75 Call(BUCY) BUCYRUS INTL INC NEW CO...	$3,756.90
	03/24/10	Unassigned		4 XQX Jan 22 '11 $75 Call(BUCY) BUCYRUS INTERNATIONAL I...	$3,312.90
	03/23/10	Unassigned		3 F Jan 22 '11 $15 Call(F) FORD MOTOR CO SHORT...	$544.71
	03/23/10	Unassigned		17 F Jan 22 '11 $15 Call(F) FORD MOTOR CO SHORT...	$3,123.98
	03/23/10	Unassigned		10 OZL Jan 22 '11 $22.50 Call(MRVL) MARVELL TECHNOLOGY ...	$2,444.33
	03/23/10	Unassigned		1 VAA Jan 22 '11 $260 Call(AAPL) APPLE INC SHORT...	$1,325.20
	03/23/10	Unassigned		1 VAA Jan 22 '11 $260 Call(AAPL) APPLE INC SHORT...	$1,332.19
	02/18/10	Unassigned		4 OQI Jan 22 '11 $70 Call(CREE) CREE INC COM SHORT...	$3,332.90
	02/18/10	Unassigned		8 ZJM Jan 22 '11 $40 Call(TCK) TECK RESOURCES LTD CL B ...	$4,545.84
	02/18/10	Unassigned		2 VAA Jan 22 '11 $230 Call(AAPL) APPLE INC COM SHORT...	$3,430.41
	02/18/10	Unassigned		1 VAA Jan 22 '11 $230 Call(AAPL) APPLE INC COM SHORT...	$1,716.18
	02/18/10	Unassigned		1 VAA Jan 22 '11 $230 Call(AAPL) APPLE INC COM SHORT...	$1,709.19
	02/17/10	Unassigned		8 ZJM Jan 22 '11 $40 Call(TCK) TECK RESOURCES LTD CL B ...	$4,441.84
	02/16/10	Unassigned		4 OQI Jan 22 '11 $65 Call(CREE) CREE INC COM SHORT...	$3,816.90
				Total Sold Short	**$148,827.47**

Transaction History

| Transactions | Check Summary | Deposit Summary | Categories | Reports |

Date	Type	Description	Amount
09/08/09	Sold Short	6 HIG JAN-10 $25 CALLS (HIGAE) @ $2.98	1,775.44
09/15/09	Sold Short	56 NLY OCT-09 $18 CALLS (NLYJS) @ $0.45	2,469.72
09/15/09	Sold Short	5 HIG JAN-10 $27 CALLS (HIGAT) @ $3.64	1,816.18
09/15/09	Sold Short	1 HIG JAN-10 $27 CALL (HIGAT) @ $3.65	356.24
09/18/09	Sold Short	6 X JAN-10 $55 CALLS (XAK) @ $4.02	2,403.42
09/18/09	Sold Short	4 MET OCT-09 $41 CALLS (JAJJE) @ $1.14	448.97
09/18/09	Sold Short	4 JPM OCT-09 $46 CALLS (JPMJY) @ $1.40	552.97
11/04/09	Sold Short	10 EWZ JAN-11 $85 CALLS (ZYLAQ) @ $7.12	7,104.28
11/04/09	Sold Short	18 FXI JAN-11 $50 CALLS (VHFAF) @ $3.96	7,106.25
11/04/09	Sold Short	4 AAPL JAN-11 $230 CALLS (VAAAW) @ $20.16	8,052.78
11/04/09	Sold Short	20 EEM JAN-11 $46 CALLS (ZALAT) @ $2.80	5,576.78
11/05/09	Sold Short	1 GOOG JAN-11 $630 CALL (OUPAR) @ $43.33	4,324.13
11/06/09	Sold Short	1 GOOG JAN-11 $630 CALL (OUPAR) @ $44.78	4,469.13
11/06/09	Sold Short	20 EEM JAN-11 $46 CALLS (ZALAT) @ $2.86	5,696.78
11/09/09	Sold Short	11 EWZ JAN-11 $90 CALLS (ZYLAR) @ $6.82	7,485.52
11/09/09	Sold Short	14 FXI JAN-11 $55 CALLS (VHFAG) @ $3.05	4,251.34
11/09/09	Sold Short	3 FXI JAN-11 $55 CALLS (VHFAG) @ $3.06	915.71
11/09/09	Sold Short	1 GOOG JAN-11 $640 CALL (OUPAT) @ $44.55	4,446.13
11/09/09	Sold Short	2 AAPL JAN-11 $240 CALLS (VAAAX) @ $18.99	3,796.39
11/09/09	Sold Short	1 AAPL JAN-11 $240 CALL (VAAAX) @ $19.00	1,891.20
11/09/09	Sold Short	1 AAPL JAN-11 $240 CALL (VAAAX) @ $18.98	1,897.19
11/11/09	Sold Short	4 GS JAN-11 $210 CALLS (VSDAU) @ $18.70	7,468.79
11/13/09	Sold Short	9 FCX JAN-11 $95 CALLS (OBQAS) @ $12.50	11,234.93
11/16/09	Sold Short	15 SSO JAN-11 $43 CALLS (ZKBAQ) @ $4.69	7,015.51
11/16/09	Sold Short	10 QLD JAN-11 $65 CALLS (ZVXAO) @ $6.90	6,884.29
11/16/09	Sold Short	9 FCX JAN-11 $100 CALLS (OBQAT) @ $11.55	10,379.95
12/02/09	Sold Short	5 TCK JAN-11 $45 CALLS (ZJMAI) @ $4.90	2,438.17
12/02/09	Sold Short	5 TCK JAN-11 $45 CALLS (ZJMAI) @ $4.83	2,403.17
12/14/09	Sold Short	10 ZJM Jan 22 '11 $45 Call @ 4.88	4,864.34
12/21/09	Sold Short	10 ZJM Jan 22 '11 $45 Call @ 4.67	4,654.34
12/21/09	Sold Short	10 ZXV Jan 22 '11 $240 Call @ 43.70	43,687.34
12/21/09	Sold Short	10 VFN Jan 22 '11 $120 Call @ 30.84	30,827.67

Transaction History

Transactions	Check Summary	Deposit Summary	Categories	Reports

Date	Type	Description	Amount
11/09/09	Sold Short	6 EWZ JAN-11 $90 CALLS (ZYLAR) @ $6.80	4,067.38
11/09/09	Sold Short	1 GOOG JAN-11 $640 CALL (OUPAT) @ $44.68	4,459.13
11/09/09	Sold Short	11 EEM JAN-11 $48 CALLS (ZALAV) @ $2.75	3,008.64
11/09/09	Sold Short	1 AAPL JAN-11 $240 CALL (VAAAX) @ $18.81	1,872.20
11/09/09	Sold Short	1 AAPL JAN-11 $240 CALL (VAAAX) @ $19.05	1,896.20
11/11/09	Sold Short	2 GS JAN-11 $210 CALLS (VSDAU) @ $18.42	3,674.40
11/13/09	Sold Short	3 FCX JAN-11 $95 CALLS (OBQAS) @ $12.52	3,745.65
11/16/09	Sold Short	7 SSO JAN-11 $43 CALLS (ZKBAQ) @ $4.70	3,276.64
11/16/09	Sold Short	3 QLD JAN-11 $65 CALLS (ZVXAO) @ $6.90	2,059.69
11/16/09	Sold Short	2 QLD JAN-11 $65 CALLS (ZVXAO) @ $6.80	1,350.46
11/16/09	Sold Short	3 FCX JAN-11 $100 CALLS (OBQAT) @ $11.51	3,442.66
11/17/09	Sold Short	3 SSO JAN-11 $43 CALLS (ZKBAQ) @ $4.54	1,359.70
11/17/09	Sold Short	3 SSO JAN-11 $43 CALLS (ZKBAQ) @ $4.55	1,362.70
11/17/09	Sold Short	1 SSO JAN-11 $43 CALL (ZKBAQ) @ $4.56	447.23
11/17/09	Sold Short	5 QLD JAN-11 $65 CALLS (ZVXAO) @ $6.90	3,438.15
12/14/09	Sold Short	10 ZJM Jan 22 '11 $45 Call @ 4.85	4,834.34
12/15/09	Sold Short	10 ZJM Jan 22 '11 $45 Call @ 4.75	4,734.34
12/21/09	Sold Short	5 ZXV Jan 22 '11 $240 Call @ 43.70	21,841.67
12/21/09	Sold Short	3 ZXV Jan 22 '11 $240 Call @ 43.56	13,065.40
12/21/09	Sold Short	9 VFN Jan 22 '11 $120 Call @ 30.84	27,744.50
12/21/09	Sold Short	1 VFN Jan 22 '11 $120 Call @ 30.80	3,079.16
12/23/09	Sold Short	5 ZJM Jan 22 '11 $45 Call @ 4.73	2,353.17
12/24/09	Sold Short	8 VFN Jan 22 '11 $125 Call @ 32.21	25,757.31
11/04/09	Sold Short	5 EWZ JAN-11 $85 CALLS (ZYLAQ) @ $7.12	3,548.14
11/04/09	Sold Short	9 FXI JAN-11 $50 CALLS (VHFAF) @ $3.95	3,540.12
11/04/09	Sold Short	2 AAPL JAN-11 $230 CALLS (VAAAW) @ $19.61	3,912.39
11/04/09	Sold Short	6 EEM JAN-11 $46 CALLS (ZALAT) @ $2.80	1,675.43
11/04/09	Sold Short	3 EEM JAN-11 $46 CALLS (ZALAT) @ $2.81	832.72
11/06/09	Sold Short	8 FXI JAN-11 $50 CALLS (VHFAF) @ $4.00	3,185.89
11/09/09	Sold Short	5 EWZ JAN-11 $90 CALLS (ZYLAR) @ $6.89	3,433.15
11/09/09	Sold Short	9 EEM JAN-11 $48 CALLS (ZALAV) @ $2.75	2,460.15
11/09/09	Sold Short	1 AAPL JAN-11 $240 CALL (VAAAX) @ $19.03	1,894.20
11/09/09	Sold Short	1 AAPL JAN-11 $240 CALL (VAAAX) @ $19.02	1,901.19
12/02/09	Sold Short	5 TCK JAN-11 $35 CALLS (ZJMAG) @ $8.41	4,197.13
12/10/09	Sold Short	2 GCZ Jun 19 '10 $107 Call @ 10.71	2,136.44

Transaction History

Transactions	Check Summary	Deposit Summary	Categories	Reports

Date	Type	Description	Amount
08/20/09	Sold Short	5 MET SEP-09 $39 CALLS (JAJID) @ $1.16	568.22
08/20/09	Sold Short	6 WDC SEP-09 $34 CALLS (WDCIH) @ $0.93	545.47
08/20/09	Sold Short	6 MDR SEP-09 $25 CALLS (MDRIE) @ $0.85	497.47
08/20/09	Sold Short	4 X SEP-09 $45 CALLS (FBJII) @ $2.27	896.96
08/24/09	Sold Short	2 NOV JAN-10 $38 CALLS (NONAY) @ $6.00	1,190.46
11/04/09	Sold Short	6 EWZ JAN-11 $85 CALLS (ZYLAQ) @ $7.13	4,265.38
11/04/09	Sold Short	10 FXI JAN-11 $50 CALLS (VHFAF) @ $3.94	3,924.36
11/04/09	Sold Short	3 AAPL JAN-11 $230 CALLS (VAAAW) @ $20.09	6,016.59
11/04/09	Sold Short	6 EEM JAN-11 $46 CALLS (ZALAT) @ $2.77	1,657.43
11/04/09	Sold Short	3 EEM JAN-11 $46 CALLS (ZALAT) @ $2.78	831.71
11/04/09	Sold Short	2 EEM JAN-11 $46 CALLS (ZALAT) @ $2.79	548.48
11/05/09	Sold Short	1 GOOG JAN-11 $630 CALL (OUPAR) @ $43.45	4,336.13
11/06/09	Sold Short	1 FXI JAN-11 $50 CALL (VHFAF) @ $4.00	391.23
11/06/09	Sold Short	9 FXI JAN-11 $50 CALLS (VHFAF) @ $3.95	3,540.12
11/04/09	Sold Short	1 EWZ JAN-11 $85 CALL (ZYLAQ) @ $7.16	707.23
11/04/09	Sold Short	1 FXI JAN-11 $50 CALL (VHFAF) @ $3.94	385.23
11/04/09	Sold Short	1 AAPL JAN-11 $230 CALL (VAAAW) @ $19.62	1,953.19
11/04/09	Sold Short	1 EEM JAN-11 $46 CALL (ZALAT) @ $2.81	272.24
12/21/09	Sold Short	1 VFN Jan 22 '11 $120 Call @ 31.08	3,103.17
12/21/09	Sold Short	1 ZXV Jan 22 '11 $240 Call @ 43.95	4,390.13
12/11/09	Sold Short	4 VHP Jan 22 '11 $50 Call @ 6.35	2,532.92
12/11/09	Sold Short	4 VGO Jan 22 '11 $80 Call @ 9.23	3,684.89
12/11/09	Sold Short	4 VJN Jan 22 '11 $65 Call @ 4.70	1,872.94
12/11/09	Sold Short	4 VBT Jan 22 '11 $55 Call @ 4.42	1,760.94
12/11/09	Sold Short	4 VP Jan 22 '11 $60 Call @ 6.12	2,440.92
12/14/09	Sold Short	4 VKO Jan 22 '11 $60 Call @ 4.26	1,696.94
12/15/09	Sold Short	4 VMU Jan 22 '11 $80 Call @ 9.13	3,644.89
12/15/09	Sold Short	4 ZHB Jan 22 '11 $60 Call @ 6.45	2,572.92
12/15/09	Sold Short	8 ZJM Jan 22 '11 $45 Call @ 4.75	3,785.88
12/21/09	Sold Short	5 ZXV Jan 22 '11 $240 Call @ 43.56	21,771.68
12/21/09	Sold Short	8 VFN Jan 22 '11 $120 Call @ 30.67	24,525.34
12/24/09	Sold Short	6 VFN Jan 22 '11 $125 Call @ 32.46	19,466.98

Transaction History

Alerts | Transfer Money | Bill Pay | Help

| Transactions | Check Summary | Deposit Summary | Categories | Reports |

Date	Action	Description	Amount
04/29/09	Sold Short	3 ATI JAN-10 $35 CALLS (YFQAG) @ $5.30	1,579.71
04/29/09	Sold Short	2 JPM JAN-10 $35 CALLS (WJPAG) @ $6.55	1,300.47
04/29/09	Sold Short	2 JPM JUN-09 $35 CALLS (JPMFB) @ $2.72	534.49
04/29/09	Sold Short	2 BUCY JUL-09 $20 CALLS (HBUGD) @ $3.25	640.49
04/29/09	Sold Short	4 MDR AUG-09 $15 CALLS (MDRHC) @ $3.35	1,328.97
04/29/09	Sold Short	2 JPM JUN-09 $35 CALLS (JPMFB) @ $2.72	534.49
04/29/09	Sold Short	5 CLF JAN-10 $20 CALLS (YCPAA) @ $6.23	3,103.17
04/29/09	Sold Short	5 MDR JAN-10 $17.50 CALLS (YAEAW) @ $3.37	1,673.21
04/29/09	Sold Short	5 BUCY JAN-10 $20 CALLS (YHBAD) @ $5.40	2,688.19
05/01/09	Sold Short	3 ATI JAN-10 $35 CALLS (YFQAG) @ $6.95	2,074.70
05/01/09	Sold Short	4 JPM JAN-10 $35 CALLS (WJPAG) @ $5.75	2,288.95
05/05/09	Sold Short	3 ATI JAN-10 $40 CALLS (YFQAW) @ $6.48	1,933.71
05/05/09	Sold Short	5 FWLT JAN-10 $25 CALLS (YNMAE) @ $4.70	2,338.19
05/05/09	Sold Short	5 FWLT JAN-10 $25 CALLS (YNMAE) @ $5.00	2,488.19
05/08/09	Sold Short	5 FWLT JAN-10 $25 CALLS (YNMAE) @ $5.40	2,688.19
05/18/09	Sold Short	4 WFC JAN-10 $30 CALLS (FHUAD) @ $4.00	1,588.96
05/04/09	Sold Short	2 FCX JUN-09 $50 CALLS (FCXFJ) @ $3.21	632.49
05/04/09	Sold Short	2 JPM JUN-09 $35 CALLS (JPMFB) @ $2.55	500.49
05/29/09	Sold Short	3 FWLT JUN-09 $25 CALLS (UFBFE) @ $2.50	739.74
05/01/09	Sold Short	4 CLF JAN-10 $25 CALLS (YCPAU) @ $6.74	2,684.94
05/01/09	Sold Short	2 MOS JAN-10 $45 CALLS (LXWAI) @ $7.90	1,570.46
05/01/09	Sold Short	4 BUCY JAN-10 $25 CALLS (YHBAE) @ $4.91	1,952.95
05/05/09	Sold Short	4 FWLT JAN-10 $25 CALLS (YNMAE) @ $4.55	1,808.96
05/06/09	Sold Short	4 FWLT JAN-10 $25 CALLS (YNMAE) @ $3.90	1,548.96
05/06/09	Sold Short	4 FWLT JAN-10 $25 CALLS (YNMAE) @ $4.01	1,592.96
05/06/09	Sold Short	3 ATI JAN-10 $40 CALLS (YFQAW) @ $6.98	2,083.70
05/08/09	Sold Short	3 ATI JAN-10 $40 CALLS (YFQAW) @ $7.01	2,092.70
05/08/09	Sold Short	6 FWLT JAN-10 $25 CALLS (YNMAE) @ $5.30	3,167.42
05/18/09	Sold Short	5 MDR JAN-10 $22.50 CALLS (YAEAX) @ $2.60	1,288.22
05/18/09	Sold Short	4 WFC JAN-10 $30 CALLS (FHUAD) @ $4.00	1,588.96
06/01/09	Sold Short	8 BUCY JAN-10 $35 CALLS (HBUAG) @ $4.70	3,745.91
06/01/09	Sold Short	9 NYX JAN-10 $30 CALLS (YVXAU) @ $5.50	4,935.13
06/01/09	Sold Short	2 FCX JAN-10 $55 CALLS (YPXAK) @ $12.00	2,390.44

21

USD - US DOLLAR

Trades

Trade Date	Settlement Date	Trade Time	Action	Quantity	Symbol	Price	Principal Amount
12/24/2009	12/28/2009	12:11:26 pm	Sell to Open	-10	+VFNAE	32.400000	-32,400.0000
12/21/2009	12/22/2009	12:32:08 pm	Sell to Open	-10	+VFNAD	30.740000	-30,740.0000
12/21/2009	12/22/2009	1:44:26 pm	Sell to Open	-2	+ZXVAX	43.610000	-8,722.0000
12/21/2009	12/22/2009	1:44:26 pm	Sell to Open	-8	+ZXVAX	43.680000	-34,944.0000
12/14/2009	12/15/2009	3:24:36 pm	Sell to Open	-20	+ZJMAI	4.840000	-9,680.0000
12/10/2009	12/11/2009	3:38:03 pm	Sell to Open	-10	+GOPFZ	64.530000	-64,530.0000
11/25/2009	11/27/2009	2:49:13 pm	Sell to Open	-10	+ZHSAA	10.000000	-10,000.0000
11/16/2009	11/17/2009	2:48:24 pm	Sell to Open	-10	+ZVXAO	7.000000	-7,000.0000
11/09/2009	11/10/2009	11:38:28 am	Sell to Open	-20	+ZYLAR	6.760000	-13,520.0000
11/05/2009	11/06/2009	12:04:16 pm	Sell to Open	-40	+VHFAF	3.980000	-15,920.0000
11/04/2009	11/05/2009	11:52:28 am	Sell to Open	-37	+ZALAT	2.800000	-10,360.0000
09/18/2009	09/21/2009	11:31:23 am	Sell to Open	-1	+XAK	4.000000	-400.0000
09/18/2009	09/21/2009	11:31:23 am	Sell to Open	-1	+XAK	4.000000	-400.0000
09/18/2009	09/21/2009	11:31:23 am	Sell to Open	-4	+XAK	4.000000	-1,600.0000
09/18/2009	09/21/2009	11:31:23 am	Sell to Open	-4	+XAK	4.000000	-1,600.0000
09/18/2009	09/21/2009	12:28:52 pm	Sell to Open	-9	+JPMJY	1.350000	-1,215.0000
09/18/2009	09/21/2009	12:28:52 pm	Sell to Open	-9	+JAJJH	1.690000	-1,521.0000
05/14/2009	05/15/2009	2:33:11 pm	Sell to Open	-2	+YNMAE	4.200000	-840.0000
05/14/2009	05/15/2009	2:34:02 pm	Sell to Open	-2	+HBUAE	4.700000	-940.0000
05/14/2009	05/15/2009	2:36:28 pm	Sell to Open	-2	+FHUAU	4.600000	-920.0000
05/14/2009	05/15/2009	2:42:35 pm	Sell to Open	-2	+YAEAU	3.100000	-620.0000
05/14/2009	05/15/2009	2:53:41 pm	Sell to Open	-2	+CLFAS	5.800000	-1,160.0000
05/20/2009	05/21/2009	11:41:26 am	Sell to Open	-2	+CLFGS	5.200000	-1,040.0000
05/27/2009	05/28/2009	11:39:44 am	Sell to Open	-2	+HBUGE	4.300000	-860.0000
05/27/2009	05/28/2009	11:40:15 am	Sell to Open	-2	+MDRHD	3.100000	-620.0000
05/27/2009	05/28/2009	12:07:24 pm	Sell to Open	-2	+UFBHE	3.800000	-760.0000

USD - US DOLLAR

Trades

Trade Date	Settlement Date	Trade Time	Action	Quantity	Symbol	Price	Principal Amount
05/01/2009	05/04/2009	12:36:20 pm	Sell to Open	-15	+YCPAU	6.310000	-9,465.0000
05/01/2009	05/04/2009	1:41:20 pm	Sell to Open	-15	+YHBAE	4.910000	-7,365.0000
05/05/2009	05/06/2009	12:09:52 pm	Sell to Open	-15	+YNMAE	4.600000	-6,900.0000
05/06/2009	05/07/2009	3:17:12 pm	Sell to Open	-15	+YFQAW	6.900000	-10,350.0000
05/07/2009	05/08/2009	11:47:17 am	Sell to Open	-15	+UNEAR	2.200000	-3,300.0000
05/07/2009	05/08/2009	12:25:49 pm	Sell to Open	-15	+UNEAR	2.200000	-3,300.0000
05/12/2009	05/13/2009	3:37:53 pm	Sell to Open	-15	+YNMAE	4.700000	-7,050.0000
05/18/2009	05/19/2009	3:47:53 pm	Sell to Open	-15	+FHUAD	4.000000	-6,000.0000
05/19/2009	05/20/2009	11:11:20 am	Sell to Open	-15	+YAEAX	2.750000	-4,125.0000
06/01/2009	06/02/2009	10:46:28 am	Sell to Open	-2	+YVXAU	5.500000	-1,100.0000
06/01/2009	06/02/2009	10:46:28 am	Sell to Open	-6	+YVXAU	5.500000	-3,300.0000
06/01/2009	06/02/2009	10:46:28 am	Sell to Open	-2	+YVXAU	5.500000	-1,100.0000
06/01/2009	06/02/2009	3:30:29 pm	Sell to Open	-10	+YMPAI	5.100000	-5,100.0000
06/01/2009	06/02/2009	3:41:45 pm	Sell to Open	-10	+HBUAG	4.700000	-4,700.0000
06/02/2009	06/03/2009	3:33:02 pm	Sell to Open	-1	+CLFAF	6.320000	-632.0000
06/02/2009	06/03/2009	3:33:02 pm	Sell to Open	-9	+CLFAF	6.310000	-5,679.0000
06/11/2009	06/12/2009	9:50:06 am	Sell to Open	-10	+YAEAX	5.000000	-5,000.0000
07/15/2009	07/16/2009	3:13:01 pm	Sell to Open	-10	+SPJAJ	6.300000	-6,300.0000
08/07/2009	08/10/2009	12:45:33 pm	Sell to Open	-10	+WDCAF	4.900000	-4,900.0000
08/13/2009	08/14/2009	3:01:07 pm	Sell to Open	-10	+JPMIX	1.530000	-1,530.0000
08/20/2009	08/21/2009	2:28:57 pm	Sell to Open	-10	+FBJII	2.320000	-2,320.0000
08/21/2009	08/24/2009	9:43:47 am	Sell to Open	-1	+JAJIC	2.000000	-200.0000
08/21/2009	08/24/2009	9:45:08 am	Sell to Open	-9	+JAJIC	2.000000	-1,800.0000
08/26/2009	08/27/2009	3:33:28 pm	Sell to Open	-10	+HIGIN	1.150000	-1,150.0000
09/08/2009	09/09/2009	12:26:16 pm	Sell to Open	-4	+HIGAE	3.000000	-1,200.0000
09/08/2009	09/09/2009	12:26:16 pm	Sell to Open	-6	+HIGAE	3.000000	-1,800.0000
09/09/2009	09/10/2009	12:03:02 pm	Sell to Open	-10	+HIGAE	3.200000	-3,200.0000
09/15/2009	09/16/2009	1:30:27 pm	Sell to Open	-60	+NLYJS	0.450000	-2,700.0000
09/15/2009	09/16/2009	2:13:52 pm	Sell to Open	-10	+TXYAR	2.300000	-2,300.0000

Transaction History

| Transactions | Check Summary | Deposit Summary | Categories | Reports |

07/15/09	Sold Short	2 STT JAN-10 $50 CALLS (SPJAJ) @ $6.30	1,250.46
08/04/09	Sold Short	3 STT JAN-10 $50 CALLS (SPJAJ) @ $8.20	2,449.68
08/19/09	Sold Short	4 X SEP-09 $45 CALLS (FBJII) @ $2.27	896.96
08/20/09	Sold Short	4 MET SEP-09 $39 CALLS (JAJID) @ $1.21	472.97
08/20/09	Sold Short	5 MDR SEP-09 $25 CALLS (MDRIE) @ $0.95	463.22
08/20/09	Sold Short	2 X SEP-09 $45 CALLS (FBJII) @ $2.31	452.48
08/20/09	Sold Short	9 WDC JAN-10 $30 CALLS (WDCAF) @ $5.30	4,755.09
08/21/09	Sold Short	4 JPM SEP-09 $45 CALLS (JPMII) @ $1.20	468.97
09/09/09	Sold Short	4 MET OCT-09 $39 CALLS (JAJJD) @ $1.91	752.97
09/09/09	Sold Short	6 HIG JAN-10 $25 CALLS (HIGAE) @ $3.30	1,967.43
09/09/09	Sold Short	6 HIG JAN-10 $25 CALLS (HIGAE) @ $3.13	1,865.44
09/11/09	Sold Short	4 X OCT-09 $47 CALLS (FBJJX) @ $3.20	1,268.95
09/14/09	Sold Short	5 HIG JAN-10 $27 CALLS (HIGAT) @ $3.24	1,616.18
09/14/09	Sold Short	1 HIG JAN-10 $27 CALL (HIGAT) @ $3.22	313.24
09/14/09	Sold Short	2 STT JAN-10 $55 CALLS (SPJAK) @ $4.90	970.47
09/15/09	Sold Short	4 WDC OCT-09 $36 CALLS (WDCJI) @ $2.00	788.96
09/15/09	Sold Short	2 CLF JAN-10 $30 CALLS (CLFAF) @ $5.00	990.47
09/18/09	Sold Short	4 X JAN-10 $55 CALLS (XAK) @ $4.05	1,612.94
09/18/09	Sold Short	5 MET OCT-09 $41 CALLS (JAJJE) @ $1.17	577.22
09/08/09	Sold Short	6 MDR SEP-09 $26 CALLS (MDRIL) @ $1.00	587.47
09/08/09	Sold Short	6 HIG JAN-10 $25 CALLS (HIGAE) @ $3.00	1,787.44
09/09/09	Sold Short	3 HIG JAN-10 $25 CALLS (HIGAE) @ $3.16	945.71
09/09/09	Sold Short	2 HIG JAN-10 $25 CALLS (HIGAE) @ $3.15	628.47
09/09/09	Sold Short	1 HIG JAN-10 $25 CALL (HIGAE) @ $3.17	308.24
09/09/09	Sold Short	6 HIG JAN-10 $25 CALLS (HIGAE) @ $3.20	1,907.44
09/11/09	Sold Short	6 HIG JAN-10 $26 CALLS (HIGAO) @ $3.25	1,937.43
09/14/09	Sold Short	5 NOV OCT-09 $39 CALLS (NONJB) @ $3.00	1,488.20
09/15/09	Sold Short	80 NLY OCT-09 $18 CALLS (NLYJS) @ $0.45	3,531.59
09/16/09	Sold Short	10 TXT JAN-10 $22.50 CALLS (TXTAX) @ $2.00	1,984.41
09/17/09	Sold Short	4 JPM OCT-09 $45 CALLS (JPMJI) @ $2.00	788.96
09/18/09	Sold Short	4 X JAN-10 $55 CALLS (XAK) @ $4.13	1,644.94
09/18/09	Sold Short	4 X JAN-10 $55 CALLS (XAK) @ $4.10	1,632.94
09/18/09	Sold Short	4 X JAN-10 $55 CALLS (XAK) @ $4.09	1,628.94
09/18/09	Sold Short	5 BUCY JAN-10 $40 CALLS (HBUAH) @ $2.95	1,467.20
09/18/09	Sold Short	5 BUCY JAN-10 $40 CALLS (HBUAH) @ $2.96	1,472.20
09/18/09	Sold Short	5 MET OCT-09 $41 CALLS (JAJJE) @ $1.23	607.22
09/18/09	Sold Short	4 MET OCT-09 $41 CALLS (JAJJE) @ $1.19	468.97
09/18/09	Sold Short	5 MET OCT-09 $41 CALLS (JAJJE) @ $1.15	563.22
09/18/09	Sold Short	5 NOV OCT-09 $45 CALLS (NONJI) @ $1.32	652.22
09/18/09	Sold Short	4 JPM OCT-09 $46 CALLS (JPMJY) @ $1.28	504.97
09/18/09	Sold Short	4 JPM OCT-09 $46 CALLS (JPMJY) @ $1.31	512.97
09/21/09	Sold Short	4 UYM OCT-09 $29 CALLS (UUZJC) @ $1.76	692.97
09/21/09	Sold Short	3 SSO OCT-09 $35 CALLS (SOJJI) @ $1.35	394.73
09/21/09	Sold Short	4 UWM OCT-09 $28 CALLS (ULXJB) @ $1.35	528.97

Transaction History

Transactions	Check Summary	Deposit Summary	Categories	Reports

04/22/09	Sold Short	3 BUCY JUL-09 $20 CALLS (HBUGD) @ $2.51	742.74
04/22/09	Sold Short	2 JPM JAN-10 $35 CALLS (WJPAG) @ $6.77	1,344.47
04/22/09	Sold Short	3 BUCY JAN-10 $20 CALLS (YHBAD) @ $4.79	1,426.72
04/22/09	Sold Short	2 NOV AUG-09 $34 CALLS (NONHF) @ $4.70	930.48
04/22/09	Sold Short	2 NOV JAN-10 $35 CALLS (YMPAG) @ $6.73	1,336.47
04/22/09	Sold Short	2 JPM JUN-09 $35 CALLS (JPMFB) @ $3.11	612.49
04/21/09	Sold Short	3 CHK JUL-09 $22.50 CALLS (CHKGQ) @ $1.33	388.74
04/21/09	Sold Short	3 CHK JAN-10 $22.50 CALLS (WZYAX) @ $3.30	979.73
04/16/09	Sold Short	3 CLF JAN-10 $20 CALLS (YCPAA) @ $5.44	1,621.71
04/16/09	Sold Short	4 BUCY JUL-09 $20 CALLS (HBUGD) @ $2.64	1,044.98
04/16/09	Sold Short	3 CLF JUL-09 $20 CALLS (CLFGD) @ $3.40	1,009.73
04/16/09	Sold Short	4 CHK JUL-09 $22.50 CALLS (CHKGQ) @ $2.10	828.98
04/16/09	Sold Short	3 MDR AUG-09 $17.50 CALLS (MDRHW) @ $2.70	799.73
04/16/09	Sold Short	3 MDR JAN-10 $17.50 CALLS (YAEAW) @ $4.00	1,189.72
04/16/09	Sold Short	2 PBR JAN-10 $37.50 CALLS (YMOAU) @ $5.78	1,146.48
04/16/09	Sold Short	4 BUCY JAN-10 $20 CALLS (YHBAD) @ $4.85	1,928.96
04/16/09	Sold Short	4 CHK JAN-10 $22.50 CALLS (WZYAX) @ $4.00	1,588.96
04/16/09	Sold Short	2 PBR JUL-09 $36 CALLS (PBRGH) @ $3.52	694.49
04/13/09	Sold Short	4 BUCY JUL-09 $20 CALLS (HBUGD) @ $2.48	980.98
04/13/09	Sold Short	4 BUCY JAN-10 $20 CALLS (YHBAD) @ $4.70	1,868.96
04/06/09	Sold Short	3 STT AUG-09 $30 CALLS (STTHX) @ $9.33	2,788.74
04/06/09	Sold Short	5 MDR AUG-09 $15 CALLS (MDRHC) @ $2.84	1,408.25
04/06/09	Sold Short	5 MDR JAN-10 $15 CALLS (YAEAZ) @ $4.12	2,048.24
04/06/09	Sold Short	3 STT JAN-10 $30 CALLS (WRHAX) @ $11.49	3,436.74
04/03/09	Sold Short	4 CLF JAN-10 $20 CALLS (YCPAA) @ $7.02	2,796.99
04/03/09	Sold Short	4 CLF JUL-09 $20 CALLS (CLFGD) @ $4.72	1,876.99
04/03/09	Sold Short	3 STT AUG-09 $30 CALLS (STTHX) @ $8.86	2,647.74
04/03/09	Sold Short	2 NOV AUG-09 $30 CALLS (NOVHF) @ $7.00	1,390.50
04/03/09	Sold Short	5 MDR AUG-09 $15 CALLS (MDRHC) @ $3.03	1,503.25
04/03/09	Sold Short	5 MDR JAN-10 $15 CALLS (YAEAZ) @ $4.37	2,173.24
04/03/09	Sold Short	3 STT JAN-10 $30 CALLS (WRHAX) @ $11.14	3,331.74
04/03/09	Sold Short	2 NOV JAN-10 $30 CALLS (YMPAF) @ $9.23	1,836.49
04/01/09	Sold Short	2 MOS JAN-10 $40 CALLS (LXWAH) @ $12.26	2,442.48
04/01/09	Sold Short	4 MS JAN-10 $20 CALLS (WWDAD) @ $8.59	3,424.97
04/01/09	Sold Short	2 PBR JAN-10 $30 CALLS (YMOAF) @ $7.50	1,490.49
04/01/09	Sold Short	4 MS JUL-09 $20 CALLS (MSGD) @ $6.42	2,556.97
04/01/09	Sold Short	2 FCX AUG-09 $35 CALLS (FPAHG) @ $9.42	1,874.48

25

Transaction History

Alerts | Transfer Money | Bill Pay | Help

| Transactions | Check Summary | Deposit Summary | Categories | Reports |

Date	Action	Description	Amount
04/02/09	Sold Short	4 MS JAN-10 $22.50 CALLS (WWDAX) @ $7.20	2,868.97
04/02/09	Sold Short	2 MOS JUN-09 $45 CALLS (MOSFI) @ $6.68	1,326.49
04/02/09	Sold Short	2 MOS JUN-09 $45 CALLS (MOSFI) @ $6.20	1,230.49
04/02/09	Sold Short	4 CLF JAN-10 $20 CALLS (YCPAA) @ $7.30	2,908.97
04/02/09	Sold Short	4 CLF JUL-09 $20 CALLS (CLFGD) @ $4.96	1,972.97
04/02/09	Sold Short	2 MOS JAN-10 $45 CALLS (LXWAI) @ $11.21	2,232.48
04/02/09	Sold Short	2 FCX JAN-10 $40 CALLS (YPXAH) @ $11.79	2,348.48
04/02/09	Sold Short	2 FCX JAN-10 $40 CALLS (YPXAH) @ $11.57	2,304.48
04/02/09	Sold Short	3 NOV AUG-09 $30 CALLS (NOVHF) @ $6.64	1,981.72
04/02/09	Sold Short	2 FCX AUG-09 $40 CALLS (FCXHH) @ $8.96	1,782.48
04/02/09	Sold Short	2 PBR JAN-10 $35 CALLS (YMOAG) @ $7.03	1,396.49
04/02/09	Sold Short	2 PBR JUL-09 $34 CALLS (PBRGB) @ $4.98	986.49
04/02/09	Sold Short	2 PBR JUL-09 $34 CALLS (PBRGB) @ $4.66	922.49
04/02/09	Sold Short	3 NOV JAN-10 $30 CALLS (YMPAF) @ $8.67	2,590.72
04/02/09	Sold Short	4 MS JUL-09 $22 CALLS (MSGV) @ $5.41	2,152.97
04/21/09	Sold Short	3 BUCY JUL-09 $17.50 CALLS (HBUGA) @ $3.20	949.73
04/21/09	Sold Short	3 BUCY JAN-10 $20 CALLS (YHBAD) @ $4.21	1,252.72
04/17/09	Sold Short	5 BUCY JAN-10 $20 CALLS (YHBAD) @ $4.84	2,408.19
04/09/09	Sold Short	6 WFC JUL-09 $17.50 CALLS (WFCGT) @ $4.31	2,573.44
04/09/09	Sold Short	4 STT AUG-09 $32 CALLS (STTHF) @ $9.32	3,716.91
04/06/09	Sold Short	4 STT AUG-09 $32 CALLS (STTHF) @ $8.20	3,268.99
04/03/09	Sold Short	5 CLF JUL-09 $20 CALLS (CLFGD) @ $4.49	2,233.24
04/03/09	Sold Short	8 MDR AUG-09 $15 CALLS (MDRHC) @ $3.03	2,409.99
04/24/09	Sold Short	2 PBR JUL-09 $35 CALLS (PBRGG) @ $2.65	520.49
04/21/09	Sold Short	5 CHK JUL-09 $20 CALLS (CHKGD) @ $2.28	1,128.23
04/17/09	Sold Short	5 BUCY JUL-09 $20 CALLS (HBUGD) @ $2.77	1,373.22
04/17/09	Sold Short	5 CLF JUL-09 $25 CALLS (CLFGE) @ $2.26	1,118.23
04/17/09	Sold Short	5 CHK JUL-09 $22.50 CALLS (CHKGQ) @ $2.26	1,118.23
04/17/09	Sold Short	3 STT AUG-09 $35 CALLS (STTHG) @ $7.48	2,233.70
04/17/09	Sold Short	4 JPM JUN-09 $35 CALLS (JPMFB) @ $3.11	1,232.97
04/13/09	Sold Short	5 BUCY JUL-09 $20 CALLS (HBUGD) @ $2.48	1,228.22
04/09/09	Sold Short	2 MOS JUN-09 $45 CALLS (MOSFI) @ $5.58	1,106.48
04/09/09	Sold Short	3 CLF JUL-09 $20 CALLS (CLFGD) @ $4.08	1,213.72
04/09/09	Sold Short	3 STT AUG-09 $35 CALLS (STTHG) @ $7.50	2,239.70
04/09/09	Sold Short	5 MDR AUG-09 $15 CALLS (MDRHC) @ $3.16	1,568.21
04/09/09	Sold Short	2 NOV AUG-09 $34 CALLS (NONHF) @ $5.49	1,088.48
04/09/09	Sold Short	2 FCX AUG-09 $44 CALLS (FCXHZ) @ $7.30	1,450.47
04/09/09	Sold Short	2 PBR JUL-09 $36 CALLS (PBRGH) @ $4.10	810.48
04/09/09	Sold Short	3 MS JUL-09 $24 CALLS (MSGY) @ $4.50	1,339.72

USD - US DOLLAR

Trades

Trade Date	Settlement Date	Trade Time	Action	Quantity	Symbol	Price	Principal Amount
04/06/2009	04/07/2009	3:58:00 pm	Sell to Open	-15	+STTHF	7.920000	-11,880.0000
04/15/2009	04/16/2009	4:08:44 pm	Sell to Open	-15	+HBUGD	2.590000	-3,885.0000
03/17/2009	03/18/2009	12:46:27 pm	Sell to Open	-10	+FCXEG	5.200000	-5,200.0000
03/17/2009	03/18/2009	12:49:34 pm	Sell to Open	-10	+NOVEF	3.600000	-3,600.0000
03/17/2009	03/18/2009	12:50:43 pm	Sell to Open	-10	+MSGD	6.200000	-6,200.0000
03/17/2009	03/18/2009	1:04:43 pm	Sell to Open	-10	+MOSFH	8.000000	-8,000.0000
03/17/2009	03/18/2009	1:07:27 pm	Sell to Open	-8	+PBRGY	5.600000	-4,480.0000
03/17/2009	03/18/2009	1:07:27 pm	Sell to Open	-2	+PBRGY	5.600000	-1,120.0000
03/18/2009	03/19/2009	3:18:38 pm	Sell to Open	-5	+FCXEG	6.100000	-3,050.0000
03/18/2009	03/19/2009	3:20:04 pm	Sell to Open	-10	+MDRHC	2.500000	-2,500.0000
03/18/2009	03/19/2009	3:18:38 pm	Sell to Open	-5	+FCXEG	6.100000	-3,050.0000
03/18/2009	03/19/2009	3:20:04 pm	Sell to Open	-10	+MDRHC	2.500000	-2,500.0000
03/18/2009	03/19/2009	3:32:22 pm	Sell to Open	-2	+MSGD	7.000000	-1,400.0000
03/18/2009	03/19/2009	3:32:22 pm	Sell to Open	-3	+MSGD	7.000000	-2,100.0000
03/18/2009	03/19/2009	3:33:00 pm	Sell to Open	-5	+MOSFH	7.700000	-3,850.0000
03/18/2009	03/19/2009	3:36:31 pm	Sell to Open	-5	+NOVEF	3.500000	-1,750.0000
03/18/2009	03/19/2009	3:39:26 pm	Sell to Open	-5	+PBRGY	6.300000	-3,150.0000
03/19/2009	03/20/2009	2:17:16 pm	Sell to Open	-5	+MDRHC	3.000000	-1,500.0000
03/19/2009	03/20/2009	2:17:17 pm	Sell to Open	-9	+SIIGY	3.400000	-3,060.0000
03/19/2009	03/20/2009	2:17:31 pm	Sell to Open	-1	+SIIGY	3.400000	-340.0000
03/25/2009	03/26/2009	3:40:27 pm	Sell to Open	-15	+GSGS	25.690000	-38,535.0000
03/23/2009	03/24/2009	1:51:07 pm	Sell to Open	-15	+CXJHD	3.380000	-5,070.0000
03/23/2009	03/24/2009	3:49:17 pm	Sell to Open	-15	+WFCGT	3.600000	-5,400.0000
03/26/2009	03/27/2009	12:19:49 pm	Sell to Open	-9	+CLFGD	3.600000	-3,240.0000
03/26/2009	03/27/2009	12:19:38 pm	Sell to Open	-4	+CLFGD	3.600000	-1,440.0000

Transaction History

| Transactions | Check Summary | Deposit Summary | Categories | Reports |

Date	Type	Description	Amount
03/26/09	Sold Short	8 CLF JUL-09 $20 CALLS (CLFGD) @ $3.60	2,865.99
03/26/09	Sold Short	10 PBR JAN-10 $30 CALLS (YMOAF) @ $9.35	9,338.45
03/26/09	Sold Short	6 GS JUL-09 $95 CALLS (GSGS) @ $27.93	16,749.41
03/26/09	Sold Short	10 NOV JAN-10 $25 CALLS (YMPAE) @ $12.72	12,708.43
03/23/09	Sold Short	4 SII JUL-09 $27.50 CALLS (SIIGY) @ $2.85	1,129.00
03/23/09	Sold Short	2 SII JUL-09 $27.50 CALLS (SIIGY) @ $2.80	558.49
03/23/09	Sold Short	3 USO APR-09 $32 CALLS (UBODF) @ $1.85	544.75
03/23/09	Sold Short	1 GLD APR-09 $94 CALL (GLDDP) @ $3.00	291.25
03/23/09	Sold Short	10 WFC JUL-09 $17.50 CALLS (WFCGT) @ $3.70	3,684.48
03/19/09	Sold Short	6 SII JUL-09 $27.50 CALLS (SIIGY) @ $3.45	2,057.49
03/19/09	Sold Short	10 MDR AUG-09 $15 CALLS (MDRHC) @ $3.05	3,034.49
03/18/09	Sold Short	3 MOS JUN-09 $40 CALLS (MOSFH) @ $8.20	2,449.74
03/18/09	Sold Short	6 MS JUL-09 $20 CALLS (MSGD) @ $7.27	4,349.48
03/18/09	Sold Short	4 PBR JUL-09 $27.50 CALLS (PBRGY) @ $6.40	2,548.99
03/18/09	Sold Short	4 NOV MAY-09 $30 CALLS (NOVEF) @ $3.93	1,561.00
03/18/09	Sold Short	3 FCX MAY-09 $35 CALLS (FCXEG) @ $6.10	1,819.74
03/17/09	Sold Short	3 MOS JUN-09 $40 CALLS (MOSFH) @ $8.16	2,437.74
03/17/09	Sold Short	6 MS JUL-09 $20 CALLS (MSGD) @ $6.26	3,743.48
03/17/09	Sold Short	3 PBR JUL-09 $27.50 CALLS (PBRGY) @ $5.76	1,725.74
03/17/09	Sold Short	1 PBR JUL-09 $27.50 CALL (PBRGY) @ $5.77	568.25
03/17/09	Sold Short	4 NOV MAY-09 $30 CALLS (NOVEF) @ $3.67	1,457.00
03/17/09	Sold Short	3 FCX MAY-09 $35 CALLS (FCXEG) @ $5.28	1,573.75
03/26/09	Sold Short	3 CLF JUL-09 $20 CALLS (CLFGD) @ $3.60	1,069.75
03/26/09	Sold Short	5 PBR JAN-10 $30 CALLS (YMOAF) @ $9.38	4,682.23
03/26/09	Sold Short	3 GS JUL-09 $95 CALLS (GSGS) @ $28.03	8,402.71
03/26/09	Sold Short	5 NOV JAN-10 $25 CALLS (YMPAE) @ $12.70	6,342.22
03/19/09	Sold Short	4 SII JUL-09 $27.50 CALLS (SIIGY) @ $3.44	1,365.00
03/19/09	Sold Short	7 MDR AUG-09 $15 CALLS (MDRHC) @ $3.04	2,114.74
03/17/09	Sold Short	2 MOS JUN-09 $40 CALLS (MOSFH) @ $8.07	1,604.50
03/17/09	Sold Short	3 MS JUL-09 $20 CALLS (MSGD) @ $6.25	1,864.74
03/17/09	Sold Short	2 PBR JUL-09 $27.50 CALLS (PBRGY) @ $5.75	1,140.50
03/17/09	Sold Short	2 NOV MAY-09 $30 CALLS (NOVEF) @ $3.67	724.50
03/17/09	Sold Short	2 FCX MAY-09 $35 CALLS (FCXEG) @ $5.37	1,064.50
03/26/09	Sold Short	2 CLF JUL-09 $20 CALLS (CLFGD) @ $3.60	710.50
03/26/09	Sold Short	1 GS JUL-09 $95 CALL (GSGS) @ $27.94	2,789.24

28

Transaction History

| Transactions | Check Summary | Deposit Summary | Categories | Reports |

10/23/08	Sold Short	2 CLF JAN-10 $35 CALLS (YCPAZ) @ $9.24	1,838.49
10/23/08	Sold Short	2 WLT JAN-10 $35 CALLS (YZGAG) @ $10.80	2,150.49
10/23/08	Sold Short	2 FCX JAN-10 $30 CALLS (YPXAF) @ $7.00	1,390.50
10/23/08	Sold Short	2 X JAN-10 $40 CALLS (WYSAH) @ $10.30	2,050.49
10/23/08	Sold Short	2 PRU JAN-10 $35 CALLS (YKYAG) @ $11.50	2,290.49
10/23/08	Sold Short	2 BTU JAN-10 $35 CALLS (LLWAG) @ $10.00	1,990.49
10/23/08	Sold Short	2 PBR JAN-10 $25 CALLS (YMOAE) @ $6.40	1,270.50
10/23/08	Sold Short	2 SWN JAN-10 $30 CALLS (LVXAF) @ $7.20	1,430.50
10/23/08	Sold Short	2 BUCY JAN-10 $25 CALLS (YHBAE) @ $5.47	1,084.50
10/23/08	Sold Short	1 EEM JAN-10 $25 CALL (YVKAE) @ $4.10	401.25
10/23/08	Sold Short	1 EWZ JAN-10 $40 CALL (WKBAZ) @ $5.40	531.25
10/23/08	Sold Short	2 CHK JAN-10 $25 CALLS (WZYAE) @ $6.00	1,190.50
10/23/08	Sold Short	2 WFC JAN-10 $35 CALLS (WWRAG) @ $5.00	990.50
10/22/08	Sold Short	1 EEM JAN-10 $25 CALL (YVKAE) @ $4.75	466.25
10/22/08	Sold Short	1 EWZ JAN-10 $40 CALL (WKBAZ) @ $7.10	701.25
06/10/08	Sold Short	1 AAPL JUL-08 $190 CALL (APVGR) @ $8.00	791.25
06/10/08	Sold Short	1 CSX JUN-08 $65 CALL (CSXFM) @ $2.30	221.25
06/10/08	Sold Short	3 BUCY JUL-08 $75 CALLS (HIKGO) @ $3.70	1,099.75
05/30/08	Sold Short	1 MA JUL-08 $330 CALL (GSYGF) @ $10.00	991.25
05/27/08	Sold Short	2 CLF JUN-08 $97.50 CALLS (CGJFK) @ $4.60	910.50
05/27/08	Sold Short	2 CSX JUN-08 $65 CALLS (CSXFM) @ $3.40	670.50
04/24/08	Sold Short	1 CLF MAY-08 $160 CALL (CGJEL) @ $7.74	765.25
04/18/08	Sold Short	2 AKS MAY-08 $70 CALLS (AKSEN) @ $4.41	872.50
04/16/08	Sold Short	3 RIO MAY-08 $40 CALLS (RIOEH) @ $1.11	322.75
04/16/08	Sold Short	3 RIO MAY-08 $40 CALLS (RIOEH) @ $1.07	310.75
04/16/08	Sold Short	1 MA MAY-08 $240 CALL (MALEU) @ $9.34	925.25
04/16/08	Sold Short	2 FDG MAY-08 $65 CALLS (FDGEM) @ $3.44	678.50
04/16/08	Sold Short	2 FDG MAY-08 $65 CALLS (FDGEM) @ $3.40	670.50
04/09/08	Sold Short	2 ANR MAY-08 $50 CALLS (ANREJ) @ $3.73	736.50
04/08/08	Sold Short	2 WLT MAY-08 $70 CALLS (WLTEN) @ $5.71	1,132.50
04/08/08	Sold Short	2 ANR MAY-08 $50 CALLS (ANREJ) @ $3.80	750.50
04/07/08	Sold Short	2 WLT MAY-08 $70 CALLS (WLTEN) @ $5.54	1,098.50
04/01/08	Sold Short	5 ISRG APR-08 $370 PUTS (IJAPN) @ $44.25	22,117.13
04/01/08	Sold Short	4 MA APR-08 $240 PUTS (MALPU) @ $12.71	5,076.98

SECURITIES PURCHASED OR SOLD (Continued)

TRADE DATE	SETTLEMENT DATE	DESCRIPTION	SYMBOL/ CUSIP	TRANSACTION TYPE	QUANTITY	PRICE	AMOUNT PURCHASED	AMOUNT SOLD
03/24/08 15:27	03/25/08	CALL CAL MAINE FO APR 035 CBOE EXP 04/19/2008 OPEN CONTRACT	X QKMDG	Sold	-1	4.5400		445.25
03/24/08 15:27	03/25/08	CALL CAL MAINE FO APR 035 CBOE EXP 04/19/2008 OPEN CONTRACT	X QKMDG	Sold	-3	4.5000		1,347.73
03/24/08 14:38	03/25/08	CALL RESEARCH IN APR 105 **** EXP 04/19/2008 OPEN CONTRACT	XRULD105	Sold	-4	10.8100		4,316.96
03/25/08 12:52	03/26/08	CALL INTUITIVE SU APR 280 **** EXP 04/19/2008 OPEN CONTRACT	XAXVD280	Sold	-5	53.7600		26,871.96
03/25/08 14:16	03/26/08	CALL MASTERCARD APR 210 **** EXP 04/19/2008 OPEN CONTRACT	XMALD210	Sold	-4	23.1400		9,248.90

Transaction History

Alerts | Transfer Money | Bill Pay | Help

Transactions | Check Summary | Deposit Summary | Categories | Reports

Date	Type	Description	Amount
10/23/08	Sold Short	1 EWZ JAN-10 $35 CALL (YEKAG) @ $7.20	711.25
10/23/08	Sold Short	1 CLF JAN-10 $35 CALL (YCPAZ) @ $9.22	913.25
10/23/08	Sold Short	1 WLT JAN-10 $35 CALL (YZGAG) @ $10.80	1,071.25
10/23/08	Sold Short	1 FCX JAN-10 $30 CALL (YPXAF) @ $7.00	691.25
10/23/08	Sold Short	1 X JAN-10 $40 CALL (WYSAH) @ $10.30	1,021.25
10/23/08	Sold Short	1 PRU JAN-10 $35 CALL (YKYAG) @ $11.50	1,141.25
10/23/08	Sold Short	1 BTU JAN-10 $35 CALL (LLWAG) @ $10.00	991.25
10/23/08	Sold Short	1 BAC JAN-10 $25 CALL (WBAAE) @ $4.70	461.25
10/23/08	Sold Short	1 PBR JAN-10 $25 CALL (YMOAE) @ $6.40	631.25
10/23/08	Sold Short	1 SWN JAN-10 $30 CALL (LVXAF) @ $7.20	711.25
10/23/08	Sold Short	1 BUCY JAN-10 $25 CALL (YHBAE) @ $5.31	522.25
10/23/08	Sold Short	1 EEM JAN-10 $25 CALL (YVKAE) @ $4.10	401.25
10/23/08	Sold Short	1 CHK JAN-10 $25 CALL (WZYAE) @ $6.00	591.25
10/23/08	Sold Short	1 WFC JAN-10 $35 CALL (WWRAG) @ $5.00	491.25
06/16/08	Sold Short	2 FMC JUL-08 $75 CALLS (FMCGO) @ $6.00	1,190.50
06/10/08	Sold Short	2 AAPL JUL-08 $190 CALLS (APVGR) @ $8.00	1,590.50
06/10/08	Sold Short	1 CSX JUN-08 $65 CALL (CSXFM) @ $2.20	211.25
06/10/08	Sold Short	5 BUCY JUL-08 $75 CALLS (HIKGO) @ $3.70	1,838.24
05/27/08	Sold Short	4 CLF JUN-08 $97.50 CALLS (CGJFK) @ $4.60	1,828.99
05/27/08	Sold Short	4 CSX JUN-08 $65 CALLS (CSXFM) @ $3.40	1,349.00
04/18/08	Sold Short	3 AKS MAY-08 $70 CALLS (AKSEN) @ $4.41	1,312.75
04/16/08	Sold Short	5 RIO MAY-08 $40 CALLS (RIOEH) @ $1.11	543.25
04/16/08	Sold Short	5 RIO MAY-08 $40 CALLS (RIOEH) @ $1.08	528.25
04/16/08	Sold Short	1 MA MAY-08 $240 CALL (MALEU) @ $9.34	925.25
04/16/08	Sold Short	3 FDG MAY-08 $65 CALLS (FDGEM) @ $3.40	1,009.75
04/16/08	Sold Short	3 FDG MAY-08 $65 CALLS (FDGEM) @ $3.40	1,009.75
04/09/08	Sold Short	3 ANR MAY-08 $50 CALLS (ANREJ) @ $3.73	1,108.75
04/08/08	Sold Short	3 WLT MAY-08 $70 CALLS (WLTEN) @ $5.72	1,705.75
04/08/08	Sold Short	3 ANR MAY-08 $50 CALLS (ANREJ) @ $3.73	1,108.75
04/07/08	Sold Short	3 WLT MAY-08 $70 CALLS (WLTEN) @ $5.54	1,651.75
04/01/08	Sold Short	7 ISRG APR-08 $370 PUTS (IJAPN) @ $45.02	31,504.58
04/01/08	Sold Short	3 ISRG APR-08 $370 PUTS (IJAPN) @ $44.25	13,272.67
04/01/08	Sold Short	6 MA APR-08 $240 PUTS (MALPU) @ $12.71	7,617.46

USD - US DOLLAR

Trades

Trade Date	Settlement Date	Trade Time	Action	Quantity	Symbol	Price	Principal Amount
03/07/2008	03/10/2008	3:06:56 pm	Sell to Open	-10	+MALCQ	8.400000	-8,400.0000
03/10/2008	03/11/2008	2:56:31 pm	Sell to Open	-10	+MONCC	4.900000	-4,900.0000
03/24/2008	03/25/2008	2:24:08 pm	Sell to Open	-10	+RULDL	11.230000	-11,230.0000
03/24/2008	03/25/2008	3:25:56 pm	Sell to Open	-10	+AKSDK	3.200000	-3,200.0000
03/24/2008	03/25/2008	4:07:17 pm	Sell to Open	-10	+QKMDG	4.500000	-4,500.0000
03/25/2008	03/26/2008	2:42:03 pm	Sell to Open	-10	+MALDB	23.200000	-23,200.0000
03/25/2008	03/26/2008	4:19:55 pm	Sell to Open	-4	+AXVDV	54.870000	-21,948.0000
03/25/2008	03/26/2008	4:19:55 pm	Sell to Open	-2	+AXVDV	54.380000	-10,876.0000
03/25/2008	03/26/2008	4:19:55 pm	Sell to Open	-4	+AXVDV	54.470000	-21,788.0000
04/01/2008	04/02/2008	10:29:07 am	Sell to Open	-10	+IJAPN	44.930000	-44,930.0000
04/01/2008	04/02/2008	10:46:30 am	Sell to Open	-10	+MALPU	12.640000	-12,640.0000
04/07/2008	04/08/2008	2:54:25 pm	Sell to Open	-10	+WLTEN	4.700000	-4,700.0000
04/08/2008	04/09/2008	4:10:19 pm	Sell to Open	-10	+ANREJ	3.700000	-3,700.0000
04/14/2008	04/15/2008	12:16:20 pm	Sell to Open	-4	+AXVDJ	73.170000	-29,268.0000
04/16/2008	04/17/2008	12:17:54 pm	Sell to Open	-10	+FDGEM	3.200000	-3,200.0000
04/18/2008	04/21/2008	1:15:44 pm	Sell to Open	-10	+AKSEN	4.480000	-4,480.0000
04/18/2008	04/21/2008	1:38:35 pm	Sell to Open	-10	+VEV	2.550000	-2,550.0000
05/27/2008	05/28/2008	1:57:58 pm	Sell to Open	-10	+CSXFM	3.400000	-3,400.0000
05/28/2008	05/29/2008	10:37:12 am	Sell to Open	-10	+GTIFE	1.700000	-1,700.0000
06/16/2008	06/17/2008	9:51:50 am	Sell to Open	-5	+FMCGO	6.000000	-3,000.0000
09/09/2008	09/10/2008	3:51:09 pm	Sell to Open	-4	+RSXWS	13.600000	-5,440.0000
09/09/2008	09/10/2008	3:51:12 pm	Sell to Open	-4	+RSXWS	13.600000	-5,440.0000
09/09/2008	09/10/2008	3:51:15 pm	Sell to Open	-2	+RSXWS	13.600000	-2,720.0000
09/11/2008	09/12/2008	9:59:01 am	Sell to Open	-3	+EEVLD	20.000000	-6,000.0000
10/23/2008	10/24/2008	11:35:58 am	Sell to Open	-3	+YMOAE	6.580000	-1,974.0000
10/23/2008	10/24/2008	11:35:58 am	Sell to Open	-3	+WYSAH	10.970000	-3,291.0000
10/23/2008	10/24/2008	11:35:58 am	Sell to Open	-3	+YHBAE	5.360000	-1,608.0000
10/23/2008	10/24/2008	11:35:58 am	Sell to Open	-3	+YPXAF	6.810000	-2,043.0000
10/23/2008	10/24/2008	11:35:58 am	Sell to Open	-3	+LLWAG	10.060000	-3,018.0000
10/23/2008	10/24/2008	1:17:46 pm	Sell to Open	-3	+YZGAG	11.230000	-3,369.0000

USD - US DOLLAR

Trades

Trade Date	Settlement Date	Trade Time	Action	Quantity	Symbol	Price	Principal Amount
10/23/2008	10/24/2008	1:52:11 pm	Sell to Open	-3	+LVXAF	7.360000	-2,208.0000
10/23/2008	10/24/2008	2:31:17 pm	Sell to Open	-3	+WWRAG	4.610000	-1,383.0000
10/23/2008	10/24/2008	3:16:44 pm	Sell to Open	-3	+WZYAE	5.600000	-1,680.0000
10/23/2008	10/24/2008	4:42:09 pm	Sell to Open	-3	+YKYAG	10.700000	-3,210.0000
10/23/2008	10/24/2008	4:42:09 pm	Sell to Open	-3	+YCPAZ	7.400000	-2,220.0000
10/23/2008	10/24/2008	4:42:09 pm	Sell to Open	-3	+WBAAE	4.850000	-1,455.0000
10/24/2008	10/27/2008	10:04:09 am	Sell to Open	-3	+WKBAZ	5.000000	-1,500.0000
10/24/2008	10/27/2008	10:04:09 am	Sell to Open	-3	+YVKAE	2.740000	-822.0000
10/31/2008	11/03/2008	10:54:22 am	Sell to Open	-3	+FCXEG	4.800000	-1,440.0000

Daily Account Activity

Trade Date	Settlement Date	Activity	Quantity	Trade #	Currency	Price	Subtracted	Added
		PURCHASES AND SALES						
USD - US DOLLAR								
+MALCR: 02/14/2008	02/15/2008	Mastercard Inc Cl A Mar 2008 190.00 Call Sell to Open	-6.0000	55404134	USD	18.130000	0.00	-10,858.36
+MALOD: 02/14/2008	02/15/2008	Mastercard Inc Cl A Mar 2008 220.00 Put Sell to Open	-6.0000	55404130	USD	21.950000	0.00	-13,150.33
+MFPOE: 02/14/2008	02/15/2008	Monsanto Co New Mar 2008 125.00 Put Sell to Open	-6.0000	55408606	USD	12.130000	0.00	-7,258.39
+MONCA: 02/14/2008	02/15/2008	Monsanto Co New Mar 2008 105.00 Call Sell to Open	-6.0000	55408602	USD	14.550000	0.00	-8,710.38
+PMJCA: 02/14/2008	02/15/2008	Petroleo Brasileiro Sa Petrobr Sponsored Adr Mar 2008 105. Sell to Open	-6.0000	55404128	USD	13.770000	0.00	-8,242.38
+PMJOE: 02/14/2008	02/15/2008	Petroleo Brasileiro Sa Petrobr Sponsored Adr Mar 2008 125. Sell to Open	-6.0000	55404136	USD	12.770000	0.00	-7,642.39

Transaction History

| Transactions | Check Summary | Deposit Summary | Categories | Reports |

Date	Type	Description	Amount
03/07/08	Sold Short	5 MA MAR-08 $185 CALLS (MALCQ) @ $8.65	4,317.21
02/25/08	Sold Short	4 FWLT MAR-08 $80 PUTS (UFGOP) @ $5.05	2,012.98
02/25/08	Sold Short	2 FWLT MAR-08 $80 PUTS (UFGOP) @ $5.07	1,012.48
02/25/08	Sold Short	2 FWLT MAR-08 $80 PUTS (UFGOP) @ $5.12	1,022.48
02/25/08	Sold Short	2 FWLT MAR-08 $80 PUTS (UFGOP) @ $5.08	1,014.48
02/20/08	Sold Short	5 FLS MAR-08 $105 PUTS (FLSOA) @ $7.72	3,852.21
02/15/08	Sold Short	10 FWLT MAR-08 $75 PUTS (UFBOO) @ $7.90	7,888.42
02/15/08	Sold Short	10 FWLT MAR-08 $65 CALLS (UFBCM) @ $8.35	8,338.41
02/13/08	Sold Short	7 PBR MAR-08 $105 CALLS (PMJCA) @ $14.90	10,420.64
02/13/08	Sold Short	7 MON MAR-08 $105 CALLS (MONCA) @ $13.23	9,251.65
02/13/08	Sold Short	7 PBR MAR-08 $125 PUTS (PMJOE) @ $12.34	8,628.66
02/13/08	Sold Short	7 MON MAR-08 $125 PUTS (MFPOE) @ $13.76	9,622.65
02/13/08	Sold Short	5 MA MAR-08 $220 PUTS (MALOD) @ $20.47	10,227.14
02/13/08	Sold Short	5 MA MAR-08 $190 CALLS (MALCR) @ $21.15	10,567.14
01/04/08	Sold Short	2 MA JAN-08 $200 CALLS (MALAT) @ $8.60	1,714.48
01/04/08	Sold Short	2 AAPL JAN-08 $190 CALLS (APVAR) @ $7.95	1,584.48
01/03/08	Sold Short	1 MOS JAN-08 $100 CALL (MOSAT) @ $4.91	490.24
01/03/08	Sold Short	1 MOS JAN-08 $100 CALL (MOSAT) @ $4.88	483.25
01/02/08	Sold Short	1 FWLT JAN-08 $155 CALL (UFGAK) @ $7.60	755.24
01/02/08	Sold Short	1 FWLT JAN-08 $155 CALL (UFGAK) @ $7.90	789.23
12/21/07	Sold Short	1 FSLR JAN-08 $260 CALL (HJQAY) @ $21.41	2,136.22
12/21/07	Sold Short	3 MON JAN-08 $115 CALLS (MFPAC) @ $3.95	1,178.74
12/21/07	Sold Short	2 FWLT JAN-08 $165 CALLS (UFGAM) @ $6.39	1,272.49
12/21/07	Sold Short	2 RIG JAN-08 $145 CALLS (RIGAI) @ $3.87	768.49
12/21/07	Sold Short	2 AAPL JAN-08 $195 CALLS (APVAS) @ $8.51	1,696.48
12/21/07	Sold Short	2 MA JAN-08 $210 CALLS (MALAB) @ $10.69	2,132.47

Transaction History

Alerts | ⟫ Transfer Money | Bill Pay | ? Help

| Transactions | Check Summary | Deposit Summary | Categories | Reports |

Date	Type	Description	Amount
03/07/08	Sold Short	3 MON MAR-08 $105 CALLS (MONCA) @ $6.72	2,009.73
03/07/08	Sold Short	2 MA MAR-08 $185 CALLS (MALCQ) @ $9.50	1,894.48
02/26/08	Sold Short	3 RIG MAR-08 $145 PUTS (RIGOI) @ $5.16	1,541.74
02/26/08	Sold Short	3 MON MAR-08 $125 PUTS (MFPOE) @ $6.42	1,919.73
02/22/08	Sold Short	3 RIG MAR-08 $135 CALLS (RIGCG) @ $7.06	2,111.73
02/22/08	Sold Short	3 MON MAR-08 $110 CALLS (MONCB) @ $8.67	2,594.73
02/22/08	Sold Short	3 MON MAR-08 $120 PUTS (MFPOD) @ $8.18	2,447.73
02/22/08	Sold Short	3 PBR MAR-08 $125 PUTS (PMJOE) @ $11.16	3,341.72
02/22/08	Sold Short	5 FWLT MAR-08 $77.50 PUTS (UFGOW) @ $6.53	3,257.22
02/22/08	Sold Short	5 FWLT MAR-08 $70 CALLS (UFBCN) @ $6.73	3,357.22
02/22/08	Sold Short	3 PBR MAR-08 $110 CALLS (PMJCB) @ $11.16	3,341.72
02/22/08	Sold Short	2 MA MAR-08 $210 PUTS (MALOB) @ $15.25	3,044.47
02/22/08	Sold Short	2 MA MAR-08 $190 CALLS (MALCR) @ $14.93	2,980.47
02/22/08	Sold Short	3 RIG MAR-08 $140 PUTS (RIGOH) @ $6.03	1,802.74
12/21/07	Sold Short	1 FSLR JAN-08 $260 CALL (HJQAY) @ $21.44	2,139.22
12/21/07	Sold Short	3 MON JAN-08 $115 CALLS (MFPAC) @ $3.96	1,181.74
12/21/07	Sold Short	2 FWLT JAN-08 $165 CALLS (UFGAM) @ $6.45	1,284.49
12/21/07	Sold Short	2 RIG JAN-08 $145 CALLS (RIGAI) @ $3.97	788.49
12/21/07	Sold Short	2 AAPL JAN-08 $195 CALLS (APVAS) @ $8.46	1,686.48
12/21/07	Sold Short	2 MA JAN-08 $210 CALLS (MALAB) @ $10.58	2,110.47
12/24/07	Sold Short	1 MON JAN-08 $115 CALL (MFPAC) @ $5.43	538.25
12/24/07	Sold Short	4 JEC JAN-08 $100 CALLS (JECAT) @ $2.90	1,152.99
12/24/07	Sold Short	1 FWLT JAN-08 $165 CALL (UFGAM) @ $7.76	771.24
12/24/07	Sold Short	1 RIG JAN-08 $145 CALL (RIGAI) @ $5.40	535.25
12/24/07	Sold Short	1 AAPL JAN-08 $200 CALL (APVAT) @ $9.50	945.24
12/24/07	Sold Short	3 MOS JAN-08 $95 CALLS (MOSAS) @ $5.56	1,661.73
12/24/07	Sold Short	1 MA JAN-08 $210 CALL (MALAB) @ $12.03	1,198.24
01/02/08	Sold Short	2 AAPL JAN-08 $195 CALLS (APVAS) @ $8.57	1,708.48
01/02/08	Sold Short	3 FWLT JAN-08 $155 CALLS (UFGAK) @ $7.90	2,363.72
12/31/07	Sold Short	6 NOV JAN-08 $75 CALLS (NOVAO) @ $2.30	1,371.48
12/31/07	Sold Short	2 MON JAN-08 $115 CALLS (MFPAC) @ $4.10	810.49
12/31/07	Sold Short	1 RIG JAN-08 $145 CALL (RIGAI) @ $3.60	351.25
12/31/07	Sold Short	1 AAPL JAN-08 $200 CALL (APVAT) @ $9.00	891.24
12/31/07	Sold Short	1 MOS JAN-08 $95 CALL (MOSAS) @ $5.33	528.25
12/31/07	Sold Short	1 MOS JAN-08 $95 CALL (MOSAS) @ $5.50	541.25
12/31/07	Sold Short	1 MA JAN-08 $210 CALL (MALAB) @ $9.80	971.24
01/02/08	Sold Short	4 JEC JAN-08 $95 CALLS (JECAS) @ $4.10	1,632.98
01/02/08	Sold Short	6 MON JAN-08 $110 CALLS (MONAB) @ $6.40	3,831.45
01/02/08	Sold Short	3 SPWR JAN-08 $130 CALLS (QSUAW) @ $7.72	2,309.72
01/03/08	Sold Short	2 JEC JAN-08 $95 CALLS (JECAS) @ $5.60	1,110.49
01/03/08	Sold Short	1 FWLT JAN-08 $160 CALL (UFGAL) @ $9.00	891.24
01/04/08	Sold Short	4 MA JAN-08 $200 CALLS (MALAT) @ $8.77	3,500.95
01/04/08	Sold Short	4 AAPL JAN-08 $190 CALLS (APVAR) @ $7.90	3,152.96

Daily Account Activity

Trade Date	Settlement Date	Activity	Quantity	Trade #	Currency	Price	Subtracted	Added
		PURCHASES AND SALES						
USD - US DOLLAR								
+AXVAR:		Intuitive Surgical Inc New Jan 2008 350.00 Call						
12/11/2007	12/12/2007	Sell to Open	-20.0000	51544089	USD	22.030000	0.00	-44,022.28
+FCXAB:		Freeport-Mcmoran Copper & Gold Jan 2008 110.00 Call						
12/07/2007	12/10/2007	Sell to Open	-20.0000	51427969	USD	6.440000	0.00	-12,842.76
+SGRAN:		Shaw Group Inc Jan 2008 70.00 Call						
12/07/2007	12/10/2007	Sell to Open	-18.0000	51426978	USD	3.850000	0.00	-6,895.35
12/07/2007	12/10/2007	Sell to Open	-2.0000	51450072	USD	3.840000	0.00	-753.47
+UFBAZ:		Foster Wheeler Ltd Shs New Jan 2008 150.00 Call						
11/30/2007	12/03/2007	Sell to Open	-6.0000	51070072	USD	10.450000	0.00	-6,250.38
11/30/2007	12/03/2007	Sell to Open	-14.0000	51070074	USD	10.440000	0.00	-14,586.24
+APVAR:		Apple Inc Jan 2008 190.00 Call						
11/30/2007	12/03/2007	Sell to Open	-20.0000	51044810	USD	12.280000	0.00	-24,522.58
+GOQAT:		Google Inc Cl A Jan 2008 700.00 Call						
11/30/2007	12/03/2007	Sell to Open	-10.0000	51044814	USD	44.120000	0.00	-44,094.80
+MALAT:		Mastercard Inc Cl A Jan 2008 200.00 Call						
11/30/2007	12/03/2007	Sell to Open	-10.0000	51044806	USD	16.400000	0.00	-16,375.22
+RIGAH:		Transocean Inc New Shs Jan 2008 140.00 Call						
11/30/2007	12/03/2007	Sell to Open	-20.0000	51083685	USD	7.110000	0.00	-14,182.74
+RULAE:		Research In Motion Ltd Jan 2008 125.00 Call						
11/30/2007	12/03/2007	Sell to Open	-10.0000	51044820	USD	11.150000	0.00	-11,125.30
+AXVAR:		Intuitive Surgical Inc New Jan 2008 350.00 Call						
12/11/2007	12/12/2007	Sell to Open	-18.0000	51544283	USD	22.030000	0.00	-39,606.35
12/11/2007	12/12/2007	Sell to Open	-2.0000	51544287	USD	22.330000	0.00	-4,442.92
+FCXAB:		Freeport-Mcmoran Copper & Gold Jan 2008 110.00 Call						
12/07/2007	12/10/2007	Sell to Open	-20.0000	51428015	USD	6.440000	0.00	-12,829.76
+SGRAN:		Shaw Group Inc Jan 2008 70.00 Call						
12/07/2007	12/10/2007	Sell to Open	-20.0000	51426984	USD	3.850000	0.00	-7,649.84
+RULAE:		Research In Motion Ltd Jan 2008 125.00 Call						
11/30/2007	12/03/2007	Sell to Open	-10.0000	51023844	USD	11.360000	0.00	-11,324.80
+UFBAZ:		Foster Wheeler Ltd Shs New Jan 2008 150.00 Call						
11/30/2007	12/03/2007	Sell to Open	-9.0000	51062214	USD	10.450000	0.00	-9,371.33
11/30/2007	12/03/2007	Sell to Open	-11.0000	51062222	USD	10.440000	0.00	-11,447.29
+RIGAH:		Transocean Inc New Shs Jan 2008 140.00 Call						
11/30/2007	12/03/2007	Sell to Open	-20.0000	51045204	USD	7.110000	0.00	-14,169.74
+MALAT:		Mastercard Inc Cl A Jan 2008 200.00 Call						
11/30/2007	12/03/2007	Sell to Open	-10.0000	51023828	USD	16.410000	0.00	-16,374.72
+GOQAT:		Google Inc Cl A Jan 2008 700.00 Call						
11/30/2007	12/03/2007	Sell to Open	-10.0000	51071109	USD	43.070000	0.00	-43,034.32
+APVAR:		Apple Inc Jan 2008 190.00 Call						
11/30/2007	12/03/2007	Sell to Open	-20.0000	51023838	USD	12.250000	0.00	-24,449.58
+APVAT:		Apple Inc Jan 2008 200.00 Call						
12/26/2007	12/27/2007	Sell to Open	-3.0000	52317003	USD	9.860000	0.00	-2,933.44
+HJQCX:		First Solar Inc Mar 2008 250.00 Call						
12/28/2007	12/31/2007	Sell to Open	-3.0000	52430957	USD	47.500000	0.00	-14,225.27
+MALAB:		Mastercard Inc Cl A Jan 2008 210.00 Call						
12/26/2007	12/27/2007	Sell to Open	-2.0000	52302883	USD	9.880000	0.00	-1,952.95
12/26/2007	12/27/2007	Sell to Open	-1.0000	52302889	USD	9.770000	0.00	-955.47
+MONDA:		Monsanto Co New Apr 2008 105.00 Call						
12/28/2007	12/31/2007	Sell to Open	-3.0000	52430955	USD	15.600000	0.00	-4,655.41
+MOSCR:		Mosaic Co Mar 2008 90.00 Call						
12/28/2007	12/31/2007	Sell to Open	-3.0000	52430925	USD	14.540000	0.00	-4,337.42
+QSUAY:		Sunpower Corp Cl A Jan 2008 140.00 Call						
12/26/2007	12/27/2007	Sell to Open	-3.0000	52316999	USD	9.820000	0.00	-2,921.44

Daily Account Activity

Trade Date	Settlement Date	Activity	Quantity	Trade #	Currency	Price	Subtracted	Added

PURCHASES AND SALES

USD - US DOLLAR

Trade Date	Settlement Date	Activity	Quantity	Trade #	Currency	Price	Subtracted	Added
+APVAT:		Apple Inc Jan 2008 200.00 Call						
12/26/2007	12/27/2007	Sell to Open	-10.0000	52317757	USD	9.860000	0.00	-9,824.82
+HJQCX:		First Solar Inc Mar 2008 250.00 Call						
12/28/2007	12/31/2007	Sell to Open	-5.0000	52430941	USD	47.500000	0.00	-23,722.12
+JECAT:		Jacobs Engr Group Inc Del Jan 2008 100.00 Call						
12/28/2007	12/31/2007	Sell to Open	-10.0000	52418100	USD	2.900000	0.00	-2,864.93
+MALAB:		Mastercard Inc Cl A Jan 2008 210.00 Call						
12/26/2007	12/27/2007	Sell to Open	-10.0000	52302879	USD	9.770000	0.00	-9,734.83
+MONDA:		Monsanto Co New Apr 2008 105.00 Call						
12/28/2007	12/31/2007	Sell to Open	-5.0000	52430961	USD	15.600000	0.00	-7,772.37
+MOSAS:		Mosaic Co Jan 2008 95.00 Call						
12/26/2007	12/27/2007	Sell to Open	-10.0000	52318703	USD	5.670000	0.00	-5,634.89
+MOSCR:		Mosaic Co Mar 2008 90.00 Call						
12/28/2007	12/31/2007	Sell to Open	-5.0000	52430927	USD	14.540000	0.00	-7,242.37
+QSUAY:		Sunpower Corp Cl A Jan 2008 140.00 Call						
12/26/2007	12/27/2007	Sell to Open	-10.0000	52304275	USD	9.790000	0.00	-9,754.83
+RIGAJ:		Transocean Inc New Shs Jan 2008 150.00 Call						
12/27/2007	12/28/2007	Sell to Open	-2.0000	52359219	USD	4.030000	0.00	-782.97
12/27/2007	12/28/2007	Sell to Open	-8.0000	52359221	USD	4.020000	0.00	-3,183.93
+APVAR:		Apple Inc Jan 2008 190.00 Call						
01/04/2008	01/07/2008	Sell to Open	-10.0000	52651596	USD	8.180000	0.00	-8,144.85
+JECAS:		Jacobs Engr Group Inc Del Jan 2008 95.00 Call						
01/02/2008	01/03/2008	Sell to Open	-10.0000	52516333	USD	4.040000	0.00	-4,004.91
+MALAT:		Mastercard Inc Cl A Jan 2008 200.00 Call						
01/04/2008	01/07/2008	Sell to Open	-10.0000	52655292	USD	8.890000	0.00	-8,854.84
+APVAS:		Apple Inc Jan 2008 195.00 Call						
01/02/2008	01/03/2008	Sell to Open	-10.0000	52553345	USD	8.610000	0.00	-8,574.84
+MALDT:		Mastercard Inc Cl A Apr 2008 200.00 Call						
12/31/2007	01/02/2008	Sell to Open	-1.0000	52484112	USD	31.700000	0.00	-3,148.44
+MONAB:		Monsanto Co New Jan 2008 110.00 Call						
01/02/2008	01/03/2008	Sell to Open	-10.0000	52516341	USD	6.650000	0.00	-6,614.87
+QSUAW:		Sunpower Corp Cl A Jan 2008 130.00 Call						
01/02/2008	01/03/2008	Sell to Open	-10.0000	52516337	USD	7.720000	0.00	-7,684.86
+RIGAH:		Transocean Inc New Shs Jan 2008 140.00 Call						
01/02/2008	01/03/2008	Sell to Open	-10.0000	52516347	USD	7.500000	0.00	-7,464.86
+MALCR:		Mastercard Inc Cl A Mar 2008 190.00 Call						
02/13/2008	02/14/2008	Sell to Open	-1.0000	55334473	USD	21.470000	0.00	-2,125.46
02/13/2008	02/14/2008	Sell to Open	-9.0000	55334479	USD	21.550000	0.00	-19,361.26
+MALOD:		Mastercard Inc Cl A Mar 2008 220.00 Put						
02/14/2008	02/15/2008	Sell to Open	-10.0000	55402972	USD	22.900000	0.00	-22,864.72
+MFPOE:		Monsanto Co New Mar 2008 125.00 Put						
02/13/2008	02/14/2008	Sell to Open	-10.0000	55319381	USD	13.790000	0.00	-13,754.82
+MONCA:		Monsanto Co New Mar 2008 105.00 Call						
02/13/2008	02/14/2008	Sell to Open	-10.0000	55318919	USD	12.850000	0.00	-12,814.83
+PMJCA:		Petroleo Brasileiro Sa Petrobr Sponsored Adr Mar 2008 105.						
02/13/2008	02/14/2008	Sell to Open	-10.0000	55323803	USD	14.820000	0.00	-14,784.81
+PMJOE:		Petroleo Brasileiro Sa Petrobr Sponsored Adr Mar 2008 125.						
02/13/2008	02/14/2008	Sell to Open	-10.0000	55320599	USD	12.500000	0.00	-12,464.84
+UFBCM:		Foster Wheeler Ltd Shs New Mar 2008 65.00 Call						
02/15/2008	02/19/2008	Sell to Open	-10.0000	55468446	USD	8.310000	0.00	-8,274.88
+UFBOO:		Foster Wheeler Ltd Shs New Mar 2008 75.00 Put						
02/15/2008	02/19/2008	Sell to Open	-8.0000	55468448	USD	7.730000	0.00	-6,151.91
02/15/2008	02/19/2008	Sell to Open	-2.0000	55468454	USD	8.050000	0.00	-1,586.97

Daily Account Activity

Trade Date	Settlement Date	Activity	Quantity	Trade #	Currency	Price	Subtracted	Added
		PURCHASES AND SALES						
USD - US DOLLAR								
+DEJH:		Deere & Co Oct 2007 140.00 Call						
09/06/2007	09/07/2007	Sell to Open	-10.0000	46611210	USD	4.900000	0.00	-4,881.90
09/11/2007	09/12/2007	Sell to Open	-10.0000	46786169	USD	5.490000	0.00	-5,471.39
+FCXJS:		Freeport-Mcmoran Copper & Gold Oct 2007 95.00 Call						
09/05/2007	09/06/2007	Sell to Open	-9.0000	46553837	USD	3.490000	0.00	-3,123.93
09/05/2007	09/06/2007	Sell to Open	-1.0000	46553839	USD	3.480000	0.00	-346.98
09/11/2007	09/12/2007	Sell to Open	-10.0000	46786439	USD	3.600000	0.00	-3,581.42
+FLRJG:		Fluor Corp New Oct 2007 135.00 Call						
09/05/2007	09/06/2007	Sell to Open	-10.0000	46553055	USD	5.030000	0.00	-5,011.90
09/11/2007	09/12/2007	Sell to Open	-10.0000	46786257	USD	5.000000	0.00	-4,981.40
+NOVJG:		National Oilwell Varco Inc Oct 2007 135.00 Call						
09/05/2007	09/06/2007	Sell to Open	-10.0000	46553053	USD	6.250000	0.00	-6,231.88
09/11/2007	09/12/2007	Sell to Open	-10.0000	46786265	USD	6.660000	0.00	-6,641.37
+RFYJX:		Research In Motion Ltd Oct 2007 85.00 Call						
09/06/2007	09/07/2007	Sell to Open	-10.0000	46609282	USD	6.150000	0.00	-6,131.88
09/11/2007	09/12/2007	Sell to Open	-10.0000	46786249	USD	5.550000	0.00	-5,531.39
+RZJJB:		Garmin Ltd Ord Oct 2007 110.00 Call						
09/06/2007	09/07/2007	Sell to Open	-10.0000	46611398	USD	6.530000	0.00	-6,511.88
09/11/2007	09/12/2007	Sell to Open	-10.0000	46785939	USD	5.310000	0.00	-5,291.39
+APVJH:		Apple Inc Oct 2007 140.00 Call						
09/14/2007	09/17/2007	Sell to Open	-8.0000	46973242	USD	7.000000	0.00	-5,567.89
+FCXJA:		Freeport-Mcmoran Copper & Gold Oct 2007 105.00 Call						
09/26/2007	09/27/2007	Sell to Open	-2.0000	47476699	USD	5.400000	0.00	-1,056.97
09/26/2007	09/27/2007	Sell to Open	-5.0000	47476701	USD	5.400000	0.00	-2,692.44
09/26/2007	09/27/2007	Sell to Open	-5.0000	47476703	USD	5.400000	0.00	-2,692.44
+FCXJT:		Freeport-Mcmoran Copper & Gold Oct 2007 100.00 Call						
09/17/2007	09/18/2007	Sell to Open	-8.0000	47018515	USD	5.500000	0.00	-4,367.91
+FLRJG:		Fluor Corp New Oct 2007 135.00 Call						
09/14/2007	09/17/2007	Sell to Open	-8.0000	46972558	USD	6.300000	0.00	-5,007.90
+NOVJG:		National Oilwell Varco Inc Oct 2007 135.00 Call						
09/14/2007	09/17/2007	Sell to Open	-8.0000	46974904	USD	6.700000	0.00	-5,327.89
+NOVJY:		National Oilwell Varco Inc Oct 2007 57.50 Call						
09/26/2007	09/27/2007	Sell to Open	-3.0000	47476705	USD	5.700000	0.00	-1,685.46
09/26/2007	09/27/2007	Sell to Open	-9.0000	47476707	USD	5.500000	0.00	-4,936.40

Transaction History

Transactions | Check Summary | Deposit Summary | Categories | Reports

Date	Type	Description	Amount
09/17/07	Sold Short	9 SLB OCT-07 $100 CALLS (SDBJT) @ $5.50	4,935.18
09/17/07	Sold Short	12 FCX OCT-07 $100 CALLS (FCXJT) @ $5.30	6,342.91
09/14/07	Sold Short	9 RIMM OCT-07 $90 CALLS (RFYJR) @ $5.30	4,755.18
09/14/07	Sold Short	6 PCP OCT-07 $135 CALLS (PCPJG) @ $5.50	3,287.45
09/14/07	Sold Short	3 PCP OCT-07 $135 CALLS (PCPJG) @ $5.50	1,647.72
09/14/07	Sold Short	9 NOV OCT-07 $135 CALLS (NOVJG) @ $7.00	6,285.16
09/14/07	Sold Short	9 DE OCT-07 $140 CALLS (DEJH) @ $4.90	4,395.19
09/14/07	Sold Short	15 CAM OCT-07 $90 CALLS (CAMJR) @ $3.50	5,230.67
09/14/07	Sold Short	9 AAPL OCT-07 $140 CALLS (APVJH) @ $7.00	6,285.16
09/28/07	Sold Short	12 RIG OCT-07 $110 CALLS (RIGJB) @ $7.00	8,382.88
09/26/07	Sold Short	12 RIMM OCT-07 $100 CALLS (RULJT) @ $7.20	8,622.87
09/26/07	Sold Short	3 SLB OCT-07 $100 CALLS (SDBJT) @ $7.00	2,089.72
09/26/07	Sold Short	3 NOV OCT-07 $135 CALLS (NOVJG) @ $11.50	3,439.70
09/26/07	Sold Short	4 FCX OCT-07 $100 CALLS (FCXJT) @ $9.00	3,588.95
09/26/07	Sold Short	3 DE OCT-07 $140 CALLS (DEJH) @ $6.50	1,939.73
09/26/07	Sold Short	5 CAM OCT-07 $90 CALLS (CAMJR) @ $5.00	2,488.22
09/26/07	Sold Short	12 FLR OCT-07 $140 CALLS (FLRJH) @ $7.00	8,382.88
09/26/07	Sold Short	12 GRMN OCT-07 $120 CALLS (RZJJD) @ $5.40	6,462.91
09/26/07	Sold Short	9 AAPL OCT-07 $155 CALLS (APVJK) @ $5.00	4,485.19
09/26/07	Sold Short	3 AAPL OCT-07 $155 CALLS (APVJK) @ $5.40	1,609.73
09/26/07	Sold Short	2 AAPL OCT-07 $155 CALLS (APVJK) @ $5.20	1,030.49

Transaction History

Transactions | Check Summary | Deposit Summary | Categories | Reports

Date	Type	Description	Amount
09/17/07	Sold Short	6 SLB OCT-07 $100 CALLS (SDBJT) @ $5.50	3,287.45
09/17/07	Sold Short	6 FCX OCT-07 $100 CALLS (FCXJT) @ $5.50	3,287.45
09/14/07	Sold Short	6 RIMM OCT-07 $90 CALLS (RFYJR) @ $5.30	3,167.46
09/14/07	Sold Short	4 PCP OCT-07 $135 CALLS (PCPJG) @ $5.50	2,188.97
09/14/07	Sold Short	6 NOV OCT-07 $135 CALLS (NOVJG) @ $7.00	4,187.44
09/14/07	Sold Short	6 DE OCT-07 $140 CALLS (DEJH) @ $4.90	2,927.46
09/14/07	Sold Short	8 CAM OCT-07 $90 CALLS (CAMJR) @ $3.50	2,785.96
09/14/07	Sold Short	6 GRMN OCT-07 $110 CALLS (RZJJB) @ $4.80	2,867.46
09/14/07	Sold Short	4 AAPL OCT-07 $140 CALLS (APVJH) @ $6.90	2,748.96
09/18/07	Sold Short	5 MHS OCT-07 $90 CALLS (MHSJR) @ $3.00	1,488.23
09/28/07	Sold Short	9 RIG OCT-07 $110 CALLS (RIGJB) @ $7.00	6,285.16
09/28/07	Sold Short	6 GRMN OCT-07 $120 CALLS (RZJJD) @ $7.00	4,187.44
09/27/07	Sold Short	11 CAM OCT-07 $90 CALLS (CAMJR) @ $7.00	7,683.64
09/26/07	Sold Short	9 RIMM OCT-07 $100 CALLS (RULJT) @ $7.20	6,465.16
09/26/07	Sold Short	3 NOV OCT-07 $135 CALLS (NOVJG) @ $11.50	3,439.70
09/26/07	Sold Short	3 FCX OCT-07 $100 CALLS (FCXJT) @ $9.00	2,689.71
09/26/07	Sold Short	9 DE OCT-07 $140 CALLS (DEJH) @ $6.50	5,835.17
09/26/07	Sold Short	6 FLR OCT-07 $140 CALLS (FLRJH) @ $7.00	4,187.44

Daily Account Activity

Trade Date	Settlement Date	Activity	Quantity	Trade #	Currency	Price	Subtracted	Added
			PURCHASES AND SALES					
USD - US DOLLAR								
+APVJH:		Apple Inc Oct 2007 140.00 Call						
08/31/2007	09/04/2007	Sell to Open	-10.0000	46402637	USD	8.260000	0.00	-8,242.35
08/31/2007	09/04/2007	Sell to Open	-5.0000	46415126	USD	8.270000	0.00	-4,126.17
+AXVJF:		Intuitive Surgical Inc New Oct 2007 230.00 Call						
09/13/2007	09/14/2007	Sell to Open	-15.0000	46916986	USD	13.150000	0.00	-19,693.66
+MDRJT:		Mcdermott Intl Inc Oct 2007 100.00 Call						
08/31/2007	09/04/2007	Sell to Open	-15.0000	46402305	USD	4.140000	0.00	-6,183.62
+SDBJT:		Schlumberger Ltd Oct 2007 100.00 Call						
08/31/2007	09/04/2007	Sell to Open	-15.0000	46402641	USD	3.600000	0.00	-5,373.63
+ZQNJT:		Amazon Com Inc Oct 2007 95.00 Call						
09/21/2007	09/24/2007	Sell to Open	-15.0000	47298362	USD	2.330000	0.00	-3,463.91
+CAMJP:		Cameron International Corp Oct 2007 80.00 Call						
08/28/2007	08/29/2007	Sell to Open	-12.0000	46168454	USD	2.500000	0.00	-2,982.42
08/28/2007	08/29/2007	Sell to Open	-3.0000	46168470	USD	2.520000	0.00	-738.47
+DEJG:		Deere & Co Oct 2007 135.00 Call						
08/28/2007	08/29/2007	Sell to Open	-15.0000	46162990	USD	3.950000	0.00	-5,889.87
+FCXJQ:		Freeport-Mcmoran Copper & Gold Oct 2007 85.00 Call						
08/28/2007	08/29/2007	Sell to Open	-12.0000	46199225	USD	5.000000	0.00	-5,982.37
08/28/2007	08/29/2007	Sell to Open	-3.0000	46199253	USD	4.930000	0.00	-1,461.46
+FLRJE:		Fluor Corp New Oct 2007 125.00 Call						
08/28/2007	08/29/2007	Sell to Open	-6.0000	46169926	USD	5.570000	0.00	-3,330.24
08/28/2007	08/29/2007	Sell to Open	-6.0000	46169948	USD	5.530000	0.00	-3,306.26
08/28/2007	08/29/2007	Sell to Open	-3.0000	46169974	USD	5.340000	0.00	-1,590.30
+MHSJR:		Medco Health Solutions Inc Oct 2007 90.00 Call						
08/28/2007	08/29/2007	Sell to Open	-15.0000	46165556	USD	2.140000	0.00	-3,174.92
+NOVBD:		National Oilwell Varco Inc Feb 2008 120.00 Call						
08/23/2007	08/24/2007	Sell to Open	-2.0000	45935672	USD	12.050000	0.00	-2,399.95
+NOVJE:		National Oilwell Varco Inc Oct 2007 125.00 Call						
08/28/2007	08/29/2007	Sell to Open	-15.0000	46161566	USD	5.670000	0.00	-8,469.83
+PCPJG:		Precision Castparts Corp Oct 2007 135.00 Call						
08/28/2007	08/29/2007	Sell to Open	-15.0000	46166670	USD	7.350000	0.00	-10,989.80
+RFYJP:		Research In Motion Ltd Oct 2007 80.00 Call						
08/28/2007	08/29/2007	Sell to Open	-15.0000	46166674	USD	5.700000	0.00	-8,514.83
+RIGJA:		Transocean Inc Ord Oct 2007 105.00 Call						
08/28/2007	08/29/2007	Sell to Open	-12.0000	46183551	USD	3.280000	0.00	-3,918.40
08/28/2007	08/29/2007	Sell to Open	-3.0000	46183555	USD	3.610000	0.00	-1,065.47
+RZJJA:		Garmin Ltd Ord Oct 2007 105.00 Call						
08/28/2007	08/29/2007	Sell to Open	-10.0000	46183525	USD	4.680000	0.00	-4,662.40
08/28/2007	08/29/2007	Sell to Open	-5.0000	46183529	USD	4.770000	0.00	-2,367.45
+FCXJA:		Freeport-Mcmoran Copper & Gold Oct 2007 105.00 Call						
09/26/2007	09/27/2007	Sell to Open	-11.0000	47475835	USD	5.300000	0.00	-5,793.38
09/26/2007	09/27/2007	Sell to Open	-4.0000	47475837	USD	5.300000	0.00	-2,113.95
+FCXJT:		Freeport-Mcmoran Copper & Gold Oct 2007 100.00 Call						
09/17/2007	09/18/2007	Sell to Open	-12.0000	47016591	USD	5.500000	0.00	-6,561.86
+NOVJY:		National Oilwell Varco Inc Oct 2007 57.50 Call						
09/26/2007	09/27/2007	Sell to Open	-3.0000	47475823	USD	5.600000	0.00	-1,655.46
09/26/2007	09/27/2007	Sell to Open	-12.0000	47475825	USD	5.600000	0.00	-6,701.86
+PCPJG:		Precision Castparts Corp Oct 2007 135.00 Call						
09/14/2007	09/17/2007	Sell to Open	-10.0000	46992775	USD	5.400000	0.00	-5,364.89
09/14/2007	09/17/2007	Sell to Open	-1.0000	46992777	USD	5.400000	0.00	-538.48
09/14/2007	09/17/2007	Sell to Open	-1.0000	46992779	USD	5.400000	0.00	-538.48
+RFYJR:		Research In Motion Ltd Oct 2007 90.00 Call						
09/14/2007	09/17/2007	Sell to Open	-12.0000	46993167	USD	5.100000	0.00	-6,081.87
+RULJT:		Research In Motion Ltd Oct 2007 100.00 Call						
09/26/2007	09/27/2007	Sell to Open	-1.0000	47474425	USD	7.400000	0.00	-718.47
09/26/2007	09/27/2007	Sell to Open	-5.0000	47475805	USD	7.400000	0.00	-3,692.43
09/26/2007	09/27/2007	Sell to Open	-2.0000	47475807	USD	7.400000	0.00	-1,476.96
09/26/2007	09/27/2007	Sell to Open	-7.0000	47475829	USD	7.300000	0.00	-5,099.40

Transaction History

| Transactions | Check Summary | Deposit Summary | Categories | Reports |

Date	Type	Description	Amount
11/13/07	Sold Short	9 RIMM JAN-08 $110 CALLS (RULAB) @ $13.70	12,315.07
11/13/07	Sold Short	2 GOOG JAN-08 $650 CALLS (GOOAJ) @ $45.50	9,090.37
11/13/07	Sold Short	9 FCX JAN-08 $100 CALLS (FCXAT) @ $8.90	7,995.13
11/13/07	Sold Short	6 AAPL JAN-08 $170 CALLS (APVAN) @ $15.40	9,227.36
10/22/07	Sold Short	6 AAPL NOV-07 $175 CALLS (APVKO) @ $9.00	5,387.42
09/28/07	Sold Short	9 RIG OCT-07 $110 CALLS (RIGJB) @ $7.00	6,285.16
09/28/07	Sold Short	6 GRMN OCT-07 $120 CALLS (RZJJD) @ $7.00	4,187.44
09/27/07	Sold Short	11 CAM OCT-07 $90 CALLS (CAMJR) @ $7.00	7,683.64
09/26/07	Sold Short	9 RIMM OCT-07 $100 CALLS (RULJT) @ $7.20	6,465.16
09/26/07	Sold Short	3 NOV OCT-07 $135 CALLS (NOVJG) @ $11.50	3,439.70
09/26/07	Sold Short	3 FCX OCT-07 $100 CALLS (FCXJT) @ $9.00	2,689.71
09/26/07	Sold Short	9 DE OCT-07 $140 CALLS (DEJH) @ $6.50	5,835.17
09/26/07	Sold Short	6 FLR OCT-07 $140 CALLS (FLRJH) @ $7.00	4,187.44
12/07/07	Sold Short	30 SGR JAN-08 $70 CALLS (SGRAN) @ $3.85	11,523.33
12/07/07	Sold Short	21 FCX JAN-08 $110 CALLS (FCXAB) @ $6.43	13,483.05
12/07/07	Sold Short	9 FCX JAN-08 $110 CALLS (FCXAB) @ $6.44	5,789.16
11/30/07	Sold Short	30 RIG JAN-08 $140 CALLS (RIGAH) @ $6.57	19,683.20
11/30/07	Sold Short	22 MA JAN-08 $200 CALLS (MALAT) @ $15.89	34,936.97
11/30/07	Sold Short	30 AAPL JAN-08 $190 CALLS (APVAR) @ $12.20	36,572.95
11/30/07	Sold Short	30 FWLT JAN-08 $150 CALLS (UFBAZ) @ $10.57	31,683.02
11/29/07	Sold Short	20 GOOG JAN-08 $700 CALLS (GOQAT) @ $33.79	67,563.96
11/29/07	Sold Short	6 GOOG JAN-08 $700 CALLS (GOQAT) @ $33.92	20,343.19
11/29/07	Sold Short	4 GOOG JAN-08 $700 CALLS (GOQAT) @ $33.56	13,420.79
11/29/07	Sold Short	29 ISRG JAN-08 $330 CALLS (AXVAC) @ $23.42	67,895.21
11/29/07	Sold Short	1 ISRG JAN-08 $330 CALL (AXVAC) @ $23.68	2,363.22
11/29/07	Sold Short	8 MA JAN-08 $200 CALLS (MALAT) @ $12.95	10,349.85

Transaction History

Alerts | Transfer Money | Bill Pay | Help

Transactions	Check Summary	Deposit Summary	Categories	Reports

Date	Type	Description	Amount
06/14/07	Sold Short	10 HAL JUL-07 $35 CALLS (HALGG) @ $2.10	2,084.47
05/18/07	Sold Short	10 CVX JUN-07 $80 CALLS (CVXFP) @ $3.30	3,284.45
05/18/07	Sold Short	10 GS JUN-07 $230 CALLS (GPYFF) @ $7.00	6,988.40
05/18/07	Sold Short	10 FWLT JUN-07 $95 CALLS (UFBFS) @ $4.03	4,018.44
05/18/07	Sold Short	10 TSO JUN-07 $120 CALLS (TSOFD) @ $4.40	4,388.44
05/18/07	Sold Short	10 NOV JUN-07 $95 CALLS (NOVFS) @ $2.53	2,518.47
05/14/07	Sold Short	10 CAT JUN-07 $75 CALLS (CATFO) @ $3.00	2,984.46
05/10/07	Sold Short	10 MRO JUN-07 $105 CALLS (MROFA) @ $4.70	4,684.43
05/09/07	Sold Short	10 CI JUN-07 $165 CALLS (CIFM) @ $3.08	3,068.46
05/09/07	Sold Short	10 CLF JUN-07 $75 CALLS (CLFFO) @ $3.02	3,008.46
05/09/07	Sold Short	10 RS JUN-07 $65 CALLS (RSFM) @ $2.37	2,358.47
05/09/07	Sold Short	10 MA JUN-07 $140 CALLS (MALFH) @ $5.75	5,738.42
05/08/07	Sold Short	10 PCP JUN-07 $110 CALLS (PCPFB) @ $4.81	4,798.43
05/08/07	Sold Short	10 FWLT MAY-07 $75 CALLS (UFBEO) @ $2.00	1,984.47
05/07/07	Sold Short	10 PCU MAY-07 $85 CALLS (PCUEQ) @ $2.00	1,984.47
05/07/07	Sold Short	10 AAPL JUN-07 $105 CALLS (QAAFA) @ $2.50	2,484.47
05/04/07	Sold Short	10 MDR JUN-07 $60 CALLS (MDRFL) @ $1.81	1,798.48
05/04/07	Sold Short	10 RIG MAY-07 $90 CALLS (RIGER) @ $3.00	2,984.46
05/02/07	Sold Short	10 OIH JUN-07 $160 CALLS (OIHFL) @ $5.95	5,938.41
04/26/07	Sold Short	10 FCX JUN-07 $70 CALLS (FCXFN) @ $3.01	2,998.46
04/26/07	Sold Short	10 RTI MAY-07 $100 CALLS (RTIET) @ $2.60	2,588.47
04/26/07	Sold Short	10 SHLD MAY-07 $190 CALLS (KDUER) @ $4.55	4,538.44
04/26/07	Sold Short	10 NOV MAY-07 $85 CALLS (NOVEQ) @ $2.11	2,098.47
04/26/07	Sold Short	5 GS MAY-07 $230 CALLS (GPYEF) @ $3.00	1,492.23
04/26/07	Sold Short	5 GS MAY-07 $230 CALLS (GPYEF) @ $3.01	1,497.23
04/26/07	Sold Short	10 ATI MAY-07 $115 CALLS (ATIEC) @ $3.88	3,868.45
04/26/07	Sold Short	10 MA MAY-07 $110 CALLS (MAEB) @ $3.40	3,388.45
04/26/07	Sold Short	10 TSO MAY-07 $120 CALLS (TSOED) @ $4.28	4,268.44
12/11/07	Sold Short	20 GOOG JAN-08 $720 CALLS (GOQAD) @ $29.00	57,980.12
12/11/07	Sold Short	12 ISRG JAN-08 $350 CALLS (AXVAR) @ $23.06	27,662.57
12/11/07	Sold Short	8 ISRG JAN-08 $350 CALLS (AXVAR) @ $23.21	18,557.72
12/07/07	Sold Short	23 SGR JAN-08 $70 CALLS (SGRAN) @ $3.88	8,902.62
12/07/07	Sold Short	7 SGR JAN-08 $70 CALLS (SGRAN) @ $3.85	2,689.70
12/07/07	Sold Short	21 FCX JAN-08 $110 CALLS (FCXAB) @ $6.42	13,462.05
12/07/07	Sold Short	9 FCX JAN-08 $110 CALLS (FCXAB) @ $6.43	5,780.16
11/30/07	Sold Short	30 RIG JAN-08 $140 CALLS (RIGAH) @ $6.57	19,683.20
11/30/07	Sold Short	30 AAPL JAN-08 $190 CALLS (APVAR) @ $12.20	36,572.95
11/30/07	Sold Short	25 FWLT JAN-08 $150 CALLS (UFBAZ) @ $10.57	26,405.84
11/30/07	Sold Short	5 FWLT JAN-08 $150 CALLS (UFBAZ) @ $10.58	5,282.17

Transaction History

Transactions	Check Summary	Deposit Summary	Categories	Reports

11/29/07	Sold Short	30 RIMM JAN-08 $125 CALLS (RULAE) @ $10.70	32,073.01
11/29/07	Sold Short	15 GOOG JAN-08 $700 CALLS (GOQAT) @ $34.59	51,868.96
11/29/07	Sold Short	15 GOOG JAN-08 $700 CALLS (GOQAT) @ $33.92	50,867.97
11/29/07	Sold Short	22 ISRG JAN-08 $330 CALLS (AXVAC) @ $23.80	52,338.70
11/29/07	Sold Short	8 ISRG JAN-08 $330 CALLS (AXVAC) @ $23.68	18,937.71
11/29/07	Sold Short	15 MA JAN-08 $200 CALLS (MALAT) @ $12.98	19,458.45
11/29/07	Sold Short	9 MA JAN-08 $200 CALLS (MALAT) @ $13.00	11,689.08
11/29/07	Sold Short	6 MA JAN-08 $200 CALLS (MALAT) @ $12.95	7,765.38
11/13/07	Sold Short	12 RIMM JAN-08 $110 CALLS (RULAB) @ $13.50	16,182.76
11/13/07	Sold Short	2 GOOG JAN-08 $650 CALLS (GOOAJ) @ $45.60	9,110.37
11/13/07	Sold Short	16 FCX JAN-08 $100 CALLS (FCXAT) @ $9.00	14,379.78
11/13/07	Sold Short	10 AAPL JAN-08 $170 CALLS (APVAN) @ $14.50	14,484.28
10/22/07	Sold Short	12 AAPL NOV-07 $175 CALLS (APVKO) @ $9.00	10,782.84
09/28/07	Sold Short	12 RIG OCT-07 $110 CALLS (RIGJB) @ $7.00	8,382.88
09/26/07	Sold Short	12 RIMM OCT-07 $100 CALLS (RULJT) @ $7.20	8,622.87
09/26/07	Sold Short	3 SLB OCT-07 $100 CALLS (SDBJT) @ $7.00	2,089.72
09/26/07	Sold Short	3 NOV OCT-07 $135 CALLS (NOVJG) @ $11.50	3,439.70
09/26/07	Sold Short	4 FCX OCT-07 $100 CALLS (FCXJT) @ $9.00	3,588.95
09/26/07	Sold Short	3 DE OCT-07 $140 CALLS (DEJH) @ $6.50	1,939.73
09/26/07	Sold Short	5 CAM OCT-07 $90 CALLS (CAMJR) @ $5.00	2,488.22
09/26/07	Sold Short	12 FLR OCT-07 $140 CALLS (FLRJH) @ $7.00	8,382.88
09/26/07	Sold Short	12 GRMN OCT-07 $120 CALLS (RZJJD) @ $5.40	6,462.91
09/26/07	Sold Short	9 AAPL OCT-07 $155 CALLS (APVJK) @ $5.00	4,485.19
09/26/07	Sold Short	3 AAPL OCT-07 $155 CALLS (APVJK) @ $5.40	1,609.73
09/26/07	Sold Short	2 AAPL OCT-07 $155 CALLS (APVJK) @ $5.20	1,030.49

Daily Account Activity

Trade Date	Settlement Date	Activity	Quantity	Trade #	Currency	Price	Subtracted	Added
		PURCHASES AND SALES						
USD - US DOLLAR								
+MDRFM:		Mcdermott Intl Inc Jun 2007 65.00 Call						
06/05/2007	06/06/2007	Sell to Open	-2.0000	41505169	USD	15.570000	0.00	-3,099.44
+MROGZ:		Marathon Oil Corp Jul 2007 62.50 Call						
06/04/2007	06/05/2007	Sell to Open	-10.0000	41383827	USD	7.500000	0.00	-7,475.36
+RIGGA:		Transocean Inc Ord Jul 2007 105.00 Call						
06/04/2007	06/05/2007	Sell to Open	-10.0000	41394820	USD	2.450000	0.00	-2,424.94
+TEXGR:		Terex Corp New Jul 2007 90.00 Call						
06/04/2007	06/05/2007	Sell to Open	-10.0000	41392492	USD	2.680000	0.00	-2,654.93
+XTQGZ:		Express Scripts Inc Jul 2007 62.50 Call						
06/04/2007	06/05/2007	Sell to Open	-10.0000	41394816	USD	2.530000	0.00	-2,504.94
+APVJH:		Apple Inc Oct 2007 140.00 Call						
09/14/2007	09/17/2007	Sell to Open	-3.0000	46973476	USD	7.000000	0.00	-2,075.45
09/14/2007	09/17/2007	Sell to Open	-9.0000	46973482	USD	7.000000	0.00	-6,286.38
+FCXJA:		Freeport-Mcmoran Copper & Gold Oct 2007 105.00 Call						
09/26/2007	09/27/2007	Sell to Open	-11.0000	47475835	USD	5.300000	0.00	-5,793.38
09/26/2007	09/27/2007	Sell to Open	-4.0000	47475837	USD	5.300000	0.00	-2,113.95
+FCXJT:		Freeport-Mcmoran Copper & Gold Oct 2007 100.00 Call						
09/17/2007	09/18/2007	Sell to Open	-12.0000	47016591	USD	5.500000	0.00	-6,561.86
+NOVJG:		National Oilwell Varco Inc Oct 2007 135.00 Call						
09/14/2007	09/17/2007	Sell to Open	-12.0000	46974140	USD	6.500000	0.00	-7,761.85
+NOVJY:		National Oilwell Varco Inc Oct 2007 57.50 Call						
09/26/2007	09/27/2007	Sell to Open	-3.0000	47475823	USD	5.600000	0.00	-1,655.46
09/26/2007	09/27/2007	Sell to Open	-12.0000	47475825	USD	5.600000	0.00	-6,701.86
+PCPJG:		Precision Castparts Corp Oct 2007 135.00 Call						
09/14/2007	09/17/2007	Sell to Open	-10.0000	46992775	USD	5.400000	0.00	-5,364.89
09/14/2007	09/17/2007	Sell to Open	-1.0000	46992777	USD	5.400000	0.00	-538.48
+RULJT:		Research In Motion Ltd Oct 2007 100.00 Call						
09/26/2007	09/27/2007	Sell to Open	-1.0000	47474425	USD	7.400000	0.00	-718.47
09/26/2007	09/27/2007	Sell to Open	-5.0000	47475805	USD	7.400000	0.00	-3,692.43
09/26/2007	09/27/2007	Sell to Open	-2.0000	47475807	USD	7.400000	0.00	-1,476.96
09/26/2007	09/27/2007	Sell to Open	-7.0000	47475829	USD	7.300000	0.00	-5,099.40
+RZJJB:		Garmin Ltd Ord Oct 2007 110.00 Call						
09/14/2007	09/17/2007	Sell to Open	-5.0000	46996311	USD	4.800000	0.00	-2,372.45
+APVKO:		Apple Inc Nov 2007 175.00 Call						
10/22/2007	10/23/2007	Sell to Open	-1.0000	48736588	USD	9.000000	0.00	-878.47
10/22/2007	10/23/2007	Sell to Open	-17.0000	48736590	USD	9.000000	0.00	-15,274.22
+FLRKL:		Fluor Corp New Nov 2007 160.00 Call						
10/19/2007	10/22/2007	Sell to Open	-15.0000	48682362	USD	7.100000	0.00	-10,607.30
10/19/2007	10/22/2007	Sell to Open	-3.0000	48682364	USD	7.100000	0.00	-2,125.45
+GOOKH:		Google Inc Cl A Nov 2007 640.00 Call						
10/18/2007	10/19/2007	Sell to Open	-1.0000	48631362	USD	28.800000	0.00	-2,858.44
10/18/2007	10/19/2007	Sell to Open	-1.0000	48631364	USD	28.800000	0.00	-2,878.44
10/18/2007	10/19/2007	Sell to Open	-2.0000	48631366	USD	28.800000	0.00	-5,756.90
10/18/2007	10/19/2007	Sell to Open	-1.0000	48631368	USD	28.800000	0.00	-2,878.44
10/18/2007	10/19/2007	Sell to Open	-5.0000	48632035	USD	28.600000	0.00	-14,292.27
10/18/2007	10/19/2007	Sell to Open	-5.0000	48632037	USD	28.600000	0.00	-14,292.27
10/18/2007	10/19/2007	Sell to Open	-2.0000	48632039	USD	28.600000	0.00	-5,716.90
10/18/2007	10/19/2007	Sell to Open	-1.0000	48632041	USD	28.600000	0.00	-2,858.44
+NOVKV:		National Oilwell Varco Inc Nov 2007 72.50 Call						
10/19/2007	10/22/2007	Sell to Open	-18.0000	48682890	USD	4.200000	0.00	-7,512.84
+APVAN:		Apple Inc Jan 2008 170.00 Call						
11/13/2007	11/14/2007	Sell to Open	-8.0000	50106314	USD	15.100000	0.00	-12,047.79
11/13/2007	11/14/2007	Sell to Open	-8.0000	50106316	USD	15.280000	0.00	-12,191.79
+AXVAA:		Intuitive Surgical Inc New Jan 2008 310.00 Call						
11/16/2007	11/19/2007	Sell to Open	-1.0000	50397145	USD	18.000000	0.00	-1,778.46
11/16/2007	11/19/2007	Sell to Open	-17.0000	50398228	USD	18.000000	0.00	-30,573.99
+FCXAT:		Freeport-Mcmoran Copper & Gold Jan 2008 100.00 Call						
11/13/2007	11/14/2007	Sell to Open	-18.0000	50106312	USD	9.150000	0.00	-16,422.70
+GOQAR:		Google Inc Cl A Jan 2008 690.00 Call						
11/26/2007	11/27/2007	Sell to Open	-25.0000	50698884	USD	38.797000	0.00	-96,933.46
+RULAB:		Research In Motion Ltd Jan 2008 110.00 Call						
11/13/2007	11/14/2007	Sell to Open	-18.0000	50106310	USD	14.400000	0.00	-25,872.56
+GOQAB :		Google Inc Cl A Jan 2008 710.00 Call						
11/30/2007	12/03/2007	Sell to Open	-20.00	51016094	USD	38.600000		$-77,148.77

Daily Account Activity

Trade Date	Settlement Date	Activity	Quantity	Trade #	Currency	Price	Subtracted	Added
		PURCHASES AND SALES						
USD - US DOLLAR								
+GOQAT:		Google Inc Cl A Jan 2008 700.00 Call						
11/29/2007	11/30/2007	Sell to Open	-10.0000	50989946	USD	36.170000	0.00	-36,134.42
+MALAT:		Mastercard Inc Cl A Jan 2008 200.00 Call						
11/29/2007	11/30/2007	Sell to Open	-4.0000	50987021	USD	13.250000	0.00	-5,273.90
11/29/2007	11/30/2007	Sell to Open	-6.0000	50987023	USD	13.000000	0.00	-7,770.86
+RULAE:		Research In Motion Ltd Jan 2008 125.00 Call						
11/29/2007	11/30/2007	Sell to Open	-10.0000	50975773	USD	10.700000	0.00	-10,664.81
+APVKL:		Apple Inc Nov 2007 160.00 Call						
10/01/2007	10/02/2007	Sell to Open	-20.0000	47752854	USD	8.080000	0.00	-16,122.71
10/03/2007	10/04/2007	Sell to Open	-10.0000	47903692	USD	8.400000	0.00	-8,374.85
+CAMJS:		Cameron International Corp Oct 2007 95.00 Call						
10/03/2007	10/04/2007	Sell to Open	-16.0000	47877861	USD	4.000000	0.00	-6,367.86
10/03/2007	10/04/2007	Sell to Open	-4.0000	47877863	USD	4.000000	0.00	-1,594.96
+CAMKA:		Cameron International Corp Nov 2007 105.00 Call						
10/18/2007	10/19/2007	Sell to Open	-30.0000	48625087	USD	3.650000	0.00	-10,900.27
+DEKK:		Deere & Co 2007 155.00 Call						
10/18/2007	10/19/2007	Sell to Open	-30.0000	48621775	USD	5.580000	0.00	-16,690.18
+FCXKY:		Freeport-Mcmoran Copper & Gold Nov 2007 120.00 Call						
10/11/2007	10/12/2007	Sell to Open	-30.0000	48308891	USD	6.630000	0.00	-19,840.13
+FLRKM:		Fluor Corp New Nov 2007 165.00 Call						
10/11/2007	10/12/2007	Sell to Open	-20.0000	48299705	USD	6.610000	0.00	-13,170.25
10/11/2007	10/12/2007	Sell to Open	-10.0000	48299709	USD	6.600000	0.00	-6,575.37
+GOOKP:		Google Inc Cl A Nov 2007 580.00 Call						
10/01/2007	10/02/2007	Sell to Open	-20.0000	47758652	USD	25.180000	0.00	-50,322.18
10/03/2007	10/04/2007	Sell to Open	-10.0000	47904282	USD	25.780000	0.00	-25,754.58
+LMTKC:		Lockheed Martin Corp Nov 2007 115.00 Call						
10/12/2007	10/15/2007	Sell to Open	-30.0000	48378557	USD	2.370000	0.00	-7,060.33
+MALKM:		Mastercard Inc Cl A Nov 2007 165.00 Call						
10/05/2007	10/09/2007	Sell to Open	-30.0000	48038211	USD	9.280000	0.00	-27,790.01
+MDRKL:		Mcdermott Intl Inc Nov 2007 60.00 Call						
10/05/2007	10/09/2007	Sell to Open	-30.0000	48038209	USD	2.529900	0.00	-7,540.02
+MONKS:		Monsanto Co New Nov 2007 95.00 Call						
10/12/2007	10/15/2007	Sell to Open	-30.0000	48378555	USD	3.030000	0.00	-9,040.30
+NOVKQ:		National Oilwell Varco Inc Nov 2007 85.00 Call						
10/11/2007	10/12/2007	Sell to Open	-30.0000	48299713	USD	3.000000	0.00	-8,950.30
+OIIKP:		Oceaneering Intl Inc Nov 2007 80.00 Call						
10/01/2007	10/02/2007	Sell to Open	-20.0000	47759558	USD	2.920000	0.00	-5,802.87
10/03/2007	10/04/2007	Sell to Open	-10.0000	47903958	USD	2.530000	0.00	-2,504.94
+RFYJT:		Research In Motion Ltd Oct 2007 75.00 Call						
10/05/2007	10/09/2007	Sell to Open	-10.0000	48034044	USD	38.750000	0.00	-38,730.88
10/05/2007	10/09/2007	Sell to Open	-10.0000	48034048	USD	38.400000	0.00	-38,380.89
+RIGKD:		Transocean Inc Ord Nov 2007 120.00 Call						
10/12/2007	10/15/2007	Sell to Open	-2.0000	48380029	USD	3.000000	0.00	-598.98
10/12/2007	10/15/2007	Sell to Open	-28.0000	48380033	USD	2.890000	0.00	-8,043.31
+RULKD:		Research In Motion Ltd Nov 2007 120.00 Call						
10/09/2007	10/10/2007	Sell to Open	-30.0000	48145157	USD	5.500000	0.00	-16,450.18
+SDBKB:		Schlumberger Ltd Nov 2007 110.00 Call						
10/01/2007	10/02/2007	Sell to Open	-20.0000	47761578	USD	4.000000	0.00	-7,962.83
10/03/2007	10/04/2007	Sell to Open	-10.0000	47903962	USD	3.430000	0.00	-3,404.92
+APVAO:		Apple Inc Jan 2008 175.00 Call						
11/26/2007	11/27/2007	Sell to Open	-30.0000	50704605	USD	14.320000	0.00	-42,909.78
+AXVAZ:		Intuitive Surgical Inc New Jan 2008 290.00 Call						
11/26/2007	11/27/2007	Sell to Open	-30.0000	50704603	USD	24.990000	0.00	-74,919.29
+GOQAR:		Google Inc Cl A Jan 2008 690.00 Call						
11/26/2007	11/27/2007	Sell to Open	-30.0000	50704611	USD	38.421800	0.00	-115,214.07
+MHSAT:		Medco Health Solutions Inc Jan 2008 100.00 Call						
11/26/2007	11/27/2007	Sell to Open	-30.0000	50704609	USD	4.420000	0.00	-13,210.23
+NOVAN:		National Oilwell Varco Inc Jan 2008 70.00 Call						
11/26/2007	11/27/2007	Sell to Open	-30.0000	50704613	USD	4.880000	0.00	-14,590.21
+RULAD:		Research In Motion Ltd Jan 2008 120.00 Call						
11/26/2007	11/27/2007	Sell to Open	-30.0000	50704621	USD	10.850000	0.00	-32,499.94

Daily Account Activity

Trade Date	Settlement Date	Activity	Quantity	Trade #	Currency	Price	Subtracted	Added
		PURCHASES AND SALES						
USD - US DOLLAR								
+APVJF: 10/05/2007	10/09/2007	Apple Inc Oct 2007 130.00 Call Sell to Open	-15.0000	48034490	USD	30.300000	0.00	-45,418.52
+APVKM: 10/05/2007	10/09/2007	Apple Inc Nov 2007 165.00 Call Sell to Open	-30.0000	48032674	USD	7.540000	0.00	-22,570.09
+AXVKT: 10/24/2007	10/25/2007	Intuitive Surgical Inc New Nov 2007 300.00 Call Sell to Open	-3.0000	48931753	USD	20.050000	0.00	-6,009.89
+APVJI: 10/05/2007	10/09/2007	Apple Inc Oct 2007 145.00 Call Sell to Open	-15.0000	48032668	USD	30.300000	0.00	-45,418.52
+CAMKX: 10/03/2007	10/04/2007	Cameron International Corp Nov 2007 100.00 Call Sell to Open	-30.0000	47907506	USD	3.320000	0.00	-9,910.28
+FCXKB: 10/04/2007	10/05/2007	Freeport-Mcmoran Copper & Gold Nov 2007 110.00 Call Sell to Open	-30.0000	47958917	USD	6.740000	0.00	-20,170.13
+FLRKM: 10/10/2007	10/11/2007	Fluor Corp New Nov 2007 165.00 Call Sell to Open	-30.0000	48217328	USD	5.070000	0.00	-15,160.20
+GOOKR: 10/03/2007 10/03/2007	10/04/2007 10/04/2007	Google Inc Cl A Nov 2007 590.00 Call Sell to Open Sell to Open	-25.0000 -5.0000	47885474 47885492	USD USD	23.450000 23.030000	0.00 0.00	-58,599.30 -11,490.06
+JECKQ: 10/17/2007	10/18/2007	Jacobs Engr Group Inc Del Nov 2007 85.00 Call Sell to Open	-30.0000	48558878	USD	3.700000	0.00	-11,050.27
+MALKM: 10/05/2007	10/09/2007	Mastercard Inc Cl A Nov 2007 165.00 Call Sell to Open	-30.0000	48032676	USD	9.150000	0.00	-27,400.02
+MDRKL: 10/17/2007	10/18/2007	Mcdermott Intl Inc Nov 2007 60.00 Call Sell to Open	-30.0000	48555357	USD	3.080000	0.00	-9,190.29
+MONKU: 10/17/2007	10/18/2007	Monsanto Co New Nov 2007 90.00 Call Sell to Open	-30.0000	48555361	USD	3.300000	0.00	-9,850.28
+NOVJY: 10/05/2007 10/05/2007 10/05/2007	10/09/2007 10/09/2007 10/09/2007	National Oilwell Varco Inc Oct 2007 57.50 Call Sell to Open Sell to Open Sell to Open	-10.0000 -10.0000 -10.0000	48034132 48034154 48034178	USD USD USD	19.150000 19.200000 19.220000	0.00 0.00 0.00	-19,133.18 -19,183.18 -19,203.18
+NOVKP: 10/05/2007 10/05/2007	10/09/2007 10/09/2007	National Oilwell Varco Inc Nov 2007 80.00 Call Sell to Open Sell to Open	-10.0000 -20.0000	48038213 48038215	USD USD	3.400000 3.380000	0.00 0.00	-3,351.42 -6,758.85
+RIGKD: 10/18/2007	10/19/2007	Transocean Inc Ord Nov 2007 120.00 Call Sell to Open	-30.0000	48621423	USD	2.800000	0.00	-8,350.31
+RULKD: 10/09/2007	10/10/2007	Research In Motion Ltd Nov 2007 120.00 Call Sell to Open	-30.0000	48145153	USD	5.500000	0.00	-16,450.18
+GOQAT: 11/29/2007	11/30/2007	Google Inc Cl A Jan 2008 700.00 Call Sell to Open	-10.0000	50989940	USD	35.500000	0.00	-35,474.93
+MALAT: 11/29/2007	11/30/2007	Mastercard Inc Cl A Jan 2008 200.00 Call Sell to Open	-10.0000	50987015	USD	13.250000	0.00	-13,225.27
+RIGAX: 11/26/2007 11/26/2007	11/27/2007 11/27/2007	Transocean Inc Ord Jan 2008 130.00 Call Sell to Open Sell to Open	-3.0000 -10.0000	50750680 50750682	USD USD	6.700000 6.200000	0.00 0.00	-1,994.20 -6,175.38
+RULAE: 11/29/2007	11/30/2007	Research In Motion Ltd Jan 2008 125.00 Call Sell to Open	-10.0000	50975769	USD	10.700000	0.00	-10,675.31

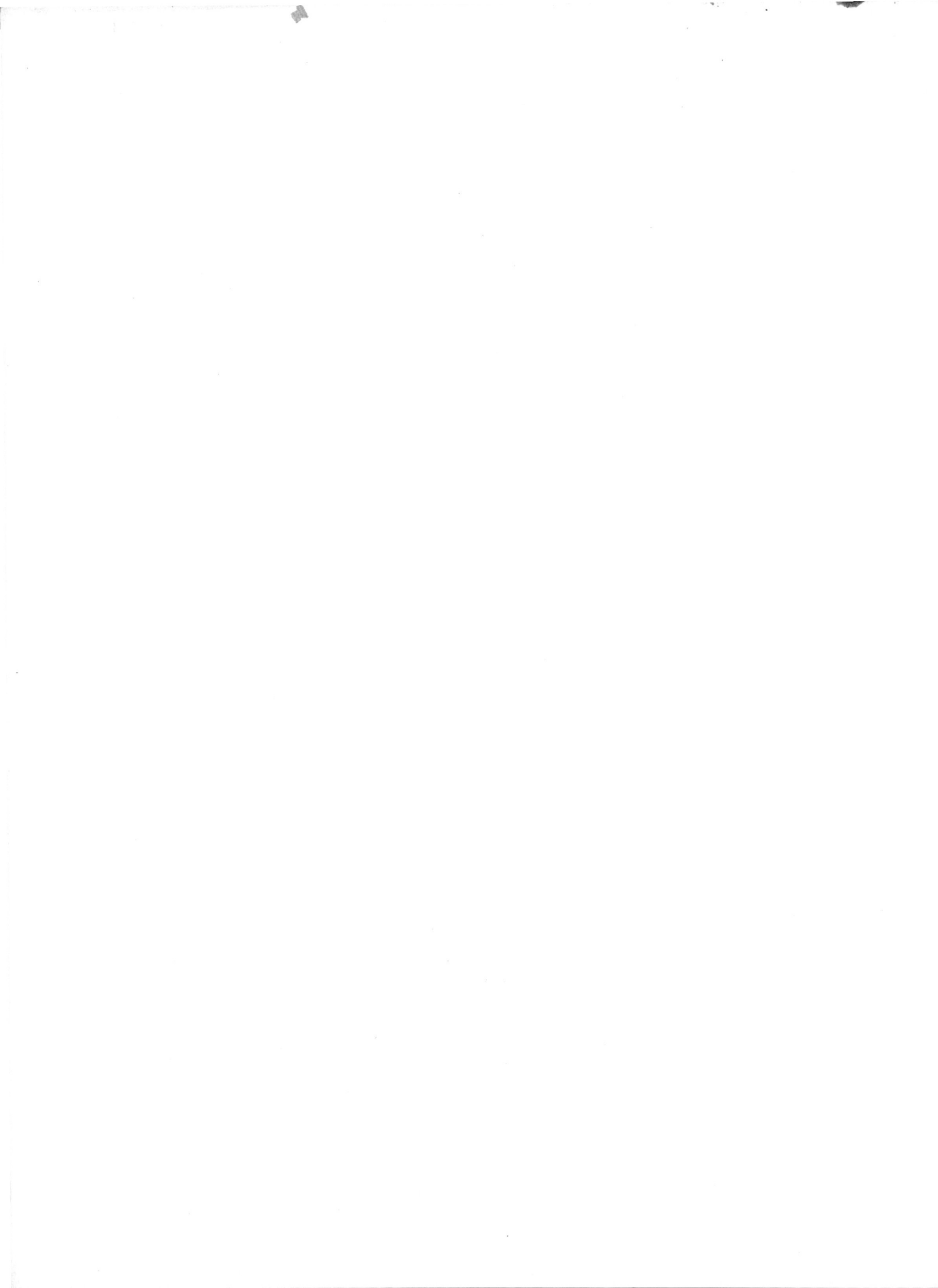